THE SUCCESSFUL CHRISTIAN IN A FAILING WORLD

Written by
Jon Adams
October 2003-June 2005

Jon Adams
604 616 0084

xulon PRESS

Copyright © 2005 by Jon Adams
Second Printing © 2006
Third Printing © 2007

The Successful Christian in a Failing World
by Jon Adams

Printed in the United States of America

ISBN-13: 978-1-59781-621-2
ISBN-10: 1-59781-621-3

All rights reserved solely by the author. The author guarantees all contents are original and do not infringe upon the legal rights of any other person or work. No part of this book may be reproduced in any form without the permission of the author. The views expressed in this book are not necessarily those of the publisher.

Unless otherwise indicated, Bible quotations are taken from The New English Bible. Copyright © 1970 by Oxford University Press and Cambridge University Press. The Interlinear Greek-English New Testament. Copyright © 1964 by Samuel Bagster and Sons Limited.

www.xulonpress.com

The Righteous perish
And *no one* takes it to heart
Isaiah 57:1

CONTENTS

Preface xiii
Chapter 1 21
Anger, Violence, and Love:
   -Anger, Love, and Politics
   -Government Programs and the Justice of Grace
   -The Sermon on the Mount: An End to Violence
   -The Sermon on the Mount: God, War, and Self Defense
   -Are There Two Kinds of Holiness?
   -Servants: What Was Jesus Getting At?
   -Prestige and the Desire for Power
   -Love and the Law: God, Courts, and the Prison System
   -A Short parable from the New Testament

Chapter 2 95
On Government:
   -Religious Freedom and the Separation of Church and State
   -Democracy and the Multi-Party System
   -Christian Support for a Democratic Government
   -Christians, Political Parties, and Capitalism

- Criticism of the Government
- Protest: Critiquing Authority
- Independence and Liberty Within a Governed Society
- Social Policy and the Population as a Resource
- A Rough Model of a Just Government

Chapter 3 157
Patriotism

Chapter 4 161
Terrorism

Chapter 5 165
Power: The Social equivalent of the Splitting of the Atom
  - Power and Violence: A Christian Defense

Chapter 6 181
The Flesh: What is It?

Chapter 7 187
Temptation

Chapter 8 191
The Church and the Gospel: Have We Forgotten?

Chapter 9 217
Prayer: The Key to Living With God

Chapter 10 223
Where is God in a World of Suffering?
  The Problem of Evil: Can God be Trusted?

Chapter 11 243
Forgiveness
Chapter 12 253
The Power of God

Chapter 13 271
Missions and the Mission Field:
   -The Call
   -Who are the Lost?

Chapter 14 295
Faith

Chapter 15 321
Society, Morality, and the Church

Chapter 16 327
Comparing Ourselves To Other Christians

Chapter 17 331
My Clear Conscience, and Your Refusal to Agree
That I Should Have It

Chapter 18 337
Guilt and Shame

Chapter 19 351
Worldliness and the Believer

Chapter 20 359
Have You Ever Been Told Just How Bad You Really Are?

Chapter 21 363
What Gives a Person Value?
   -Talents, Value and Globalization
   -A Basis for Individual Value Not Based on

Personal Success

Chapter 22 377
Intelligence

Chapter 23 381
People on the Street

Chapter 24 385
The Social Gospel

Chapter 25 397
The Rich and the Poor

Chapter 26 401
Christians and Their Families

Chapter 27 407
The Contemporary Church:
  -Music: How Should We Sing?
  -Technology
  -The Commercialization of Christian Teaching
  -Church Programs
  -Preaching: What Can be Said?
  -A Pastoral Job Description

Chapter 28 435
Praising God: What's the Point?

Chapter 29 439
Feminism: A Discussion on Vocabulary and Reality

Chapter 30 445
The Discipline of Children: Physical Punishment

Chapter 31 449
Hermeneutical Principles: Understanding the
Sayings of Jesus

Chapter 32 459
Marriage and Love

Chapter 33 463
Friendship

Chapter 34 467
Misunderstanding

Chapter 35 471
Bible College: A Defense of Openness

Chapter 36 479
In Praise of Naturalness: Some Concluding Remarks

PREFACE

The world we live in today is a world of celebrities. We seem obsessed with the lives of those who have become famous, even if this fame lasts only briefly. We closely follow what they think and what they do when they are away from the public eye, as if being famous gives these otherwise ordinary people insight into the deeper truths of life, or that, perhaps by knowing about such famous people we also can possess, even a small amount of the charisma that surrounds their magical and wealthy lives. We glorify those who, by reason of their exposure in the media, are familiar to almost everyone, and want to be like them. We know in our hearts, of course, that there is virtually no likelihood that we will ever reach such heights, but we follow these people's lives as if they were friends or relatives, and in some sense, that is truly how we see them. To a degree, we fear that if we do not become famous like them, we may end up never having any value. To be known, for almost any reason, is to be valued.

Perhaps this is how we feel because our world is so crowded that the individual is lost in the mass of humanity that surrounds it. It is difficult to feel unique, when there are over six billion other people, also seeking to be valued. In addition, modern society is so complex and compartmentalized that the solitary person becomes insignificant in the structurally bureaucratic maze that makes individual input daunting and overwhelming. The world has been explored, and few challenges can be found to make one feel truly alive and in a struggle to achieve some previously unattained dream. In this ocean of humanity it is helpful to think about two realities. The first is the impact that the Saviour alone, and later his twelve disciples had on the world. The second, is that in a church where God is taken seriously, each one of us is in a family, in which we are a brother or sister to all who worship with us.

The story of the Sunday school teacher whose witness to the Lord had a dynamic impact on D.L.Moody the world famous 19th century evangelist, is well known. But we can also trace the impact of this Sunday school teacher, person by person, down to Billy Graham, one of the most well known and loved evangelists of this generation. Without the unpretentious Sunday school teacher, perhaps none of these other evangelists would have had their particular ministries. It is not being known that is truly important. It is being in a relationship with God, where God can direct one's life, so that through this relationship we can make a difference in the world. I doubt that we genuinely believe this, but if we have a relationship with God, could there be any one more important to know? Moreover, the worth of the individual is unchangeably given an eternal value, in that the Son of God came to earth and died on a cross to save, each one of us, lost and sinful though we were.

God's plans are not determined by famous people, even by famous clergymen, but by ordinary individuals who take God seriously. I do not know the line that divides an obsession from a passion, but a passion for God will guarantee a life that has meaning in a meaningless world. It is not the church that needs to reach out to a lost humanity but individuals filled with love for a suffering and confused world. It is not programs, no matter how well thought through and presented, that will ensure the success of the church's mission. Rather, it is Spirit filled individuals who cannot help but be different from the people around them, and who speak with an authority that comes from a genuine relationship with Jesus. If the world is to be changed, this will not happen through the great plans of huge churches with vast congregations, but by individuals reaching out to neighbours and friends, sharing the gospel, being a support in times of need, and helping each new believer grow in the faith.

Along with our fascination for the famous, there is an equally unfortunate belief that as individuals we are powerless in the face of vast wealth, vast political power, and a seemingly unstoppable military might. This sense of powerlessness is agreeable to those who hold great power because it reduces the opposition they can expect from a disenchanted and disunited population. However, the feeling of virtual impotence by the majority of the population is also one of the greatest lies that can be believed. Those who hold power are always a minority compared to the vast numbers that potentially could oppose them. Were these masses to rise up as one, there would be no chance the minority claiming absolute power could survive this wave of opposition.

There is, however, another reason why this belief is a lie, and this resides in the amazing power of God that can be demonstrated for God's glory, through the life of one individual. The biblical heroes were frequently solitary, and far from perfect individuals, who stood alone against the tide of error and sin. Whether or not they succeeded, in the usual sense, they did exercise a degree of power that forced the unspiritual to confront them, and take them seriously. There are two social entities that have power: (1) a population united against an oppressive government and (2) an individual who genuinely knows God, and is strong in his or her assurance of this relationship. One individual can indeed make a great impact on an unbelieving world.

In the course of thinking about many of the ideas I have attempted to deal with here, and in reading of the experiences of those who have sought to make a positive difference in the world, I have come to believe that there is virtually nothing more oppositional to the establishment of a kingdom where the second great commandment is valued and lived, than human violence in all its Medusian forms. And further, that there is nothing more important in human relationships than the need to teach and live in a strenuous opposition to this violence in conformity to the same commandment. This violence is not limited to those forms of violence we are usually conscious of. One of the most troubling expressions of violence is that expressed in the supposed defense of moral and religious positions, and against those who have failed to measure up to these standards. This is entirely understandable in that these violent expressions attempt to protect that which is presumably one of the most valuable dimension of human and religious life. Yet, it remains violence, nonetheless. I am brought back to the revelation of the Godhead in the Lord Jesus, and find it absent, both in his ministry, and in the biblical description of love.

Yet, perhaps surprisingly, what needs to be understood, when such a book as this is read, is that the entire enterprise of living up to Jesus' standards is completely impossible. Simply because we do not have to follow the Mosaic law does not mean that what we do have to follow is doable. On the contrary, what Jesus expects is far more challenging than what was outlined in the Law. Commitment and promises to God, as much as they reveal that our heart's desire to follow the Lord sincerely, will not make us any more able to become the "good Christians" we long to be. As C S Lewis noted years ago, we need to come to the point where we realize that it is humanly impossible to be what God, paradoxically, expects of us. On the other hand, it is extremely useful to have some idea about the kind of people God does want us to become. And knowing the truth can help us turn from empty paths and understandings that we may have long considered acceptable and right.

The church today is in a time of crisis. It is not that there have not been other and different crises in the past. It could well be, in fact, that each generation is faced with its own unique challenges, and that ours is just a variation on the experience. Yet there is a specificity in our day that relates to a global destruction of religious models as explanations of human life, and, in the face of this, a radical doubt as to the reality of all religious teachings. What this means for the church is that without a deep and widespread renewal of the spiritual life of the church, in which experience, and not just proclamation is the dominant feature, the ever growing secular world around us will increasingly ignore the church as the source of any credible ideas on human amelioration. For the individual Christian, surrounded by this secularity in society, and the epistemological confusion that is at its base, faith in the validity of Christian teachings will become more and more problematic.

In concrete terms, certain questions must be asked. Does the alleged work of Christ on the cross and in the resurrection actually produce individuals who are dramatically and perceptibly different from those who do not profess any such faith? Does the teaching on salvation and sanctification actually work? Is the church qualitatively different from those unbelievers, and especially those unbelievers who are committed to other religious systems, who make up the rest of society? Are Christians perceived as different, and admired by those around them, not because they proclaim religious beliefs, but because their lives and social actions are radically at variance with the personal characteristics of non-Christians? If the sanctification of the believer, as taught in the New Testament, does not work, why are we teaching it? And if it does work, why is it so under-emphasized in the preaching of the church? And why is it that Christians are not known and recognized, around the world, by their love, holy lives and the experience of the power of God, at least to the same degree that Muslims are unjustifiably known as the source of most global terrorism?

If nothing else is gained from this work, may it be the realization that anything but a response of love does not reflect the character of the God we would like to serve and worship. I suspect that if we truly loved, there would be so many problems that would simply never be generated. A God given love for others would make impossible any action that would violate that person in the name of any other good, no matter where that good was felt to be based. A love of God and others would make realpolitik, if not impossible, then of severely truncated value. Genuine love would direct our political thinking and feeling. Love would motivate us to seek the lost. Furthermore, a love from God would be accompanied by a faith in God that knows, and is open to the power of God.

Some central beliefs about God, ones that are the very core of my faith in God's essential goodness and love, are that God is logical, that he is fair in the most serious sense, and that a biblical assertion that implies only two possibilities, i.e. either a or b, is rigidly so in God's thinking as well. Further, I believe that God is not schizophrenic, arbitrary in his actions, or intrinsically unpredictable. This of course does not mean that God can be limited or completely categorized, but rather that he does nor possess characteristics that are inherently contradictory. For me, at least, that humanity is in slavery to sin is a central belief in my understanding of God. These assumptions are the basic framework of how scripture should be understood, and are in essence simply another way to describe the nature of the Godhead as revealed in Jesus Christ. Perhaps this language seems strange and unbiblical. However, the scriptures are the source of this thinking, and if they were not found in holy writ, I doubt that we would have very much on which we could rest our faith. An intellectual knowledge is, however, only one aspect of one's journey with God. A relationship with the Father of our Lord Jesus in which we come to know, even as we are known, is crucial, and ultimately far more satisfying.

This book was written from a desire to set people free from ideas and beliefs that tie them down, and that limit them in their understanding of God, themselves, the church, and even the world around them. An honest view of ourselves and the world around us that is not satisfied with easy answers to troubling ideas, along with a solid understanding of scripture, can lead us to become free, psychologically healthy individuals who know God as a true father, and are confident in his power, even in the face of evil and intellectual confusion. What was written was also accompanied by a strong belief that if there was anything in the book that was valuable, this was so, only to the degree that it represented the truth of God. One who seeks to say the words of God can not say anything that originates in him or herself, in any real sense. I doubt that there is anything new in this book. Indeed, if there were, it would probably not express the mind of God accurately. On the other hand I have attempted to engage the mind of the reader so that he or she will begin to question what has previously been unreflectively held as true. A biblical understanding of reality, and a radical questioning of existence and the scriptures do not necessarily have to be antithetical processes.

The chapters may be read in any order. However, within each chapter there is usually a thematic development that requires one to read sequentially through the chapter. I apologize for any errors, and pray that what is read will be contemplated in an attitude that seeks truth.

CHAPTER ONE
ANGER, VIOLENCE, AND LOVE

O rge gar andros dikaiosunen Theou ouk ergatsetai—
For a person's anger cannot promote the righteousness of God. James 1:20

The world waits to see, again, the love of God dramatically expressed in the life of one person.

The sad thing about being human is that one can never escape being wronged. No matter how perfect one's life, there will always be someone who will misinterpret one's actions, and find fault with what we do. In addition, we know ourselves, and in our hearts we know quite well that we are not anywhere near being perfect ourselves. Our selfishness, impatience, greed, and simple lack of love tell us daily that we are not only the recipients of unfairness and wrong, but also the cause of these misfortunes for others. We are wronged, and in turn we do wrong to others. Indeed, in regard to our attitude to society, our "use" of morality is derived from, and expressed, in the main, in the deep seated anger, distrust, and simple lack of love we harbor in our hearts towards virtually all other human beings. It frequently does not even matter if the person we hurt is the one who acted against us. That, of course, would be the best turn of events for us, but we are willing to return the wrong to anyone we perceive to have wronged us in some other, sometimes insignificant way.

The indiscriminate fashion of our own wrongdoing is not necessarily as irrational as it first appears. Out of the plethora of hurtful acts done to us we build up a general mistrust towards all others, that sees in these others, those from the past who have wronged us. We have been hurt, and in retaliation we hurt others. This does not make these acts we do any less sinful. It does help, however, in understanding the hurt that causes such behaviour, gives us a reason for compassion towards those who wrong us, and perhaps provides an explanation for our own behaviour that can temper the guilt and self loathing that often lies just below the surface of our own conscious existence. Sadly, this understanding does not remove our separation from God, or automatically give us new hearts that refrain from such destructive ways of (re)acting.

Jesus taught that God's expectations can be summed up in two principles. We should love the Lord with all our heart and mind, and we should love our neighbour as ourselves (Matt. 22:38,39). The implication in this is that if we do these things we will not do other acts that we can find in long lists of moral injunctions, and that to fulfill these two propositions will result in the fulfilling of the essence of the Mosaic law (1 Timothy 1:5). Jesus' words also imply that sin, as it relates to both God and others, is essentially an expression of a lack of love. If this is true, then to examine one wrong is, at least from one perspective, to examine all. For if to love is to remove sin, then all sin is an expression of a lack of love. As such, the divine expectation to love is not an addition to a list of personal characteristics we are expected to possess, like patience, unselfishness, and devotion to God. Rather, all these characteristics are present in the experience of love.

As St John said, "if we say we love God but have not love for others we walk in darkness" (1 John 4:20). Indeed, if I do not steal, and do this only because I have been so commanded, yet still do not love the brother or sister, for the protection of whom such a command is devised, then no doubt there is a level of goodness in this restraining of my covetousness. However, the essence of the law has been missed. One could theoretically keep all the law, outside of the first commandment to love God, yet still hate all of humanity. This is the, not incidental reason why Jesus' statement about loving God and loving others is so radical. To reiterate, if love is the fulfillment of the law, then all sin issues from a lack of love. This being the case, in order to understand anger from God's perspective, we must understand love, for love shines light on anger, and gives reasons for why it cannot express God's moral perfection. Yet, given the depths of our sinfulness, how can we ever attain to such perfection?

If love is the expression of the character of God in humanity, then in all human discourse, in all human interactions, anger is never justified. However, having been surrounded by anger from our infancy, and having been taught about the wrath of God, virtually from our first Sunday school lessons, such a claim may need some explanation. Among several causes, anger frequently originates as a defensive reaction to previous frustrations, devaluations, hurts by others, and other people's anger directed towards us. It can also be a reaction to another's failure to do what we believe is right, good, or simply what we want. Anger is a reaction based on the assumption that there is a moral freedom to choose good in the offending person, that the clear moral good was rejected, and that this justifies the opprobrium we "passionately" express. Anger further ignores the social environment in which the individual was raised, the culture to which he or she was exposed, and the psychological environment of the home that may have damaged the person who has acted "inappropriately".

The above remarks are not theologically unfounded, nor do they contradict scripture. We compartmentalize various aspects of our thinking, keeping separate ways of thinking which would be, if they were put side by side, internally contradictory. Indeed, in the cognitively dissonant way in which we often think, we hold that all are slaves of sin as Paul asserts, and also, that society can make people better or worse. Finding an individual (Christian) who did not believe society can influence behaviour, would be a difficult task. The problem of how society can make people "better or worse", while at the same time, asserting that, according to the scriptures, we cannot improve ourselves, is usually ignored by an appeal to the idea that it is the perfection of God to which we cannot attain. However, the idea that there are both "good" and "bad" people in the world strongly suggests, at least theoretically, that perfection may be attained, and that character can be improved on. So in what sense can it be said that both of these ideas are correct?

At this point in the discussion let it be understood that the environmental aspects given as causes of human action are not intended to, and do not negate the belief or fact that without God's help we cannot express the character of God perfectly, and that, perhaps for any number of reasons, there are sins from which we cannot become free without the grace of God.

Anger, on a psychological level, ignores both the reasons for the anger that exist in the person becoming angry, as well as the causes of the behaviour in the person who triggers the angry response. Further, anger ignores the state of lostness and spiritual impotence that are the objective causes of all offending behaviour. The word 'objective' is used because we can misconstrue motivations for an individual's actions that are not objective, not founded in reality. If we are slaves of sin, then we need to have compassion towards those who sin, including ourselves. The fact is that we are either slaves of sin or we are not. We cannot have it both ways. This is a fundamental question, and for those who believe in the inerrancy of scripture it is essential that scriptural doctrines be maintained. One cannot be angry at the sin of another without simultaneously believing that the individual was free not to sin. If we are free not to sin, then St. Paul is in error in teaching that we are slaves to sin, for we are not! If then we are not free, not to sin, then there is no theological reason to be angry at another's sin. This is not a devaluation of the enormity of sin. Rather, it is merely an argument regarding the lack of justification for anger.

Just as anger is an emotion that is founded on reasons, so also is love an emotion that is similarly grounded on reason. Love, thus, is not simply an emotion. It is, in addition, a rational attitude that prompts behaviour, and makes other, unloving attitudes inconceivable. Anger is possible, only because we do not possess in ourselves a loving attitude towards the other, the possession of which would make it impossible to be angry with this other, for the wrong that may well have been done. An attitude of love can be maintained in several complementary ways. Firstly, we can arrive at reasons why we should be loving towards others. Secondly, through the sanctifying work of the Holy Spirit we can have a love placed in our hearts that may or may not include various reasons for the love, but is not dependant on the reasons for the strength of that love, and in doing so removes the hatred that we have been long unable to deal with. In the second method there is a combination of these two. The first, by itself is inadequate. Our anger and self love are so deep that conceptual understandings, by themselves, are unable to withstand the vicissitudes of negative or destructive human interaction. Somewhere, in an unexpected situation, we will be blindsided by a behaviour that elicits an unloving response. The truth is that we are mostly a one we do not know. Our unconscious mind is more our true self than what we are familiar with in our self conscious moments when awake. As a consequence, without the healing of our hearts by the Holy Spirit, it is inevitable that we will betray ourselves and others.

Moral judgement and displeasure *at the person* can be expressed in violence, war, a ridiculing of another's positions, and in the demonizing of a person's beliefs or actions to justify our anger (lack of love) in its various modes of expression. Anger expresses our willingness to attack, to find fault with in order to crush and, in fact, to treat the other as we would not have them treat us. Human anger is often justified by religious people as a qualitatively similar response to God's response to wrong. This, however, I would suggest, is a misidentification of our anger with God's, based on an erroneous understanding of the "wrath of God", and can only be corrected by taking seriously the ministry of Jesus as the perfect expression of God, (see John 14:7-11) and therefore of the manner in which God responds to wrong.

Anger, and the violence that lies at its heart and is frequently associated with it, is probably worst when one possesses the attitude that the wrongdoer is failing to comply with divine, and obviously decent, moral expectations. The reaction is unfortunately unacceptable, not because the other has not been guilty of these failings, but because the reaction reveals a lack of both an understanding of Salvation and a genuine love in the person making the accusations, and further, because, almost certainly these divine expectations are used as a cover for the anger and violence that reside in the heart of the 'spiritual' person making the evaluation. It is also wrong because the nature of God as expressed in Jesus, was diametrically opposed to this as an acceptable reaction to human failings.

If we accept as true the story of Jesus' forgiveness of the woman taken in adultery in John's gospel, we must also accept that only one who is perfect has the right to condemn a wrong-doer. Perhaps it is unnecessary, but what is being discussed here is condemnation. It is impossible not to evaluate an act. If this were not so it would be impossible to know if a behaviour were morally acceptable or not. Nevertheless, contrary to what we deeply wish in our hearts, namely the punishment of the person who has wronged us, Jesus, the *only* one who was and is without sin, did not employ this option.

Indeed, what this little incident shows us is that without true love we will not evaluate the behaviours of those around us whom we condemn or reject, either accurately or adequately, and that our responses to other people's behaviour, particularly "bad" behaviour, will not express God's perception of the situation. If we could observe our own dealings with God we would almost certainly be appalled at ourselves. Virtually always, our coming to God in repentance, is not an act of love on our part. Even in our receiving salvation we are using God. And the proof of God's love for us is that he lets us do this. He who loves us, and wants this love returned, as all who love want their love returned, proves the unselfishness of his love in allowing us to receive the gift of his life, while knowing full well that we come to him, only to take, to use, that we come with hard hearts, and only because we need his gift. Only a heart that loves can see as God sees.

Sin is the cancer that separates us from God and destroys human relationships, and there are many responses to this human problem that can be made. However, if one rejoices in the punishment for sin that appears to have fallen on a sinner, if one rejoices at a "terrible sinner" being sent to jail, or better yet, to hell, if one finds pleasure that a sinner has finally gotten his "just desserts" in hell or elsewhere, then one has absolutely no idea of the love of God, one has absolutely no understanding of the purpose of the incarnation, and one is only confessing to a virtually complete absence of the fruit of the Spirit. A terrible expression of violent hatred for a sinner does nothing but bring shame on the church, does not advance the kingdom of God, and is a denial of the spirit of Jesus as portrayed throughout the gospels.

It may be argued that Jesus' response to the fig tree that had no fruit (Matt. 21:18-20), and the incident in the Temple where he drove out the moneychangers (Matt. 21: 12,13) contradict this point. This interpretation suggests that Jesus' love and patience were displayed when the individual expressed regret or shame at his or her acts, but where individuals did not express such shame he was impatient and angry. In regards to the fruitless fig tree, if we interpret this act as symbolic of his judgment on Israel for rejecting his Messiahship, then the tree is not the object of his anger as the tree itself is merely symbolic, and secondly, it is irrational to be angry at a piece of vegetation for not having fruit at the particular time one wanted it. Luke 19:41,42, however states that "When he came in sight of the city (Jerusalem) he wept over it and said, "if only you had known the way that leads to peace".

This is the attitude of one filled with love. It is not the picture of one angered by a failure to act as suggested by the fig tree anecdote. Moreover, if the fig represents Israel, why was the gospel so successful among the Jews after the resurrection, and what can be made of Paul's statement in Romans 9-11? Romans 11:1 states, "I ask then, has God rejected his people? I cannot believe it.", and this is followed by verse 29 which asserts, "For the gifts and calling of God are irrevocable." If these verses are correct, then Jesus' remark regarding the fig tree, at the symbolic level is not intended to be interpreted as the nation of Israel. Therefore both on the overall interpretational level, in terms of Jesus' emotional response to Israel's rejection of him, and the irrationality of this kind of remark to a tree, anger does not seem likely as a Messianic response. This being the case, whatever the fig tree incident does mean, it is not and can not be used as an expression of Jesus' anger at those who have failed to act properly. It may be problematic, but its interpretation cannot be that Jesus got angry, either at the tree, or at the nation of Israel.

An examination of the temple incident likewise cannot be used to show that Jesus was filled with anger at the money changers. The gospels, in fact, reveal that Jesus' response to the unrepentant was not anger but a quest for their reintegration into the household of God. Indeed, the incident, as an expression of anger is uncharacteristic of Jesus' response to sin. Before his repentance, Zaccheus was a grasping tax collector who oppressed his own people. It was almost certainly Jesus' love for him, despite and in contrast to the social hatred that decent people harboured towards Zaccheus, that brought about the radical change in Zaccheus' life, and this love was revealed before Zaccheus expressed any sorrow for his sins. Further, if we examine Jesus' reactions to those who were not repentant at any stage in their encounter with the Messiah, we find that anger was not the way Jesus responded. On the cross Jesus did not rain down imprecations on those who were rejecting him. Rather he cried our "Father forgive them for they know not what they are doing." It is not then simply wrong to attribute anger to Jesus. It is illogical, given significant events in his life where such anger would have seemed justified.

Minimally, the Temple incident does not necessarily imply anger at all, and I would suggest it is our own expected angry response that injects this emotion into the event. Rather than anger, Jesus may well have been filled with such deep sorrow that what people saw may have been tears rather than an angry twisted mouth. Jesus' response to people was not, and cannot be internally contradictory and confusing. Jesus was not radically compassionate, and then unexpectedly vituperative, even in the face of deep wrong. Jesus was not inconsistently loving but continually so. Nor could we have confidence in such love if such overwhelming love was presented, only when he was alive, and then withdrawn, when and after he was crucified as "we had had our chance!" To assume such a state would be to say that the risen and glorified Christ is essentially different to the incarnate Christ when he walked this earth.

As the scripture informs us, "He is the same yesterday, today, and forever." St. John in the epistles says that perfect love casts out fear (1 John 4:18). Could we have perfect love for one who was so unpredictable? Finally, as Paul states, God commends his love towards us in that while we were yet sinners Christ died for us (Romans 5:8). This is a love for the violent hater of the Lover. It is a love that, the antithesis of an aggressive, angry response to opposition, takes into itself the violence of the other's hatred to the extent of giving up its right to live. If there is no greater love than that which gives up life for a friend (John 15:13) then surely we can only conclude that the enemies of God are His friends, for it is the sinful for whom Christ died. Whatever the two incidents mean, they do not teach the anger of the Saviour, and they do not justify our anger towards those who fail to fulfil God's commands.

Anger is not redemptive; it is legalistic. It focuses on the wrong done, and not on the redemption of the wrongdoer. As such, that is from a legal point of view, anger is totally justified. It is the moral reaction to wrong. However, to reiterate, it is not the redemptive reaction to wrong, and this is evidenced in Jesus' ministry to sinners. John the Baptist clearly expected Jesus to institute the cleansing of Israel with stern judgment, as he exclaims in Matthew, "His (Jesus, the Messiah's) shovel is ready in his hand and he will winnow his threshing floor; the wheat he will gather into his granary, but he will burn the chaff on a fire that can never go out." This has been interpreted eschatologically by Christians at various times, to refer to the end of history, though with a similar level of angry punishment to sinners. However, the context suggests otherwise. John, as the last of the Old Testament prophets, expected the end times to begin with the appearance of the Messiah who would restore Israel to its original relationship with God and punish the breakers of the Law. That, however, is not how Jesus understood and conducted his ministry. If John was condemnatory, as the gospels indicate, and as the law demanded, Jesus was forgiving and compassionate. These are two different responses to sin. To understand the difference between the ministry of John and the ministry of Jesus we have to understand the function of the law, as Paul taught it in the book of Romans. The Law was to reveal the sinfulness of humanity, not to solve this problem. John presented the law. Jesus, on the other hand, (re)presented redemption for a world that could never fulfil that law. Jesus certainly cleansed his granary, but he did it by revealing the love and power of God for a lost humanity, causing a new birth in the heart of the sinner, and not in a condemnatory judgment.

Clearly, the Christian response to wrong is not anger. This applies not only to wrong done us, but also to wrong generally, wrong in the social environment, wrong in the political world, and wrong done within one's family, even wrong done by a vicious political dictator and persecutor of the church. If we examine the life of Jesus as the gospels present it, and see this in Johannine terms as expressing the character of God the Father, we are forced to come to a troubling conclusion: anger does not express the character of God. If God does not wish us to harbor anger towards others is it logical to believe that God himself acts differently? This has implications for how a Christian should also behave, for if anger was not Jesus' way of responding to opposition, is it likely that it should be ours? If we do not have true love in our hearts, all manner of wrongdoing is fair game for our displeasure at humankind generally, mainly because there are usually good reasons for our angry response, almost literally in every direction. Moreover, the enemy of humanity depends on the continuance of the cycle of violence to continue the hurt such violence causes in the human heart. On the other hand, if the love of God truly does dwell in our hearts and minds, this will generate a paradigm, a model, a way of viewing the world that will color our behaviour and speech and make it impossible for the logical machinations that generate the justification for an angry response or attitude to succeed.

If we do have love, there will be understanding and compassion for the weak, for the poor, for the morally corrupt. Strangely, the indignation and rejection of the morally corrupt expressed by religious and secular people alike is frequently so virulent that it could be supposed that moral sins were a variety of sin beyond the grace of God, or that Christians were immune to such temptations and failings. Or perhaps the anger unconsciously reveals that such sins are familiar and dangerous possibilities one fears and struggles to deny. In addition, there will be a love for creation, for the environment, that does not express itself in an unfeeling willingness to subjugate the natural world, and in a despising of those who seek to protect it, even if sometimes unreasonably. One living in love will possess a deepening realization that other's sins are understandable, and not simply perverse and willful behaviour in defiance of known and obviously correct ways of acting.

Nevertheless, even if the behaviour of others were a blatant act of defiance against God, even such acts should generate love, and not a violent rejection and despising of the person. The judgements we pass on each other were of great concern to Jesus. In fact, Jesus' remark, "Pass no judgement and you will not be judged" (Matt.7:1) is not simply a "law". Rather, it is the expression of a moral impossibility. This impossibility does not exist in relation to our inability to conform to the injunction. Rather it exists in relation to an existential inability to make a condemnatory judgement if we have love in our hearts. Jesus' next remark is, "Why do you look at the speck of sawdust in your brother's eye (one particular failing perhaps), with never a thought for the great plank (all your sinfulness) in your own?" Jesus goes on to say "First take the plank out of your own eye and then you will see clearly (how) to take the speck out of your brother's" How do we take the plank of sinfulness out of our own eye? Is it not in the realization that such a task is beyond us, and that only the blood of Christ, the salvific work of Christ can achieve this, and then in faith taking this gift of forgiveness and cleansing, both at the time of the new birth and then day by day in our walk with God? Once we understand that Jesus alone is the way to our own "correction", we come to understand that the removal of our brother or sister's 'speck of sin' is also only through this gift and this transformation. And this explanation ignores the obvious comparison of sizes of wrong that Jesus was alluding to in the parable.

When God deals with the sin of an individual, it often appears that (he) is not interested in the one who may have wronged that individual. The feeling may well be that there is unfairness on God's part. The reason for this "one sidedness" is that God is attempting to end evil, not distribute levels of blame and punishment. The end of evil in this world begins in the heart of the person who turns from it. It is not that God is not interested in the one causing the hurt, but rather that the heart of the one wronged is more important than the "justice" of the fact of being wronged.

However, this does not mean that God is unaware or careless of the injustice done. From the scriptures we see clearly that God is deeply concerned with justice. On the other hand, punishment is less important than is the removal of evil from the human heart that causes this injustice. While God may be directing one person away from ungodliness, and apparently ignoring the wrongdoer, this is not so. The other individual is also the object of God's concern to stop evil in the world. And for that other person, God's concern will also appear just as one sided.

The recognition of our own sinfulness removes the logical possibility of judging another, and it should also logically, remove the desire to judge another. We need to remember that Jesus did not say, 'judge not if the sin is small or against someone else'. He simply said "Pass no judgement". Humility before God as to our own sinfulness leads to a unification with other sinful people that encourages compassionate interpersonal harmony, and removes the passion to find fault. Moreover, does the scripture not say that while we were yet sinners Christ died for us (Rom. 5:8), and God so loved the world that he gave his only begotten Son. (John 3:16)? Are we not all so deeply sinful that without God's grace we would never be able to become children of God? Are we not also capable of blatant rebellion? Are not the worst of people, simply mirrors of our own terrible propensity to evil? We need to view other people's terrible sins with a great deal more humility. No one knows what he or she is capable of, given the "wrong" circumstances.

And if that logic does not make an impact, ask yourself if you love others as you love yourself. Would you do for the dirty street person what you would willingly do for yourself, in order to be comfortable? Would you assist the prostitute to the same degree that you would assist your own daughter or son? As Jesus said, "If you love only those who love you, what is extraordinary about that? Even the heathen do as much." (Matt. 5: 46-48) Is there an overwhelming love in your heart for the worst of sinners, for your least favorite foreign dictator, your least liked politician? We, as Christians, need to stop thinking and reacting to what happens in the world as the pagans, the heathen, the lost, as the sinful part of our personalities do. We need to critique our hearts and our reactions in the light of the model of love that Jesus lived and taught. As Paul wrote in Romans 12:2, "Adapt yourselves no longer to the pattern of this present world, but let your minds be remade and your whole nature be transformed." This verse is not teaching us to hate the world. It is simply teaching us to think the way God would about what happens in the world. Finally, if your answer to the questions at the beginning of the paragraph is 'no', then, like me you realize how far we are from being the kind of people we should be and the world desperately needs. Together, we can only seek refuge in the forgiveness of God in Christ and with this understanding, and gratitude to God for being given what we could never earn, there will be a humility before the sinful that will not allow anger, and an unloving despising of another.

Anger, Love and Politics

If we are truly motivated by the love of God, political positions adopted by us as individual citizens will be taken from this standpoint, and not based on an impatient and angry belief in the "stupidity," greed, deceitfulness, or laziness of our fellow humans, who milk the system selfishly. Theoretically, love should have an impact, even on governmental budgets which should certainly not be based solely on the bottom line. This may seem a reasonable value in a business model, though it is not totally acceptable even here, but it should not be allowed to be the deciding factor in governmental policy. As a result, budgetary and policy priorities should necessarily be formed based upon their impact on all, including the poor, and not simply on the reaction of the business community to these policies. Christians cannot simultaneously profess to live in conformity to the love of God, seek and rejoice in such love, and at the same time harbour a hardness of heart towards their fellow human beings which verges on the malicious in the vehemence of its judgmental attitudes towards the poor as unworthy recipients of governmental assistance. If one's initial reaction to the poor is one of condemnation, if one of our first thoughts is that the poor are lazy abusers of taxpayer's money, I suggest we need to examine our hearts to discover the origin of these feelings. Are we not commanded to love lost sinners who are guilty, every day, of sin against God? And if we are expected to love the lost who continually sin, is it unreasonable for God to expect us to love the suffering poor, who may be, but are frequently not responsible for the economic state they are in. Do we imagine that God expects us to harden our hearts to their suffering because some abuse governmental programs? Moreover, are we so unaware of the life the poor live that we imagine governmental welfare provides such a life style that one may be tempted to lie, in order to achieve such governmental abundance? I actually heard one respected Christian leader make the incredible denial that there actually was such a thing as poverty and homelessness in our society, and that if there was, in some peculiar fashion, it was caused by the poor themselves.

    This is *not* a biblical position. On the contrary, it is antithetical to the broad river of loving social involvement throughout the entire scriptures which strongly advocate a compassionate support and protection of the weak, the poor and the homeless.(See Eze.18:12, Prov.14:31, Jer.7:5,6, Amos 4:1, Zech. 7:10, Psa.10:18. Psa.12:5, Psa. 82: 2-5, Psa. 146:7-9, Isa. 1:17,23, Isa. 3:11-15, Isa.10:1-3, Isa. 58, Ecc. 5:8, Deut. 14:29, Deut. 24:17, 19,20, Deut. 26:12,13, and James 2:1-17) Indeed, even if it were true, which it is not, that the poor are universally the cause of their own problems, scripture teaches a compassionate response to the weakness of such people, and not their condemnation, which the bible never engages in.

One remarkable passage among many that can be found in the scriptures is Psalm 82. This is a unique psalm in that it speaks of "gods" and "sons of a high god", and these references may indicate that it is quite old. Such terminology is reminiscent of Genesis six. Nevertheless, verses two to five are entirely consistent with the rest of scripture.

> How long will you judge unjustly
> And show favor to the wicked?
> You ought to give judgement for the weak and the orphan,
> And see right done to the destitute and downtrodden,
> You ought to rescue the weak and the poor
> And save them from the clutches of wicked men.
> But you know nothing, you understand nothing,
> You walk in the dark
> While earth's foundations are giving way.

How does one rescue the weak? How does one "see right done to the destitute and the downtrodden"? Most of us are very middle class. We have no idea how the "lower classes" live. Nor do we want to know. At those times when we may be forced to go somewhere slightly "poor" we breathe a sigh of relief when we are able to finally get back to "nice people and attractive areas". I say this because that is how I react. And the thought that I might have to dive into that messy and perhaps even dangerous milieu, if I am to be obedient to Christ, fills me with trepidation. Where will it all end? What else will I be asked to do? You see the psalm is not addressed to a limited group, such that most of us can sit back and be spectators to the wonderful work God is commanding them to do. We are all commanded to right wrong and protect the weak. The earth's foundations are giving way, and we sit back comfortably in our nice little (or big) houses and watch the news, and ridicule reality shows.

Christians should be ashamed of the hardness of heart, frequently expressed in anger at government programs to assist the poor. This anger is usually justified as a response to the laziness of the poor, their dishonesty and their manipulation of the aid programs, the inefficiency of the programs, and their budgetary impacts, but the real spring of such anger is a lack of compassion, a lack of genuine love for others and, at times a resentment, similar to that of the older brother's in the parable of the prodigal son, at the possibility that others would get something they had not worked for. We need to recollect that, as Christians, we are recipients of God's welfare program. Salvation is a treasure, not simply a hand-out, given without any labor on our part, to completely unworthy recipients. Indeed, God's welfare was gained at dreadful cost, through the struggle of the Saviour, even to the point of death. And God is not hard hearted and resentful at having to hand out this welfare to the spiritually poor world. From God's perspective, compassion is not given because of a deserving level of individual effort. Indeed, if we examine the gospels we discover in the parables, and in the dealings of Jesus with those around him, that God's gifts were particularly showered on those who were the most undeserving, the most socially despised.

Of course, in society, given human limitation, there are government programs that are not efficient in ameliorating the suffering of the poor, and there are individuals who abuse the programs that are instituted to reduce poverty; just as there are Christians (most of us) who want salvation but also want to continue living selfish lives. However, this does not negate the need for the programs generally, and only points to a need to refine and redirect this assistance, not to its abolition. The politically left, the "irrational" environmentalist, and the bleeding heart liberal, should not be despised for their concern for the unprotected of the earth, nor should the religious receive approbation for a callous opposition to such concern, masquerading as efficiency and moral accountability.

Government Programs and the Justice of Grace

Self made people, apart from often forgetting the economic and social variables they had no control of, or impact on, and that were crucial to their success, often have a philosophical difficulty regarding the justice of God's grace. Valuing self-effort so highly, the very behaviour they so deeply despise, namely the receiving of a benefit without labor and effort, becomes a stumbling block to their simple acceptance of Salvation. Perhaps this spirit of self reliance, and not simply their wealth, is why it is so difficult for the wealthy to enter the kingdom of heaven. The poor have no illusions about their ability to acquire wealth, or even to gain enough to live properly, and consequently, usually have no great difficulty in seeing themselves as poor also, before God.

One can not have a theological belief in the grace of God, and a contrary political and social belief that violently and vituperatively contradicts both this belief and the grace it teaches. If, in God's economy, justice is served by a free gift, though that free gift was "earned" by a death on the cross, then it is not intrinsically true that one must work strenuously in order to receive any material benefit, the corollary of this not being that one need not attempt to work in order to qualify for a benefit. From the scriptural perspective, in the social sphere, compassionate giving is not based on either a qualifying labour, or laziness, but rather on desperate need. That is to say, in the giving of a gift there is no necessary value placed on labor of some kind. That God provides in grace, and not according to the degree of effort is clearly seen in Matthew 20: 1-16. In this parable the landowner paid each worker the same amount, irrespective of the amount of time the laborer had spent working. The landowner's philosophy was not founded on work deserving reward but rather on the kindness of grace in the face of human need. Just as today there are those who object to any program that attempts to help the poor, those who had worked longer than those at the end of the day complained when the landowner, representing God, gave equal amounts to all. They believed the workers at the end who had not labored as they had, did not deserve the owner's generosity. However, God deems the recipient of a gift acceptable, based on need and the willingness to accept the gift.

This is true both of salvation and of any other material gift in any form. For if the gift of salvation is a gift given to an undeserving recipient, then lesser gifts cannot be withheld on the basis of the real or supposed undeserving nature of the potential recipient. In truth, the category of "deserving", from God's standpoint is both irrelevant and simultaneously a potential obstacle to the receipt of the gift. That this is true is so, not from a legal standpoint, but from the standpoint of love. Those who regard themselves deserving of the gift of God regard their relationship with the creator as one of payment for deeds done, and therefore miss both the gift and the nature of God's relationship with his creation. As such, to determine a needy individual as unworthy of government or private aid, of whatever kind, is to place oneself outside the paradigm of the thinking of God, and this is so because it is a failure to think from the standpoint of love.

Indeed, to imagine that one's wealth is the result of superior intelligence and hard work is like trying to create a nuclear explosion by using only Newtonian physics. It leaves out too much. Material wealth is not an unqualified indication of strenuous labor at all, but at times merely the result of an acquired amount of capital that can be used to access a mass market, or the result of a monopoly that guaranteed, through supply and demand, a high return on a limited asset. Further, one's ability to work hard may well be merely the result of one's individual socialization, and not an imagined personal and heroic decision to achieve great things. It may also be simply the result of having been born in an educated family where learning was valued and intellectual discipline was inculcated. It may even be the result of a happy family life, where one developed a strong sense of one's worth that allowed one to work productively, despite opposition, as a result of this sense of personal worth. Or contrawise, it may be the result of a dysfunctional family life where self hatred drives one to achieve, to prove to a disapproving parent that one can succeed. In all these, and other cases it is not the pure act of labor that achieves one's success but any number of other events and experiences that cause one to choose well and get ahead.

To reiterate, one can not rejoice in the love of God for oneself, while at the same time feeling bitterness or anger, or at least not loving one's equally undeserving brother and sister, or neighbour because of the assistance that a government has provided for that individual as a result of their poverty. Even if one were to assume that vast numbers are unworthy of the government's assistance, do we honestly imagine that we can in good conscience ignore these people so that they sink into even deeper poverty and in some cases turn to crime. Is it good sense to refuse to spend money if the result is greater expense in policing and health care? Further, how does one determine levels of deserving? Is this based on an evaluation of an individual's character? What level of suffering does a family have to endure before they are accounted worthy of our grudging assistance? If one examines the levels of government aid to corporations, are our criteria as stringent for this sector as we frequently make them for the poor? As Christians we need to read the gospels and the thirteenth chapter of Corinthians a little more seriously, and critique our lives and attitudes in the light of such extravagant, undeserving love.

The Sermon on the Mount and Breaking the Circle of Violence

We need to carefully ask ourselves a very simple question. "How much and how many of my reactions to other people are violent, impatient, and anger filled?" "Am I justifying my rejection and impatience with "reasonable" positions, and "godly" values, while I know that I do not love the person to whom I am directing my anger?" Despite all the correct theology and valid reasoning we may employ to justify our impatience and anger, these harsh responses to people only reveal the lack of the one characteristic that should be the identifying mark of a Christian. The negativity that we communicate to others hinders, in truth, our ability to reach others for Christ. The fact is that if people do not come to us to confess their sins because we come across as judgmental and harsh, then we are neither filled with love nor expressing the presence of Jesus in the world.

Love is the nature of God. It is the core of the commandments, the greatest of virtues, and the true test of one's knowledge of and relationship with God. It was also the one quality expressed by Jesus that distinguished him from the religiously correct others of his time who saw infractions as causes of rejection, anger, violence and punishment, hopefully divine punishment. We are not commanded to express a love that God does not express consistently and always (him)self, and we need to show this love, not simply because God commands it. We are so commanded because love is the very essence of the character of God. Love is the central nervous system of a redeemed universe. It is the one sine qua non quality, without which God ceases to be God. Nor is it the power of God that makes God worthy of worship; it is his love. Love does not get angry. It would not know how. It would not know how to twist the word so that it could come out as anger. Love looks for and understands causes; love seeks the good of the lawbreaker, not his/her punishment. Love is the fulfillment of the law not its executioner.

Quite understandably, people want to be loved, but they also want to be able to punish those who wrong them. We have created images of God just like that, so we can have the love, and also have the violence. But the love of God seeks the redemption and reintegration of the wrong-doer into God's family, seeks to break the circle of violence, not by executing the violent other, but by turning away that violence in expressions of love, in the overwhelming presence of love.

In the Sermon on the Mount Jesus taught us to "love (our) enemies and pray for (our) persecutors (as) only in this way can (we) be children of (our) heavenly Father who makes his sun rise on the good and bad alike." It is this radical, and seemingly impossible rejection of our human thirst for retaliation that makes us want to see in Jesus' call to turn the other cheek etc., anything but its apparently literal and simple meaning. We quite understandably do not want this to be true. Our world of balanced violence would fall apart. We imagine the evil taking over the world, unopposed, and feel relief that even if we were to obey these unrealistic commands, fortunately there are enough "sinners" left who would protect us from Jesus' illogicality. Oh, this is very much what we feel, and what we fear, just as we proclaim the beauty and loftiness of the Sermon on the Mount. Why is it that we love Jesus, and lovingly admire St. Francis and Gandhi? Is it not because they refused to respond with anger, and that they were filled with love for even the worst. And that in our hearts we know that this is the way human beings should act towards one another? And why is it, that in this generation it was a non-Christian, Gandhi who was the St. Francis who took the Sermon seriously?

In this world we are kind to those who are kind, and violent to those who are violent. Patient to those who are patient, and angry and impatient to those who are impatient. We, and the world, initiate actions toward others based upon these two principles. We attempt to create a kind of social and personal equilibrium by forcefully suppressing behaviour that threatens this social harmony. We unconsciously seek harmony because it is an approximation of God's kingdom, and because it is, in fact, distasteful and exhausting to most of us to act violently. Harmony, the goal of our violence is completely acceptable. Human beings are programmed to live at peace with one another. We simply do not know how to achieve this without force. As a result we employ both love, which we deeply long for, and violence which we deeply hate. The question we must ask, however, is, "What did Jesus teach?" Did Jesus teach, or even allow, a use of these two polar principles, or did he consistently proclaim the radically disturbing, and essentially terrifying, principle of love...and that alone?

Though we live as solitary individuals before God, we do not so live as solitary individuals in relation to one another. Righteousness and morality may have a direct connection to our relationship with God, but they have an equally direct connection to our dealings with our fellow human beings. Righteousness is also extremely practical. It is not correct behaviour, *simply* because the nature of the act is acceptable to God, or even that it reflects God's character. Righteous acts are good because they promote a de-alienated and harmonious social environment.

There are at least two fundamental ways in which the Sermon on the Mount should be understood. The first is that Jesus is giving us a picture of the human heart as God desires it, and as it was intended. For example, the lesson on divorce is not one more rule to restrict life, but rather a plea that two hearts filled with the love of God would not experience an emotional entropy that would end in the dissolution of the marriage. The second great direction of the Sermon is an answer to the question, "How does one respond to a lack of love in another human; how does one break the cycle of violence?"

When Jesus encourages us to "go the second mile", to "turn the other cheek" and to give, "not only our shirt but also as well our coat" he is not providing us with external behaviour that is somewhat masochistic. Moreover, if we were to do all these things, but still fail to have love for this other demanding and loveless person, we would have missed the intention of the example completely. What Jesus is actually presenting is a love that surprises and wins over, or at least has the possibility of winning over, the "enemy" who is wronging us. Jesus is teaching us that the cycle of violence is not overcome by defeating the enemy other by the use of force of one kind or another. Indeed he is suggesting two sides of the problem, (not simply one side of a negative injunction, i.e. not a but b). These two positions are: (1) that violence is *not* overcome by this method, and (2) that force is the *wrong* method to overcome such violence. The radical understanding he is teaching is that the cycle of violence is overcome by acts of abundant love, a love that gives more than is expected, more than is required, a love that in giving this "more", reveals a lack of resentment towards the offending other. Jesus appears to be teaching that an act of love in the face of violence is so surprising that it forces the violent individual to reconsider, and perhaps repent. Jesus is teaching that violence can be overcome by a refusal to react violently. There is, in this act of abundant love, a selflessness that is the core of the humanly impossible life of holiness that Jesus repeatedly teaches. In this teaching on violence the self has stopped holding onto things. The sense of private property has been left behind, and possessions are seen as temporarily held.

The doubling of each of these examples in the Sermon should not be seen in mathematical or in limiting terms. In each example, the other person, the violent other, puts the individual under his or her power. The initiation of the second action, the second mile, the other cheek, and the coat, represents the Christian taking that power back in the free giving of that which was violently forced on her/him. It is the refusal to strike back, while recognizing, and "forcing" the perpetrator of the violence to face, the unacceptable and even undesirable violence of the initial act. It is not passive resistance, but an active and explicit response that indicates love for the other, an other who may truly be a repulsive and hateful individual. It is an action that is intended to elicit a response in the offending other, because of its completely unexpected and willing nature. People do not normally respond to violence by acts of love. God's attitude to another's hatred is also seen in Exodus 23: 4,5 which states, "When you come upon your enemy's ox or ass straying you shall take it back to him. When you see the ass of someone who hates you lying helpless under its load, however unwilling you may be to help it, you must give him a hand with it." This is not simply a command. Rather, it is a subversive teaching to love, despite the other's attitude towards you. Jesus, in the Sermon, simply added that in his Kingdom the heart of the hated person was willing to help.

The examples of behaviour, or even the set of injunctions in the Sermon on the Mount, should not be seen primarily as laws, but rather as negative or positive remarks, describing what love does or does not do. Matthew 5: 21,22 is not a refining of the law of murder, but an expression of the fact that any kind of rejection of another person is a failure to love, and that it is the lack of love that "ends one in the fires of hell" to use the biblical imagery.

Even the teaching on secret devotion to God and alms giving is an aspect of love in action. The lack of secrecy in prayer etc. reveals the self's desire to be superior to others, the desire of the ego to be praised. It is an unconscious confession that the public response to the religious behaviour is of more importance than the religious act itself. At least part of an understanding of the section on the exaltation of the self above others, apart from the fact that this reveals a psychological feeling of personal inadequacy, is that this behaviour shows the individual's lack of the sense of oneness with other people. And a sense of human oneness is an aspect of the presence of love in an individual.

Yet, while the possibility that love can remove the violence in an individual exists, and only this kind of behaviour is an expression of the character of God, there will never be a guarantee that such behaviour will remove all violence this side of the Kingdom of God. In this non-violent war there will be casualties, just as there are in 'ordinary' wars. As Matthew 5: 12 states, "in the same way they persecuted the prophets before you." Jesus may have been filled with love, but a look at his own life shows the sacrifice and seriousness of taking the ways of God to heart.

It needs also to be said that the use of love does not preclude the exercise of force. While we may lack the ability to restrain the violence of others, God possesses such power, and it would be unreasonable to believe that the ability and right to restrain the sinful was contrary to God's love. If, for example, we were to see a child being kidnapped do we believe that attempting to stop this violence and probable tragedy would be contrary to the Sermon on the Mount? Certainly we should attempt to stop all acts of crime and violence. It is not the stopping that is taught against but rather the violent anger and hatred that is usually associated with these acts that Jesus was focusing on. Within limits, this acceptability of restraining force justifies the existence, at least in some form, of police forces, if not the military. Nevertheless, it still must be said that it is not force that destroys violence. Force may restrain the expressions of violence but only love can change the violent heart.

Yet the more we contemplate the words of Jesus on the mount the more we come to realize that while we may be quite happy that in the dispensation of a redeemed world achieved through the salvific work of Christ, we do not have to obey the ceremonial aspects of the law of Moses, Jesus has not left us standards that are any less impossible than those parts of the law that express eternal values. Indeed, if anything, Jesus has presented the even more impossible task of possessing all encompassing love, and living this love in such a way that one may not be able to protect oneself from the violence of a hate filled humanity. To begin this task, despite what we may have been taught, despite our societal obsession with revenge in the name of justice, despite our instinctual response to lash out, despite all these things and more, if we want to follow God, if we want an end to violence, individually and globally, and if we want to pursue those qualities we most admire in the depths of our hearts, we must begin by philosophically rejecting, anger and its variants as justifiable reactions to wrong.

In the Sermon on the Mount, Jesus is teaching a love that is selfless, a missionary kind of love that actively seeks to remove violence and unite a fragmented society. It is a foolish love, a love that is impossible and ridiculous to the heart that is not fully possessed by the God, who alone is capable of such love. It is a love that does not see a hated enemy in any other individual. It is also the paradigm by which the entire ministry of Jesus must be understood.

The Sermon on the Mount and War

And yet let one caveat be added to this. It is a caveat of failure, but it is pragmatic. The position of Jesus is the position of ultimate love and ultimate faith. To have faith and to know that one has it are not the same experience as desiring to have faith. Faith is the position Isaiah took in Jerusalem when it was besieged (I am taking the book of Isaiah at face value here and not questioning its date or authorship.), and then, protected by God, escaped destruction. If one does not genuinely have faith one should not put oneself and others in harms way. When Jesus was with his disciples they were safe. They were also surrounded by his faith. However, just before he was crucified, Jesus said to them in Luke 22:35,36, "When I sent you out barefoot without purse or pack were you ever short of anything? "No", they answered. "It is different now. Whoever has a purse had better take it with him, and his pack too; and if he has no sword, let him sell his cloak to buy one." A problematic section, don't you agree?

Perhaps Jesus was admitting that the disciples did not possess sufficient faith at that time to do what was ideally both true and possible. Perhaps Jesus was allowing a second, lower level of (faith) behaviour. Perhaps Jesus was teaching that if you do not have genuine faith in this world, then you definitely need to protect yourself from its harshness and violence. It is neither easy nor pleasant to write this interpretation but it may be the truth. That the disciples lived under the umbrella of Jesus' faith and relationship with the Father is clear from John 17:11,12, "I am to stay no longer in the world, but they are still in the world...When I was with them, I protected by the power of thy name those whom thou hast given me." Coupled with Luke 22, Jesus seems to be suggesting that maintaining the level of faith and protection the disciples experienced during His earthly ministry would be more difficult after he was gone, and that there was a high possibility it would not be maintained.

To digress a little, it is also true that virtually no matter who is presenting the idea of non-violence, in the depths of the heart of this individual is the belief, like a rock hard nut secreted away in the sub-conscious, that there are times when war is justified. If one attempts to take Jesus seriously, one comes to the point where one is forced to conclude that violence is never acceptable. But I believe that this secret reservation stays in the heart unless an exceptionally high level of spirituality exists, where God removes this in a revelation of his power that makes the reservation simply unnecessary.

The great pacifist Thoreau, when confronted with the slavery issue and the imminent execution of John Brown who was convinced that a violent confrontation with the forces supporting slavery was the only way the system would ever be destroyed, decided that in some situations, violence was permissible. This does not mean that he was correct, but it does show that even the most pacifistic can be lead to see a limitation to the non-violent approach. And the force of this argument is powerful indeed. Gandhi said, when asked if Hitler could be defeated non-violently, "He could be defeated but there would be many casualties." He is also reported to have said, however, that if a mad dog were to roam through one's village one killed it. How does one, non-violently defeat a madman who has his finger on the button of a nuclear device and is going to push it ? How does a nation state, "turn the other cheek"? Do governments respond differently to individuals? As the world learned during the Second World war, appeasement does not stop a maniacal dictator. Nevertheless, failure to convert the violent is not a proof of the error of Jesus' method. Jesus did not say, "try this, and if it doesn't work return to violence". There is something absolute about Jesus' teaching in the Sermon that is not amenable to tinkering.

We must go back to Jesus. Can Jesus be trusted on this? Surely what is absolutely needed in this situation is a level of spirituality that is simply not contemplated by most Christians. We need to be in such a place with God that we can exercise the word of faith, expecting God to confirm it. When we wear bracelets that spell out WWJD, (what would Jesus do?), we need to realize that Jesus himself did not know what he would do until he was led by the Spirit. When Jesus said he did whatever the Father told him he was not simply saying that he obeyed the Mosaic law without fault. He was led by the Spirit to answer and teach what the Father wanted for each particular individual and social situation in which Jesus found himself. You cannot know what Jesus would do in every situation unless you are in a close relationship with God such that you also are led by the Spirit of God.

This does not imply you cannot act unless God tells you to. Life has its obligations and necessities, and we do them without thinking whether we should. Not all life is an aspect of religious obligation. You do not have to ask God if you can have a coffee...though you must be surrendered to him so that if, for some exceptional reason God did not want you to, you do not. We need to be open to that extremely unusual direction. But it is extremely unusual. We do not need specific divine guidance for every action we contemplate doing. The scripture says, "I being in the way the Lord led me." (Genesis 24:27) In the midst of completely normal activity, God will guide one. However, there are some issues of such tremendous importance that only the wisdom of God is sufficient, and only a deep spirituality will make this a possibility.

The thing is, the Christian's walk is not totally one of the mind discovering biblical truths that will fit every situation. We are supposed to be in a relationship with the Godhead that includes genuine communication, and this does not simply mean us praying to God. It also includes God speaking to us, and at times specifically guiding us. If Jesus is always with us, doesn't that imply that he will speak to us?

So what does that have to do with the Christian's attitude to war? That Jesus taught the unacceptability of violence seems inescapable. This attitude is tied, perhaps inseparably, to radical love which would not consider engaging in violence towards the one loved (the enemy). (See 1Cor. 13: 4-7) Perhaps, in a world of violence, in a world of war, God's way of bringing about peace is by waging radical love. The Jews who passively let themselves be led into the concentration camps were not committing violence, but they were also not making a radically positive statement. The Nazis were not confronted by their own guilt in the face of this passivity. And perhaps I would have done and been the same. No one can find fault with those millions who died. But they weren't making any symbolic statements either.

If we examine the lives of St. Peter and St. Paul we find that at times God miraculously preserved them from harm: Peter was released from jail by the angel, Paul was bitten by the snake but not harmed, was stoned and left for dead and then rose up and travelled to another town. We also know that both were almost certainly killed by the Roman government. Paul, in 2 Corinthians 11: 23-27, gives a long list of his sufferings, among which he says, "Five times the Jews have given me thirty-nine strokes, three times I have been beaten with rods, once I was stoned" To act in the way of love is not to be secure from the violence of those to whom one goes to express that love.

Perhaps that is where the problem lies for us. If we follow the path of divine love we want a guarantee that we will be safe. We want an outcome that is equivalent in success to the peace that follows from a successful war. Maybe that is why Jesus said, "Blessed are the peacemakers for they shall be called the children of God" Jesus appears to be claiming that those who genuinely follow him will ultimately be successful. However, do we truly believe this? The unbelieving part of our personalities is a vast hidden land that needs, and lacks, God's habitation. To reject war, we need a vibrant faith that sees God's ultimate victory over a violence, that at times seems invincible.

I would suggest that if we do not have, or have not had, a close walk with God, any expressions of faith in this idea do not count for much. Religious knowledge is not a knowledge of ideas relating to God. These ideas may be correct, and they may be the basis of a real knowledge of God, but that is all they are. If the ideas we have do not flow out in actions, we had better come to a moment of inner self realization, and ask God for a deeper life with him. Isn't this also what James in his epistle says? This is not about salvation faith. Rather it is about a faith that changes how a life is led, that changes the environment, particularly the social environment, around us. However, lest we become too discouraged in all this, we should also realize that faith at times is like an underground river, flowing but unseen. We may also have more faith than we realize. Sometimes the truest things we hold are below our conscious awareness. To say that our faith is small is not to say that we have no faith at all. Jesus can take that small spark of faith and fan it into a flame. But we do need to understand ourselves accurately.

While it is clear that a violent attitude towards another individual or state must be rejected according to the Sermon on the Mount, and further, that acts of love, even in the face of multifarious acts of violence, as positive responses to this violence, are the teachings of the Sermon, do these principles imply a categorical rejection of self defense?

Firstly, and without qualification, it must be asserted that the Sermon on the Mount describes God's model for how human relations should operate. Secondly, and I do not know how this conclusion can be avoided, the Sermon teaches that violence should not be violently opposed. Once again, though, is one justified in defending oneself? The practical truth is that a life lived in love and righteousness will defend one, to some degree, against the resentments of most. This seems true even for nations. States that interact on the global level in a fair and compassionate fashion have less likelihood of being attacked by other nation states. As one author has written, "it is not only the axe that is to blame, it is also the tree." If a nation acts violently, or only in its own interests, it can expect to be hated, and even attacked. The desire to control the world is not a particularly Christian ambition, and opposition to this global policy of control will certainly include the perception that such a state is a threat to other states. Massive "defense" spending in order to guarantee superiority, is also not likely to decrease the threat of attack on such a state. Instead, it will paradoxically increase this threat.

Global self interest, as state policy, is no less unchristian than unrestricted individual self interest. One may want to be left alone but obligations to other human beings, whether as individuals or in terms of states, remain as divine expectations. A massive reduction in the possibility of being attacked will, nevertheless, be achieved if an individual or state acts from the standpoint of loving, "self interest". Such a behavioural orientation is not impractical or other worldly. In fact, it is decidedly of this world. Genuine Realpolitik would not needlessly antagonize other nations by short-sighted actions that, even in the short term were only marginally successful, and in the long term were cumulatively disastrous. A nation that deceives itself into thinking it can act solely in its self interest , with no negative side effects, is not acting in a hard headed and decisive fashion. Rather it is acting recklessly and unintelligently. There are, thus, acceptable modes of self defense.

Are these, however, the only acceptable forms of self defense? Matthew 8: 5-13, Luke 7:1-10, Acts 10: 1-48 all mention Roman Centurions who acted in godly ways. In the Gospels the centurion asked Jesus to heal a servant, and in Acts, the Centurion Cornelius had a vision in which an angel told him to visit, what turned out to be St Peter. In none of these stories did either Jesus or the apostle tell the centurion he was engaged in a murderous occupation and should resign or desert. Each was praised for the faith and godliness of his life. Now these incidents can be interpreted simply by suggesting that God was not trying to solve all their spiritual problems at once. However, there is no indication in the text that this should be the interpretation. And if there is no explicit indication for that interpretation, is there not a tacit implication that their occupations were not regarded by Jesus or Peter as inherently sinful?

Moreover, when Jesus was being tried by Pilate, he is asked, "What have you done? Jesus replied, 'My kingdom does not belong to this world. If it did, my followers would be fighting to save me from arrest...'" (John 18: 35,36) There are three implied ideas here: (1) that fighting is not in itself wrong, and (2) that in earthly governmental arrangements, fighting is not necessarily wrong, at least in the protection of the state or its people, and (3) that Jesus does not expect us to violently and forcibly seek to impose the kingdom of God. The third implication must necessarily be true as Jesus specifically states that his kingdom is not of this world. Further, this interpretation of the kingdom of God is consistent with all of Jesus' teaching regarding the institution of the kingdom throughout his earthly ministry.

What the scripture seems to present us with, then, is two positions. The first is the Messianic position expressed in the Sermon on the Mount. This position describes God's ideal stand on human relationships which teaches that the response to violence is not a response in kind. There are no excluding conditions. In that it is ideal does not necessarily imply that it is therefore unachievable. That is how we usually understand "ideal", but this should not be the interpretation with regard to God's standards. In Christ, and in Him alone, the impossible is made possible. The second position can be loosely identified with the Mosaic Law. The catchword for this position could be "Moses gave you". This is the pragmatic position given in the Torah because of the inability of the human heart to perfectly express the character of God.

If one looks at both of these positions, the conclusion not only appears to be, but is that in the kingdom of God there is no violence of any kind. This is clearly seen in Hosea 2: 18,19,

> Then I will make a covenant on behalf of Israel with the wild beast, the birds of the air, and the things that creep on the earth [all sources of violence] and I will break bow and sword and weapons of war and sweep them off the earth, so that ALL living creatures may lie down without fear.

This is God's attitude to war. And those who seek to express this kingdom, here and now, can be seen as the kind of "first fruits" of James 1:18, who act in the way that Jesus described in the Sermon. This is similar to the Catholic understanding of monasteries as examples, "islands" of the Kingdom of God while existing 'prior' to this kingdom.

Nevertheless, these parallel positions seem to indicate that God accepts the fact that not everyone understands, or even wants to understand God's kingdom principles, and that the problem of violence is so deeply entrenched in human thought and behaviour that we are afraid to live by God's standards. We are, in fact, paralyzed by this fear, and can not seem to see any other workable alternative. In this accepted but unacceptable level of understanding, God understands that this will result in behaviour that, while seeking a "just" peace, will involve violence and war.

One final comment in relation to war and those who are engaged in it. Despite the fact that Scripture, particularly the teaching of our Saviour, teaches us to love our enemies, and not attempt to annihilate them, it is also true that there are genuine Christians who attempt to walk with God, and who serve in the armed forces, just as did the godly Roman centurions who were praised for their faith and devotion. I believe they are wrong in their support of military action. But I also believe that they walk day by day in a state of acceptance before God, clothed in the perfect righteousness of Jesus, and because these people are in submission to God in their hearts, God finds pleasure in their devotion, just as Jesus did towards the centurion. If I believe they are unfortunately wrong in their understanding, then perhaps it is also true that my unrealized sins are far worse, and I am much more in need of God's grace. God takes us where we are, and most of the time this includes erroneous attitudes to aspects of life. God accepts us where we are, sometimes in spite of the sin that we cannot overcome at that particular time in our lives. God also accepts us as we are when this includes mistakes in understanding his word on particular subjects. We never know perfectly, and we never act perfectly. There are, no doubt, thousands of godly soldiers, sailors and airmen who love God and seek to love their fellow human brothers and sisters, while continuing in the military. Unfortunately, on this point, I believe they are incorrect, and I deeply understand how they can be so.

Are There Two Levels of Holiness?

The violence in the world is a pure reflection of the sinfulness within the human heart. Several times Jesus said words to the effect, "Moses gave you that because of the hardness of your hearts". There seem to be two levels of appropriate behaviour suggested in Jesus' statement. One is the level of those who are still, to one degree or another controlled by sin or whose lives are controlled or unavoidably impacted by the sinfulness of others, and the other is that state of soul and being which completely expresses the character and desire of God. Was Jesus saying that Moses had made a mistake? Jesus was definitely implying that Moses did not describe human behaviour the way God would prefer it. To accept both positions as expressing some level of truth it seems that we must view certain aspects of the Law of Moses as acceptable, only because we, as individuals and societies, are too sinful to live at the level of the Kingdom of God. This is not a remark that is deprecatory of Judaism, any more so than what Jesus, himself a Jew, said to other Jews was anti-Jewish.

For first century Christians the law was a source of instruction and a cause of controversy. James, as he is described in Acts, appeared to see all aspects of the law as necessary, in addition to having faith in Christ as Redeemer.

Paul sought to teach the perfection of the law as an instructor to show humanity's complete inability to achieve God's perfect standard, and saw the law in historically pre-soteriological (redemptive) terms. Jesus, on the other hand, evaluated parts of it as laws for 'second level' living. Jesus saw the law as a mixed system that at times did not reveal a kingdom without violence, did not describe a kingdom permeated by love. At this level, the Mosaic law is a law for a society that assumes and accepts human weakness, just as our own legal system does. How else can Matthew 19:3-8 be understood? However, as such it is a law for a society that does not operate on the principle of love.

Lest we begin to think, however, that as Christians we are above that level and society, we need to be reminded that the more we meditate on the Sermon on the Mount the more radically troubling it becomes for us, as we discover we are completely incapable of "submitting" to it. I would go further and claim that we are unwilling to submit to it. We very much live as individuals with the mindset, and on the spiritual level of the Deuteronomic society, and indeed living in a sinful world we may to some degree be forced, by the sinfulness of others, to live at such a level. In addition, the law of the Sermon on the Mount is no different to the Mosaic law. Neither are capable of fulfillment by any of us in our own strength.

The appeal to a difference between murder and killing as evidencing personal and impersonal motivations, that allow for an exception to the teachings of the Sermon, also seems less than convincing. Though it is easy to see the selfishness contained in my murdering someone. The mass killing of human beings in a war is not significantly less personal, simply because it is undergone by a society as a collective group. Hatred is essential in an army in order to motivate ordinary "non-murderous" individuals to kill people they do not know. Further, the true reasons nation states go to war is usually for ideas that do not even approach altruism. It is highly doubtful that there is anything impersonal about a war.

It should also be noted that, when Israel sought to have a king, God continued to guide and support them. The situation, however, also continued to be an abandonment of God. Israel sought a king because they did not trust God to protect them sufficiently. If we do not have the faith to live at the Sermon on the Mount level, then perhaps, for example, we will also need to buy a sword (invest out GNP in military hardware and in the training of an army). The religious acceptance of war seems a good example of second level spiritual living. I wish I could, but I do not see how the teachings of the Sermon on the Mount can be found to be compatible with any belief in the rightness of war. It seems to stretch credulity a little too far to assert that my self defense is unacceptable, but the violent defense of another is justifiable and that a war of self defense or against a tyrant constitutes a sufficient basis for a just war. I deeply respect those who hold such opinions, and understand their dilemma. It could be perhaps that God "uses" the unacceptable actions of some to limit or remove the greater evil of others. The truth is I wish I could also believe this. Jesus may accommodate our weakness, but it does not make the weakness any more acceptable.

Along the lines of God's second best theology just alluded to, I also suspect that God will, at least look kindly on certain actions as done in good conscience, and for the best of reasons, even though they are not what God would desire. The scripture may very well present two levels of "acceptable" behaviour. However, if we really did live at the spiritual level of the Sermon, I do not think, for example, that we would have a military. Matthew 5:44, Luke 6:27, states, "You have learned 'love your neighbour, and hate your enemy', but what I tell you is this: love your enemies and pray for your persecutors." And similarly in Luke,

"Love your enemies, do good to those who hate you.". Frankly, I do not see a way around the implications of these positions. Surely it is our fear and our lack of faith that leaves us at such a low spiritual level, even if, to some degree, God accepts us at this level.

Like Paul who felt constrained to write after he had declared that salvation was by grace and not by works, "shall we sin therefore that grace may abound? God forbid", so it must be declared before God that such a low level of spirituality is not where we as a church, and as individuals should be. We are not where we should be, and we should at least admit to ourselves our true position in relation to the terrifying perfection of God's standard, and from that self realization, at least confess that the position of the Sermon on the Mount is truly Jesus' desire for the church generally, and for us as individuals. It must also be, if the scriptures are to be believed, a level that, with the sanctifying work of the Holy Spirit, is attainable.

If one is filled with the love of God, solving the problems of human sinfulness, error, ambition, greed, and perhaps even stupidity (if such a category can exist in the heart of one filled with the love of God) by violence will not be contemplated. *Revenge,* in the name of justice, war, the passionate desire to see criminals punished, and celebration at this punishment, are all attitudes that are part of the web and woof of societal and hate-filled thinking. It is the thinking of those who are lost, even if it is paradoxically found in the hearts of those who claim to trust Jesus for their own forgiveness from eternally damning sin. These attitudes are antithetical to the teachings of the gospels, the teaching of Jesus in his earthly life, and contrary to Jesus' attitude to his victimizers when, according to such societal attitudes, he would have been most justified in expressing fierce and divine wrath at sinful behaviour towards himself as the divine ruler of the universe.

It may be thought that when confronted with violence and its results one should express more love to the victim of this violence than to the perpetrator. This appears a natural reaction to evil, and containing the feelings of compassion for the weak as it does, seems the correct Christian response. Nevertheless, I would suggest that the love contained in the heart of the Redeemer, does not operate in this fashion. The love that God would have us express to the victim of wrongdoing is unrestrained, except by variables outside its power, such as a rejection or misunderstanding of that love. The love to the wrongdoer can only be similarly unlimited, just as the love of God was unrestrained in the incarnation and the crucifixion. It is not that the Christian should express more love towards the victim, but rather that the heart, as God would have it, should be consumed by a passion for the appearance of the kingdom of God, in whatever situation the Christian finds her or himself in. God's love for the sinner is not reduced by wrongdoing, anymore than there is a lessening of this love for one to whom wrong is done.

There may be two kinds of holiness, the Mosaic and the Messianic, and both may have a scriptural basis. The presence of evil in the world makes imperfection difficult, if not impossible, to avoid. Nevertheless, for the Christian there can be victory over sin, and the impossible level of goodness presented by Jesus in his ministry, is possible as we are transformed into his image by the Spirit of God in our hearts. Without this transformation we all live at varying levels of the Mosaic Law.

Violence, Power and Servants

The two poles of Jesus' teaching, with regard to how we are to act toward another person, are seen in his teaching on violence, and in his teaching on power. "He who will be great among you shall be a servant." As the model of this, just so we wouldn't miss the point, though we have always seem to do so, Jesus, the omnipotent God became a human being and made himself vulnerable to the whims of other human beings.(Philippians 2:5-8) He refused to do violence when violence was done to him, and he refused to demand his position as the creator of the universe, even with his disciples. In a synthesized version of Luke chapter 22, and Matthew 20 :25-28 Jesus said,

> You know that in the world rulers lord it over their subjects, their great men make them feel the weight of authority, and those in authority are called their country's "benefactors". But it shall not be so with you. Among you, whoever wants to be great must bear himself like the youngest, the chief of you like a servant. And whoever wants to be first must be the willing slave of all- like the Son of Man. For who is greater, the one who sits at table or the servant who waits on him? Surely the one who sits at table. Yet here am I among you like a servant.

In this upside down model, a leader is a servant. He was not a servant in word only, claiming this position while actually acting contrary to this, as we do. As such, Jesus washed the disciples' feet, a demeaning act that only a servant would do. Jesus did not do this to initiate even one more religious ritual whose meaning is usually lost in its repeated enactment. The value and purpose of the act was in its implication. What he was showing was that, if one actually was a leader there should be no pride, no attitude that less prestigious tasks were below one, no sense that the leadership role gave one a position that precluded the performance of menial tasks, indeed no idea that some jobs are in themselves demeaning, and in particular, that a position of power did not abrogate the obligations of selfless love. Once, after St Francis had become famous for his humility, poverty and compassion, he was at a dinner with some princes of the church. He was eating a piece of bread for which he had begged on the streets before he came to the dinner. He offered a piece to a cardinal who took and kept it. In Francis' heart and in his actions he saw himself as the lowest, as one of the poorest in an identification with the poor and with Christ in his poverty. Even though he was with the leaders of society he humbled himself, not holding himself as one of the powerful as they were, even though that is exactly what he was, as their invitation had shown.

An occupation is fulfilled in the operation of its tasks. Whatever the position one holds, that position does not give the holder the right to assume a superiority and power over others, especially in areas outside of the occupation's specific operation. However, regardless of these attitudes of power, the idea of servant-hood is that we are each to consider what we do as actions to benefit and strengthen others. All occupations, according to Jesus' teaching, are other directed. If one is a plumber, this is to be seen as benefiting others who need such services. If one is a cashier, this too is to be done as a service to others, and if one happens to be the CEO of a multi-national company, this also is to be accomplished, not solely for oneself and the stock options it affords, but for the benefit of the huge global community affected by the company. Clearly then, to operate a company solely for the profit it generates for the shareholders, is unchristian.

Does this teaching disturb you? It certainly does me. What Jesus is telling us is personally disrupting. The nature of work in the contemporary world is that one is employed for the economic benefits that will accrue. Whatever non-economic satisfaction accompanies a job is also self directed. In fact, we usually choose an occupation because it appeals to us. We definitely do not work so that others will benefit. I suspect that even the ministry is chosen mainly because we are interested in such work. Our reasons for working are not what Jesus had in mind here. It is not that our reasons for working at something are sinful. Rather it is that we do not possess the one reason God seeks in human interactions, selfless service. Jesus speaks one language. In fact, if he were a singer he would be singing only one song, in an endless variation, all the time. It may have a number of verses, but it would be saying just one thing. That one thing would be love. Jesus was not acting as a servant, only when he washed the disciples feet. His total ministry was an expression of this. The emptying of the prerogatives of godhead in the act of incarnation was an expression of this, and indeed is the example of behaviour and attitude for all who hold leadership roles of any kind, formal and informal. In all Jesus' words and deeds he sought the good for those he encountered.

A couple of balancing notes to this must be that the term "servant" implies one person in relation to another. There are situations in which an individual is not in relation to another, but exists only in relation to the situation, for example eating, swimming or walking along a beach at sunrise . That one must be in the state of servant-hood in relation to others, does not imply that one must not ever act for one's own benefit. The second point is that servant-hood was not employed by Jesus to assert our subservience to God. Rather, what he sought to teach was an individual's attitude of selflessness towards other people, all other people.

What then is the purpose of servant-hood? On one level it certainly goes to the core of our pride and disallows it. Yet while this is clearly important, it has another more significant purpose. Acting as a servant means that one identifies with the weakest. One who acts on this level of humility is approachable. The powerless do not fear the "servant", and in this environment of safety, in the removal of social barriers that alienate one person from another, there is a healing of humanity. Is it not, that Jesus became a servant so that we could approach the Godhead without fear? The taking on of servant-hood is a manifestation of love, for it is the laying aside of those qualities and attitudes that separate humanity. Servant-hood quietly says that the desire for superiority over another person no longer exists. It is a removal of the psychological and social armor that makes both the "wearer" and the observer social antagonists. Servant-hood is the necessary condition for the encouragement of social harmony and integration. In servant-hood there is a crucifixion of the desire to oppress and dominate others. The goal of servant-hood, on the national level, is the abandonment of the ambition to conquer and dominate. Because of this, servant-hood is not simply an action or actions. Rather, it is an attitude that will underlie these actions. Servant-hood is an expression of love, and the crucifixion of self.

Prestige and the Desire for Power

Western society has created a taxonomy of power and prestige in which occupations are graded as to their importance, and to the degree that they are remunerated. Jesus teaches us however, that the temptation to assume superiority because of the social estimation of a task should be vigorously fought against. Luke 22:26 tells us, "the most important must bear himself like the youngest". The willing humbling of the 'highest' can not ever be taken for granted. It is something that seems to be a constant struggle, and indeed we understand that this will be so, if only because we are all extremely tied to the belief, for example, that certain jobs give a person the right to great prestige and social importance, and we seek those positions if at all possible. In addition, it is rather unlikely that we have never thought, "My car is better/worse than his. My house is worth more/less than my sister's' My income is so little I must have no value". All these thoughts are examples of how we either feel superior to others, or feel ashamed in relation to another's success. As others have pointed out, as a race we seem obsessed with seeing and finding an almost infinite number of ways in which we are superior to the people around us.

The psycho-dynamics of this exhortation by Jesus are quite complex. Pride and the desire for power, pleasure at being powerful, (in)sensitivity for the feelings of those with less power, are all part of the state of soul that is behind the injunction. St. Francis regarded this issue as of such great importance that the loss of "position" was part of the spiritual impoverishment each of the brothers had to submit to. In addition, the leadership of his group rotated so that one person did not feel the position was permanently his. Social background had nothing to do with who was chosen to be the monastic leader. The leader, in fact, was not called 'father' but rather 'mother', to even further reduce the idea of power over others that leadership seems to suggest. St. Francis himself made a point of never becoming ordained as a priest, and remained only a deacon, (a word which interestingly comes from the Greek word *diakonos* meaning a servant) throughout his life.

The problem of "superiority" cannot be solved simply by individuals attempting to restrain their pride. There must be systemic, organizational, and educational changes that do not encourage the feeling of superiority over people. As religious people we may have been taught to give respect to people in certain positions. This, in reality, only reinforces the person's belief that there is something in them that is worthy of the subservience others give them. On top of that, however, such an attitude contradicts the simple command to act 'as the youngest'. The respect we give to the powerful should, in fact, be refocused and directed towards those who do not have any of what society regards as power. Respect sounds like a valuable attitude, but in reality, if it is given only to those with "socially valuable" positions, (and who frequently demand it), it only feeds the human weakness for superiority.

Even in the church, ecclesiastical positions are given a respect usually not derived from the value of their ministry but from the power they are able to exert in the church. If we examine our reactions to, and relationships with people with power in the church we may be surprised to discover that our delight in being singled out by a person with influence, for example, stems not from either genuine respect or love, but from our perception of that individual as one possessing power, and that in being singled out we have been allowed to participate in this aura of power. Moreover, we judge success by the level of power and prestige we or others have accumulated during our lives. Jesus taught that this should not be the way Christians think, or the way they relate to one another.

Just after the second president of the United States was elected, and before the White House was built, there was a fire in a building near where he was staying. He rushed out and helped carry buckets of water with other people who had gathered to help. This is a good example of "a servant" attitude. The attitude we should have towards one another is one of love. We should not have "a position" to maintain. Love removes the need for imposed respect. Servants do not lord it over others. Obviously they cannot, because they are not the ones with power, and in perceiving oneself as a servant one is unlikely to act as one who has power over others.

Modern society may have a high degree of social mobility, but it is nevertheless riddled with divisions. It is not simply India that is divided by caste. To be a servant is to dealienate society, to remove the barriers that separate us from one another in society, to the degree that the humble individual becomes a sister and brother to the lowest, and the lowest is unashamed in the presence of the most powerful. How will God act in the spiritual world of heaven? We will never be equal to God, and God will never divest (him)self of the characteristics of Godhead. However, surely the kenosis, the emptying of the God qualities of the Lord Jesus Christ in his coming to this earth, indicates that the almighty creator is lovingly approachable, and that he does not seek fear in his followers. After all, was Jesus merely putting on an act when he was in human form?

Of course, the world is full of people who regard themselves as important and superior, and it is not only the political world that is replete with such people, along with the symbols of power that gratify the egos of those who possess it. The Christian should not simply accept this societal attitude without question. Of course, it does mean that we must give up our ambitions to be held to be of importance. As human beings we do not really need to be told that this attitude is wrong. We naturally resent being patronized or demeaned by those in power. Unfortunately, this tendency to be corrupted by power exists even in those who most resent it. It is not enough to realize the evil it does to us. We also need to understand that it is evil, when we are the ones who are given power. Jesus' servant teaching was not intended simply to suggest organizational changes and teach the general equality of all humans. Rather, Jesus wanted us to realize that the desire for power, and its heartless expression in demeaning others, reveals a lack of love in the individual acting in this way. To be a servant in the heart is to love, and to have, or want to have a place of superiority over others is to fail to love.

In Jesus' model there are no holders of power who selfishly control others, and impose their own version of correct policy, behaviour or belief on other people. There are no superior and inferior classes of people. There may be varieties of social function, and even of inherent social power within that function, but one cannot profess to be a servant, while at the same time seeking to control others and acting in a dictatorial fashion that communicates one's social, economic or intellectual superiority over others. There cannot be a grasping at power, or a joyous intoxication in one's "glory". There must be a belief in, and a feeling of human equality among people, a perception of equality with others where the ego does not think of raising itself above others in its own conceit. The actually powerful are not alone in being guilty of this sin.

Nevertheless, it should not be understood that Jesus was teaching that different individuals should not have different levels of authority in the performance of certain social tasks. In this sense, Jesus possesses divine power and authority from the Father, which is above others, as we see in the scriptures which relate that on the Mount of Transfiguration, God told the disciples, "This is my beloved Son, hear him." Nor was Jesus teaching that we should masochistically desire to be doormats to other people, and allow all manner of evil to be done out of a false belief that we should never take a position of opposition to other people. Jesus was frequently forced to oppose, contradict and act against the desires of other people. We need to ensure, however, that we do this in a fashion that reflects the loving character of Christ, and not from the aggressiveness of a lost and angry world.

For a Christian there should be no, either instituted or unofficial, positions of power, so constituted that they allow the ego to glory in its own importance, that lead it to seek to make others feel inferior, and that, in fact, give others a feeling of shame because of their lack of such status. There are, of course, understandable reasons for the human desire to be important. Perhaps the most common experience we have had as individuals is being informed, usually impatiently, of our mistakes and weaknesses, from our parents, teachers, friends and even complete strangers. These personal devaluations leave us with the desire, and sometimes obsession, to be found acceptable to people in the ways that society has decided are criteria for success. One of these criteria for this success is superiority over others. Yet despite these mitigating and understandable reasons, the desire to be superior to other people remains essentially destructive, and ultimately leaves us alone in an unfriendly world.

It appears, as one implication of the servant attitude, that no task is socially demeaning. If all tasks are done in an attitude of love and for the benefit of others, how could any such tasks in themselves be demeaning? In the same sense, the body of Christ, in which all believers are part, is made up of individuals with differing ministries, all of which are honorable. As we see in 1 Corinthians 12:14-26, all social occupations acceptable to God are honorable and essential to the wellbeing of the human community. And in that all such activities contribute to the functioning of society, and are inter-dependent, all occupations are both valuable and essential. Labor, not simply the high paying form, is an activity that should generate self respect and a sense of worth. That a community cannot go without garbage collectors is soon evident when there is a strike of these workers. Who is to say that their labor is of less value than the CEO who directs a successful company? Indeed we could continue without our complex capitalist economy, but we would be in deep distress if we did not have people who removed our mountains of waste. At the risk of sounding more politically extreme than is intended, the high salaries we pay to certain sectors of the society only accentuate the sense of worthlessness that most people feel in relation to a society that evaluates people in terms of their income and wealth. And to these people we willingly assign power and respect. Say what you will. Such an attitude of worthlessness so generated is not one that God finds pleasure in.

In teaching servant-hood and greatness,(Matt.23:11, Matt. 20:24-28, Mark 10:44, John 13:12-15) Jesus is not teaching us that we should feel, or artificially attempt to act as if we are inferior to others. We may not be objectively inferior at all. Rather, Jesus is employing the language of power, and turning it upside down. He is turning the social understanding of greatness on its head. Jesus teaches that greatness is to be found in the act and attitude of serving, and not in the possession of power and wealth. We ascribe greatness to one who has amassed power over others, for example through wealth, military success or rank, political standing, or through leadership in an economic enterprise. Jesus, however, is specifically asserting that these are not God's criteria for greatness at all. To be a success, one must love. Indeed, if one wishes to be great with God, if one wants to be a success, one must seek the wellbeing of others, and be willing to do this, though it brings us neither recognition nor reward.

Does the society in which we live see any difference between it and the Christian? Apart from a general, and not very deeply disturbing feeling that the religious world does not approve of the values of contemporary Western society, is Jesus' radically different and revolutionary set of human attitudes towards our fellow human beings presented to it in any vigorous and compassionate fashion? If our society is becoming more and more insensitive and violent, is it because we Christians are not living the love that Jesus taught in the Sermon? If there were just one person possessed by the radical love of God as Jesus and St Francis were, our societies would rush to be in his or her presence, lives would be changed and the brutal self centred lifestyle that is in our face every time we turn on the TV would be shown as the empty and useless thing that it is.

People long for authenticity. They long for a love that is not condemnatory. They long for the truth expressed in the simple heart of a caring person. If people are seeking satisfaction outside Christianity it is mainly because we, the Christians, are not showing them what it really means to be a Christian, and what the power of God can achieve in the lives of those who love God.

We Christians have bought deeply into the idea that success is measured in monetary and asset terms, that our value is determined by the size of our bankroll or the brand of our car. Despite the fact that we are Christians, we have been socialized to believe, and even more so to feel, that these ungodly (that is to say not expressing the character of God) ways of looking at people are, in fact, the truth. And it must be admitted, it is not easy to be unimpressed by power. It is not easy to see people simply as children of God, or even, simply as human beings, and not as economic beings. Yet it is time to leave these values behind and conform our thinking and acting to the beautiful, and individual affirming qualities and character of Jesus Christ. It is time we stopped being indistinguishable from non-Christians.

Apparently 57% of Americans go to church on a regular basis. With this number the world should be overturned for the Kingdom of God. With this percentage attending church the US should be known around the world for its love and Christian character, and not for the size of its military and its willingness to use it. However, because the church is not filled with the life changing love of the Saviour this is not the situation, and it is no better in other, so called Christian countries. It is not beliefs that make one a Christian example.

It is the way one lives. Specifically it is the behaviour of approachable love.

The only title true love can possibly take in relation to another person is that of one who serves, a worker. One who serves, regards him or herself, only in terms of the activity itself, and not in relation to the social critique of that activity, except as this regards his or her employer. A servant does not boast, attempt to show others the brilliance of his or her intellect or position or seek power over others. In God's "workforce" a servant is truly humble, and seeks only two things: the strengthening of others and the glory of God. It is only good works that should not be hidden under a bushel. We need to imitate the Saviour who, though he held the power of the universe and its continuation in his hands, chose to appear among us as one who was as weak as we are. Jesus chose to become a servant because, given his love for us, that was all he could become. It was an expression of this love.

The truth is that the call to servanthood is simply a call to love. It is love under another name. This is, of course, because in the kingdom of God, love fills the heart, and love must serve. Love does not strive for power. In this sense, the expression of self-centred power is the antithesis of love. If love is the motivation, the central thesis point that achieves true harmony and success, then in the unredeemed world in which we live, power is the equally central anti-thesis that achieves harmony and success through the forced submission of others.

The rejection of power divisions by Jesus not only has impacts on how we act towards others, it also casts doubt on our understanding of familiar biblical terms. In this regard the term "kingdom" can only be a misnomer, as a "kingdom" is, in essence, a state of rank, superiority and inferiority, unequal possession and control of resources, and the conferring of power and privilege, usually as the result of accidental birth in a monarchical or noble family. Even more importantly, however, it implies the imposition of the ruler's will over an unwilling population. There is a violence within the term that is internally contradictory to a realm where all are united in love and perfect wisdom. As Jesus said when Pilate asked him if he was a king, "King is your word." (John 18:37) As such, perhaps the kingdom of God should not be called a kingdom at all, though what it is, seems in truth, to be a mystery. It is equally true that the "political system of God" is unlikely to be a democracy, as the need for a democracy is founded on human ignorance (the limitations of human knowledge) and the inability of humans to govern fairly and well without the countervailing balance of opposing humans, who are also limited, and must also be limited in their ability to exercise power over other human beings.

Choosing the path of servanthood is not, however, an irrational leap of faith. Just as there are reasons for desiring power, punishment and revenge, so there are valid reasons for rejecting these paths. If we do not see that the passion for violence and control is an endless cycle of violence and spiritual ugliness, and that the path Jesus taught is the way of healing and joy, then we are doomed to continue with unhappiness, and destined to continual societal unrest and suffering. It has long been known that both violence and love produce results, at times strikingly similar results. And yet, can we risk choosing one over the other? Can God be trusted to look after things (and this is a serious question) if we choose to faithfully follow what Jesus appears to be teaching? That, indeed, is the question we must all ask ourselves, and the answer we finally arrive at will determine if we are truly different from the world or not. Choosing to be non-violent, to bless and not curse those who may very well be in the wrong, is not an easy choice. One's whole being may cry out for some kind of satisfactory imprecation, if not punishment to fall on the wrong-doer. It is not that by choosing to forego hatred the evil doer will magically disappear. Rather, if we do not choose the path of love the cycle of violence will never be broken.

Love and the Law: God and the Legal System

A man and a woman appear in court. They have been charged with tormenting two children from the age of one till they were teens, abusing them, forcing them to wear diapers even as they grew to be adolescents, and confining them in cribs that were too small for their juvenile bodies. The courts sentence them to less than a year of jail time with the probability of early parole. We cry out for a stiffer sentence, and probably believe justice has not been well served. A well respected man is defamed and shamed in front of his colleagues. The accusation is withdrawn but the damage has been done and the man seeks to sue to regain his good name. How does the Christian emphasis on love relate to these situations, and indeed, what should our position on jail as a form of punishment be?

When one is wronged, to the extent that laws appear to have been broken, one can either take someone to court to achieve justice, or decide not to seek one's rights, in a move that is geared to remove violence from social interaction. The problem is not, however, as simple as it may appear from the above choices. Would we allow criminals to go free if we choose this second model of behaviour?

In the scriptures there appear to be two principles, two methods of dealing with social evil. One is the traditional recourse to the law, and the other is the principle, exemplified best perhaps, in the teaching of the Sermon on the Mount. However, there are at least three basic intentions in seeking the right. One is the achieving of a moral and/or legal justice, another is a quest for retaliation, and the third is the search for a reconciliation of humans in a world of harmonious relationships. If one believes that ultimate good is achieved through the employment of the justice system of law, trials, imprisonment and fines, then this is the method used to achieve this end. Nevertheless, even if ultimate good may not be either achieved or desired through this process, a lower level of righteousness, goodness or perhaps justice in the non-legal sense of the word, is sometimes achieved through a recourse to the courts. If, however, one is convinced that this route has historically failed to make any genuine gains, then one may follow the path of absolute forgiveness in not seeking a legal resolution to the wrongs done one. The desire for retaliation, on the other hand, can find no justification anywhere in the teaching of either Jesus or the apostles.

As problematic as it truly is, I believe that Jesus taught that the removal of inter-human evil is not found in a seeking of logical and legally derived fairness. This is further evidenced, both from a scriptural point of view and from the simple observance of human conflict situations. One does not win, simply by proving that one was right and blameless. Indeed, the human obsession with attempting to prove to another angry person that one was not to blame, while appearing to be logic based, fails to achieve peace virtually every time it is attempted. This, at times legal quest seeks to determine the relative degrees of truth in a person's complaint and find one individual, for example, right and the other at fault. This path seeks to place blame. And the truth of the matter is that there is a powerful sense of rightness to this method in that blame can frequently be justly placed. However, this approach does not achieve reconciliation between people, nor does it encourage the growth of love. It does not remove evil from society, and does not heal the injury that has been caused. Moreover, Jesus did not teach that if love does not work, then we are free to "slap the other person's cheek" back.

In the world as it now is, however, to limit the destructiveness of wrong done, and to control selfish and malevolent behaviour, the legal system has the potential to be effective as a restraining force. Moreover, in a society's being law based, the exercise and justification for extreme acts of retaliation are taken out of the control of those involved in wrong as victims, and theoretically placed in the dispassionate hands of legal practitioners, thus bringing the level of societal violence down to a more manageable level. The legal system, then, does not deal with either the origin or the removal of evil in society, but only with its restraint.

The Sermon on the Mount was preeminently a teaching directed to individuals responding to social issues of disharmony. In this sense, perhaps despite one's immediate reaction to the contrary, it does not seem to have been specifically intended as a pattern to be instituted by governments. If Islam suffers from the problem of excessively focusing on religious governance at the expense of the individual, Christianity has the problem of propounding principles for the individual that are problematic for implementation in a religious, or indeed any form of government. Indeed, it must be said that though the Old Testament was directed primarily to the nation of Israel, the New Testament seeks a holy response, not from groups or societies but from individuals. To reiterate, the focus of the New Testament is the individual in her or his relationship to God, within the church, and towards other individuals. This is certainly not to suggest that the New Testament is only interested in the individual in his or her rather selfish relationship with God. The individual's social obligations are of exceeding importance in New Testament teaching. What is not taught is the specific nature of governmental behaviour in an evil world, and indeed the very existence and definition of "government", as opposed to administration, implies the simultaneous existence of those who do not want to be governed.

Jesus' teaching on the mount is a radical abandonment, on the level of the individual, of the search for justice as we usually understand it. Not only the Mosaic law, but all law is a quest for the ascription of blame and rightness. The problem, perhaps, for the Christian is that neither the gospel nor Jesus in his teaching, appear to work on that principle. For Jesus, and also for St Paul, it is better to be defrauded and wronged than to fight for one's right and thus ultimately destroy the possibility of a harmonious relationship that may exist between conflicting individuals.

However, this does not imply that one does not possess rights, anymore than it is correct to assume that God does not care how one treats other individuals. Neither, does it mean, though one may not be "allowed" to seek "revenge" for wrongs done one, that one has not, in fact, been wronged, perhaps severely. Nor does it necessarily imply that one should not, either individually or collectively seek to achieve just and humane conditions of fairness in society. Martin Luther King and Gandhi both actively sought to achieve justice by means of explicitly non-violent, and compassionate means based on the Sermon on the Mount. When struck they did not strike back. In utilizing the law, and in seeking to generate legislation that would protect and free, they sought to change social conditions, not cause harm to those who had wronged them.

Nevertheless, I believe that the rejection of redress in the Sermon on the Mount remains so total in its apparent range of implication that any activity that opposes evil in society becomes problematic. James 5:8-10 appears on the face of it to be a good example of this non-active response to evil. The Christian seems reduced to "oh well, don't worry about it." as a response to all societal wrong. And this seems as equally troubling, on the practical level, as fighting people, literally or in court.

On the other hand, perhaps James, rather than being the exemplar of non-action, as it appears at first glance, actually provides the key to how evil should be opposed. Throughout most of chapter five, James is denouncing the wealthy for their selfish lives in the face of societal destruction. Verse five states: "You have lived in pleasure on the earth and lived riotously; you have satisfied your hearts in/during a day of slaughter." This is not a silent acceptance of wrongdoing. So where does the "silent acceptance" idea spring from? Verse nine warns against blaming other people for one's troubles and teaches us not to murmur against others. Thus, when James claims that the wealthy have been partly to blame for the suffering of the negatively wealthy, he is complaining. However, he apparently contradicts this stance in verse nine, when he tells the rest of us not to murmur against wrongdoing,. Now either James is internally inconsistent, or verse nine is actually referring to an angry attitude of lovelessness in the face of this suffering, and not to the unacceptability of pointing out error and unbecoming behaviour. These are the alternatives as far as I can see. Either James is inconsistent, or it is acceptable to point out error.

In seeking a solution to this apparent difficulty, if not impossibility, one needs to recollect that there are both Old and New Testament precedents for an employment of avenues of opposition (e.g. the court system) to wrong in society. When Paul was arrested in Jerusalem and ultimately sent to Rome for an appeal to the "Supreme Court", and even at certain times during his missionary journeys, he used the courts and the law to attempt to remain free. Further, Amos 5:7-13 portrays the legal system, though it can be subverted, as a place where justice can, or at least should be dispensed. Amos proclaims:

You that turn justice upside down
And bring righteousness to the ground
You that hate a man that brings the worngdoer to
    court
And loathe him that speaks the whole truth
For all this, because you levy taxes on the poor
Though you have built houses of hewn stone
You shall not live in them
Though you have planted pleasant vineyards
You shall not drink wine from them
For I know how many your crimes are
And how countless your sins
You who persecute the guiltless, hold men to ransom
And thrust the destitute out of court.

    This section deals explicitly with governmental wrong, the abuse of power, the use of wealth to assert lies, and the consequent subversion of justice. However, it also implies the real potential of the court, both legal and of public opinion, to assure the rightness of societal human interaction. It is also clear from history, both past and contemporary, that if wrong is not opposed, the power of evildoers to hide the light of truth and fairness increases. Incidentally, to "persecute the guiltless" means, among other things, to employ lies to destroy the credibility of those who have done no wrong. Indeed, the denial of the truth and the use of lies is a repeated theme throughout this passage.
    It appears then that wrong can be opposed. It is the methodology, the strategy whereby this is done, and the subjective intent that is important in this opposition. If one opposes only to benefit oneself, and with no concern for the one who has done the evil, the opposition is flawed. All opposition to wrong should be conducted with the intent of creating harmonious and loving human relationships, not simply to create the kind of moral society we, in the cold-

ness of our compassionless hearts may believe is correct. Any struggle which seeks violence to, or the punishment of the wrong-doer fails the criteria of holy New Testament living. However, the entire bible, including the Sermon on the Mount is an expression of opposition to evil, both social and individual, and this opposition is not presented as cold and passionless. Jesus, in his death and resurrection was not only dealing with the terrible alienation from God that we humans experience, but also with the problem of evil itself. As Mel Gibson has reminded us, the events leading up to his, Christ's, death are called the "passion of Christ", and not simply God's solution to evil.

Despite these remarks, however, it remains extremely difficult to generate specific strategies for social behaviour that oppose evil from the standpoint of Jesus' teaching, though the teaching, directed to the individual, very clearly has potentially powerful social impacts. Moreover, from the New Testament, it seems evident that the church is not seen as a protest movement, but rather as a dynamic influence, "leaven" that changes the society through the radical transformation of individual behaviour. However, in that the radical transformation of the individual is an implied negative critique of social behaviour antithetical to the nature of Christ, this critique does not preclude the possibility that the church, or parts of it, could, in certain situations, overtly express this negative evaluation in socio-political action of some sort.

However, while it seems to be acceptable to oppose evil on the societal level, it does not follow that all evil should be opposed. Before one becomes too emotional in one's response to that comment, certain ideas should be considered. Did St. Paul attempt to destroy the institution of slavery? Was this not attempted because he secretly supported the institution? Nothing in his writings indicates such a stance. Indeed, he recommends that if freedom is offered it should be taken. However, he seems to have accepted that as an institution, it was the law of the day. We may wish that he was more specific in his opposition to such an inhuman institution. However, while asserting certain values and practices that weakened, if not negated the inhumanity of the institution, he did not actively oppose it. In addition, Jesus did not go out of his way to oppose the Roman occupation of Israel, though he no doubt regarded it as a continual act of violence against a people.

There may be reasons that relate to an individual's or a society's very survival that make opposition to evil pragmatically impossible. It is far from clear, for example that a Gandhian protest movement, which is an extension of the Christian individual response in the arena of mass action, would even be able to operate in some political regimes, let alone be successful. Imagine such a movement being attempted in Nazi Germany or the Soviet Union.

Further, there may be strategic reasons that relate to the church's standing in society that make opposition to certain problems unproductive. For example, the church surely should not be continually taking positions against every error in society, at the risk of appearing solely interested in the society's level of morality, rather than in its redemption. One may feel heroic in opposing all evil, but wisdom, and even compassion do not always go along with such heroics. The church certainly does have a mission, but this mission does not include attempting to solve all of society's moral weaknesses by utilizing a strategy of opposition.

There are wrongs done one that affect only oneself. These wrongs can relate to one's ego, one's property, one's time, and can be borne with the help of God, and indeed may even generate a situation where the wrongdoers can discover, not anger and resentment but our love as fellow sinners and potential children of God. There are other wrongs that may have been inflicted on individuals and whole groups within society that can be opposed in a more active and organized fashion. Whether individually or collectively, however, wrong can only be opposed from an attitude of love for the one or the society that has committed the wrong. If love is the fulfillment of the law, then opposition to lawlessness can only be conducted "successfully" from that position of love.

It does not follow that if we should not seek retribution, for the sake of social healing, that society does not have the right to protect itself from those who would harm it. There are individuals among us who are quite willing to cause others to suffer in any number of ways, and who should be apprehended. There will always be a need for prisons. What there is no need for is the attitude of utter indifference to these criminals that we as members of the society almost universally possess. The sad fact is, however, that once criminals are imprisoned, or sentences have been carried out, we feel no more involvement in their lives. This does not imply, however, that there should not be places where threats to society can be put to protect that society.

I am well aware that there are many Christians who feel that criminals should be punished. Emotionally, I share this attitude with them. It needs to be asked, however, what the purpose of punishment is. Is punishment merely to inflict some variety of pain on an individual? If that is its sole function and objective, does this not sound a little sadistic? Do we punish children only to cause them pain? I doubt than any parent would agree to this as a goal. Even if punishment is supported as an acceptable form of response to wrong, it surely has a loftier end. Parents who cause pain surely do so in order to teach their child. If this is so with our children, why should it not be doubly so with criminals? And if teaching, in order to induce a change in behaviour is the primary end of punishment generally, shouldn't the teaching of a criminal also be the primary end of imprisonment?

However, though there are certainly attempts by the prison authorities and the government to provide educational and other means of positive attitude change in the prison population, this usually has limited success. As a society we generally feel that the only action that is truly available to us is a combination of length of jail time and the deprivation of personal freedom. We have little confidence that programs of any kind in jail will have a deep impact, and our only satisfaction, in the main, is that the criminal is at least temporarily, off the streets and not threatening our safety. As Christians our attitudes are essentially no different to those of other members of society in this regard. In other words, as Christians we are virtually bankrupt of ideas that possess any redemptive potential when it comes to the criminal population. Let me suggest that the major cause of this lack is that we simply do not care about these people. Indeed, if we do expend any energy in their regard it is only to express pleasure that they are put behind bars, and that they are moral failures whom, in our hearts, we despise, even as we fear them.

We Christians need to understand that what Jesus was teaching, on the Mount and virtually throughout his entire ministry, was a description of his kingdom. Jesus was not presenting principles that would make allowance for our sinfulness, but rather positions that exemplified the perfect nature of the Kingdom, without sin, even if in a world with sin. In that sense he was not teaching us what we should do, from a legal perspective, with a genocidal murderer or a dishonest politician. Rather, he was instructing his followers on how they should react internally to the evil that would be done to them, on the nature of the heart of a citizen of the heavenly kingdom. These reactions excluded, for example, an angry, violent response, and a rampant desire to sue, that was grounded only on a wish for retaliation.

In Exodus 18, under the guidance of Jethro, his father-in-law, Moses set up a system of courts that settled cases based on their level of difficulty with Moses as the final arbiter of "difficult questions". The courts were constituted, not only to decide religious questions, but rather all interpersonal problems the people of Israel had with each other. This system of judges was presumably the basis, at least the literary basis of the system of justice in the time of the judges, though the hierarchical efficiency of Jethro's system seems absent in the book of Judges. When Jesus refused to judge between two brothers over the division of their family assets in Luke 12:14, he was referring to this general legal system. He was also pointing out the radical difference between the Mosaic law and the principles that form the basis of the Kingdom of God.

In the face of the seemingly "totally other" nature of the kingdom of Jesus, we must ask ourselves, "Are we truly members of this spiritual kingdom? Do our actions conform to this kingdom, or are we stimulated by the same motivations as those who have not been transformed by his Spirit and his love?" It is so well understood that social behaviour is motivated, in the main, by self strivings that we take this for granted as the justification for our sense of justice. If my brother takes control of all or most of my parents' assets, we believe that justice has not been served. However, this sense of (in)justice is often based on resentment, and the desire of the self for as much as is possible. We will accept equality, but we definitely want something.

The warning Jesus gave in the passage in Luke was against covetousness. The message in the parable Jesus gave immediately following this warning was that the primary goal of human life, rather than being the accumulation of possessions, was a relationship of harmony with God (verses 16-20). However, it was not simply covetousness, nor was it simply a message intended to cause a fear of God if one was not prepared for death, that Jesus was focusing on. Rather, what Jesus wanted us to consider was a life that was NOT motivated by self. As surprising as it well may be, Jesus understood the terrifying inner revolution in accepting such a proposition. Our entire lives are built around the belief that if we are to be safe in this world we must fight (insert 'compete') against others to guarantee such safety.

Luke 12:22-31, where Jesus claims that God can be trusted to look after us, expresses not simply Jesus' command that we trust God, and that we should put God first (v. 31), but more importantly his understanding that we find such a proposition absolutely terrifying in its vulnerability to the savagery of the world and the selfishness of other people who are like us. In fact, Jesus goes out of his way to calm our fears on this issue. Perhaps the startling thing about the passage is that Jesus does not say that what the gentiles seek is sinful, but rather that God knows that we need exactly those things that the gentiles seek. If then it is the centrality of the self that Jesus is finding fault with, it is the opposite of this, a life of completely programmed non-self-centredness, that Jesus wishes us to be driven by, a selfless-ness that is just as powerful in its all encompassing passion.

When Jesus refused to divide the family assets between the two brothers he was not asserting that the other brother had done no wrong. Quite conceivably the other brother may have been acting with as much covetousness as the brother who had received nothing. Jesus was critiquing, not the specifics of this case but the motivation behind a legal quest to enforce justice for one's own benefit. It was not the court system in its totality that was at stake in this story. Nor was Jesus necessarily accusing the brother of the covetousness that he was warning against.

What Jesus actually said was that (a) his ministry was not to be a judge between people, (b) that his ministry was to teach that the orientation and nature of the heart were his primary concerns, and (c) that one's primary aspiration should be the kingdom of God and a trust in God as a divine parent to provide what one needed. Giving the illustrations of the lilies and the birds of the air was not intended as a teaching that we should not work to attain our daily necessities, however, nor that the material things one may seek are in themselves essentially evil. Jesus was thus teaching against greed, covetousness and living without faith in God, but not necessarily against actively seeking those things that one needed. It seems impossible to live in this world without seeking that which the self needs. Indeed, much of daily life appears to be selfishly based. It is moreover acceptable to seek these necessary "things". What is not acceptable is a heart that is corrupted by selfishness, anger, greed and other sinful attitudes, and which does not seek above all else, the kingdom of God and the good of the other person. The teaching of Luke 12 is, indeed, that there *are* needs of the self, and that, given the caveat of the conditions above, seeking these needs is not intrinsically sinful. Thus, while a heart motivated by selfless love would not seek the recourse of the law as regards certain inter-human dilemmas, this does not imply that there would never be a recourse to the law as an arbiter of other issues.

In this issue it is crucial to understand that what Jesus sought was not justice as we understand it, as the equal balance of dues between people. The spirit of the Mosaic law is seen in Exodus 21:23,24 "Whatever hurt is done, you shall give life for life, eye for eye, tooth for tooth, hand for hand, foot for foot, burn for burn, bruise for bruise, wound for wound." Lest we rush to the conclusion that this paradigm is brutal and we have happily left it behind, this is essentially the basis of our own legal system which is also based on the philosophy that a certain act requires an equal and fair response, just as the Mosaic law attempts to achieve. A murderer should get a certain amount of time in jail, a thief should get a sentence that reflects an equivalent amount of suffering to that caused by the act of theft, and so on. However, throughout Jesus' ministry, and not simply in the Sermon on the Mount, Jesus teaches us that this is not the paradigm that God works from. Those who are keen on the death penalty, ignoring the sociological data that shows the death penalty does not significantly impact levels of extreme crime, need to read the gospels with an eye on the perspective from which Jesus comments on problems we would understand as justice and fairness issues. The equal response model is not the one Jesus teaches, either as the method to reduce inter-human conflict, or as expressing the nature of the character of God that Jesus wishes us to personify.

It may be argued, however, that this Messianic argument sounds fine, but that this is not the way the world works. And indeed it does not. Galaxies crash into each other self destructively; volcanoes and earthquakes follow the courses they must, irrespective of the destruction and suffering they cause; animal predators hunt down and savagely kill their prey, sometimes eating it while it still lives. This is the world we live in, and not an ideal world of unselfish activity where no action results in the suffering of another creature, human or otherwise. Christians must be rigorously consistent here. Do we believe that Jesus represented the exact expression of God, or was he "radically different" to the God of the Old Testament? Personally, I do not believe there is much teaching on this problem that is genuinely satisfying. Nevertheless, whatever the enormous questions this may raise, if one accepts Jesus as the exact image of God, then the God of the previous millenia must be the same type of God as the revelation of the Godhead in Jesus.

What this means in regards to this legal discussion, is that while we see wrong or crime or sin as requiring a balanced measure of punishment, God views this situation of wrongdoing as necessitating an action that includes a completely additional dimension to our two dimensional thinking. For God, the resolution of "crime/sin" is *not* found in punishment but in repentance. This is God's attitude now, it was universally so in the past, and it will be forever. The grace of God towards the sinner in salvation, every other act of goodness towards us, the teaching of Jesus on the response to violence by love, and Jesus' teaching on forgiveness, are all apparently irrational behaviours that approach the removal of wrong from an entirely different dimension to the balanced punishment model we, both Christians and pagans, almost universally employ.

The difference between the way we see the world and the way Jesus saw it is that what Jesus was presenting was a paradigm for the removal of evil. He was not presenting paths for solutions to particular problems resulting from the sinfulness of particular human hearts. Rather, he was solely teaching those behaviours and attitudes which characterize inhabitants of God's kingdom. The particular actions such people would engage in would necessarily flow from the changed nature of these inhabitants, and the behavioural principle that would be the driving force of these individuals would result from a new birth that would create this new motivating principle within them.

As such Jesus was not teaching that there should not be solutions to social and inter-human conflict situations that appeared to ignore the standards of the Kingdom of God. Put positively, there could be solutions to social problems that appeared to ignore the true characteristics of the Kingdom, but that these should be understood to be confessions of failure to live at the Kingdom level. As Jesus put it, "Moses gave you that because of the hardness of your hearts but in the beginning (i.e. in a perfect state) it was /is not like that". What this means is that divorce, for example, is impossible if each person were to possess a heart that reflected the character and love of God, but that in the world of sin this may be a necessary path in order to avoid even worse or further evil. Further, in the same way that Jesus' teaching on God's provision did not preclude the possibility that one could engage in labour to provide for one's needs, so in the search for one's needs one might, if one possessed a heart in conformity with the Kingdom, use the courts to achieve those or other needs.

Because Jesus refused to be a judge between the two brothers does not mean that God is not interested in social justice. Indeed, justice and truth are tied inextricably together in the search for social peace and fairness. Exodus 23:2 states, "you shall not favour the poor man in his suit." Merely because one is poor does not mean that truth must be sacrificed in any decision involving such a person. Indeed, four verses further in this chapter, verse six states, "You shall not deprive the poor man of justice in his suit." Shoddy appearance, lack of social connections, in fact all those things that might generate in middle class people a feeling of superiority towards the poor must be spurned in a Christian's loyalty to the truth of a poor individual's quest for fairness. Nor is it simply a matter of truth alone. God is evidently especially concerned with the lot of the poor, as seen in its special mention in this chapter, and as such, so should we be. Justice and truth express the character of God. That Jesus died to express the character of a Kingdom without sin should not lead us to conclude that Jesus was not interested in justice.

While it is not acceptable to God to seek litigation from a standpoint of greed, retaliation, or anger, the use of the law for self defense is another matter. Clearly, there are strong Old and New Testament precedents showing how the legal system can protect the poor, the alien, widows and other weak members of society, and that if the weak cannot do so themselves, then others need to stand in the breach for them. St. Paul himself employed the legal system in an attempt to both protect himself and have himself found innocent of wrong. To reiterate, Jesus was saying that it was the heart that was of primary concern in human interaction, and not the legal fairness of a situation. If one's heart sought the Kingdom of God above all else and was filled with love, then other decisions in the other areas of human life would fall, or at least had the chance to fall into their proper place. Indeed, with such a heart, one was free to seek justice in whatever direction was appropriate.

A Short Parable from the New Testament

But the lawyer wanting to vindicate himself said to Jesus, "and who is my neighbour?" Jesus replied, A man was on his way to work in Washington DC. In fact, he was an under secretary in a government department. He was extremely well dressed but on the way he experienced insulin shock and fell to the ground as if he were drunk. He had his arms outstretched so that passers by could see his medic alert bracelet, but none stopped to notice. All the decent people walked by him, or even over his body without stopping to see what was wrong. If there were any Christians in the crowd they also walked past him, preferring to believe that he was an alcoholic, and not worthy of their time.

But an Iraqi Muslim student who was also walking along the street on the way to university came upon him, and when he saw him he was moved to pity. He noticed the star of David around the sick man's neck and ignored it as he hailed a passing cab. He helped the man up, put him into the cab and went with him to a hospital where the doctors and nurses were quickly able to heal the sick man. Later the American government worker offered the Muslim $100, but the student refused. He then offered to take the student for a meal at a restaurant, but this also was refused. He was told that he was simply doing what his father had taught him. And Jesus asked, "which of these people do you think was neighbour to the man who fell ill on the street?" The lawyer answered, "The one who showed him kindness." And Jesus said, "Go and do as he did." Luke 10:28-37 (Not an invented story)

Dear Father, I need you more than I understand in my most religious moments. It is not enough that my ideas are right. I am faced with an evil world, where friendship is shallow and not dependable, and viciousness is just below the surface. The cruel remark is so easy, and finding those who truly love is usually a futile search, so that I end being forced to accept acquaintances in lieu of lovers. And I am no different. I also am the cause of suffering, just as these others are the source of my suffering. I am not able to respond with love, and I do not have the strength not to feel the cruelty and anger of the world as a whip on my own back.

Somehow you must place in me this wholeness. Somehow I must hunger for you as if this really were the most important exercise in which I could be involved. My lack of prayer reveals I do not believe it is, even while I proclaim just such a truth. If you do not place this knowledge and desire in me, I have no hope. John said that we love Him because He first loved us. Cause me to know that love, and love others as your love was poured out for me.

CHAPTER TWO
ON GOVERNMENT

Democracy is chosen, not because the will of the people is universally good, but because, in this era of human sinfulness, the alternatives to a democratic form of government are universally evil.

Why Christians can support a non-Christian government: Democracy and Christianity.

The purpose of a democratic government is the well-being of the people, the encouragement, and the legislation of right and sensible action, and the balancing and limitation of the power of groups and classes over other groups and classes. That these, essentially humanitarian principles exist, implies that they also exist for societies other than one's own, and that the oppression of other societies is not supported by such beneficent and democratic principles. In that the purpose of government is the well-being of people, it would be inconsistent for such a government to seek to expand its control over other people, against the wishes of these others. Moreover, the criterion whereby a government can be positively evaluated is the degree to which it has a salutary effect on its people. A democratic government is not an entity separate to the people, but rather is the express representative of the people in their opinions and wishes.

A democratic government does not exist for its own sake, is not justified in the development of policies at variance with the wishes of the majority of the people and contrary to the values of the majority, and its continuance is justified only as it sees itself to be subservient to the society which chose it to represent them and for their interests. A democratic government therefore does not govern its people, for such a separation of entities does not exist. Rather, a democratic government balances the powers of opposing groups so that any group in society is not disadvantaged by any other group. Where the government does not balance these opposing interests, or fails to express the will of the people, it is oppressive, in violation of the democracy it exists to protect, and needs to be democratically removed.

Government can and must be seen therefore as a human activity, done for the support and amelioration of human life, as a civic obligation towards one's neighbours, and not as an exercise in the use of power. Indeed power, either on the local, state/provincial or federal and even international levels, should not be conceived of as the goal of a Christian's political ambition, or the goal of the political party to which a Christian belongs. As unsophisticated as it sounds, the loss of an election is preferable to the abandonment of the principles that ideally are the core of a political party's reason to exist.

Religious Freedom and the Separation of Church and State

That politically involved Christians frequently come across as more concerned with forcing society to conform to the moral tenets of the scriptures, than as those possessing a heart for the people, a love of country and a burning passion to leave this world a little better than they found it, or at least to struggle in the attempt to achieve such an improvement, is not simply unfortunate, it is tragic, and a cause for alarm regarding the state of the church. Indeed, most Christian political rhetoric is devoid of love. It is angry, and there is little or nothing attractive in its repetitious statements about our country's having left its supposedly pure Christian roots. Indeed, Christians are frequently marked, not by a joy for life, or even a joy in God, but by being "so seriously against", what must appear to unbelievers as virtually everything. Rather than being for life and filled with a joyful freedom, Christians appear unhappy and unable to enjoy anything around them. They seem to know what they are against, but be ignorant of what they are supposed to be for. While Jesus said "if I am lifted up I will draw all people to me", Christians frequently are so lacking in inner freedom that they succeed only in driving people away from Jesus.

Most religious political commentary, surprisingly by the evangelical wing of the church, carries with it, or seems to carry the implication that society can be redeemed by legislation, that a government can turn a society back to God by the force of its legislative authority, and that a "moral" country is an acceptable country. Indeed, the church seems to have abandoned evangelization as the primary mission of the church, and substituted in its place the redemption of the country by the return to a sound moral base and good family values, and even more importantly, a government motivated and controlled by the word of God.

Is morality the goal of the Christian church? Would a moral country satisfy God's standards? Paradoxically, though a truly moral country would be pleasing to God on at least one level, a society believing itself to be moral, only from the level of moral tenets, could prove to be one of the hardest to penetrate with the Gospel. If our goal is a moral country , have we also considered the attitude of heart that frequently goes with such an understanding? Why was it that, according to St. Paul, the purpose of the law was not to instill righteousness, but to awaken the awareness of moral failure in the light of divine moral and religious standards? This Pauline teaching does not imply that God did not expect people to conform to divine standards. In this sense prophetic calls to societal reformation should not be understood to contradict Pauline teaching. If the Law was intended to reveal sin, then the prophetic exhortations, though they demanded behavioural change, must also be understood in this light. That is, they also were intended to reveal sin. There is a divine strategy here that, in our concern to strengthen morality, we appear to be missing. Do we not believe in the absolute inability of the sinner to redeem and transform him or herself? Has our country become so populated by born again people, and yet not been significantly changed, that we have given up on salvation as a method of change, and taken in its place a morality imposed by legislation? Does the church not believe that the process of becoming holy is solely dependent on the Holy Spirit making real the salvific work of Christ on the Cross?

Why then is there such an emphasis on morality and the law, when it is clear from the very Bible, that is repeatedly appealed to, that the law, not simply the Mosaic law but any law, is totally incapable of producing the kind of societal change that the Moral Majority seek, and that this is only accomplished through the indwelling Spirit producing the character of God in the individual, by writing the law of God on his or her heart? Moreover, if this section of the evangelical wing of the church responds that they understand the necessity of the Spirit to transform the heart, why is there such an emphasis on a "reformed" society, along with the millions of dollars that go to achieving this band aid solution? One's true beliefs are seen in the behaviours that we engage in, and not from the words that these behaviours essentially contradict. Why is there so much emphasis on morality, when Jesus is the end of the law as a method of adequate transformation, its *finis* (end) and *telos* (goal), to all who believe? (Rom. 10:4) It is not moral that people need to become but saved and sanctified.

It is not that, as Christians we can live without morality. Rather, what is being critiqued is the abandoning of an emphasis on the transformative power of the Cross, evidenced in an obsession with societal morals. Would it not be better to exert all this energy and money on more effective evangelization, more gospel centred preaching, and a greater and genuine dependence on the Holy Spirit to transform lives? Indeed, it may well be claimed that the decay of social standards is the result of the decay in the spirituality of the church, and its de facto drift away from solid biblical teaching that is Christ centred and transformative.

Government does have a major role to play in society in protecting the powerless, working for social justice, and in fostering societal harmony, but it does not have the role of imposing morality on society. And it certainly does not have the role of imposing what would certainly be the moral viewpoints of a particular group of people claiming to be the true interpreters of scripture for the rest of society. The Catholic Inquisition and the Protestant Puritan Commonwealth in England are perfect examples of one religious viewpoint being violently imposed on a population. Examples in other religions of this tendency of religion when it possesses political power could easily be given. The danger is not, I would suggest, solely in the religion, or in the nature of religion generally, but in the abysmal willingness of the human heart to abuse power, and to do both psychological and physical violence to other human beings who appear to disagree with them.

The real danger, and the terrible reason religious groups must not be allowed to take political power, is that it is not only possible, but entirely probable, that even an extremely religious person who holds political power, while affirming a vast variety of acceptable theological positions or beliefs, would not have the two qualities that are essential in the religious governing of people, and these are a genuine, deep and passionate love for the weakest and the worst, and secondly, a humble heart that understands that his or her level of understanding, particularly with regards to God, is limited and quite likely to be, at least partially erroneous as a result of this intellectual limitation. The hallmarks of a religiously motivated government would inevitably be dogmatism and an intolerance of opposition.

As for religion, the purpose of government cannot be the propagation and support of one religion, but the protection of the freedom of all religions. Freedom of religion does not necessarily imply the qualitative equality of all, or even some religions. However, it is the environment in which there is the least likelihood that religious oppression will occur, and in which the truth, perhaps as one sees it, can prosper without the hindrance and resentment that governmental support of one religion would certainly engender, and which in the long run hinders the acceptance of truth. Freedom of religion should create the environment in which true religion can flourish, but not by an equal propagation by the government.

Government cannot support or even encourage one religion over another for the primary reason that historically this has led to the violent oppression of those in the society who hold views contrary to the beliefs held by the religious group possessing political power. The essence of democratic government is compromise. However, such a method of resolution is anathema to a solely religious understanding as, from this viewpoint, one can not compromise God's principles. This being the case, it is virtually impossible for groups who seek to conform both their lives and the lives of those in society, to what they perceive to be God's standards, to operate within the governmental level of a democratic system without either abandoning or weakening their level of commitment to certain principles, sedulously avoiding religious issues, or attempting to limit, subvert, or negate the democratic process itself. Thus, in order to minimize the influence of the government on religious observance, and the impact of extremist religion on government, it is essential that there continues to be a rigorous separation of state and religion.

Those who argue for the retention of religious terminology in the dialogue of the nation and in expressions of citizenship, rather than seeking to bring the nation back to its "pure beginnings" are, in fact, intentionally or unintentionally rejecting the separation of church and state upon which the country is actually and legally based. That there remained religious content in governmental conversation, such as "under God", and oaths on the bible, well into the twentieth century reflected the religious nature of the founders and the overall religious unity of feeling of the nation up to the present time. This was acceptable while this was the case. Yet it was an inconsistency that was waiting for a time when such religious assumptions would be questioned as universal and generally accepted.

The fact remains that the country is a secular democracy. It was founded on this principle, and the division of state and religion is an explicit admission that, as far as the government of the country is concerned, the country is not a theocracy. When individuals and organizations seek to "reassert" a religious essence into the constitutional nature of the country, such an eventuality, were it to succeed, would negate the definitely constitutional separation of the state from religion. Nor is this longed for intertwining of the state with religion simply with religion generally. As it is expressed in North America, the association of the state with religion desired by some, is specifically with a Judeo-Christian expression of religion. Buddhist, Moslem or Hindu religious sentiments would certainly be excluded by those seeking a retention of religious expression in the life of governmental and educational life. Ironically, those very people who despair at the secularity of the nation and seek a "resurgence" of religion in the state would be the very ones (from their point of view) who would support the separation of church and state in order to defend such an exclusion.

Such a union might be acceptable to some degree if the nation was populated by only Jews and Christians. Today this is clearly not so, and the expressions we hold dear in governmental confessions do not reflect the pluralistic societies that North America has become. Either these non-Christian segments of our societies are to be accepted equally with Jews and Christians as full citizens with rights to respect for their varying beliefs, or they are second class citizens. Though the founding group of individuals was predominantly made up of Christians of some sort or another, the state that they founded was explicitly secular and non-religious. We may wish to turn the clock back. We may wish that the nation had remained essentially Christian. We may wish that the general tenor of the nation was more spiritual, but we have no legal basis on which to force this into being. We cannot "take back "our public schools for God, for example, because they were never religious schools in the first place.

That this discussion must be carried on again at this time in history after centuries of its being enshrined in the consciousness of the population, is so because, after centuries of the church's believing that its goal was spiritual and evangelical, sections of the church, unfortunately often evangelical, and it should not be assumed that I am not an evangelical myself, now appear to believe that the government should be dominated by either religious groups or their supporters in order to return the state to its supposedly original pristine godly position. There have always been deeply religious, godly people in government, and such a situation has rarely been a problem as, up to the present no organized attempt has been contemplated to subvert a democratic government, by means of the democratic process itself, so as to institute a "theocracy". However, I would assert that that is exactly what Christian religious groups who are seeking both to influence and control the political life of the country are attempting. They may not admit this publicly, or even perhaps to themselves, but this is the logical conclusion to the installation of their programs.

Granted, religious groups in North American democratic countries nay not see themselves as attempting to subvert the democratic process, and it would almost certainly be unfair to accuse most of the Christians involved in these organizations of consciously contemplating such a move. However, the intrinsic character of puritan movements, which these contemporary politically activist movements are, is such that compromise on godly principles is impossible. There is no talk at present of taking over the government, but I would assert that this is so, only because at this moment, there is little likelihood that such an attempt would be successful. Nevertheless, the central goals, epistemological basis of their beliefs, and the inviolability of these beliefs, make the worst case scenario a necessary conclusion, given a sufficient level of political power.

This problem, as most already know, is not solely a problem for the Christian church and the West. It is a global phenomenon whose causes will not be dealt with here. The fact is though, that the philosophy of Divine control behind political involvement by religious groups is virtually identical, whether it is in Iran by Muslims, in the United States by Christians, or in Israel by ultra-orthodox Jews.

Such a position is not an attack on the church, or even a part of the church. Nor is it an attack on religion generally, as even a casual reading of other parts of this book will readily reveal. For a certain number of deeply religious people, however, there is not, and can not be, a separation of church and state. Such an idea is tantamount to blasphemy, as there cannot be an area of human life where God is not involved in some fashion, or at least possesses evaluative rights. For a religious body to support the separation of church and state, I would suggest there are three positions on which this is possible: (a) a belief that until the establishment of the Kingdom of God at the end of the world a secular and inferior system of government is acceptable and possibly instituted by God, (b) there is a need to protect the church from the encroachment of the state, and the state from the encroachment of the church, and (c) the individual has not sufficiently reflected on what such a separation implies in relation to the prerogatives of God.

On the pragmatic level, the second position is totally justified as a legal defense of both church and state, and is the core of the position taken in this section.. What the above claim regarding the practical need for such a separation asserts is the historic impossibility of religious people to refrain from violence and oppression when they hold the reins of state power, the concurrent belief that the future would be no different were this to occur once again, and that such a religious state so constituted would not be a genuine theocracy, but only a government under the power of a religious hierarchy.

However, while there must then be a separation between the state and religious organizations, this separation, should not operate in such a fashion that, contrary to the principle of freedom of religion itself, the state restricts a religious group, or obstructs such a group in the expression of its beliefs and in its desire to spread its beliefs, in the name of that very freedom which the state believes itself to be defending. In the, essentially new environment of immigrant pluralistic societies, the religious freedom of one group cannot be restricted in the defence of the purported religious freedom of another if no laws are being broken, no violence is being engaged in or encouraged, and no property rights are being trespassed. In the area of religious freedom the laissez faire model of the capitalist system should be invoked, allowing the "market place" to determine the success of particular religions.

Moreover, the enlargement of one group, at the expense of another group, whatever that group, can not be the justification for a restriction on any religious group. Neither should statements of difference, from whatever group, be seen as harmful, or necessarily malevolently intended. It is clearly in the nature of religions to differ in their beliefs. It is not logical, given this fact, to impute the statement of differences by any group in reference to another group, to religious, or racial hatred or discrimination. Indeed, only an incitement to violence would justify such a charge. If a particular religion did not believe it understood the metaphysical world better than any other, group there would be no reason for it to exist.

Indeed, the existence of a religious group, by definition, implies that it sees itself as theologically or spiritually superior to other religious groups in relation to its understanding of divinities and other metaphysical entities. A religion's belief in its superiority is an issue only for those who wish to cause dissension, or for those who having no particular religion, see either no difference between religions, or seek to employ a false liberalism, that would pressure all groups to deny essential differences. Further, societal values should not determine a limitation on any religion's expression of rejection of these societal values on the condition, as already expressed, that such expressions do not incite violence, or encourage actual discrimination in relation to aspects of life that are not connected to such beliefs. Nevertheless, within the environment of free and peaceful religious expression, a government must be sensitive to the possibility of specious claims of discrimination made by one group to limit another group's ability to function as a dynamic religion with the right to express its views freely, even if the spreading of these views impacts on, or is disquieting to the group making such a claim. To say that all religions are thus adequately protected, is to say that our particular religion is adequately protected.

Democracy and the Multi-Party System.

The form of government that exists in much of the developed world today is representative democracy. It would probably be more accurate to call this form of government representative multi-party democracy, as this is both the extant system and that held to genuinely allow free expression of popular difference of opinion. In this system, usually one representative is chosen by a region within a state, and this person theoretically represents the region's population in governmental debate. In a multi-party system the representative from the party that wins the most votes in a regularly held election is said to be the representative of the total population of the region, even though he or she truly represents only the party to which he or she belongs and consequently the minority or majority who voted for this individual.

This is one of the problems of the multi-party system, as the minority of electors voted for another party with potentially very different ideas on how the government should act. The question then is, "to what degree does a representative genuinely represent the total population she or he comes from?" Nevertheless, even if there were not a multi-party system, the question of any representative truly representing the total population would still exist as the representative can not be expected to have been supported by the entire population of the region. Indeed successful representation can only be achieved, to any degree, by the simple goodwill of the representative.

Genuine representation of the people's desires should be the goal of any democratic government. That there are times when a people's desires will be destructive cannot be used as an argument against government being a representative body, for the counter argument that the government should not be representative opens government up to the kind of tyranny that government by the people seeks to protect a population from. In any case, that governments at times already follow the shallow thinking of a people can, I believe, be seen in some of the legislation that presently exists. There are enough problems associated with a democratic government without imagining unlikely possibilities that are supposed to weaken the argument for true representation.

The representational form of democracy is chosen because it is inconceivable that every individual in a population would be able to participate in the political debate. It is probably rightly assumed that in such a situation nothing would ever be accomplished. However, the limitation of popular input into the government decision making process, to the periodic election of "representatives", takes this logistical difficulty to an extreme and, I would suggest, unacceptable length. One reason why this extremely limited representation may not easily be abandoned is that the governmental oligarchy so created is unwilling to share power with the people in any truly significant manner. That the elected body is, in fact, an oligarchy is clear, for the total number of representatives elected is tiny compared to the total population, and because even within this number there is a core of powerful people, the cabinet, who are the true directors of the business of government. This is simply a statement of fact.

If this form of representative administration continues, in order to approximate the democracy we claim to live under, it should at least be incumbent then that the representative be constitutionally obliged to seek and take into consideration, if not rigidly follow, the views of the section of the population she or he has been chosen to represent, while being free to follow the dictates of conscience, logic and party solidarity in all other issues. While there still exists the need for a small chosen decision making body, parliament, the congress or even a Cabinet, popular input, either sought or unsolicited could be made part of the decision making process, and not simply as this impacts on the popularity of the governing party or is derived from a poll. This input could be directed generically to the government and then passed on to the parties and independents, perhaps on a daily basis, to do with as they saw fit. The reason why this gathering of ideas is essential, is that the governing body, as a democratic institution, must reflect popular opinion. While allowing that such input is clearly dangerous, as the population may not be as socially advanced as the government, and the people may also be unaware of sensitive information the government possesses, it is equally true that the people may be more reflective of constitutional and social values than the government itself. It is also necessary, at times, to balance the power of the government so that it does not abuse its power and effectively cease being a representative body.

It should also be noted that most people do not vote for an individual as their particular representative, but rather vote for this person as the representative of a party. Thus, there is another layer of abstraction in that the party is seen as the representative of the people, and most people do not, in the slightest, conceive of the elected representative as the one chosen to channel their particular concerns and desires. Indeed, most of the time an elector's concerns and needs have only a tenuous connection to what any level of governmental administration deals with. Thus, representation by an individual, this crucial aspect of democracy, limited though it already is, is not, in reality part of the political philosophy of the electorate, even though they assent to it, almost as a creedal belief.

However, there may still be good and sufficient reasons why such a party system of representation should continue, at least to some degree and in some form. Even with a relatively small population, decisions have to be made, and further, there must be a process for doing this in the event of an equal division of opinion. The greater the population the more there exists the need for a body to make laws etc. for, and in the place of the general population. There needs to be therefore an administrative executive, and a parliament or congress for example, that is entrusted to make these decisions. The British system of royal assent to bills is acceptable only in that it is truly a pro forma step, and not a violation of the will of parliament. The American presidential system that allows for a real veto of congressional will, though the president is elected by the people, is more problematic. As a balance of power with the congress it has value, but in that it is a denial of the right of the people's elected body, the congress, to represent the people, it is nondemocratic. Apart from the fact that such a system consumes a great deal of debate time in political gamesmanship, there are other systems of national leadership that are more democratic, and perhaps would be more efficient. Nevertheless, some form of executive decision making must be in place, and thus, there are built in limits to the degree a democracy can in fact be democratic.

Nevertheless, despite these difficulties, throughout history the electorate has been periodically increased. Initially the possession of land was a deciding criterion, and for centuries women were not permitted to vote. However, vested interests have given way to political pressure and the force of rational argument, and as a result of these changes, criteria to be met by a potential voter have been consistently reduced over the centuries to the simple requirement of citizenship and a minimum age. That the number of those allowed to vote has consistently been increased, allows the possibility that the traditional resistance to a greater participation in the democratic process by the population, because of the inability of all the population to participate in the decision making process beyond the periodic choosing of representatives and the governing party, may also be reduced. Adequate reasons for this hope exist very simply as a result of advances in communication technologies and the increasing level of education throughout the population.

It must be admitted that there is almost certainly no perfect political system and the creation of political parties is an understandable result of the need for legislative success and governmental stability. To the degree that parties express the wishes and attitudes of a mass of individuals they can be valid expressions of democratic political activity. However, political parties as they exist today, are in essence, non-democratic entities in which the individuality of the members is of little worth, the conscience of the member is frequently denied free expression, and the rationality and possible good sense of the legislation being considered in the legislature is routinely ignored in an attempt to obstruct and deny parliamentary and future electoral success to the governing party. In addition, there is, at times, a tension between the positions of the individual members of a political party and the electoral region that sent the representative, regarding views that democratically demand expression, and the strategic and particular needs of the party to accomplish social and political goals consistent with its party platform.

This is especially true in Canadian politics where there is no freedom to vote with an opposition party on any vote other than a small number, specifically described as conscience votes. These, however, do not cover all cases where one's conscience is involved in the topic being debated. Further, the conscience and simple honesty of the individual member is virtually always crushed by one part or another of the party platform that each member must agree to support. It is highly unlikely that all members of a party will completely agree with a party platform, which anyway is usually an electoral device shaped to appeal to a wide range of popular interests. This conflict is resolved by an appeal to the violence model. The party "whip" enforces compliance to the platform and voting activity of the member with threats of expulsion (and therefore almost certain political oblivion) or other forms of party sanction such as access to the leader, refusal to support the member's private bill proposals to the House, or the denial of a cabinet position in the event of the party's success electorally. For a Christian, party solidarity is, at times untenable and, in any case, is a denial of the very democracy that we claim to support and be governed by.

The party solidarity model is, in fact, the simplest, least creative and most destructive of the entire democratic political process that could have been chosen. It is though, the easiest method to administer to achieve party success. However, that is simply not enough justification to employ it. Indeed, the mindless, lock step refusal of opposition parties both to support progressive legislation, to deny the governing party legislative success and acknowledge that the government is acting properly (though of course the governing party usually has the votes to ignore the opposition) is childish, irrational, a travesty of the democratic purpose to govern well, and one of the main causes for the widespread popular mistrust and refusal to respect the very legislative process that should be held in high regard as the expression of the meditations of the nation's wisest and best citizens.

It is well known that opposition members frequently comment on the value and validity of governmental legislation with government members, and then vote against the legislation in solidarity with their party, and on that sole basis. This does not serve the public good, and may well be in opposition to the wishes of the member's respective electorates. Indeed, even if the above reasons were to be ignored, it is shameful behaviour, and is only equalled by the completely ridiculous and predictable negative reaction to absolutely everything short of motherhood issues, that both opposition parties and the government express to the media about each other's positions, occasionally before they adopt these very policies themselves. In fact, this appalling "theatre of the absurd" is so lacking in integrity that humor is the only response one can usually muster. What we are laughing at, is really the blatant lying that we know full well is being expressed. It is a rather disingenuous exercise then, for politicians to wonder at the lack of respect for, and interest in the political process and its institutions when their own obvious lack of integrity is the order of the day!

Within and among political parties, therefore, there must be developed mechanisms where conscience and rationality are allowed to be expressed in a vote on legislative matters without the differing party member being punished or expelled for such opposition or support. There is no reason, for example, why motions to be voted on, where these do not conflict with specific party platform positions, should not be free votes where any member of the House can vote one way or the other without such a vote being seen as either a vote of confidence in the government that requires the holding of an election if the governing party loses the bill voted on, or lack of overall support for one's party.

Party solidarity was not, of course, developed to deny the integrity of the individual and there are obviously strong reasons for its existence. However, its execution is iniquitous in its virtual enforcement of dishonesty, and therefore of sin. Though it may be true that those who refuse to deny either the rationality of a legislative position proposed by the government, or refuse to silence their own conscience and vote against their own party, should be willing to suffer for such a principled stand, it is equally correct to assert that such a predicament should not be the order of the day. Further, until a nation's citizenry stands up and refuses to accept such an intolerable state of affairs, until they demand that the legislative bodies take rationality, honesty and democracy seriously, lack of integrity and (essentially) bad government will continue. Moreover, that such an appeal will almost certainly be seen as unrealistic and quixotic only strengthens the point that rationality and integrity need to reenter the political arena.

Expulsion, and an inability to perform as a representative of the district from which one comes should not be the results of such a stand. A stand based on the integrity of the representative is the very essence of democracy, and must inevitably result in the strengthening of the democratic process, the effectiveness of the assembly and an elevation of the respect the population has for its elected representatives. The freedom of the member to differ from his or her party is essential for the integrity of the member, the genuine practice of democracy, and for public confidence in the integrity of the entire political process, and its participants. Indeed, were such stands allowed, and were such stupidities abandoned, there would almost certainly be such a return of interest by the people in the governing process, and support for the government (whatever party) that the change would resemble a social revolution whose impact would reverberate around the world, and possibly even cause tyrannies to tremble.

Sadly however, I do not expect this to happen because party organizers would fear that respect for another party would weaken support for their own party and reduce the enmity between parties, particularly at the grassroots level, and this enmity is the very fuel of the electoral process. The continual focusing on the failures and inadequacies of other parties and their representatives appears to be the dominant method of justifying a party's existence. That on most issues the majority of mainstream parties have shared objectives and understandings is not mentioned. And anyway, the collegiality of the House is not of much value in the mudslinging of a campaign. And yet the political strategists who continue such dishonesty and irrationality are, I strongly believe, mistaken, for in an atmosphere of honesty, the true policy and ideological differences would stand out in stark clarity and provide clear popular choices that would more surely guarantee a political party's continued existence if they had any deserving validity. Further, such integrity would give credence to remarks on the times genuine opposition and differences were expressed, and elevate the public debate from the shallowly rhetorical, to one of a true discussion of hopefully serious ideas.

Christian Support for a Democratic Government

The church in the developed world regards a democratic form of government as virtually an arm of its national and global mission. Democracy and Christianity seem to go together as a hand fits a glove. When, however, did democracy become a biblical teaching? Why, moreover, should a Christian support a democratic government, particularly if that government does not actively support and promote Christianity? Is democracy the only form of government a Christian could support? These are incredibly important questions. Christians in democratic countries have been brought up, on the whole, to support democracy as a positive and good political system. They take this position for granted. However, they are also taught to support whatever governmental system they find themselves in as a result of a particular interpretation of a biblical teaching that governments are instituted by God. As such, from that particular teaching, democracy is not at all unique. In addition, as democracy must protect the rights of all citizens under its jurisdiction, it is not capable of actively promoting Christianity. Indeed the whole concept of government by the people can actually be seen, not simply as theologically problematic, but as outright rebellion against God, in that the people assert their right to govern themselves, and do not give this right to God.

These are not simple questions, and those who enlist the religious right into their ranks should not be naïve about the internal contradiction that exists in Christians as to the primacy of the democratic process as it impinges on Christian values and teachings. A Christian government, that is a government run by Christians for the propagation and implementation of biblical teaching, by its very definition, could not be democratic. A democratic government must reflect, or at least take into account, diverse and opposing positions. It must allow secular viewpoints, indeed protect all viewpoints, and allow the free expression of divergent and even problematic opinion. This would be impossible for a Christian government, (or for that matter a government by any religious group). A democratic government controlled by one particular religion would soon degenerate into an, at best, benevolent dictatorship. However, this does not imply that a Christian can not support and defend a democratic government. The position only asserts that a Christian government could not long be democratic.

The issue of "rebellion against God" may be answered by asking if the right to self government is indeed an assertion that the individuals making such a claim are simultaneously asserting that they do not submit to the governance of God. I would claim that people making the democratic claim are not necessarily, in the ordinary and philosophical sense, making such a claim. Rather, what they are, in fact, asserting is that in relation to other human beings, they are categorically unwilling for one person, or group, or groups of people to exercise control over them, such that their desires, needs and inalienable rights as humans are denied, or only arbitrarily taken into account. They are further asserting, I would suggest, a belief in human nature that is in conformity with the biblical teaching on the sinfulness of all humans, that human beings, including themselves, are not to be credulously trusted to further the good of society at the expense of their own self-ish objectives, and indeed, that such a trust, in relation to a putatively Christian government, would invariably be betrayed in a refusal to countenance a variety of widely based social concerns. Further, they are making an evaluation in which, as a result of an examination of history, they find no reason to believe that the handing over of governmental power, and the abrogating of their own historically prior personal independence to any group or person would result in anything other than oppression, degradation and violence. As a consequence, an assertion of the validity and rightness of democracy as a system of government is not identical to, and does not necessarily imply as a corollary, an act of rebellion against God, or a refusal to be controlled by God.

The idea that governments are instituted by God is insidious in its simple and powerful appeal. This is so because much of the violence in the world is governmentally caused; wars are governmental instruments, and state violence , predominantly, but by no means only in the developing world, of unnamable variety and degree against citizens, is widespread. The Geneva Convention is apparently violated by most intelligence agencies, even from the "good" countries, who routinely brutalize their prisoners both male and female. The truth is that governments achieve submission to their dictates because they wield power and the threat of violence against those who would oppose them. Indeed, this being the case, to understand a government as instituted by God surely comes close to blasphemy and the imputation of evil to the Godhead. Surely it also assumes that God is not particularly interested in the moral nature of the government (as God has instituted it) nor in the motives of those who took power or possess power, just so long as there is a (any) government. And yet, even a casual reading of the books of Kings would reveal that this is definitely not the case.

When Jesus encouraged us to "render to Caesar what is Caesar's and to God what is God's" he was not providing a theological imprimatur to governments in general but rather acknowledging that there can be claims by governments that are worthy of support. That this encouragement was not a blanket encouragement to total submission is clear from the final half of the statement, "and render to God what is God's", which implies the distinct possibility that divine obligations may well contravene governmental law and require the individual to disobey the government under which the individual finds him or herself. Clearly this must be the interpretation, because Caesar himself would have regarded all his whims as requiring obedience, and not only those decided not to be contrary to the will of God. It surely also implies the absolute impossibility of any attitude along the lines of "my country right or wrong".

Rousseau may have believed that the state needed a religion that would be subservient to the state, and that Christianity was not suited for this task, however, though he was correct on the second point, this view is deeply flawed for two important reasons. The first is that from a Christian point of view there is no earthly institution that can demand a higher level of allegiance, and the second is that to agree to such a position of subservience to the state, or to the will of the majority expressed in legislation, could potentially result in citizens and Christians being obligated to participate in inhumane and sinful acts. The Nazi Holocaust is but one example of such a possibility. The state is a human creation, and as such is inherently open to error. As such, though the conscience can not be claimed to be infallible, the conscience must always be asserted to be superior to the dictates of the state.

The founding fathers of the American experiment strongly believed in the obligation of the citizenry to hold the government accountable, and to fight against the diminishing of democratic freedoms. Neither from a democratic nor from a religious point of view is it wise or acceptable to be anything other than vigilant and critical of the actions of all levels of government, and in all situations, not excluding, and particularly with regards to war.

Short of simply rejecting this biblical teaching, which is, in fact, not widely taught throughout the scriptures, in what sense can these verses be understood? The teaching, indeed, must not be taken simply at face value. Actually, Romans 13, is completely at odds with Paul's own experience with both Jewish and Roman authorities. Further, statements in this chapter contradict Old Testament prophetic utterances against governments both Jewish and pagan. Old Testament prophecies and moral pronouncements against government oppression of the people, and particularly the poor, fly in the face of the claims made in the chapter. With the exception of 1 Peter 2:13 which also teaches a submission to governments, or at least in relation to conforming to acceptable behaviour, nowhere else in the bible is there a statement that governments are described as "God's agents working for your good", except for particular punishments intended by God and using a 'pagan' nation, such as in Isaiah 10:5, "The Assyrian! He is the rod that I wield.". No such blanket claim about this institution is made anywhere in the OT, and the Gospels do not portray governments as anything other than essentially oppressive and cruel. Can the Roman persecution of the church be seen as "God acting for the church's good"? Were the Stalinist slaughter of millions of Ukrainians, the Turkish slaughter of vast numbers of Armenians, Hitler's genocide against the Jews, and the Japanese army's slaughter in Nanking acts of "God's agents" working for "our" good? If an interpretation of the sacred text flies in the face of the irrefutable facts of existence we need to take a hard second look at the interpretation we have put on the text.

Nor should it be understood that each government was initially instituted by God but that some government somehow became corrupted, and therefore ..what? Not then so instituted? Even if a government has been instituted by God, this does not grant it the right to claim such a divine protection if its acts have become blatantly contrary to the will of God. At that point, as the Chinese traditionally expressed it, the government loses the support of heaven. The tenth chapter of Isaiah begins,

> Shame on you! You who make unjust laws
> And publish burdensome decrees,
> Depriving the poor of justice,
> Robbing the weakest of my people of their rights,
> Despoiling the widow and plundering the orphan.
> What will you do when called to account,
> When ruin from afar confronts you? (Verses 1-3)

These verses do not suggest that governments have a blanket blessing from God simply because they exist. Nor do they encourage the belief that governments consistently act in the interests of the people, as Romans 13 seems to suggest. In fact, as God appears to see the situation, the government described in these verses is specifically acting, "not as agents for the people's good" but as the enemy of righteousness and God (him)self. These verses in Isaiah, among others, do not suggest any blanket level of support for a government if it acts in ungodly ways.

In what sense then can a government be seen as instituted by God? Certainly it cannot be in the choice of the individuals who become the government, for on the whole many of the people who appropriate tremendous political power often do so by violent means, much bloodshed or as a result of greed, ambition, and pride. It would also, quite reasonably, not be so in governments that actively promote anti-Christian behaviour or seek to destroy the church. Given these conditions, such an institution as divinely placed, can only be so in regards to its support of a rational and harmonious organization of society, the fair division of societal resources, the protection of the weak, the protection of the natural world from rampant economic predation, the establishing of an environment in which the church can grow, and in the encouragement of such behaviour.

Given the logical possibilities, (or impossibilities) of an apparently literal understanding of these verses in Romans, that is to say an inadequately critiqued understanding of the teaching of Romans 13, it is tragically incorrect to interpret scripture on government to mean that all governments are established by the will of God, and should therefore be obeyed, not opposed, and not severely, if necessary, criticised. In fact, to assert that all governments are the expression of the will of God on earth either implicates God in the evil that they do, or it is simply wrong, except to the degree that these governments express the nature of God. Jesus may have been extricating himself from a trap when he stated, "Render to Caesar what is Caesar's and to God what is God's", but this does not negate the truth of his remark. Governments should be obeyed only to the degree that they conform to the principles of social behaviour set forth in the scriptures.

Not every law enacted however has an immediate relationship to a biblical teaching. Speeding limits, for example, do not seem to have much to do with biblical teachings or, at times, even simple rationality . However, while this may usually be the case, speeding can endanger the lives of others, and such behaviour certainly falls within the realm of biblical teachings. In addition, while a law may not be an expression of a specific scriptural stand, as Romans 13 states, "they (the authorities) do not carry the sword (gun, nightstick...) in vain". Clearly a law may be morally good and beneficial, neither moral nor immoral, or morally evil and destructive.

Whatever the case, the government does have the power to impose its authority. Indeed, it is this very power which forces us to confront the potential sacrifice that opposing the government may entail. Jesus, in being faithful to God's plan for his life, ran headlong into a confrontation with the authorities, and was totally aware of this inevitability throughout his earthly ministry. The result for Jesus was his crucifixion. We can see this also in the early chapters of the book of Acts. When Peter in response to the Sanhedrin's command not to preach the gospel, stated, "We must obey God rather than men", we are all in support of his correct stance. However, the result of his refusal to submit is seen in the following verses. The Sanhedrin sent for the apostles "and had them flogged...The apostles went out from the Council rejoicing that they had been found worthy to suffer indignity for the sake of the Name." (Acts 5: 27-42) Opposing the government in a "rendering to God what is God's" may have serious consequences. That one is standing for the right does not make these results any less severe.

Many deeply religious people believe that only a theocracy can perfectly fulfill God's requirements. A religious government however, simply because it is based on religious principles is not necessarily an expression of a theocracy, but only of a sacerdotal system, a system of priestly power. A theocracy, as the name implies, is government by God, not by a body of supposed representatives of God. The biblical basis for such an interpretation, even if it is a rather rough hewn model, is found in the Old Testament books of Judges and Samuel. There was no government in this time of theocracy. There was no government by a body of priests, and there certainly was no government by a monarch. It was precisely a government that the people wanted, and that both God and Samuel found so disturbing. Nor can it be said that the judges were, in effect, the government. They did not always exist, and appear to have been raised up, from time to time, usually to free the people from the oppression of foreign control. They did not make laws, did not tax the people, and did not create even a tiny standing army.

Samuel regarded this open ended, rather anarchic system in which "There was no king in Israel and all did what was right in their own eyes." (Judges 17:6) as perfectly agreeable. Why else would he have been so upset at its possible dissolution? We are usually taught that this state of human freedom was an indication of the sinfulness of the Israelites and of humanity in general. However, though they did frequently turn away from God, it was also the foundation of the theocracy that Samuel was so upset about abandoning as, in reality, a decision to abandon this form and choose a king was an abandoning of God. And, according to the scriptures, this is also how God viewed the move. A theocracy then, from the biblical perspective, is in actuality a form of non-government, not a form of priestly, clergy driven government.

It is suggested that, just as with the theoretical perfection of the Mosaic law, the existence of a theocracy, in the biblically understood sense, in a world where sin exists, appears not to be a possibility. If then a theocracy is not a possibility, lesser forms of government may be theoretically acceptable as interim forms. That this is true can be seen in the fact that, while stating a non-theocratic government was not perfect, God himself chose the leader of this less than ideal popularly demanded government. Democracy may therefore be theoretically possible as an acceptable governmental model that can be supported by Christians, and conceivably other religious groups, as one such interim form. The question then becomes, "Is democracy an acceptable interim form, and are there characteristics about democracy that make it a better form than other governmental models?"

It could be argued that this secondary form of government was acceptable to God only as long as the king ruled righteously and in submission to God. This is a significant point, and one which, incidentally, argues against the notion that all governments are instituted by God. The point, however, is that this "less than theocratic" form of government was acceptable to God. What this indicates is that non-theocratic governments are presumably acceptable to the degree that they govern justly, are not oppressive, seek the protection of the weak of society, and do not oppose the work of God. The fact that governments can become oppressive and unjust does not negate the possibility of non-theocratic forms of government being acceptable to God.

If it is still asserted that all governmental systems except a theocracy, and not a priestly theocracy, are sinful, we need, I believe, to take another look at the purpose of the law in the mind of God. According to the Old Testament, the theocracy that existed prior to the institution of a monarchy, came in the period of the Mosaic law. Like the Mosaic law, a theocracy was, and remains, the ideal; with a theocracy as the ideal state of governance. This is so because only God can be trusted with the governance of people. Only God has the perfect love and wisdom needed, not to oppress dissidence. Indeed, to momentarily digress, it is strange that when thinking of the love and justice of God we focus on the love of God in relation to ourselves as individuals, but immediately focus on the justice and wrath of God when we consider societies, as if societies are not simply social constructs made up of individuals.

The law, however, was intended, according to St. Paul in the book of Romans, to teach us that, by ourselves, we could never be perfect; we could never fulfill the law. The Law thus had a heuristic, a teaching purpose. A theocratic state was not intended for a humanity that was not redeemed and sanctified, but rather was intended as a perfect model for a perfectly redeemed humanity, just as the Law is the model of the perfect kind of behaviour of a redeemed and sanctified people.

Unfortunately, so far there has never been a perfectly sanctified humanity, and the history of religious governance only reveals that the administrators of such an intended form almost invariably resort to violence in an attempt to impose their perceived standards of divine behaviour in the face of contrary opinion and differing behaviour. An imposed theocracy is neither demanded nor workable in the present age for perhaps similar reasons as to why righteousness is not forcibly imposed on the world. Both scenarios would not work.

I, for one, would fear a religious government as much as I would fear a fascist, totalitarian one because, once again, religious governments have historically been as equally violent, oppressive and willing to shed rivers of blood as any fascist dictatorship that has ever existed. Just as holiness can not be imposed (e.g. by the Law), so also a theocracy cannot be imposed, and God does not seem interested in imposing such a government or it would already exist or have existed. Indeed, to reiterate, God did not force a theocracy on the people when they expressed a desire for a non-theocratic form of government. In the same way that perfect sanctification is an act of God in the individual, so a theocratic government will seemingly become real only when the Kingdom of God is perfectly enshrined in the hearts of all individuals, and as such, a theocratic government will be the expression of such a state. It is erroneous, therefore, to teach that, for a Christian, a theocratic government is the only correct or acceptable form of political organization that can be supported.

Why then should a democratic form of government be seen as the best form? From the outset, I believe that if any form of non-democratic government ruled from love, this would, in time transform itself into an equivalent form of governance as a democracy. In fact, if this condition of love existed, a mon-archy, oligarchy or dictatorship, for example, would end by transforming itself into a democratic form as a result of its positive valuation of the individual. Further, it would do this in conformity to the model of leadership that Jesus taught, i.e. the leader as servant. A non-democratic government, in valuing all, would seek to meet the needs of all above itself. It would seek the opinions of all in the formulation of policy and law because, in humility, this leadership would understand that no individual or small group of individuals was capable of knowing and understanding enough to comprehend the realities of a large population, the universe of technology, and the socio-economic requirements of a national population. It would understand that, though there need to be experts, at times the lowliest individual can have essential wisdom. The dictatorship or oligarchy would further understand that it is selfish to control resources and wealth while there is poverty and suffering, and that to possess wealth, and be unwilling to share it with others, is an expression of sinfulness and selfishness. Finally, this leadership would not seek to impose its will by violence, as this would contravene the very principle of love of others that motivate servant-like behaviour. The "monarch" thus, would renounce his kingship as irrelevant, and institute a form of collective administration that would, in effect, be a democracy.

It may be asked if God (him)self will renounce his kingship. Once again, part of the answer to this may be that the term is an earthly one, assigned to God from a time when monarchy was the dominant form of government. As such it should be understood somewhat metaphorically. That such a distinction is possible is indirectly supported by Jesus' remark, "If you disbelieve me when I talk to you about things on earth, how are you to believe if I should talk about the things of heaven?" (John 3:12) That Jesus used earthly imagery indicates he was adapting his conversation to fit our linguistic and experiential limitations. As to whether God would give up his kingship, the simple answer may well be that God could not give up being God. Is God separate and beyond us? Of course the answer is 'yes'. What we will be ultimately, and what union with God actually means, may also be part of the answer to the question. That on earth a ruler motivated by pure love would give up his or her supremacy and disproportionate control of resources, however, is beyond question.

Democracy is necessary for two apparently unrelated reasons. Firstly, democracy ideally proclaims the equality of the individual citizen and his or her right before God and other humans to respect, fairness and openness to opportunities for a fulfilled human life. Secondly, democracy is needed to balance the power of individuals and groups who would restrict or deny the very rights and protections that the first reason asserted. Modern democracy grew out of the growing economic power of the middle class that was frustrated by the nobility's traditional control over the levers of political and economic power. Democracy then, was the philosophical justification of one class's clamor for political input in policies that impinged on its interests. This historical jockeying for power was incipiently reflected in one of the most significant documents of social justice, the Magna Carta of 1215 which, among other things, expressed the historically earlier struggle of the nobility for a balancing degree of power, vis a vis the monarch, in the limitation of the king's right to arbitrarily increase taxation.

Modern democracy, then, essentially sprang from the self interest of particular classes, and not from a philosophical search for governmental fairness. However, this does not mean that the continuing quest for political power over the affairs of one's class existed as a completely evil and essentially self centred movement. The history of government has been, and remains, the history of power over others. That in a non-democratic government this power is centred in the hands of a few, and held for the benefit of those few, results in degrees of social, psychological, economic and spiritual impoverishment for the many. If power is held for the benefit of those in power, then power held by the few, necessarily results in the loss of benefit for the majority. Democracy, by spreading power more evenly throughout society attempts to spread the benefits of human life more equitably throughout society, and justifies this struggle in the name of fairness, and the prehistoric, pre-societal right of all to independence, equality and the individual quest for security and happiness(which should not be simply assumed to equate with self centredness as Muggeridge and others have unfortunately understood this quest).

By limiting the degree of power held by any one group or individual, it is hoped that there will be a more just sharing of obviously limited resources among the greater population, and thus allow for a richer development of the human spirit. The Jeffersonian Declaration of Independence is not an assertion of selfishness as a positive value, but rather of the value of all humans, and their right to live a life where each is free to develop to the limit of their power and talents, free from oppressive governments or groups so as to be able to live a happy life, to the degree that such a freedom allows one. Potentially, such rights as expressed in the Declaration, are the secular expression of the obligations that one person has towards another from God's point of view. Ideally, rights are not the weapon we brandish against others in an alienated understanding of society as warring members against whom one must struggle, but delineations of the limits and domains of justice and decency that are due from all to all. These claims to decent and respectful behaviour are the foundation of the democratic form of government. As such, they are not antithetical to Christian values, and indeed conform to that sense of equality and compassionate human interaction which is taught in scripture.

Christians, Political Parties and Capitalism

Christians probably support the democratic process by voting, as much as or more than any other group. This is not unexpected, as they are aware of the impact of legislative debate on both the quality of life and their ability to function freely as Christians. On top of this, Christians quite simply try to do the right thing as citizens of the country they live in. We tend to take this for granted, but what is it in the various political parties that leads Christians to support one party over another? Unless this choice is made for non-religious reasons, voting for a political party surely reveals a belief that one particular party conforms more closely than others to Christian ideals. How is it, however, that one Christian can support one party as "more Christian", while another can view this same party as almost diabolical, and support another, also as "more Christian"?

It appears evident that when competing parties are chosen by Christians, these individuals are employing differing criteria in the making of such a decision. Each sees particular values being emphasized by the parties, and based upon the values that each person believes are important, chooses a party that conforms most closely to these personal values. In doing so, the ideals of the "non-chosen party" that are valued by other individual Christians as important, are deemphasized or ignored. It seems rather futile to suggest the following, but the questions one must ask of oneself are, "are the values I hold to be important, in conformity with actual Christian values, and are the values I am comparing in each of these parties of a relatively equal level of biblical significance?" For example, does the sin of laziness outweigh the need for compassion for the poor? In addition, "are my sociological beliefs supported by the evidence?" Are the poor, for example, in such an economic state because they are lazy? Is my support for the death penalty (if one, in fact, does support this) a biblically defensible position, or is it really a pragmatic position predominantly founded on fear, or a certain view of justice?

My concern, apart from the right or wrongness of certain positions, is that such positions, whatever they are, are often arrived at without sufficient information, serious reflection, or solid biblical analysis. I would suggest that we Christians arrive at conclusions too rapidly, after too little thought, and often based mainly on our emotions. Further, we accept too readily the understandings and positions of our pastoral leadership on political matters, assuming, perhaps, that the spirituality of the minister must indicate that his or her political remarks or innuendoes necessarily reflect the mind of God.

One of the most deciding and divisive issues in choosing a political party is the concept of the political "left and right". This is a complex problem, but if I may, a rejection of the left based upon its totalitarian, fascist, anti-human history globally, can be seen as similar to a rejection of Christianity, based upon Christianity's history of violence and oppression when the church has been in power. Christianity has certainly been guilty of great wrong in the past, though this wrong was certainly done for what was believed at the time to be noble reasons. However, this does not imply that the teachings of Christianity and the bible are invalid because of these historical events. The behaviour of the church, from the intra-church violence at the time of the formulation of the historic creeds relating to the nature of Christ, to the Crusades, the Inquisition, the Catholic and Protestant burnings of "heretics", and to the Salem witch hunts, does not necessarily have any interpretational value in terms of the validity of the Christian gospel and the scriptures, shameful though it is.

In exactly the same way, the tyrannical actions of communists worldwide may, but do not necessarily have anything to say about Marxism as a doctrine. We would certainly assert that the terrible deeds done by the church had nothing to do with true Christian doctrine. Might this not also be true about Communism? I do not say Marxism-Leninism because I believe Lenin adapted, and essentially negated the praiseworthy essence of Marxism in order to maintain political power in Russia, during and after the October revolution. Marx may have spoken of a revolution of workers against capitalists, but it was Lenin and the Bolsheviks who got rid of genuine workers' committees set up in various cities to administer local governments, and it was the Bolsheviks who created the secret police organizations in the newly created Russian republic, instituting the oppressive forces that would terrorize the Soviet people until the demise of the USSR.

Further, Marx's early work, the Grundrisse is more a humane outline of societal development than it is a blueprint for violent revolution. The essentially compassionate nature of the society described by Marx in the Grundrisse cannot simply be denied by later, predominantly Leninist developments. Lenin's "contribution" to communist thought was intended to justify the non-implementation of Marxism until state power had destroyed the bourgeois enemies of the working class. As such, Lenin's contribution was similar to the theoretical positions taken by Christians, both Catholic and Protestant, to justify their own violent and oppressive actions in defense of Christianity, though in direct contradiction to the spirit of love and forgiveness that is the core of the Christian Gospel.

I ask the reader's forbearance to suggest that a study of the essential Marx would reveal a social system that would compare favourably with how we, as Christians, would see an ideal society. Das Kapital, Marx's later economic view of his system, is essentially the nuts and bolts analysis of what he wrote in Grundrisse, an early Marxian work. I would also like to ask Christians who are used to comparing Marx to the Devil, if their reaction to what I have written here is one of amazement and disgust. If you are used to speaking of Marx in decidedly negative terms, this discussion might be a little like being under water and wondering when one was going to get to the surface.

As Christians, however, we seek the truth. And this search at times must be undergone with concurrent feelings of antipathy generated by previous understandings of what we have perceived as antagonistic to the Christian position. So my question is, "Do we seek the truth, or do we decide to stay at a level of knowledge that may in fact be made up of some degree of error, if not complete error?" If after study you decide that my understanding of early Marx is inaccurate, I will be happy for you. At least you have sought the truth.

The fact is though, that I am not interested in defending Marx. Rather, what I seek is a balanced view of the political world based on real knowledge and genuine thought that generates a tolerant understanding of other sincere positions that are not intrinsically anti-Christian. Further, I would like to assert that political and religious historical behaviour, while casting a shadow on the associated belief system, can not be utilized to evaluate the political or religious system on which the behaviour was supposedly based.

I assure you, I am probably as Christologically based as you are, and I ask for, not patience but a willingness to explore a new way of thinking. For a Christian, Marxism has a decided value if one has forgotten that beyond North America, Europe, Japan and Australia, for example, there is a world of moderate to extreme economic suffering. In addition, *some* of the major causes of this suffering are the selfish hoarding of wealth by the developed West, an obsession for profit that has no loyalty to any country, and the shameful exploitation of ordinary men and women, particularly in

Third World countries where European and North American companies move and set up their factories because they can then pay their workers a mere pittance, even in comparison to wages in these already poor countries. The purpose of these moves is not the economic development of the Third World to which they have no intrinsic interest, but rather so that they do not have to pay their workers in the Developed World, particularly North America, wages and benefits acceptable in this part of the globe.

This move to Third World countries, of course, results in the loss of jobs for thousands of workers in the Developed World, predictable familial suffering caused by the loss of income, and societal dislocation, the economic impacts of which must be born, to some degree, by the governments of the developed countries as they attempt to reintegrate these unemployed workers into the work force. Frankly, this ignoring of the impacts on real human beings in the quest for economic gain, despite the "advance" that has, at times resulted as a consequence is not new. The enclosure laws in Britain and the social dislocation caused by industrialization itself are historic evidences of this disregard for the human consequences of this kind of economic readjustment. The human suffering so caused is apparently of no concern to the companies moving to these Third World countries. Moreover, any appeal to economic laws that such development necessarily increases the standard of living in these Third World countries ignores the economic realities on the ground, which almost always resoundingly demonstrate the continued impoverishment of the workers of these transplanted companies, except for the tiny managerial elite who are the national representatives of these companies, and who are rewarded, just as previous colonial nations supported and were generous to nationals who were loyal to their continued colonial control.

Given the profit making potential of the low cost goods in the Developed World to which they eventually are exported, the wages of these, at times almost indentured workers, is often so paltry that the impact on the standard of living for the workers, and the country generally is proportionally minimal. Global experience further reveals that where the Third World workers have the temerity to ask for or demand higher, more fair wages, they are frequently harassed, ignored, fired or the company simply moves to another even poorer location on the globe where even less needs to be paid for the products that we in the West pay relatively enormous amounts, given the low cost of their production. Moreover, in addition to the unreasonably low wage, these employees frequently work in situations where labour laws, enacted to protect and benefit the workers, are both minimal and rarely enforced.

The significant difference, in fact, between the cost asked for by developing countries for the products they themselves have produced, and the cost of products of Western companies produced in these Developing countries is indicative of the economic intent of the move to the Developing country. Indigenous products usually reflect the low cost of production and, to the amazement of most consumers, are relatively inexpensive. Western goods produced in these Developing countries , on the other hand are priced as if they bore the labor cost of production in a developed country, despite the fact that they have not been produced in the West.

In this situation Marxism can awaken in the Christian a sense of justice and compassion, and particularly in South America it, and not Christianity, has been the catalyst for reflections on social justice issues. Yet Marxism should not be necessary at all for Christians to be aware of such issues. However, as a result of our relatively wealthy lives, the human tendency is to forget others and believe that if all is well with us, then all must be well with the rest of the world. Were it not for our blindness to the suffering of others, and our ignoring of the scriptural references to the social responsibilities of Christians to other human beings, Marxism would be totally unnecessary. Potentially, Christianity teaches all and more than Marxism does as regards a compassionate and just society. In addition, in Christ we have the means to experience a radical change of heart that has the potential to produce a society or community of a quality, even more socially healing than Karl Marx was ever able to envisage; this despite the fact that, in the face of a brutal and dehumanizing nineteenth century system of production, the ideational source of Marxism was essentially the Christian vision of a caring, non-alienated society.

One does not have to be a Marxist to value the social view of Marxism positively. Nor does one have to believe in and support the violence of the class struggle, or Marx's atheism, to see that the kind of society envisioned by Marx is particularly close to a Christian one, where there is equality, justice, a provision of basic needs for all, an end to the dehumanization and shame of the weak by the selfish and powerful, and a concern for and feeling of oneness with all others in society. And yet, if I may, what deeply troubles me is that there will be some who read these lines, and in hatred at all that Marxism is for them, will not hear the non-Marxism of these passages, and will not think through the attempt to create balanced compassionate thinking.

And yet I would no more want to see a communist form of government put into place than I would want to see a Christian one that was not instituted by God. Both systems have historically proven that when given political power, in order to maintain that power and impose their worldviews on the population, they fail miserably and become tyrannical. It is not the systems themselves that are necessarily at fault, but rather the failure of the human heart to resist its own evil. A mass produced "sanctification" of society does not work. Redemption occurs, one heart at a time, and any attempt to shortcut this will always fail.

Indeed the intention in all the discussion on Marxism is not to elevate Marxism, but to question the usually, almost instinctual rejection of "non-right" parties by Christians, as if *anything* left is "an enemy of God". A concern for social justice, decent wages, and universal health care, for example, is not an ungodly concern. Indeed, it is a completely biblical interest and expresses God's concerns. It does not threaten the freedom and democracy of the nation, and it certainly does not mean that those seeking such benefits secretly desire a communist system of government, or are the dupes of that tiny number remaining who do. We need to believe that there are many people of good will, both on the left and on the right who, while having differing political philosophies, are passionate in their love for their country, for the wellbeing of the people, and in the radical defense of the democracy they have been fortunate enough to have been born in.

Practically speaking, whatever the historic weaknesses of capitalism there are, capitalism does allow an environment where societal and individual freedoms can exist. My statement, of course, may be partly incorrect. It could well be that democracy allows an environment where capitalism can exist. It must be strongly stated, however, that capitalism is not a Christian doctrine. Further, the driving forces of capitalism are decidedly non-Christian. Capitalism, (as opposed to traditional and usually marginally efficient methods of exchange and profit making), as an accumulation of vast amounts of capital that can be used to control markets in the production of goods, encourages greed, selfishness, and were it not controlled by legislation, a numbing indifference to the wellbeing and happiness of the people who produce the goods companies sell.

Nevertheless, this greed, selfishness and indifference are not necessarily intrinsic parts of capitalism but rather the unfortunate outcomes of sinful hearts reacting to real or imagined wealth, (and social power). Capitalism could be perhaps the most efficient generator of wealth so far conceived, and could be used for the benefit of humanity. It could simply be, and already is, an incredible motivator of creativity and invention. It could be, as it is to the degree that wealth is fairly shared in developed countries, a means to raise the standard of living, spread education, and improve the level of health care in a society. To some degree it is all these positive things. What it is not, is a doctrine of the Christian church and the system God wishes to be followed globally.

Christians must be careful not to identify Christianity with Capitalism. Free enterprise is simply one valuable but flawed system of exchange, and despite its much praised status, is not essentially Christian. As a system it is not found anywhere in the bible. The accumulation of wealth is not a doctrine taught in the bible. The vast gap between the rich and the poor, either in the West or even more so in the Developing World, is not encouraged in the bible, nor is the greed associated with capitalism advocated in the bible. Moreover, the arrogance of wealth is not set forth as biblically praiseworthy. At the best, capitalism is a neutral system of exchange. At the worst it is a justification for extreme selfishness, a covert justification of global national hegemony, and a denial of the obligation of the second great commandment. This does not mean that as Christians we cannot engage in capitalist enterprises. Indeed, it would almost certainly be impossible to function in this society if we did not. However, capitalism must never be regarded as a system that cannot be faulted, and those who criticize it as those who are enemies of the Gospel.

Do not forget that, historically, in Central and parts of South America, as well as, at the very least, in the thinking of certain sections of law enforcement in the rest of North America, the defense of the poor, and the search for virtually any form of social fairness is regarded merely as evidence of leftist and Marxist backing, and those who support such things, as Marxists, or Marxist dupes. In this model, a Christian who attempted to seek aid for a poor family, or a bishop who attempted to defend the poor, would be seen as communists, as indeed they have been. If you take the time to go over Jesus' words, to and regarding the poor, there is no doubt he also would be so accused. Do the research. Question your own beliefs and opinions. If you truly do believe in the inerrancy of scripture, make certain that your attitudes and beliefs are in genuine conformity to the thinking of God and the scriptures.

Finally, to sum up what some will no doubt describe as this Marxist section, though it is most definitely not so, I will end by stating that if I were to choose between living in a capitalist or communist environment I would choose the capitalist system every time, if for no other reason than the fact that for capitalism to flourish it must allow freedom and creativity. What I have attempted to suggest has been that an ascription of evil to all that is politically left is, at the least, unnecessary. Hopefully, it has been shown that many of the values of the left are, in fact, decidedly Christian, and that in the same way an imputation of evil to Christians cannot follow from the evil that Christians have done, so an imputation of evil to the philosophies and values of the left (and certainly not all on the left are communists) cannot follow from the evil done by Leftists and Communists.

What criteria then can be employed to assist us choose a political party to support? Initially it needs to be stated that no political party will completely express Christian values. Further, in most, if not all parties there will be aspects of a party's political platform that contravene Christian principles. One needs to be hesitant in condemning one party for supporting non-Christian policies, if the party one does support also contains non-Christian policies in its platform. If the primary value in Christianity is love-compassion, then it seems logical to suggest that a party that most strongly appears to support justice issues and to be compassionate to the weakest in society should therefore be supported. Simply being a Christian should also not be the deciding criteria for support of a candidate, and the political party to which the proclaimed Christian belongs. We are sadly aware of our own inconsistencies, and consequently we should not be surprised that "Christian" politicians will not necessarily vote or act in a consistently Christian fashion. Indeed, the best person as an elected representative may not be the Christian at all.

Finally, Christians should not be naïve about public expressions of "faith" by politicians. Such statements do not necessarily reveal the true state of the politician's heart, and only an evaluation of the politician's voting record may show whether such a person acts with honest and compassionate concern. Moreover, support for a politician, solely based on his or her "religious" statements may mean that decidedly non-Christian legislation is given a chance of success.

There has been a decline in the level of democracy practiced in the West over the last fifty years. The rights and freedoms of the citizenry have been slowly and seemingly inexorably eroded in a relentless drive to satisfy the ambitions for power of a small number of individuals, who hide behind the democratic process, and exploit it in order to achieve this power. That this has been attempted in the name of the defense of the nation does not make the diminution of freedom any less insidious. Tyrants have always justified oppression in the name of the preservation of the state, and a purportedly free population ceases to be free if, in the so called defense of freedom, these freedoms are taken away to the point of irrelevance. Only the temporary state of war can justify a withholding of freedoms, and the declaration of a state of war to legitimize this oppression, in an actual period of peace, makes virtually perpetual the cessation of genuine freedom that is the hallmark of a democratic state. As this relates to issues of justice, trust, truthfulness and liberation from oppression, this is not simply a political dilemma but also, and more importantly, a religious one. It is also one which Christians have, on the whole, chosen not to examine in their willingness to trust those who claim for themselves the mantle of righteousness. This trust, however, has occasionally, if not frequently, been abused.

The erosion of our freedoms from governmental intrusion and oppression has been made possible, in part, because we have simply taken for granted the solidity of the democratic nature and institutions of our society. We have been told so frequently that we live in a democracy that any questioning of the health of this democracy has been deemed unnecessary, or even worse, unpatriotic. We have, in fact, lost a credible sense of what a democracy should be, and need to be reawakened as to the "shape" of a genuinely democratic system. We need to rediscover the democracy that the country was founded on, and understand the need for the rights and freedoms enshrined in the constitutions that are intended to direct the political leadership in the land of our choice. Rather than only being taught the simple mythologies surrounding its founding, we need to become politically sophisticated as to the concepts that motivated the individuals who struggled to create a land of freedom from oppression. There need to be created incisive and motivating courses in democracy, at all levels of our nation's educational systems so that we, as citizens, have a clear understanding when these freedoms are being surreptitiously taken from us, and what is at stake in their removal.

Democracy is not something that is won at one moment of historic time, and then assumed to be capable of sustaining itself. Democracy is a state that must be continually protected, not only by its government, but occasionally even from its government. One of the bulwarks in this protection is a politically educated and aware citizenry. The power of a functioning democracy should not be seen to rest in the government, but more so in the hearts and minds of a committed and educated citizenry.

Acting as a Christian in the political realm is not a simple matter. A political system where no input from the citizenry is desired or expected removes the need for a Christian to reflect on such issues. If one exists in a democracy, however, one is forced to decide on the theological correctness of such involvement, and the kind of support such an opportunity demands. As Christians we need to possess a belief that our lives should be conducted in such a manner that the lives of those around us, the natural world, and society in general, are improved as a result of our having lived. There is much good a Christian in politics can achieve. We should not forget, however, that deep and genuine inner change is the result of a relationship with God brought about by becoming a child of God, just as John 1:12 and 3:16 declare. Political activity should not be seen as a substitute for either evangelism or the sanctifying work of the Holy Spirit.

Criticism of the Government.

When it comes to a criticism of the government, Christians suffer from a deeply seated reluctance to find fault with anyone and anything in a position of authority. Christians are taught not to criticize their pastoral leadership, and they are taught not to judge. This leaves them extremely open to being manipulated by unscrupulous leaders, and unwilling to conclude that the government is made up of characters who do not necessarily have any allegiance to the moral sensitivities that they possess as Christians. Further, one of the greatest difficulties for a citizenry is that evil, ambitious, and heartless people do not look any different to the people they meet at school, at work and at church.

Hannah Arendt, in her work on the trial of Adolph Eichmann for war crimes committed during World War 11 as a Nazi functionary, developed a concept that bears more thought than it usually gets. This concept is the "banality of evil". Despite the horror and the genocide that Eichmann had participated in, he was not a psychotic. He had engaged in murder as if it were part of a production line in a factory, and almost with as much detachment. If Eichmann had been met on the street before he became a mass murderer he probably would have been seen as a delightful and cultured man. One of the most significant reasons we hesitate to impute wrong to our political leaders is that they look like us.

As citizens and as Christians, in fact particularly as Christians, we must become more sophisticated in our approach to our national leaders. Firstly, we need to understand that in political life there are two principles: (1) say what the electorate wants to hear, and (2) hide the real reasons for policy decisions from the voters, and keep as much as possible secret for as long as possible. On the rare occasion when a truly spiritual Christian becomes a national leader these principles are less operative, but as stated, such a situation is rare.

One of the things Christians want to hear from political aspirants and leaders is that they are Christians. No one can see into the human heart, but this claim should be treated with a high degree of incredulity, what the Missouri folk are famous for, "show me". In an electorate in which there is a high level of religious observance, it is virtually political suicide not to profess some degree of religious allegiance.

In Canada the first Prime Minister, John A. MacDonald joined the fiercely Protestant Orangemen, and then formed an alliance with the staunchly Catholic, Etienne Cartier. In a dominantly Christian country like the US, what presidential candidate would not attempt to proclaim himself a Christian if that were possible. It really is about time we stopped taking political confessions of faith at face value. Louis XIV, at the age of sixty, added to the Notre Dame cathedral, and built a gorgeous chapel in his palace to show the sincerity of his faith. This did not stop him, nevertheless, from waging senseless wars, exercising an incredibly huge ego, arresting anyone who built a palace larger than he possessed, and pretentiously claiming that, l'etat c'est moi, "I am the state". His religious behaviours may have had a level of personal sincerity, but they did not prevent his acting in non-Christian ways in other political and civil areas of his life. At the best, a confession of faith should be treated as a private aspect of a politician's life, and not as a deciding determinant of how he or she will act in office.

Governments must be held accountable, and there must exist the greatest level of transparency possible. Failure to establish these principles will inevitably result in governmental actions contrary to the will of the people, and at times contrary to the constitution. Secondly, this failure runs the risk of a government's refusal to admit to wrong policy decisions, with all the human suffering that such denials can entail. Secrecy allows the powerful to exert an arrogance that feels itself above the law, and above the millions who chose the government to make their lives even a little better and more secure. This refusal to admit failure is, on the other hand, quite understandable. We as individuals fear such admissions equally strongly. If one admits to failing, the chance that he or she will be metaphorically stoned to death by one's fellows, including one's brothers and sisters in Christ, is extremely high.

A government's denials, however, have tragic repercussions that can affect whole nation states. Immediately following World War 2, the British government refused to assist two Germans accused of war crimes, though these two had worked with the British government to avoid the war, and had, in fact, sought British help in assassinating Adolph Hitler before he could lead Germany into the war. The British government had ignored their requests, and had therefore been partly to blame for the war itself. It was this blame that the government was apparently attempting to avoid by refusing to admit that the two Germans were almost certainly not guilty. By coming forward, the British government would have shown that they had ignored the warnings, and consequently failed to adequately protect its own people. A lack of legislated accountability and transparency processes makes the likelihood of unacceptable, if not criminal governmental decisions almost inevitable. Often the real intent of sealing government documents for long periods of time is not the nation's security, but merely the protection of the government's reputation.

It is a sin to hate the individuals who make up the government. It is not a sin, however, to find fault with one's government, and indeed it is the act of a patriot. Criticism does not imply that one does not love one's country. It should also be remembered that no government is perfect. There will be mistakes, no matter who leads a country, and those in government, on both sides of the floor, understand this. There can come times, nevertheless, when a government's direction is so terribly misguided and unacceptable to the people that it would be wrong not to oppose the government. The election of representatives is not the only time a population can express its opinions in ways that should influence government decision making, and a government should not assume that once it has been elected a people's obligation is to silently allow the government do what it likes. Indeed, the reality is just the opposite.

A citizen's obligation is to hold the government accountable to decency, the will of the people, and the defense of the constitution. Rather than weakening a government, popular opposition to unacceptable governmental policies strengthens the validity of the government. A government that governs contrary to the law and humanitarian social values, does not deserve to continue in office. It does not deserve to be strengthened. Tragically, those times when silent support is most demanded by governments, and when honest criticism is most absent, namely periods of military conflict, are also those times when a government must be held most accountable, and potentially, most opposed.

The decision to go to war should not be made in the tense atmosphere of the highest intellectual and oppositional paralysis, imposed in the name of patriotism and enforced through fear by the nation's security agencies . One may end up being in error, but it is not patriotic to support horrendously wrong policy decisions. Nor, indeed, is it scriptural. Exodus 23:2 states, "You shall not be led into wrongdoing by the majority, nor when you give evidence in a lawsuit shall you side with the majority." The implications of this injunction are rather widespread, but they certainly include not blindly following the majority in support of a government intent on wrongfully engaging in a war. One is not promoting Christian principles by mindlessly supporting terrible, and at times, essentially evil governmental leadership.

Protest: Critiquing Authority

For a Christian, the continuance and support of social peace is almost an article of faith. However, despite the fact that we are usually socialized to submit to authority, (not almost as if this was the expression of God himself, but actually as this expression), dissent and opposition to authority are not in themselves evil. Indeed, submission to authority can, at times be the evil that must be fled from. Initially, dissent can be seen as simply the justified expression of the democratic process through non-legislative means. A democratically elected body does not possess the right to govern contrary to the expressed will of the majority, and as the representative of a people it has an obligation to be sensitive to these wishes. Given the inherent limitations to genuine democracy that representative government already entails, dissent from the populace should be seen as an adjunct to democratic governance, and understood and accepted as part of the democratic process.

Dissent, noisy and disorganized as it usually presents itself, is not evil because of the way it appears, anymore than organized and orderly shameful government is good because of this accidental appearance. Dissent is evil only in relation to evil objectives and strategies it may espouse. Christians should not distance themselves from the rest of society, or part of that society, only on the basis of the disturbing nature of public opposition to the temporary authority. Indeed, as long as the dissent is not intentionally violent, and does not hold violence to be a method of achieving its ends, Christians should support any form of protest that has positive and socially beneficial goals.

We should be aware, however, that in this world, it is extremely difficult, and perhaps impossible, to completely separate evil from any social event that seeks success. In any progressive movement there will be some level of self centred activity, and ambitious people have used progressive social movements for their own ends from the beginning of time. This reality does not mean that Christians should abandon all socially dissenting activity. Rather, there should be a deepening of commitment to the progressive nature of the dissent, so that the chance of genuine social benefit is strengthened. If good people separate themselves from potentially positive movements, the result will almost inevitably be either the failure of the praiseworthy attempt, or a weakened success that must await another, and not inevitable tide of rising public support some time in the future. This is certainly the lesson in the failure of the American constitution to abolish slavery. The US had to wait almost three generations before the tide of public passion surged again, a lost moment of possibility that resulted in the untold suffering, devastation and death of the Civil War, eighty years later. As it has been said many times: "evil succeeds when good people choose not to act."

Moreover, the sinfulness of the unsaved is not a satisfactory reason to withhold support for social movements that propose positive ends. The lost are not another, and unrecognizable race of beings. Nor are they without any feelings and strivings for the good. We all know non-Christians who have good qualities, and some also who are decidedly and apparently better people than we are ourselves. Sin has not left us so completely that we can not find a common ground of support with the lost in the struggle for a better society. A good and acceptable goal is not made evil by its support by predominantly unsaved individuals. Involvement in social protest does not, indeed, necessarily imply that one possesses a faith in the establishment of a utopian society.

Further, as Christians we should not automatically assume that ideas generated outside the church are, because of that fact, necessarily wrong and unworthy of praise. We need to remember that Jesus was moved deeply by the scribe in Mark 12:28-34, commending his level of understanding even though it did not necessarily indicate that he was within the "kingdom of God". One does not have to be a Christian to have social positions that deserve support and commendation.

It is not only wrong, never to critique authority, it is dangerous. The world is not completely peopled by decent people. Rather, as power accumulates in an organization or state, ruthless, ambitious, and self serving people gravitate to this power, as if to a drug that will satisfy their self centred and destructive cravings. Government then is inevitably made up of a combination of good and hard working public servants, and those who are in this social enterprise to satisfy less noble ends. This being the case, it is clear that no government should be naively viewed, as if its power holders are all honorable people. In the minds of these less than honorable individuals, dissent is a hateful challenge to their untrammeled ambitions that may range from simply selfish goals to policies that they believe are correct, and should be implemented without opposition or consideration. For these individuals, the freedoms of democracy, supposedly enshrined in the constitution, the bill of rights, and in law, are inefficiencies that should be either ignored or subverted. Rather than protecting good government, a failure to support acceptable protest is an abrogation of one's social and civic responsibilities. There are times when not to dissent results, not in the health, but in the weakening, and even overthrow of good governance.

Not only should it be said that protest is an acceptable form of democratic expression. That right to protest can not be claimed to reside in the government, such that it alone has an inherent prerogative to grant the right to protest. Perhaps in the cause of social harmony it is allowable to seek "permission" from the government to hold a protest. This would certainly follow the example of Jesus in Matthew 17: 24-27 where Jesus, after stating that he actually had no obligation to pay the temple tax says, "But as we do not want to cause offence…". However, in reality the government does not possess the right to grant the citizenry permission to protest. The government does, on the other hand, have the right to demand an observance of reasonable laws, and a refraining from arbitrary violence, this last not implying that there is a violence that is not arbitrary and therefore acceptable. In that popular protest is a demonstration against governance, it is reasonable that the government against which the protest is engaged should not possess the right to deny or effectively negate this protest.

In a similar manner, the government does not have an intrinsic right to permit or refuse the formation and practice of labor unions, as unions reflect the right of free individuals to bargain for reasonable conditions and withhold their labor in the event of unrighteous conditions. Similarly, the government does possess the right to limit unions in practices that are unfair and illegal outside the valid operation of the protection of the workers.

And yet there is one more point that needs to be made. As well as there exists a need for government to be actively critiqued, all opposition to government must likewise be carefully scrutinized. It is time for Christians to become more politically aware, and realize that malicious and decidedly non-democratic groups are perfectly willing to use, and have used, the religious community, not to achieve proclaimed Christian objectives, but merely to gain sufficient electoral momentum and support to attain political and governmental power and objectives. Those who wish to replace a government, attempt to focus on its failures. In an attempt to muster opposition to the government, this is done, as regards the Christian community, by focusing on these failings as they relate to Christian teachings. However, unless the religious community is willing to be cynically manipulated by a party or group that merely purports to be similarly outraged by these failings, we need to remember that the political world does not only attract honest and socially minded individuals. Not only a party's platform, but also, and perhaps more importantly, its personnel and their practices need to be thoroughly examined. It is an admirable thing to be "harmless as doves", but for our own protection, if nothing else, we also need to be as wise as the serpents who seek to manipulate us.

Independence and Liberty Within a Governed Society

We Christians have (quite correctly) been taught so effectively that we are sinful egocentric beings that any suggestion that individual independence might not be contrary to the scriptures comes across as almost certain heresy. However, sinfulness and the claim of independence are not necessarily semi-synonymous terms, nor are holiness and freedom necessarily antithetical. The scriptures do teach that we should live unselfish lives in which, for the good of others, we sometimes need to submerge our own wishes and freedoms for the well being of these others. If, however, we have an unquestionable obligation to obey God, we have no such obligation to our fellow humans. In relation to others, we are under the obligations of love, but this does not imply an obligation to blanket obedience. Moreover, before we are citizens we are free beings, and while this freedom can be stolen and chipped away for less than honorable reasons, the innate right to freedom and independence of action is inalienable. It is upon this one, simple but profound right, that all democracies stand or fall, and it is upon this that a democracy must be evaluated.

There are few things a government depends on more than a subservient population. Opposition to a government is always, and understandably so, annoying, but with some governments it is viewed as a totally unacceptable and hateful attack to be crushed. Yet, to reiterate, the truth is that before we are citizens of a country we are free beings who have the right not to submit to the claims of subjection imposed by any government on its citizens. Indeed the dominant reason governments seek to impose their rule as absolutely as possible is to make the accomplishment of their will as easy as possible. For most of humanity's history the population of a country has been seen merely as a source of revenue, and as bodies to be expended in battle. The reason that free democracies usually have, at least a slightly more enlightened attitude to their citizenry, is that in an advanced democracy, the nation has usually developed a value for human life , and secondly, that democracy carries within it, the idea that individuals possess the right to direct the administration of their country.

Citizens, simply by reason of their habitation in a country, do not lose the freedom with which they are born. A citizen may have his or her freedom reduced to virtual non existence by the government under which she or he lives, but the right to freedom is inalienable, and can not be lost, even were the majority of the population to approve such a subjugation. No social contract can deprive a human being of this primitive right, and no historic abrogation can take away the right to freedom a human being possesses simply by being. Further, there is no social debt that can be invoked that has the power to deprive an individual of the right to a freedom and an existence, independent of the government under which that person lives. And though it may be correct to assert that the safeguards that are afforded an individual by inclusion in a society justify the limitation of one's freedom, this limitation is acceptable only to the extent that the individual is, in fact, governed justly and is granted that security.

The freedom of an individual given to an administration is not sold, or permanently handed over, but temporarily entrusted to that administration. The obligations of citizenship do not supercede the native right to freedom that exists with being human. Citizens never become the property of a government, and no government has the right to demand absolute obedience of any individual. As such, submission and obedience to a government can never be absolute, nor can the government take such submission for granted. Of course, governments possess the power to provide or deny an individual freedom. However, a government does not possess the power to give something that was never theirs. Freedom is not the property of the government, but solely that of the individual. With William Wallace in late Medieval Scotland, and countless millions since him, the passion for freedom is a cry of the human heart that God himself hears and understands.

Social Policy and the Population as a Resource

In the feudal era in Japan, during the rule of the Tokugawa family, and before modernization following the Meiji "restoration" of Imperial rule, the nation was divided into nobles related to the old Imperial line, the samurai or warrior class, and non samurai, who made up the majority of the population. Farmers were seen as resources who supplied the rice which was the currency of the period, a lord's fief, or area under his control, being measured in terms of the amount of rice it produced. The farmers' welfare was of importance to any wise feudal lord as his wealth depended on the stability of the farming peasant class. These peasants were looked after, not because they were valued in themselves, but only for the economic and military importance of the rice crop. Taxation was oppressive, but not usually to the point of being ultimately destructive to the peasant family. Social policy was determined as it impacted the political and macro-economic situation of the nation.

However, from both a Christian and a democratic point of view, the population of a country is not a resource, which should be manipulated, and "looked after", in order to achieve a maximum economic output, or to guarantee a stable and educated workforce. Social policy should not be designed merely to satisfy economic models and economic efficiencies, rather than the simple welfare of the people. The population of a country needs to be aware of the model that is driving governmental social policy, for this will impact the allocation of funding to programs related to the general population, and indicate for whom the policy or policies exist.

For its part, the government exists, not to meet the labor needs of the dominant class, but only to guarantee the security and well being of the population as a whole, not excluding the upper economic classes. The government is, and remains, only the representative of the people as a whole, and objectives that run counter to this do not reflect this very simple, democratic and humanitarian goal.

A Rough Model of a Just Government

While it is sometimes difficult to know which political party one should support, the essential direction of a government is clearly outlined in Psalm 72, traditionally held to be the last psalm of King David. David prays that God will give him a sense of justice so that he will be able to "judge the people rightly" (v. 2) David goes on to describe what just government is. It is instructive that he does not mention a balanced budget, or an increase in defense spending. He first focuses on justice in legal considerations. "To deal out justice to the poor and suffering" (v 2) It seems noteworthy that he does not simply say that he should deal out justice-to all. Justice is assumed in this outline to be most unlikely, and the law prejudicial, when the poor and suffering are concerned. Does anyone doubt that the poor usually receive a lower quality of justice in our lands of the free and the brave?

David then progresses to the economy.. "May hills and mountains (the land's natural resources) afford thy people peace and prosperity in righteousness." (v3) David, and presumably God also, understand that without economic profitability and surplus, the people will suffer. Economics is tied to righteousness. Prosperity is not assumed to be impossible without righteousness, but unjust economic practices, practices that are definitely exemplified in the capitalist mantra of the "bottom line by any possible means" (the justification, for example, of removing a production plant to a Third World country and putting people out of work), from God's perspective, fail the criterion for success.

David also sees the government to be that of the "institutional" individual, and its function to be the well-being of the population. Just as individuals are under a moral obligation to feed the poor out of their plenty, so the government has an obligation to generously supply the needs of the poor and suffering from its tax reserves. Verse four states, "He shall give judgment for the suffering (he will make legislation that meets the needs of the suffering) and help those of the people who are needy" Perhaps it is true that "big government is out" but that does not abrogate the government's obligation and compassionate responsibility to give to the poor and suffering the necessities of life, generated by the economic success of the nation's economy mentioned in the previous verse.

David sees the power of the government as a tool to limit that of selfish and oppressive groups or people. There is a realization that not all in the population are decent, and that greed for wealth, or simply power, will motivate some and lead to an oppression of the people. Oppression does not simply mean restricting individual liberties, or unjustly imprisoning people. Oppression is an unfair and excessive demand for payment, careless of the individual's ability to pay. Oppression is the fixing of an essential commodity, gasoline, for example, knowing that the population has no choice but to pay the amount that has been determined by simple greed and the artificial manipulation of supplies. God is more concerned with compassionate behaviour, and the fulfillment of the second commandment, than he is about payment dates and normal economic and even legal obligations.

Verse four states, " He shall crush the oppressor", and verses 12-14 tell us, "For he shall rescue the needy from their rich oppressors, the distressed who have no protector. May he have pity on the needy, and the poor, deliver the poor from death. May he redeem them from oppression and violence, and may their blood be precious in his eyes."

Let no one say that God is not interested in the welfare of the poor and needy, or in the treatment that is meted out to them. There is an exceedingly rich body of scripture that absolutely refutes this, along with the heartlessness that is the motivation against such teaching. The King, in these verses, sees the government as putting itself in the role of the protector of the powerless. When the scripture says" may he deliver…may he redeem…" David is placing the power and resources of the government at the disposal of the poor, because that is the obligation of the powerful, and that is the responsibility of those with economic influence.

Good government involves a valuation of the weak and downtrodden as worthy of the resources, economic, physical, legislative and judicial, of the government, and in their support and protection.

A government that defends the weak will certainly be one of justice and fairness. Verse 17 of this psalm states, "So shall all peoples pray to be blessed, all nations tell of his happiness." The activities of a government are diverse, but economic and legal fairness, and protection of the poor and suffering are the primary concerns of a good government. People do not migrate to a country because it has the best military in the world, and governments are not respected simply because they have the largest GDP on the planet. A nation is respected by others, and loved by its citizens, if it is believed to govern fairly, and if it limits and balances the power of competing groups so that they do not oppress the people. You make up your own mind. But if this psalm is correct, the most important activities of a government concern the supply of justice and the provision of necessities to a population, either by the creation of an economic environment that allows economic success for all, or through the supply of goods to those unable to do this for themselves. And further, no other concern can negate the obligation to meet these needs. This section of scripture deals with economics, law and welfare. Why do you think it did not cover military might, or glorify the accumulation of wealth or the submission of the population to the government?

Chapter 3
PATRIOTISM

If one wishes to consider patriotism, one of the first things one should realize is that most of the inhabitants of every country on the globe possess the attitude that they are citizens of the best country in which one could live, and that even if they feel distaste for their government, they will fight to defend it against any foreign invader. It is not logical however, to imagine that they are all correct in this belief. Naturally, if this is true, it is equally logical to question whether I am correct in assuming this about my own country. Patriotism is the psychological attitude of love and integration with the location in which one has resided for a lengthy period of time, or from one's birth. There is nothing particularly objective about this attitude. An Innuit presumably loves the Arctic, while a Tahitian loves the islands, ocean and warmth of his or her country, and each would feel at a terrible loss if their place of residence was somehow switched. Patriotism is clearly not the result of an objective evaluation of the land one loves, but is rather a psychological attachment to any region one joins oneself to, and is reasonably able to successfully subsist in.

In addition, patriotism is probably an attitude that is beyond most people's control. Rather than being a choice, it seems more similar to the feeling of comfort we come to experience with the familiar, and with the social and geographical territory that make up one's inner 'land'. Further, patriotic feelings can be altered, and either enlarged or diminished. The inhabitants of each German principality prior to German unification no doubt felt this towards their small territory, to the degree that they were comfortable in that land. However, with unification with the larger Prussian state, the love of one's nation shifted, to be focused on the greater homeland of Germany.

The problems associated with patriotism are that it confuses subjective feelings with objective realities, that it is excluding of other human beings, and that it is the basis on which state violence, expressed in war, finds its firmest support. Patriotism divides the world of humanity into one of, "us and them", and exclusion is not a particularly Christian attitude or value. Patriotism is, nevertheless, a very human reaction to a geographical location. It provides a sense of belonging in a world where such a state is sometimes necessary for survival, and provides a social context that gives some degree of meaning and value to one's self, as an otherwise solitary individual. Patriotism has resulted in acts of ultimate bravery, endurance to suffering, and expressions of deep unselfishness. On the other hand, we are well aware that it has also resulted in imperialistic schemes, and even genocidal campaigns. Clearly, while holding the defenders of one's land in truly deep respect, patriotism, especially one's own, should not be viewed uncritically.

The love of one's land should never eclipse the love one should possess for all humanity as God's children. Nor should one be blinded by the cynical exploitation of love of country by politicians for their own selfish, dangerous and immoral purposes. As Christians, we are citizens, not only of particular countries, but of the heavenly city, to which we owe an allegiance that far, far transcends any loyalties we may have to earthly states.

CHAPTER 4
TERRORISM

One of the great differences between war and terrorism is that wars tend to have a definite and limited duration, clearly defined targets that possess military value and easily identifiable combatants. Terrorism derives, at least part of its power, from the fact that it is amorphous, apparently almost endless, the combatants are indistinguishable from ordinary citizens, and that its targets are virtually impossible to accurately predict. In a strange fashion the indiscriminate killing of acts of terror provides a moral argument that negates any moral power that the terrorists seem to assert, in regards their ultimate objectives. If the lives of the victims are of no value, then the lives of the terrorists and those who support them also have no value. And if injustice is the accusation of the terrorist, along with the implicit claim for human dignity and rights that this suggests, then there is an equal claim that can be made for the rights and dignity of the victims of these terrorists acts that should preclude these victims of terror from the fate that terrorists meet out to them. If one group has a right to justice, then the other group has an equal right. To deny the rights of one group, is to deny the rights of the other.

This, of course, will have no impact on such acts, as those who kill other human beings almost certainly, as evidenced by this willingness to kill and maim, do not see the victims of their rage as humans in the first place. The dehumanization of the other, evidenced in killing, is unfortunately but the extreme extension of the more shallow dehumanization of the other that is the way we, as sinful human beings, act in our daily lives. The litmus test of this is found in our answer to the second great commandment, to "love our neighbour as we love ourselves".

If we would be unwilling to do for a total stranger what we would willingly do for ourselves then we are not loving our neighbour as ourselves. Clearly, what we are doing in this is devaluing an other human being. Others do not have the value that we put on ourselves. The descent into the abyss of complete denial of value for others is not inevitable, but it is understandable, and in some situations virtually inevitable. Whatever feelings of regret go through a terrorist's mind before the final moments of the act, the decision to end scores or hundreds of lives, effectively provides evidence that these victims have no value except in terms of state or organizational blackmail, and in order to achieve political ends. In indiscriminately killing others, the terrorist also becomes evil, in the same way that other evil people may have done evil to the terrorist. The evil done to them is returned in kind to others, who may or may not be responsible for the initial, and even continued evil done to the terrorist. To act in an unjust way to others in response to the injustice of others, is to become unjust oneself.

Acts of violence do not spring, causeless, as if from a "vacuum". This does not always mean that the victim has been guilty of any wrong to the perpetrator of violence. The Jews did not deserve the holocaust, any more than any other race that has endured genocidal madness deserved its fate. It is logical, however, to look at the historical record, to attempt to understand what drives terrorists in their willingness to kill. Because a terrorist group engages in such acts does not necessarily imply that the target of their acts is guilty of genuine wrong. This may or may not be the case. It is, of course, equally incorrect to assume that there must be no reason at all for the acts of terror, that the motivation for these acts resides in the twisted psyches of the violent, and that one's country or group is blameless. This also, may or may not be correct.

One of the most damaging decisions, as to the value of human life, occurred in the decision to bomb civilian targets during World War II. What qualitative difference is there between carpet bombing a city, and exterminating scores of thousands of people in a concentration camp? If one is terribly wrong, how can the other be acceptable? If the murder of defenseless civilians, or surrendered POWs is a war crime, isn't the fire bombing of civilian targets like Dresden and Tokyo, if not on the same scale, equally criminal? Allied bombing policies during the War severely weaken the moral credibility of the victorious powers in their pursuit of Nazi and Japanese war criminals. There certainly is a difference between the Allied and Axis policies generally, and the extent of governmental criminality is also significantly distinct, but the decision, nevertheless, opened the door, perhaps permanently, and further than it may already have been, to the acceptability of targeting civilians for the purposes of military and political policies and ends. The fact that such a policy has now been given a harmlessly sounding name, "all out war", and can be studied as to its efficiency in promoting military objectives, does nothing to remove the criminality of attacking and killing defenseless people. Distance from the victims of military weaponry does not inversely reduce the guilt involved in such "sterile" killing.

A state must, or at least will, defend itself against those who seek to kill its citizens in acts of terror. As states, and as citizens within these states, however, it is not enough simply to attack this kind of enemy. The more highly human rights, human dignity, and basic human survival needs are valued, the more the value of human life is taught and lived, the more a state admits to and abandons its historic errors, and moves towards a stance in defense of all humanity, and not only its own, the less likely there will be the grounds for violent acts against it. The supposed state maturity in enacting foreign policy independently of humanitarian concerns and socially shared values of decency, assures neither the value of the alliance so made with an immoral government, nor the protection of the (decent) state from the anger of the people in the totalitarian state who suffer under such a government. Realpolitik, as do all acts of selfishness, ultimately harms the perpetrator. Even towards relatively "good" states, there may be acts of terror, but the justification of these acts will be powerfully undermined. For a Christian, the final solution to terrorism can not be the death and destruction of the terrorist, but his or her discovery of the Jesus who understands wrong, and dealt with it in his crucifixion. Ultimately, a loving heart and the vigorous pursuit of just societies, are the goals of one who follows Jesus on this very violent earth.

Chapter 5
POWER: THE SOCIAL EQUIVALENT OF THE SPLITTING OF THE ATOM

If it is true, in some sense, that all power is derived from God, it is also true that God does not control all power that exists in the universe. This must be granted in that to believe otherwise would be to believe that God was responsible for every single act done in opposition to (him), and against his essential nature. Energy may have a form of objectivity, but power is the ability to achieve an end. The power of the atom is that which holds the universe together, but it may also be used to destroy humanity, or at least to annihilate a vast proportion of it. Power, in itself, is not something to be feared. What is to be feared is the holding of power in the hands of one, or a group, whose nature is antithetical to that of God. In these hands power is destructive, and can only be destructive.

If this statement is true, then we as Christians need to take the question of who has power much more seriously than we usually do. It is, moreover, not enough to evaluate an individual only by the criterion of his or her moral proclivities, but by a whole class of standards with implications regarding a range of impacts on the complete spectrum of human activity. If one focuses on one or two criteria and believes that negative impacts all result from these areas, one will fail to see other, perhaps equally, or more destructive aspects that have impacts on a wider range of human behaviours and activities. One's character is of such importance in the realm of social power, that the question of who wields it is of prime importance. In this regard, character flaws in an individual should be evaluated by their impacts. Moral flaws impact the individual's own life more than they tend to do towards the rest of society. At most they negatively impact a small group, and though this impact is of extreme importance within this "small" group, the negative impact does not usually reach beyond to the greater society. Rampant deceit, an ambition to possess power, inordinate pride, and even psychological disturbance, however, can be radically destructive to a society governed by individuals so disposed. These and other character defects can impact vast segments, and even the whole of society.

As Christians we need to examine how Jesus perceived social power. This has been dealt with, to some degree, in the section on servanthood. Jesus understood clearly that human beings possess an abiding tendency to abuse power, and taught that to counter this proclivity we should act as servants to one another, not lording it over others but regarding all, as of more importance than ourselves. Indeed, Jesus saw the power model as so diametrically opposed to the Kingdom of God that he framed his ministry around the paradigm of that of a lowly worker, in fact, the word often used can be translated "slave". Human nature is such that in all people, and to varying degrees, we cannot handle power over other human beings, except from the attitude of a servant. We inevitably begin to believe that we have a right to instant obedience and respect, and resent it when others fail to see this divine gift. Power over others is such that the more power we possess, and the longer we possess it, the more corrupted by it we become. This is true in every area of human endeavour, not excluding the ministry.

Power and Violence: A Christian Defense

In human beings there is a necessary connection between the possession of power, and the employment of violence. If this is also true of Christians, to the extent that Jesus specifically taught a rejection of attitudes of power, then it is true even more so in those who have not experienced the new birth, and who have no allegiance to the claims of a holy and love filled life. The willingness of those who do not love, to perform acts of extreme and deadly violence against other human beings, is a matter of historical record. The willingness of human beings to perform acts of brutality against those who they see as enemies, threats to a way of life, or as less than equally human to themselves, has been clearly documented in our generation, from the Nazi genocide, the Rwandan massacres, the terrorist killings, the death squads in Central and South America, and the vicious treatment of non-white, and particularly black, races in North America.

The human response to such violence has, throughout the millenia, been to employ an equal or greater level of violence. Violence, nevertheless, does not remove violence, but only perpetuates and reinforces it. If one adopts this form of response, one becomes, to varying degrees, the very thing against which one is fighting. On the other hand, the option of not responding at all is a false response, for it achieves nothing but the strengthening of the violent, and the success of their cause. And yet to oppose violence without the weapons of violence seems to assure a similar success. What weapons then do belong to the anti-violent Christian fighter?

As Christians we claim to be daughters and sons of the most powerful being in the universe. Is there any value in this in the physical world in which we live, or is it merely something that we feel we have to say? We usually hear of the resurrection as the proof of Jesus' conquest of sin as the justification for a belief in resurrection generally, but St Paul saw the resurrection in dynamic terms of power that had been made available to the believer. Chapter one of Ephesians, verses 18 to 21 state,

> "I pray that your inward eyes may be illumined, so that you know what is the hope to which he calls you, what the wealth and glory of the share he offers you amongst his people in their heritage, and how vast the resources of his power open to us who trust in him. They are measured by his strength and might which he exerted in Christ when he raised him from the dead and enthroned him at his right hand.

What St Paul saw and understood was that the resurrection opened to us the potential for power over all that could conceivably oppose the work and character of God. Because Jesus had risen from the dead, this was proof that he had conquered, destroyed, negated, any opposition to the mind of God that could possibly be encountered.

There was nothing that possessed more power than what was available to the believer through Christ. Paul talks about the believer knowing the vast power open to them "who trust in him". Potentially, this is available to all believers. However, we know from experience that this is not the experience of most of us. Now we have trusted Jesus for our salvation , so what is the problem? When Paul uses the word 'trust' in this verse we need to ask how it is that one comes to trust. How do you come to trust your friend, your husband, your children?

Trust in the bible is no different. We develop a trust from coming to know that the person is a certain "kind" and can be depended on, trusted. If we do not know God in the same manner, we will not and cannot trust him. It does not matter that we have been taught in church to trust God. This does not develop trust. It only develops the idea that it is appropriate to trust God. We come to trust God and know the vastness of his power in Christ Jesus by continually developing our relationship with God through submission to him, prayer and time with him, and basing our hopes for the effectiveness of this "activity" on the principle of the grace of God. That is, God comes to us and reveals himself to us, totally independently of our self effort and solely on the basis of the work of Christ on the cross. By discovering who and what God is, we come to know the vastness of his power open to us in Christ as a result of the Victory of the resurrection.

St Paul, living in one of the most violent eras of human history, saw the Christian in decidedly military terms, and as needing adequate weapons with which to oppose this violence. Chapter six of the book of Ephesians speaks of the armor of God:

> Therefore take up God's armor; then you will be able to stand your ground when things are at their worst, to complete every task, and to remain standing. Stand firm I say. Fasten on the belt of truth; for coat of mail put on integrity; let the shoes of your feet be the gospel of peace, to give you firm footing; and with all

these, take up the great shield of faith with which you will be able to quench all the flaming arrows of the evil one. For your helmet take salvation; for your sword take that which the Spirit gives you, the words that come from God. Give yourselves wholly to prayer and entreaty; pray on every occasion in the power of the Spirit. (Ephesians 6: 13-18)

Try to imagine yourself in a situation of real or potential violence; where your life is in danger, or where you are opposing groups that are absolutely willing to act brutally against you. Imagine yourself in a state where there is great persecution against you as a Christian, as a member of an illegal group. The words in the verses above will not have the harmless "spiritual", and frequently almost meaningless impact, that they usually have for Christians in the safe democracies of the West. I am not asserting that these words have no spiritual meaning. That is the very meaning that they *do* have. That is the very point of the verses. These are the primary weapons that we may possess in a very real struggle against the forces of darkness, against the violent and violence of society. These are our weapons in a situation where our lives may very well be at risk. Yet I am very conscious that I write this in the relative safety of a Western democracy.

What is being taught in these verses is not one more subjective, and inner set of truths that have no real connection to the world outside the human mind. What is being taught is the battle strategy of God. In these verses we are being offered a connection to the power of the Almighty. Paul is not suggesting here that if you have truth, integrity, and faith you will be a nice Christian. He is stating that you will be successful in your opposition to real evil, objectified in evil humans and demonic forces. The sword of the Spirit is not simply the rote quoting of the bible, but rather, and in significant addition, the words that the Spirit gives in a concrete situation of desperate need. Paul is teaching success here. He is not teaching a limited defense. Of course defense is a part of fighting, but these verses go far beyond mere defense.

We have become so used to saying the sword of the Spirit is the word of God that we pay almost no attention to what we have said. A sword is a weapon. Paul was writing to people whose lives were at risk. He was not giving a children's talk. When we come to oppose evil, particularly socially and nationally entrenched evil, we cannot avoid asking a question of self survival. What are the weapons at my disposal? If a non-violent, path of love is chosen, is there really anything in the arsenal of non-violence? To reiterate, the word of God is not simply the bible, or do we believe that God never speaks to individuals and society anymore? The word of God, as taught in Ephesians, is the word given to the believer in the time of trial by the Holy Spirit. Paul does not call this a delaying tactic, or a verbal act of desperation. The word given by God is described as a sword. If we were to use contemporary language, Paul would be saying the word of God is a Kalashnikov, or an M16. The word of God is a Kalashnikov.

The religion of Jesus is a peaceful one. Why did Paul think of a weapon when he thought of the word of God that would be given in times of crisis? What is it about the given word that made that image spring to mind for St Paul? Paul surely must have believed that the given word had a power that could be compared to a deadly weapon. In our best moments we too believe such things of God's word. The scriptures say that God's word will not return to God empty, but will accomplish what he intends it to achieve (Isa. 55:11). Once again, this is not simply the bible, but a word given fresh to meet a specific situation in contemporary time and space. The scripture is claiming that God's word is given to effectively meet differing and specific needs. Do we truly believe that God is restricted to the using of the biblical expressions in this? We need, I believe, not to become neurotically concerned that such a situation devalues, or puts at risk, the word of God as expressed in the scriptures.

St Paul is asserting that in times of crisis, risk and struggle we can expect to be given specific direction to adequately meet the needs of that situation. The experience of the church indicates that this does not always occur. Spiritual events such as the word of God powerfully defeating an opponent are usually not the experience of unspiritual people, though God can provide acts of grace, even for us. We also do not have direct insight into the mind of God to understand his intention or time frame, in either the giving or withholding of words that overcome opposition. Some words are like time bombs that wait in the unconscious of the hearer slowly doing their work before they burst to the surface of his or her awareness.

The fact is that God has not made understanding (him) and consequently possessing faith in Him an easy job. The word is a sword, powerful and effective in a complex of ways. Universal physical healing is a biblical teaching supported, if by nothing else, which it is not, by the ministry of Jesus amongst us. Yet God at times seems to hide himself from us, and we are left with mystery and confusion. I believe that God wants us to come to know and trust him in the deepest parts of our being, and not because he performs all that we, *rightly* expect of him. I believe that God wants us to know his character, in the same way, if not to the same degree, that Jesus knew the Father. God, the Father, Son, and Holy Spirit, wants us to know him, and in that relational knowledge, know that he is faithful, even when it appears that this is not so, and to have such faith because we have seen into the heart of the God, we pretend to worship.

The Successful Christian in a Failing World

There is a question, perhaps at the centre of existence, a question as to the silence of God. We should never forget that it was the second person of the trinity, the Son of God, who on the cross cried out, "My God, my God, why hast thou forsaken me?" Yet despite this, at times deeply troubling silence, God does reveal his mind to us in these situations of crisis, and these words have the spiritual power to achieve desired ends, both in us for our guidance and encouragement and in the hearts of those who oppose us.

Paul chose such a startling military image because he had experienced, in the great diversity of his life as a Christian, the results of divinely given ideas. Paul had experienced the power of the inspired word, and knew that its effectiveness was beyond human expectation. Indeed, his life and teaching reveal, not the organized summation of contemplatively reflected religious thought, but the "tried in the world" distillations from a life of pain, as well as joy, for transformation and spiritual power. Paul had discovered that God was faithful to his word, even in those times when he appeared silent and unresponsive. It is those earlier experiences of answered prayer and divine intrusion that keep us from the apparently logical conclusion of that silence, that keep us with God, despite the questions, and despite the silence.

God's word should not, however, be understood as a weapon to destroy another human being. The words of God are intended to destroy evil, not necessarily the evil-doer. During the height of the Renaissance, when Lorenzo the Magnificent lay dying, and in fear of his soul, he sent for Savonarola. Savonarola was a preacher whose passionate and violent sermons against the lifestyle and supporters of this period in European history for a time were successful in terrifying and turning the people of Florence away from the Renaissance lifestyle espoused by Lorenzo. When Savonarola came to the dying Lorenzo's bed he did not tell him the message of forgiveness and salvation. Rather, he told Lorenzo he would go straight to hell because of the evil of his life. Lorenzo would have listened and heeded anything Savanarola could have said.

Just how serious do you think God was about reconciling the world to himself when he sent Jesus into the world to be crucified and redeem it? Where do you think salvation and reconciliation fit in a list of God's priorities? God's Kalashnikov is a powerful weapon, but it is not a weapon of destruction but of peace. When one seeks to oppose cruelty and evil, one does not approach this in order to destroy the enemy, but to convert him or her, and so cause the evil to stop.

These qualities, and this success is not, nevertheless, automatically given just because we want them. We have to possess and speak the truth. We have to have integrity. We have to have a knowledge of God that generates faith. We have to be loyal to the gospel of *peace,* have to see that it is such a gospel. We have to possess salvation. And we have to be in such a place with God that (he) can, in fact, give us his words. How does Paul end this little section on the weapons of the Christian? He describes a continually developing relationship with God, grown in prayer and in the power of the Spirit, that guarantees success in the violent world that confronts those who seek to bring peace. Paul claims that truth will overcome lies, that integrity will have an impact on the mind that does not believe in or expect integrity in another human being, that faith will cause the power of God to be manifest in all (and terrible) situations, and that the words God gives will penetrate the hearts of the sinful and violent, and confront them with the truth.

It is not with abstract spiritual power that we confront the forces of darkness. The power that the Christian potentially possesses, and with which we can oppose evil, is the character and power of God. Paul in 2 Corinthians 10:4,5 states,

"The weapons we wield are not merely human, but powerful through God to demolish strongholds of false ideas." The Christian does have weapons and we as a church seem to have forgotten that the activities that go on within the church, and in its outreach include, in addition to words and logical argumentation, the wisdom, knowledge and power of God which can reach past and through erroneous positions in ways that we probably cannot even imagine. Would you agree with me that in the life of the church there is really very little that could be described as "powerful weapons of God that demolish opposition" such as Paul claimed he possessed?

This weaponry does not, however, guarantee that we will not suffer. We need to continually recall that Jesus was crucified, that Stephen, Paul, Peter, and countless other powerful Christians, were also murdered for their faith. God does not cease to be a mystery in this area. At times we will completely succeed in our ventures, and at other times success can only be seen from the standpoint of God, a standpoint that we do not now see. What is definitely guaranteed to those who live in the presence of God on earth, is that in this we will be faithful, we will "continue to stand" . We do not despise human failure in this remark. No one lives a perfect life, and failure is a possibility if we are human. We can love the one who fails, just as God loves him or her, because we ourselves are so often such failures. However, God has provided a way to come to him, and in seeking his face in prayer and silence before him we can come to a place where the power of God can be revealed, even through such weak creatures as us.

That the protection of God can not be taken for granted is seen in Paul's second letter to the Corinthians, chapter one. Paul says he "despaired of life" (v 8) Later, Paul gives his understanding of the experience. Apparently he had allowed his focus on God as protector to slip, and had begun to depend on his intelligence perhaps, to evade those who sought his life and hated the gospel. He says, " This was meant to teach us not to place reliance on ourselves, but on God who raises the dead. From such mortal peril God delivered us, he on whom our hope is fixed. Yes, he will continue to deliver us, if you will co operate by praying for us." (2 Cor. 1: 9,10)

We frequently make a leap from a particular promise of God to the assumption that, the promise having been given, we will automatically be the recipients of the fulfillment of the promise. This attitude by Christians is quite common, and if we are to take Paul's experience, and his understanding of it, seriously, we have no firm ground to make such assumptions. God will act as he sees fit, and there are no rules beyond God's character that I or anyone else can make to limit God's freedom. In addition, God often acts in grace to protect someone who does not have a particularly deep spiritual relationship. Nevertheless, according to this passage Paul's protection depended on two variables. One was Paul's conscious dependence on God to protect him, even to the point of raising him from the dead if need be, and second, that the prayers of the church were required. Paul described these prayers on his behalf as "co-operating with God'. God is faithful to his word and nature, but the power of God is not usually revealed to those who do not take their relationship to him terribly seriously.

The possibility of a close relationship to God is available to us, and the words of Ephesians encourage us to believe that there is an alternative to weakness and fear. Yet the enemy of our souls has always been aware of the gap between true faith, and a superficial adherence to faith principles that have not yet become 'real' in the heart of the 'believer'. When Hezekiah was king of Judah, the Assyrian king sent his chief eunuch to Jerusalem with these words, "What ground have you for this confidence of yours? Do you think fine words can take the place of skill and numbers?" (11 Kings 18:20). This is the crux of the issue. We actually have more faith in a strong military, or some other avenue of force than we have faith in God. This is the natural level of most humans, including most Christians. However, in reading the scripture we discover the possibility that the power of God is a superior alternative to physical power. These are the "fine words" of the eunuch's speech. The question we are confronted with as Christians is, "are they going to remain merely 'fine words', or are we going to spend the time before God so that these fine words are transformed into the power they assert themselves to be?" .

There is another set of weaponry that can at times be utilized, and that is the media. Apart from failure, evil people and groups do not enjoy seeing and hearing their violence portrayed on national television and radio around the world. Totalitarian governments, and those who perpetrate violence against a population, seek to hide their brutality from a world that, on the whole, does not support brutality. The press is universally suppressed in regions and states where violence is perpetrated against the nation's own citizens. To the degree that violent people have the power to hide the truth, this will be done, whether it be in our own country, or in another state that we are more willing to believe would do such things. If the silencing of a journalist, by whatever means, will go unpunished, this will be done.

It is the degree of power that an individual or state perceives him or itself to possess that determines whether the media will be silenced. However, in most Western democracies the media can help to protect and promote the cause of truth, justice, decency, and even the spread of the gospel. If this is doubted, recall the outrage and impact of videos of police brutality on public opinion, and the subsequent investigations of such brutality. The people, on the whole, possess a sense of decency and justice that can be appealed to in support of righteous causes.

Historically, Christians have attempted a variety of strategies to weaken the power of the violence of those who oppose them. The way in which St Francis sought to achieve this end is worth examining, both in terms of its level of success, and in regards to its overall failure. St Francis lived in a period of dramatic socio-economic turmoil. There had been several significant religious movements teaching a form of poverty similar to that which he espoused, and most had been silenced by ecclesiastical decree or execution. These movements were often seen as threats to church power and prestige, and crushed accordingly. Francis was certainly aware of the great risk he was taking, in adopting a path of poverty for himself and his followers, and from the beginning he actively confessed submission to the authority of the church. While teaching radical impoverishment, he actively encouraged friendly relations with the powerful in the church, some of whom recognized in him a level of spirituality and vulnerability that needed defending. He was, thus, able to continue his work, and make the impact on Christian thinking, both then and even now, that was positive and glorifying to God. An apostle of love, his poverty was, in fact, an expression of this love, and an identification with the poverty of Christ.

Nevertheless, the protection that he sought, and was offered under Cardinal Hugolin, who later became Pope Gregory IX, was gained at a great price. The Rule which Francis formulated for the Franciscan order was severely truncated, and radical poverty, the very essence of the movement, was reduced to that form of poverty common to all monastic orders, and in which it was possible to be individually poor, to possess little, while institutionally being the holder of enormous wealth, power and prestige. In essence, the church was not willing to admit to a poverty that was a genuine threat to its economic and political power. Even before Francis' death, the order had been transformed into an institution that could hardly be recognized as original Franciscanism.

What Francis did achieve was the historical memory of his early life, and that of his order, a vision that, ever since, has influenced and impacted the life of the church, and even the world, in the way of a beautiful fragrance. Franciscans have never been able to escape this radical and theoretically consistent Francis, even with the truncated version of his order that they have been forced to live with. Almost certainly he had no alternative, for he would have been suppressed if he had done otherwise. However, in seeking protection from those in the church who rejected his teaching, he was unable to continue the model for human social and religious life that he saw as the scripturally correct understanding of the gospels. His protector, who eventually became the Pope, was willing to allow his expression of spirituality, but saw an institutional need to regulate his followers. It is fascinating that St Francis, that most spiritual of Christians, was pragmatic to the degree that he sought political protection. One could argue that this decision was a strategic mistake which ultimately resulted in the failure of his mission. The decisions we may make to advance the causes we support may not always be accepted by fellow Christians. They may, in fact, find our choices "unspiritual". We do, however, need to take into consideration the structures of political and social power that we find ourselves living under, and this may be the reason St. Paul did not openly attack the virtually universal institution of slavery.

There is thus another dimension of, hopefully spiritual weaponry to that outlined in Ephesians 6 in the pragmatic set of human strategies we decide on, and that Francis decided on, in order to oppose power in the name of righteousness and peace. These strategies may be pragmatic, but they cannot be unethical, and merely politically opportunistic. The good is not achieved by evil means, no matter what that good may be. If, as Ephesians tells us, God is the God of the truth, any strategic calculation must include all dimensions of relevant truth, and not simply the one we are attempting to promote, no matter how crucial that particular value may seem.

The world we live in is certainly a place of violence. If those without power can be violent, then those who genuinely do possess this potential control over others will be tempted to abuse this power. What a strange world, that of all the species we are the only one that goes out of its way to cause pain and suffering, and even enjoy inflicting this pain, on members of its own species. Other animals may kill, but this is almost always done, only to satisfy the need for nourishment. Humans, on the other hand, do not live, even at that level of harmfulness. As a species we hate each other. This feeling exists at varying degrees, but resentment and violence lie just beneath the surface, waiting to be provoked. Put simply, holiness is the replacement of this violent hate with an equally pervasive love for all. The scripture teaches the Christian ways of defense against this violence, but it does not promise that we will never suffer, either as humans or as Christians.

CHAPTER 6
THE FLESH...
WHAT IS IT?

For a non-Christian such a question must seem odd, if not humorous. It is, nevertheless, a biblical concept that needs explanation in that an incorrect understanding can lead to behavioural limitations that restrict normal human living, and impose attitudes towards other Christians that are strains to fellowship, if not outright barriers to it. In some holiness teaching this term is employed frequently as signifying a state, principle, source of behaviour that should be shunned, crucified, and viewed with repulsion. Consequently, as it is the term for an important biblical concept, we need to see how it is used in the New Testament. That, in Paul's mind, it may well have been associated with a Platonic devaluation of the body as a material object, will not be discussed, as many of those who adopt this term in any serious fashion, would not regard a philosophical connection to a "biblical" teaching as having any value at all.

Many preachers appear to view the mention of Greek words as tools in the explaining of biblical concepts, as indeed they can be. Most who do this, however, are not Greek scholars, and one wonders whether the use of Greek, rather than as a useful explanatory device, is actually to give the explanation more credence than it logically deserves, or for some other not so spiritually lofty purpose. Knowledge of the subtleties of any language takes years of study to acquire, and this is not gained in the usual Greek and Hebrew courses that are required in most seminaries. However, that being said, and perhaps opening myself up to the same 'accusation', there are two words used for flesh in the NT: *kreas* Romans 14:21, and 1 Corinthians 8:13 which speaks of meat, and *sarx,* employed everywhere else, and having a variety of meanings in different contexts. Used as an adjective the words are *sarkikos* (a form of *sarx*) in 2 Corinthians 1:12 and 1 Peter 2:11, and *sarkinos* in 2 Corinthians 3:3.

Matthew 16:17 states, "flesh and blood have not revealed this...". Matthew 19:5,6 speak of a man and a woman becoming "one flesh", an idea repeated in Mark 10:8. Matthew 24:22 and Mark 13:20 both state, "..there should be no flesh saved". In all of these verses there is no negative connotation to the word flesh, which is simply used as being roughly equivalent to humanity or being. Matthew 26:41 and Mark 14:38 relate, "The spirit is willing but the flesh is weak", a description that has no necessary connection to the idea of the flesh as the source of sinful behaviour, but rather to the frequent inability of humanity to do what the conscious mind believes is appropriate action. Luke relates in chapter 3:6 "all flesh shall see the salvation of God", and in chapter 24:39 "For a spirit does not have flesh and bones." In the first reading 'flesh' is used as a metaphor for humanity, and the second verse is simply describing the human body. That flesh is not necessarily identical to sinful nature is seen in John 1:14 "and the Word was made flesh and dwelt among us." It is important to note that the same Greek word is used in all these cases, and that it therefore cannot be simply understood as the word used in Greek to signify the sinful nature. When Jesus says "that which is born of the flesh is flesh and that which is born of the spirit is spirit", in John 3:6 he is not identifying flesh with sin but rather denoting two sources and kinds of life: physical life on earth and spiritual life. It would be an unjustified and unnecessary over-interpretation to make the syllogism:

All people are flesh.
All people are sinners.
Therefore all flesh is sinful.

Jesus is not making that connection, but only pointing us to two different kinds of birth/life. That the word *sarx*/flesh can, indeed, be understood in a completely positive fashion is seen in the incident in chapter 6 of John, where Jesus speaks of "eating his flesh". Not only is this 'experience' presented in positive terms, it is also rightly understood, as Jesus later explained (6:63), in a metaphorical sense referring to the spiritual life that Jesus gives. Later in the gospel in chapter 8:15 Jesus says, "you judge according to the flesh…", not implying that people judge from their sinful natures, but merely as humans without the wisdom and knowledge of God. This is a reference to the limitation of human knowledge, and the tragic results that this can result in. Jesus is saying here that the people did not have enough information to make an accurate conclusion, not that they were acting from a sinful nature.

Progressing through the NT, Acts in 2:17, 26, 30, and 31 employ the word to speak of either the human race or the physical body, but not sinful nature. On the other hand, in the book of Romans, Paul, begins to give this word a much more theologically loaded meaning. Romans 6:19 speaks of the "weakness of the flesh", but this is stated only as the reason he has used human categories, "slavery and freedom" to explain the experience of sin, and liberation from this slavery. The spiritual immaturity of the people to whom this letter was addressed, had led him to use terminology that they would be able to understand.

Romans 7:5, however, goes much further, and states, "For when we were in the flesh the motions of sins [caused] by the law worked in our members [bodies] to produce death". The flesh is described here as that nature which is incapable of fulfilling the law, but rather allows the law to convict us of our guilt before God, and increase our separation from God. This section shows that, to Paul, the flesh is our existence without the indwelling Spirit of God who, in such a relationship, is alone able to produce the fruit of godly life. The flesh is not our body as such, but the sinful nature of our existence that lacks the indwelling presence of God. Verse 14 of chapter 7 states, "For we know that the law is spiritual, but I am fleshy [*sarkinos*] sold to sin as a slave". Paul appears to be setting up a dichotomy here of flesh and spirit. Nevertheless, it should not be concluded that flesh, the physical body, in itself is sinful, for to assert such would be to assert that the temple of the Holy Spirit, (1 Corinthians 3:16) is sinful. Jesus also walked around the Holy Land in a real physical body. Sinfulness is not found in cells, but in a lost spirit, a spirit that is not united to God, and thus cannot reveal the character of God. This surely is what Jesus was teaching in Matthew 15: 17-19 when he spoke of the source of evil, defilement, as coming from the 'heart', and not from the body. When Paul speaks in verse 6 of serving God "in newness of spirit" he is speaking of a new spiritual reality in the life of a believer, and of the inner being of a person in which the Holy Spirit newly dwells.

Chapter seven appears to end in a kind of "spiritual draw". Paul serves God with his mind, but also serves sin with the flesh (v 25) This is not, however, the end of the story, for Paul or for us. Chapter 8:2-4 tells us of the possibility of a victory over sin for the believer, while still in this world. He states, "For the law of the Spirit of life in Christ Jesus has made me free from the law of sin and death...that the righteousness of the law might be fulfilled in us." This is not an easy passage. Remember that Paul said in 7:25 that he served the law of God with his mind. In chapter 8 verse 7 he states, "the carnal [fleshy] mind is enmity against God, for it is not subject to the law of God, neither indeed can be." Paul previously stated that it was his flesh, and not his mind, that led him into sin. In the face of this, one is forced to ask if one's mind is spiritual, or fleshy and sinful. What this apparent contradiction seems to suggest is (a) that it is extremely difficult to explain the experience of sin using physical imagery, (b) that Paul's categories should not be understood as fixed, in the modern way we describe the mind and body, and (c) that Paul does not set up a strict body-spirit dichotomy. His categories float according to the lesson he is presenting. The carnal mind is also the carnal/fleshy nature.

Indeed, Paul implies just what the flesh is when he states in 8:8, "They that are in the flesh cannot please God", and then goes on in verse 9 to define who is in the flesh, or more accurately, who is not in the flesh. "But you are not in the flesh but in the Spirit if the Spirit of God dwells in you". According to the scripture then, the flesh, in relation to sin and holiness, is the nature of the individual who has not accepted Jesus as Saviour and Sanctifier, and in whom, therefore, the Spirit of God does not dwell. To be "in the flesh" then, is not to act in a certain way, so much as it is to lack the presence of the Spirit of God.

It is, nevertheless possible for a believer to live in the flesh, to live as though the Spirit of God did not dwell in one, by seeking to be holy by one's own efforts, or by not being willing to be transformed into the image of God. Paul spoke to his readers as "bretheren". That is to say, he was not speaking to unbelievers. He was, however, aware that one could have the faith that would make one a child of God, and yet live a life of spiritual defeat, if one failed to accept the sanctifying work that had also been won on the cross with the death of Christ. Indeed, the resurrection shows that Jesus not only carried the sins of the world, but also that, through the cross, completely defeated sin, and all the suffering and destruction it could cause. Clearly, victory over the power of sin in us, and not just its consequences, is part of that victory.

In Romans, then, the flesh is the nature of the individual in bondage to sin; it is the individual before the new birth in Christ. The concept of the flesh is intrinsically connected to the nature of sin in the individual. Moreover, it is not alien to the general meaning of "flesh" as equivalent to humanity, and in a real sense Paul is taking this general and universal meaning, and adding to it, to describe the universe of humanity, without God's Spirit. To act in the flesh, then, is not to act in ways that do not include God, such as playing football, but rather it is to act without faith, without the input of the Holy Spirit. In this sense normal human activity is not activity in the flesh, anymore than eating or getting married is acting in the flesh. The term, thus, should not be misused to describe an activity that simply appears to have no spiritual importance, such that normal and acceptable activity becomes unacceptable to God. Nor should it be understood that an act, judged to be not overtly spiritual, cannot be used by God for his own glory. God can take normal human activity and use it to reveal himself, particularly if that activity is consecrated to God. Naturally, this "normal human activity" cannot be normal sinful activity.

CHAPTER 7
TEMPTATION

One of the most well known verses in the bible for Christians is 1 Corinthians 10: 13. This verse tells us that we will not be tempted above our ability to resist the temptation, and that God will provide a way of escape. Along with the verse that says Jesus was tempted in all points as we are, I would say that it is also one of the least believed scriptures in the New Testament. We Christians get around this dilemma simply by not discussing what we feel is a discrepancy between our experience, and the apparent meaning of the verses. In some way, the verse is not important, despite the fact it seems so, because the Christian's ability to resist temptation is actually a function of the depth of his or her relationship with God, and the degree to which this person has been transformed into Christ's likeness. Ephesians chapter six, among other readings, teaches this very truth. Yet the problem remains.

The verse seems to be saying that when we are tempted, God will send something, a distraction or an intervention by a third party perhaps, that will reduce the temptation to a controllable level. But this is almost never what we experience, nor does it seem the experience of biblical characters in the moments of their temptation. What the bible is teaching, I suggest, is that as children of God, God has a method of giving us the strength to resist all temptation. God does provide a way of escape. God's provision in times of temptation is the resurrection life of Jesus Christ in us. Further, in terms of the process of the outworking of this resurrection life we protect ourselves by employing the armor of God, as described in Ephesians. This understanding is in conformity to biblical teaching. And in some sense, the usual interpretation of the verse is not.

Further, a blanket promise to "provide a way of escape…" to all, and independent of one's relationship with God is not scriptural. The promises of God have some relationship to the degree that we are close to God. Peter swore he would be faithful to Jesus. He then fell asleep when it would have been better to have prayed (a very human response to stress). Jesus' remark was that "the spirit was willing but the flesh was weak". Peter's ability to resist temptation was dependent on his character, and at that point, it failed.

Though we usually think of temptation as caused by the devil, it is actually a response to an idea. Even if the temptation is couched within an emotion, it is the idea of what that emotion will result in that pulls us in a certain direction. Though being tempted does not mean that one has sinned, the fact that a certain possibility can have an appeal to one may indicate that there is an area in one's life that needs God's grace and transformation. On the other hand that one can be tempted without this implying that one is sinful is surely related to the fact that we as humans do not "contain" perfect knowledge and are therefore capable of making incorrect decisions.

James 1:14, 15 tell us, "Temptation arises when a person is enticed and lured away by their own lust; then lust conceives and gives birth to sin." Lust in this verse does not suggest either sexual desire, or indeed anything sinful at all. Rather it merely refers to a desire for something which, once again, may or may not be sinful to any degree. This, indeed, must be the interpretation, because Jesus was himself tempted, and I doubt that we consider Jesus to be sinful. Perhaps the power of temptation lies in just this ambiguity, that part of the attraction is to something which is, in other conditions, entirely acceptable. In fact, it may well be other variables entirely, that make this object's attainment a sin, and not the thing itself. Of course, if one were tempted to murder someone, it would be difficult to show that there was an acceptable goal locked away somewhere in this desire.

James' description of the experience of temptation is couched in such emotive terminology that it is difficult not to conclude that it is anything but an aspect of sinful nature. One must, however, as in many other theological problems, return to the life of Christ. Apart from Jesus' experience in the wilderness at the beginning of his ministry, Jesus also was tempted, it would seem, when Peter told him that he should not die in the manner Jesus had just previously described (Matt. 16:23, Mk. 8:33). If Peter's suggestion had not found a resonant chord in Jesus, it is doubtful Jesus would have called Peter, Satan. Temptation is not then simply a Satanic appeal to our sinful nature, but more so is an appeal to an invalid decision which may or may not be sinful. Temptation from this perspective is an appeal to a choice which God does not wish.

There is another wrinkle in this problem. One may be tempted to do something which is not objectively a sin, but because one considers it a sin, the doing of that action would be a sin. To state what is probably a truism, our minds do not always lead us to the truth. In the quest to live a holy life, one can deconstruct life to such an extent that perfectly acceptable behaviour is viewed in a spiritually negative light. I suspect Satan gets great delight in this.

Life is difficult enough, without sowing additional minefields that virtually guarantee failure and sin. Rather than analyzing life into microscopic bits, as the Pharisees did, in an effort not to miss any possible sin, we need to live simply before God, in surrender to him. We need to be open to his guidance as to the acceptability of an action that is potentially problematic. If we are surrendered to God, the Holy Spirit's help is promised to us, to guide and teach us. Jesus promised this in the final chapters of John's gospel just before he was arrested (John 16: 12-15, also chapters 14-17). It is entirely possible to analyze life, and human behaviour to an extreme degree, and be incorrect in our understanding, despite the logical appeal of our conclusions. Sanctification is not the development of a complex system of rules and spiritual understandings of human action. God has not described in scripture a holy person as a neurotic personality trying fervently(in a desire to submit to God, I realize) to assure itself of its holiness. I know that of which I speak. Sanctification is a transforming and a teaching of one's heart by the indwelling Spirit of Jesus so that one can victoriously live a holy life in those areas of our heart that have been transformed. It is by being transformed into the image of Christ that temptation loses its power, just as it did in the life of the Saviour whose victory over temptation we experience through this transformation.

CHAPTER 8
THE CHURCH AND THE GOSPEL: HAVE WE FORGOTTEN?

We have been saved by grace.
Are we then sanctified by commitment?

What most human beings want more than anything else, more than money or power, or even sex, is peace. We are surrounded by a vast throng of voices, each telling us what we should be doing, thinking, feeling, and frequently finding fault with how we act. If we did not essentially agree with many of these competing voices they would not trouble us. We know we should be doing more. We realize our actions towards others are frequently unloving and selfish, and what is worse, we know the sins we have committed, even if others do not. These voices play on the CD of our virtually infallible memories within our sub-conscious, and give us no rest. We seek love because we long for another to say what we do not believe about ourselves: that we are lovable. One of the reasons it is so difficult to take the forgiveness and grace of God seriously, is that we do not seriously believe it.

Truly accepting that if we confess our sins he is faithful and just to forgive our sins and cleanse us from all unrighteousness (1 John 1:9), is a reality most of us find extremely difficult to believe. Even as Christians we must often remind ourselves that this is indeed so. Acknowledging our sin, "that's it?", we say unbelievingly to ourselves, and unwittingly to God. It is a continual mental struggle to believe that we actually and truly can come into the presence of God "just as we are", and be perfectly acceptable to God. We know that, in addition to the sinfulness that nags at us in the back of our minds, we actually don't really want to be in the presence of God in the first place. Our consciousness of sin is pervasive, and though we realize we should be a different kind of person, what we see in our lives, day after day, is often a picture of spiritual failure. We may have the right ideas and biblical positions, but we simply don't have the feelings that should accompany these ideas. We long to live from the heart, we long to possess a holiness that is unforced, but find ourselves acting only from what we believe we should be doing, from a sense of duty.

There are some who believe that the scriptures teach that we are all born sinful. Whether that is true or not, the fact remains that, at some time in our human development we have all achieved that dubious state before God. Scripture, and our experience of ourselves and others, reveal that we know none who have escaped this sorry condition. Indeed, the universal absence of pure goodness supports the scriptural claim that all have sinned and fallen short of the glory of God. The origin of such a situation, that is to say, the particular details of the origin of that situation, in some sense, is not important. Rather, what is important is the present condition of being sinful, and the consequent separation from God that such a state makes necessary. This separation from God, both in eternal terms, and in terms of our daily inability to be loving and good, makes this catastrophe the most pressing issue that could and does confront humanity.

Whether we believe that we have inherited sinfulness, or simply that we do not possess some necessary quality or characteristic, (perfect knowledge perhaps), that makes our individual fall into sin inevitable, like a computer that lacks a certain software program that results in imperfect running, is not essential to the realization of the problem. The bible describes the situation we are in as being lost. To be lost means not to know where one is, not to know how to act in the situation one finds oneself in, or to be away from one who is the true owner of the object. All these understandings seem to fit the situation we find ourselves in. The word is used metaphorically, but the experience to which it refers is far from metaphorical. We religious folk have become so used to the word that it has very little impact on our thinking. We need to hear it again, as a genuine description of our own experience, as well as others' so that, as a theological term, it can have a powerful meaning once more.

We are so used to being lost, in fact, that we find it almost impossible to imagine a *real* state of existence where this word would not describe our lives. A non-lost world lacks a sense of reality. Even Christians, who claim to understand the term, act as if salvation were just one more item we had bought at the supermarket, and not the gift bought with the death and suffering of the second person of the Godhead himself. That we do not value salvation, in our hearts, is seen in our indifference to the eternal state of a lost humanity, in our indifference to evangelism, and unfortunately in the shallowness of our relationship with God. We would probably get more excited if someone were to give us a Cadillac, than we are about the gift we say Christ has given us. We are, indeed, in a sorry state. Happily, awareness is, not just the first step but many steps toward a new attitude. It was the sinful tax collector, who would not even lift his head to heaven as he prayed, and could only confess his sinfulness, who went out of the temple forgiven (Luke 18: 10-14).

It is tempting to wonder what kind of people we would grow to be if we were surrounded by love in all our interactions with human beings. This is not a frivolous question, for we know that, to a great extent, children who are surrounded by love grow to be psychologically healthy and socially adjusted. Do we really need God's alternative to evil as much as the bible teaches us, or could we arrive at a state of goodness, with wise human help, by ourselves? This is a question that Christians cannot ignore, simply because it is not a biblical teaching. Clearly, some people are better than others, and some truly good human beings have been non-Christians.

Let me suggest two responses to this. If we take Mahatma Gandhi as one of the most loving people who have lived in the last hundred years, how did he see his own level of goodness? Gandhi used to say that he could never condemn other people who were sinners, because he was such a scoundrel himself. Obviously he did not believe he had arrived at a state of spiritual perfection.

Secondly, despite the theoretical appeal of such a "wondering", the fact remains that the world is far, far, from being anything, even as good as the Mahatma. At the best we are harmlessly selfish, and at the worst we are madmen who kill and use others for our own advantage. What we have is an existential problem of humanly unimaginable proportions, that needs a solution. Sadly, the theoretical possibility of a perfect environment producing a perfect individual is beyond the realm of reasonable probability. We have a global problem and we need a global solution. The theoretical environmental possibility may, in fact, be true, though I strongly doubt that we possess all the variables needed to produce such perfection. And the resultant state must be perfection. It cannot just be, "exceedingly good", for that implies the continued existence of some evil. Where there is some evil, there is the likelihood of more evil growing from this "tiny" amount.

Further, there must be perfect knowledge, for without such knowledge we will inevitably make mistakes that hurt and anger others who will not understand that we have "simply" acted in such a way because we "didn't know". If the lack of perfect knowledge were the one variable we did not possess, I believe that one variable would guarantee the future growth of sin, evil and suffering. Knowledge and sin are closely connected, as we see in Jesus' statement on the cross: "Father forgive them they know not what they do." Isn't at least one of the implications in this that if they had known they would not have done it? Perfect knowledge may be essential to a state of sinlessness, but this does not seem an attainable quality. If this is so, what situation or transformative act is available that can generate "good" behaviour and a freedom from sin?

Because we live in a rather morally uneven world we are quite willing to accept levels of imperfection, in other words levels of goodness. God, however, is perfect, and to live with God requires that we also must be perfect. This, indeed, was a theme to which Jesus' again and again returned in his teaching. There is nothing ambiguous in Jesus' remark, "Be perfect even as your heavenly father is perfect." It is illogical to imagine that we could simply transport the world (even just the world of humans) to heaven, and that this would be acceptable to God, and even to the humans who were so thoughtfully removed. What would the point be? And if one imagines that God simply accepts everyone, unredeemed and unsanctified, one by one, at death, and not en masse as previously suggested, isn't this also suggesting that heaven would be populated by sinful people? It is not moral improvement that is needed and required; it is a complete spiritual transformation that generates new reactions and behaviours, and ends with a perfect soul. And that is beyond any transformative process we as humans can envisage.

It is not, however, beyond God's powers of imagination. God knows we can never make ourselves as good as he wants us to be. Whether we were to live under the strict directions of the Mosaic law, or grow up in the seemingly more pagan world of a non Jewish culture, one experience would unite us all. In all societies in which people live, there is a sense of deep personal failure to be the ideal that is presented by parents and other societal teachers. Contrary to what we believe God's reaction to this to be, God actually waits for us to realize that we are spiritual failures. In fact, there is nothing God can do to help us, if we do not feel this way. Paradoxically, the perfect God who demands a similar perfection in us, waits for us to see our own spiritual impotence and lack of perfection before he can place that goodness within us. Like Alcoholics Anonymous, unless we see ourselves as we truly are, he can not help us become what we deeply long to be.

The first step then, is an admission of guilt. This can be difficult. We have learnt throughout our lives that an admission of guilt can all too soon result in rejection and punishment. We quickly learn to deny guilt, not to admit it. Yet that is what God seeks in order to remove that guilt. One of the first things we need to learn about God is that he is not like the humans who surround us. God does not pour his wrath down on us when we confess our sins. Yet a relationship with the Godhead does not come about simply through a confession of sins. God really can have nothing to do with imperfect beings. That is the quandary. How then do we go from being imperfect and sinful, to having a relationship with a holy God, if we cannot achieve this state of holiness?

Clearly, Christians do not immediately become perfect creatures. It does not take long to discover this fact. There are two stages to Christian perfection. Both are inextricably connected, and both are based on what was accomplished by Jesus on the Cross. No one really understands what Jesus experienced on the cross, but the Bible teaches that he took into himself the sins of the world. What this means is that all the sins that you (and everyone else) have ever committed, and will commit, were taken from you when Jesus took them into himself and dealt with them. Imagine a vast number of harmful bacteria entering the body, only to be attacked and destroyed by the body's immune system. Probably a bad, and definitely inadequate analogy, but hopefully useful.

Sin results in death. If there were no sin there would be no death. Sin then has a consequence, and Jesus bore that consequence himself. He died. And when he died we, as a sinful race, died also, because he had taken into himself all that we have ever been. Sin, however, did not destroy him. If Jesus had not risen from the dead, this "non-event" would have shown that sin had "won", and that the power of sin was greater than any attempt to remove that great human burden. The resurrection shows that Jesus triumphed over sin, and the evil that is associated with sin.

The first stage in God's rescue of the human race is a spiritual rebirth. Atomic energy may be extremely complex, and it may have taken a genius to discover its workings, but these workings are all around us in the world, and in the universe we eat and touch and look out on. The power that binds the universe sits quietly and simply, as if it all were no big deal. The new birth is also surprisingly simple, yet its implications and out-workings are vast, and complex, and certainly mysterious. When we come to see our deep failure and sin, and understand that Jesus has taken this burden of sin for us, we simply turn to God and ask this one who brought us forgiveness and cleansing to come into our hearts and lives. We accept him as the one who saves us from ourselves. There is no one formula that must be prayed. We turn our hearts to God, and away from sin, we understand that we can have peace with God through the one who died for us, and we thank this Jesus for taking our sins on the cross. The prayer could be as simple as, "Lord, forgive me for my sins. Come into my heart as my Saviour."

When this happens, the Holy Spirit, God in fact, comes into our spirit. This has never happened to us before, and the effect is like that of being born. It is a new experience in which we become connected to God The bible tells us that when this occurs we are made the daughters and sons of God. These are metaphorical terms to indicate to us, in earthly vocabulary, that we are as close to God as one is to one's family. There is, though, another result of this rebirth. Remember that when Jesus took our sins and died, we, in effect, died with him. When Jesus arose that first Easter Sunday (or whatever day it was) the new life he had was also the new life that we are given when we turn to him.

And just as he was and is perfect, so in Him we also are perfect. In Jesus we died when he died, and in Jesus we are now alive because he now lives. In that we were totally identified with Jesus in his death, so we are totally identified with Jesus in his perfect resurrection life. What Jesus is, we have become. Righteousness is the biblical term that means the moral perfection of God, and in the same sense that we are perfect in Jesus, we are perfectly righteous in Jesus. Jeremiah 23:6 states, "This is the name given to him: The Lord is our Righteousness." Isaiah 61:10 tells us, "Let me rejoice in the Lord with all my heart, for he has clothed me in righteousness as a garment." And finally, 1 Corinthians 1:30 says, "You are in Christ Jesus, for God has made him

(Jesus) our wisdom , our righteousness, our sanctification, and our redemption." We stand before God clothed in a righteousness that is not ours. It is the righteousness of Jesus, given to us as a gift. He loved us. We could never achieve the righteousness God demands and so he came to us, became one of us, and died for us. We poor sinners, who have turned to Jesus, have been clothed, covered by a righteousness we do not, and never could, deserve. In the new birth we become perfect before God, in Jesus.

It is this perfection that allows us to come to God in prayer, even when we know that there is a level of reality in which we are not any where near perfect. Indeed, our standing before God is totally based on the standing that Jesus has 'bought' for us with his death and resurrection. So there we have it. In our standing we are perfect, but in our hearts we are not. We still are very much strangers to God in how we think and react to the world. We are still angered when someone treats us unfairly or rudely. We still have almost no idea who God really is.

With Paul we cry out "The good that I would do, I do not, but the evil that I would not, that I do." (Romans 7: 9) The answer to our dilemma is found in the very basis of the salvation we received as a result of faith and repentance. Remember again that in Jesus we all died, and also that when he rose from the dead, we all rose from the dead as well. We need to see things as God sees them. God does not see us as sinners, but as perfect in Christ. In terms of the power to overcome sin in our lives, this applies as well. God does not see any power to achieve holiness, residing in ourselves. Rather God sees the power of the life of Jesus that has become our spiritual life, residing in us, and that is where we discover the power to overcome sin. We "attained" salvation by realizing we could do nothing to achieve righteousness before God, and we attain a holy life, a LIFE of righteousness by continuing this realization of personal impotence. When we stop continually trying to be good, when we realize that there is nothing in us that has the ability to change our behaviour and nature, and that the power we need resides in the Saviour who has already given us a perfect standing before God, then in turning to that source of "power" we begin to experience a transformation of our very nature into that of the character of God. The new life we seek is the life of Christ in us, a life whose power and influence grows as we surrender to him and come into his presence in prayer and silent waiting before him. It is the life of Christ spreading throughout our being as we place our confidence in this new life.

We have no more ability to make ourselves holy, to "act good", than we have an ability to save ourselves, to establish peace with God, by any human effort we may attempt. This, of course, is a serious problem. We must understand the Cross if we wish to understand the methodology that God has provided for deep behavioural change. Galatians 2:20 summarizes the work of the Cross and the source of the believer's new life, "I am crucified with Christ. Nevertheless, I live; yet not I , but Christ lives in me, and the life which I now live, my present bodily life, I live by faith in the Son of God, who loved me and gave himself for me." As Paul tells us, we died in Christ and rose with him to newness of life. The power to be sanctified does not reside in us, but in the Saviour. To reiterate, Christ has been made for us our wisdom, our righteousness, our sanctification and our redemption. (I Cor. 1:30) Jesus is not only the source of salvation. He is also the spring of our sanctification.

Sanctification means the setting apart for a holy purpose. It also means, in Christian terms, the process of becoming holy. We, as Christians, are sanctified in two ways. The first is the perfection that is given to us in Jesus when we become Christians, so that we can confidently say that we have a relationship to the Father, and peace with God. The second path by which we are sanctified is in the transformation of our hearts, so that the source of our behaviours conforms to, and is found in the life and character of God. In both senses, Jesus is our sanctification.

There is no point in calling people to commit themselves, ever more deeply, Sunday after Sunday, in order to follow God. There is no theological ground in demanding of a congregation that it surrender to God, if one expects this surrender to achieve what is impossible for human beings to accomplish. Of course we must be surrendered. Of course we must be committed to God. However, a thousand 'surrenders' to God will not achieve a holy life. Indeed, the assumptions of "Promise Keepers" are not New Testament at all. It is not a determination to 'keep one's promises', and self discipline that either society or the church needs. Rather it is faith in the Sanctifying life of the Risen Christ. And without a biblical understanding of the path of holiness, no genuine transformation will be achieved.

The crucial question that must be asked, and indeed it is not usually asked, is, "Throughout the scripture, when God commands individuals to conform to divine tenets of holiness, does God expect people to be able to do this?" Both in the Old Testament and in the New, does God expect people to be able to do what he commands? The question is not whether God expects people to keep the Law. God does expect people to keep the Law. The real question is, "Does God expect people to be *able* to keep the Law?" This question applies to every apparent command both in the Old Testament and in the New. If we *are* able to keep the law then it is not true that we are without strength, and Paul is teaching an incorrect doctrine, for Paul writes that "when we were yet without strength Christ died for the ungodly" (Romans 5:6)

What does this mean? Clearly we are able to be good to some degree, and Paul had a certain level of righteousness before he believed. Yet we are not able to be perfectly good, and some of us are able to be good in some areas, while continuing to sin in others. If we think of human beings as complex systems that lack a unifying principle which would result in consistent goodness, perhaps that is how we should understand ourselves in terms of sinfulness. Indeed the image of being without strength is quite good. We have the strength to achieve goodness to some degree but we lack the strength to achieve this in the totality of our behaviour. We are like a computer which can function in many or several areas, but which has become corrupted in other parts. It's as if we can run around our "building" fixing problems that arise in one place or another, but cannot fix all of the problems that keep arising. Thus we can achieve a certain level of goodness, but are incapable of achieving perfect goodness. And in fact in those areas in which we cannot be perfect we are, powerless to be so perfect. We are, as St. Paul tells us, "without strength", we are "slaves of sin", not free to be other than sinful. Now if this position is rejected, the only alternative to this "impotence model" is that human beings are capable of saving themselves; we are not without strength, and some of us, at least, do not need the grace of God in order to be accepted by God as sufficiently righteous.

There are powerful implications as a result of this impotence, for I do not believe there are many who support the alternative position just suggested. The first of these is that while the sinner is definitely guilty of having sinned, he or she could not have done otherwise. The second implication is that while evil may have been done, neither God nor any human being could, in fairness be angry at such an individual, because she or he did not possess the power to do otherwise. A slave does not have the freedom to act in any other way than within the limits of that slavery. The only justification for anger directed at one who has done wrong is that that individual had the ability, the freedom to choose otherwise, that there was an ability to act in a different fashion. It is freedom that justifies anger at sin. Either we are free not to sin, or we have no such freedom. It must be restated. Either Paul is correct in asserting that we are slaves of sin, or he is teaching error. I am not interested in any philosophical discussion on "free will". What is being discussed here is the biblical doctrine of slavery to sin. How this works; what the processes of living as if free while not being so, I do not believe will ever be satisfactorily resolved.

The discussion is solely on our freedom not to sin, and if we are not free, what the implications are in relation to our dealings with other human beings, and the implications this has on the nature of God's dealings with us as sinners. Do not imagine that I am telling God how he should act. The argument goes in exactly the opposite direction. What this is arguing is that God is not angry at the sinner because God knows the slavery that every single sinner lives under, and it would be unreasonable to be angry at an individual in such a state. God is not pleased with sinners in relation to the lives (we) live. The sinner does not cease being a sinner in such a situation. The result of being a sinner remains alienation from God and the impossibility of being in his presence if such a state of sin and rebellion continues. The results of sin are death, we are all guilty of death deserving sin, and Jesus who loved us and died for us is our only escape from this hell of sin. The need for redemption, forgiveness, the cleansing of sin and the new birth and faith in Christ as the Lamb of God slain for us, remains just as absolutely necessary. However, anger at the sinner is not a possibility if we are slaves of sin.

There seems to be a stark difference in describing humanity between the four gospels and the rest of the New

Testament. I speak of a perceived difference not a genuine contradiction in theology. Jesus makes several comments about the righteous and the unrighteous. Further, he declares where each will end at the conclusion of their lives. It is true that in Jesus' audience there were the righteous and the lost. This is, to some degree a continuation of the Old Testament division of humanity in similar ways. There are good people and there are evil people, and it seems evident that the evil deserve the anger of God. This certainly is the feeling one gets, especially in the Old Testament. I am not suggesting that this immediate "feeling" is what the OT teaches.

In this division of humanity there appears no teaching that humanity is universally in bondage to sin, as Paul, especially in the book of Romans, teaches. Yet this "contradiction" is an incorrect interpretation of the gospels and of Jesus' teaching. John the Baptist, in one of the most beautiful introductions in scripture, says of Jesus, " Behold the Lamb of God that taketh away the sin of the world." (John 1:29) If Jesus is he who removes the sin of the world, then it is fair to say that Jesus understood his ministry to be a task that humanity could not achieve on its own. Moreover, in that it was the sin of the world, Jesus must have recognized that the entire world was lost in sin. This being so, when Jesus refers to the righteous, he is not speaking of a group of individuals who have attained this position by the strength of their devotion to God and their personal holiness, any more than we Christians understand that we have righteousness independent of the grace of God.

If this is the case, then apart from this divinely attained gift, there are no righteous people, nor was Jesus implying that any could be a member of this holy group without the new birth. Without some justification in the gospels for such a position it is not enough that the rest of the New Testament teaches such a doctrine of universal moral impotence. It must necessarily be the case that the Gospels do not contradict later NT teaching. Jesus cannot teach a salvation that contradicts or is significantly different to apostolic teaching.

What we arrive at is the answer to our original question: God does expect us to conform to his law and nature but, in our own strength, he does not expect us to be able to do this. Clearly, if God does not expect us to be able to do this, God would not express anger at those who were so enslaved. Though God is passionate about the horror of sin, and though the Christian has absolutely no right to live any life other than one of holiness, God does not direct anger towards the sinner. This position is not arrived at from a "liberal" bias, independent of scriptural authority, but from an exegesis of part of one of the most central scriptural teachings, the Pauline doctrine of salvation.

Indeed, in the light of Paul's teaching, calling for surrender without an accompanying teaching on the Cross is heresy. Of course, I use that word to get attention. Nevertheless, unless a biblical, New Testament teaching on sanctification goes along with a call to commitment, there is a de facto teaching of error. I could not count the calls to surrender I have heard, but I can recall virtually no sermons in recent years on the sanctifying work of the Cross in the life of the believer. We are not saved by faith, and then made holy by human self discipline. Self discipline and strength of commitment are not New Testament concepts related to the sanctified life.

God has determined that humanity is incapable of holiness. The Law was intended to teach humanity that, when given the highest standards, we will all invariably fail. "Therefore mine own arm brought salvation" (Isaiah 63:5), as the Old Testament prophet writes. There is also a logic to this. Spiritual life exists only in God. If we can achieve holiness in our own strength, then we can assert that we have achieved God's standards by ourselves. However, the character of God, which is the character of holiness, finds its source only in God. Therefore it is not logical to assume that holiness can be achieved from a source lacking that divine source. As sinners, we did not possess the life of God. As Christians our only source of holiness is found in God. If this is true, holiness can not be achieved by any form of strenuous human effort. It is futile to say to oneself, "If I could only try harder. If I were only more surrendered to God." Just as we cannot boast of achieving salvation by our own efforts, so likewise we cannot boast of achieving sanctification by our own efforts.

Nor is sanctification a part human, part divine process. The holiness of God as taught in Romans, is based upon the death of humanity in Christ. This was not a 'half death'. Our life before God is likewise found in the resurrection of Jesus. In him we live. Our life, that is our spiritual life, is his life. The entire nature and power of our transformed life is found in the life and nature of the Son of God. The bible does not teach a kind of sanctification that goes something like, "now you do this and I (God) will do that." Sanctification is the transfer of the life of the Son to an individual who is completely unable to generate the holiness of God. It is the transfer of divine "software to a computer which will not function without such software". Yet, unless we are willing to allow God to perform this "downloading" on us we will not be changed. This passive act is the one thing God requires of us. *Make us willing, Father, to be changed into your image. Make us desire the character of God more than all else. Give us grace to seek you, for in being in your presence we are transformed into your image, and discover who you are in ways that go beyond surface human teaching.* For God does not want our best effort, either in salvation or in sanctification. Sanctification is not an exercise in behaviour modification. Nor is it a crushing of the human body's desires, or a denial of its needs, in order to achieve high levels of self control. Nor, indeed, is self control sanctification. Rather, sanctification is the placing of positive holy characteristics in the heart, so that by nature, the heart acts in a holy fashion.

Nevertheless, in what way was St Paul's life of commitment to God, prior to his becoming a Christian, different to his life of holiness, after he became a follower of Jesus? In what way were these two "holinesses" different? This question is eminently valid, given Paul's confession of failure in Romans chapter seven. And indeed even more so when we read Philippians 3: 6, in which Paul states, "concerning the righteousness which is in the law I was blameless." These two statements appear totally contradictory. Based upon this assertion in Philippians, it appears that Paul, employing his own strength of will, brought his life into conformity to the Mosaic Law. However, from Romans 7:14-25 we discover that (a) there was still an experience of sin, and (b) on the psychological level, Paul experienced a desire to submit to God that was not always followed, perhaps, by the doing of the commandments, or even the desire to do them. Paul's level of righteousness, nevertheless, must have been extraordinarily high. Why then, if he could achieve such heights of holiness by his own efforts, did he see this as inadequate, and his inner spiritual life as one of bondage to sin?

Paul's understanding of his bondage to sin was not simply that in Christ he saw a pattern of righteousness far above his own. That, though true, is not the source of his understanding. The realization that one does not act in a holy fashion from within one's nature is independent of the model of behaviour we may have. Indeed, the pattern of Christ's behaviour that we do possess, rather than being clear and unambiguous, is incomplete. Jesus' behaviour was determined by the guidance he received from his Father. Even the manner in which one lives out a life of love is unclear without guidance from God. More importantly, however, we are not directed by the scriptures to mechanically follow the pattern of love that Jesus lived out from the resources we have within us, simply as human beings. Our imitation of Christ is to come about through the continual growth of the life of Christ within us. In this sense, sanctification, as the New Testament presents it, is not an imitation of Christ's behaviour, but a divine replication that changes us into that which we long to be in our holiest moments.

There are two areas, at least, in which we are slaves of sin. Firstly, there are particular sins in our lives which we are incapable of not doing, though we know we are not acting as we should. We know we should not be sinning in a particular way, but are unable to do anything to change this. This then is a particular sin(s) for which we need the grace of God if we are to be free to act or feel as God would have us. Whether there is, in fact, a non-spiritual method of transformation that could have been used to change our behaviour, it is not 'available'.

This inability to "do" what we know we should be doing is far from uncommon, and does not relate only to specific sins we are bitterly aware of. We frequently feel we should be doing something for God (and perhaps ourselves), like praying, or reading the bible or witnessing, or maybe washing the dishes, and yet feel no desire to do this. We are as bound by sin in not desiring to do these things, and usually therefore, actually not doing them, as we are bound by a seemingly more important sin that we do engage in. We have a mental set of variables that do not provide us with the strength or desire to conform to the will of God. God then, in his grace, must place within us that necessary desire, for example, that we do not have. The giving of this needed grace is as much a part of the transforming of our hearts as we imagine the transformation of our natures is into the image of Christ. Christ in us is the divine software that, in ourselves we lack, and it is his life in us that can set us free from the seeming inability to act as we should, by giving us his nature to meet these, often mundane needs.

Secondly, the most significant way in which we are slaves to sin, and the true understanding of this experience, is discovered, not in wondering if we can become free of particular sins, independent of the grace of God, but in understanding that the core of human behaviour is found in our absolute allegiance to the self. We can, it is readily admitted, be the kind of person such that our actions reflect kind and well meaning attitudes, yet our final allegiance will be to ourselves. When Jesus asked the rich young ruler to give away all that he possessed he was not asking for the goods themselves, but seeking to show the young man (and us perhaps) that despite his "goodness" he was controlled by self interest. Jesus was attempting to show the man that he did not possess that love which is the love of the heart of God, and that neither do we.

This is not to say that unselfish acts are impossible. Or that all apparently unselfish acts are in reality selfish. This is clearly not so. We know of many who have performed such acts, even to the point of the loss of their own lives. Human beings are capable of truly unselfish and beautiful behaviour. Yet we are such people that, given the right (or wrong) set of variables we will inevitably choose ourselves over others. That despite the goodness we do express, there is an underlying stream that runs through our beings which will ultimately choose the good of the self over the good of the other. It is this underlying allegiance to the self, not a conscious choice but an existential state of being, that is the core of our imperfection. This is the "I" that was crucified with Christ so that an "I", empowered by Christ's life may live, not in ultimate allegiance to the self, but inextricably focused on the well-being of all others. It is this new "I" that generates true love, the love of the second great commandment, and allows us to fulfil this commandment by replacing our nature with the nature of Christ.

If we cannot be acceptable to God without the indwelling of the Spirit of God, does this mean that good acts done before the new birth, or acts done from simply human strength are not holy? And if these good acts done prior to faith in Christ are holy, does this not mean that everyone who has, at least some good qualities, is to that extent, holy? And does this not mean that humans do have the ability to be holy, at least to some degree? I would say that the answer to this last question must be that this is true, and that they are. When Isaiah 64:6 says, "Our righteousness is as filthy rags", this is not meant to imply that there is therefore no righteousness at all present. Perhaps Isaiah saw that despite occasional acts of goodness, and even compassion, the majority of his behaviour was not a fulfillment of the Law. Nowhere in scripture are we commanded to confess the sinfulness of all our acts. Rather we are taught to confess our sins. Further, scripture commends good acts by individuals, even when other areas of the person's life are not commendable (see Kings and Chronicles in the OT, and the story of the rich young ruler in the NT).

Lack of faith in Christ does not make good behaviour evil, and the New Testament does not teach that human beings are incapable of any level of goodness. What the scripture does teach is that we have all sinned, that we have a propensity to continue sinning, that the intellectual and spiritual structure of humans gives us the ability to imagine a system of goodness that is the opposite of the evil that is experienced and perceived, and that in our best moments we desire this goodness. Nevertheless, despite these holy desires we lack the ability to perfectly manifest the character of God (perfect love) which is the standard of perfection God desires and must have.

The morality that Jesus presented during his earthly ministry was not based on a formulation of more "finely tuned" or more accurately delineated principles than were in the law of Moses. Rather, each parable, each example of godly behaviour , each teaching related to how we should act, was predicated, based on a heart that was not centred on itself. It is in this sense that we are irretrievably the slaves of sin without the liberation that comes from an outworking of the new birth. Legislation, behaviour modification, commitment, and promises before God cannot give a person a heart that acts always and only for the other. It is only in the new birth and the transformation of the human heart by the Holy Spirit that we can achieve this level of selfless love.

As St Paul saw it clearly, "I have been crucified with Christ, nevertheless I live, yet not I, but the life that I live I live by the faith of the Son of God who loved me and gave himself for me." (Galatians 2:20) This crucified "I" is not simply 'me', but the self centred "me" that cannot turn the other cheek, that cannot love another as I love myself, that cannot give all I possess to benefit another. The core essence of sin is not the performing of specific acts that God objects to. Rather, sin is the individual's choice of itself over all other existence. Sin, then, is not found simply in the inability to perform the set of acts God has described as holy. Sin is the spiritual inability of the human heart to love unreservedly. Only in an experience of the crucified and risen life in Christ can we achieve this level of freedom from the slavery of sin.

The answer to the riddle of Paul's confession that he was a slave of sin, and yet was perfect in regards to the law is found in the very last verse of chapter seven of Romans. "In a word, I am subject to God's law as a rational being, but in my unspiritual nature I am a slave of sin." Prior to becoming a Christian (and maybe for some time after that) holiness, for Paul, was a battle against his "nature", conducted with the help of his intellect. Holiness was always a struggle, always a fight against what he would do if he allowed what he really wanted, to occur. He usually won this moral-religious war, but it was a continual fight. He was not by nature holy.

This is also our problem. We can frequently do what is right, but in our hearts, not want to do it. We can be unselfish, but realize that what we did, did not express an unselfish heart. It is the creation of an "unselfish heart" that is the essence of sanctification. And it is the possibility of unselfish acts, while experiencing a selfish heart, that is the essence of our slavery to sin. Sanctification is not merely the performance of godly acts, but the creation of a new heart, a new nature in which the Law is written on our hearts. In this new creation we do, *by nature,* what the Law of God demands. This is the difference between the motivation of the Mosaic Law and the Law of the Spirit of Life in Christ Jesus. Sanctification is the changing of our hearts so that we do the Law naturally. And that is the extremely significant point of chapters six and eight of the book of Romans.

The eighth chapter of Romans teaches us that sanctification is not a continuing of the battle against our nature. It is the replacement of our nature by another, completely different one. As it states in 2 Corinthians 5:17, "If anyone is in Christ he is a new creation; old things are passed away. Behold all things have become new." Indeed, it is the replacement of sinful human nature (that part of it that is sin oriented) with the nature of the Godhead itself. I am quite aware that some will find this understanding troubling. We have been so brought up to believe in a struggle against the sinful nature that the idea of righteous acting as an expression of one's nature may seem, not simply incomprehensible, but also erroneous. But is this not what is taught in Jeremiah 31:33 when Jeremiah states, "But this is the covenant which I will make with Israel after those days, says the Lord. I will set my law within them, and write it on their hearts."? When do we imagine that this will take place if not now? What do we imagine happened on the cross and in the resurrection? Did Paul not teach a victory over sin in a transformed life brought about by Christ's resurrected life in the believer?

This is not to suggest that there is *no* value in holy acts done, essentially against our will. However, the holiness that is taught in Romans, for example, is a radical critique of such acts. Paul regarded the holiness he had achieved under the law, that is done in his own strength, as essentially valueless before God, as a flawed righteousness. What does 1 Corinthians 13:1-3 mean if not that acts without love are of no value to the *doer* of these acts? What does, "if I give away all my possessions but have not love it does not profit me at all" (verse 3) mean, if not that the motivation of an act is essential to an evaluation of the act?

Is doing good of no value if the doing of this good does not spring from the heart? I think not. Every good act is the expression of what should be. Every good act almost certainly reveals a desire to be holy. Paul nowhere teaches that we should not do any godly act, if the act does not spring from a truly sanctified nature. Nevertheless, the teaching of the book of Romans is that the work of the Cross is to create a holy nature in the heart of the believer. The teaching of the New Testament on the holy life is not that it is a continuation of the struggle against sinful nature. Rather, the New Testament presents the holy life as a victorious transformation of the human heart, in which the character of God is lived out in the life of the believer, to increasing degrees, and becomes the genuine nature of the believer. If the spiritual life we are living is not an experience of this transformation, are we not then, in reality, still living under the dynamics and principles of the Mosaic covenant?

Can the human personality be modified? This is certainly true. Civil rights legislation shows that people can be legislated to new ways of acting. However, this modification is piecemeal. It does not reach down into the very nature of the being who needs modification, and it does not provide it with a nature that is complete in itself, without the need for modification. It is for this reason that focusing on moral improvement in a society is the wrong battle for the church. That path has been followed, and it has been found wanting. Why then should we put so much effort into pursuing it again? I realize the effort sounds worthy. That is what is so tempting about it. But that does not justify the church's efforts in a scheme that the New Testament teaches is ultimately futile.

John 1: 17 tells us that the law came through Moses, but that grace and truth came through the Lord Jesus Christ. Jesus, himself told us that we are supposed to be as conspicuous as a city set on a hill, and that people should see our good works and glorify the Father. In that grace and truth came with Jesus, the good works the world sees are not the presentation of moral standards in the manner of the Law. Rather, they are the good works that spring from the hearts of those who have experienced the "grace and truth" of the Saviour's life. It is moral actions that God wants the church to show the world, not simply a presentation of salvifically empty moral standards.

God of course, does not do the equivalent of a spiritual brain transplant. A Christian is not transformed overnight, or immediately at the time of her or his spiritual rebirth. Usually there is a major behavioural change after becoming a Christian. Though if one was brought up in a Christian home , for example, this change might not be immediately apparent. Transformation occurs over time, and may be rapid and wide-ranging, or simply consistent and gradual. There are also vast areas in us that need to be healed.

No one can adequately describe the actual process of transformation towards the character of God. Further, that sanctification involves the experiencing of the life of Christ in the believer does not necessarily imply that aspects of feeling and intellect that are part of being human are totally bypassed and irrelevant. We do learn from the things we experience, and we are changed by these events. The incarnation is surely the model for a holy life, and in that the Godhead was revealed in human form, there was a perfect and harmonious joining of humanity and Godhead which even now, two thousand years afterwards, remains a mystery. Yet somehow, the new birth gives us, as humans, a new nature that springs from the Spirit of Jesus who lives in the child of God. This also is a mystery. We experience a new nature, and this is not the result of effort on our part. It is a gift of God, just as salvation is.

As Hudson Taylor, the saintly pioneer missionary to China described it, it is an exchanged life. Our sinful nature is exchanged for the holy and loving nature of Christ. This new life is integrated into our humanity in a similar, though certainly not identical, manner to that combination in the Incarnation. We definitely do not perfectly reveal the Godhead in the fashion that Jesus did. Our lives before God and humanity are a combination of the nature of God given us in Jesus and those aspects of humanity that interact with the world and process the data that the mind receives. Without the life of Christ in us we could only evaluate what we experience, and attempt to make our behaviour conform to what we had concluded was correct. With our new nature this evaluation finds an ability to perform what is right, to the extent that the nature of Christ parallels these evaluations of spiritual correctness.

Rapid or gradual, these changes in the way we act, think and feel are dependent on the depth of the relationship we develop with God. Without times of prayer and waiting on God we will never experience, either a genuine knowledge of God, or the new life that can be ours because of Jesus' presence in our hearts and minds.

CHAPTER 9

PRAYER: THE KEY TO LIVING WITH GOD

It is difficult to write anything new or interesting on a subject that so many have written on so well over the last two thousand years. I remember, as a very young Christian walking up the stairs to a tiny Christian bookstore downtown to buy books, so many books, on the faith. One of these was a small booklet on prayer. It outlined the various types of prayer we should be engaged in: praise, confession, intercession, petition, and thanksgiving, and I attempted to direct my prayer life in this fashion. Prayer does not need, though, to be directed in regular and formulized ways for it to be effective. Nor, on the other hand, does it not possess effectiveness with God if it does. What is particularly necessary for prayer to be effective is humility and sincerity.

Prayer, like salvation is not a method of earning God's approval. When one prays one does not notch up a certain number of "airmiles" in God's book that are then translated into answers, or a level of transformed life. God's way of approaching us is always in grace. We do not earn his approval by a strenuous prayer life, and he is not overly impressed by either beautiful phrases, or lengthy prayers. If you are given to lengthy prayers, however, and have a gift for beautiful expressions that is the way you should pray. However, they are no more effective than other, more pedestrian prayers. God looks at the heart, and not at the outward appearances of our actions.

As I have written these pages I have become more and more convinced that the wonder of a Christian life lived in the love of God, and in such a closeness to God that one knows and experiences the power of God, comes from a prayer life that allows the grace and power of God to be revealed to one. Knowledge about God derived from scripture, or even another's testimony, is terribly important, but prayer is essential if this knowledge is to be transformed into a personal knowledge of God.

All the categories of prayer mentioned earlier go to make up one's experience of praying. In addition, some Christians pray in tongues. The scripture tells us that this is edifying, and St Paul wrote that he spoke in tongues more than any of his readers. Yet, there is one other "form" that should be included. This is "waiting on God'. It is not waiting, as one waits for the mailman to deliver our letters. Rather, it is simply getting alone with God, and silently being in his presence. When one comes to God, of course, one is immediately in his presence. In waiting on God, however, one attempts to silence the thoughts of one's life, and one does not utter particular prayers. C.S. Lewis, in "An Experiment in Criticism" outlines how we should come to appreciate a work of art, and describes the mental preparations for such an experience. This is a perfect description of how we begin to wait on God. He states,

> We must begin by laying aside as completely as we can all our own preconceptions, interests and associations. We must make room for [various artist's works]

by emptying out our own...We sit down before the picture in order to have something done to us, not that we may do things with it. The first demand any work of art makes upon us is surrender. Look, listen, receive. Get yourself out of the way...The many use art and the few receive it. The many behave in this like a man who talks when he should listen or gives when he should take. (Lewis, 1965, pp 18,19)

CS Lewis was writing about art, and not waiting on God but the parallels are startling. This quieting of the self is initially a little disconcerting, because we are so used to content, not silence. I suppose waiting silently is really an expression of humility, a confession that we offer nothing, and yet are in such need. Whatever the case, waiting on God gives God an opportunity to speak, to reveal himself, and equally perhaps, to silently transform our hearts into his image, and heal our psychological wounds.

God has his own time table, and we will probably wonder when anything is ever going to happen. However, do not give up. Waiting on God is one of the most wonderful ways of experiencing God's presence, his healing power, and discovering the grace of God, that are available to us as Christians. There are times when we need to stop talking to God, and allow him to speak to us.

If we decide to "try" this form of prayer, we need to set a time apart, somewhere in our busy-ness, when we will not be disturbed. You figure out when that might be. If one works downtown there are often churches that are open during the day. The Catholic and Anglican (or Episcopal) churches are usually open during the daytime in most cities and they tend to be quiet, and have comfortable pews and places to kneel.

There is not one way of praying that is superior to others. All prayer is a communication with God. And God is always waiting for us to come to him. Moreover, we do not need to feel free from sin before we come in prayer. God knows we cannot improve ourselves. That is why Jesus came and was crucified. We cannot do anything to make ourselves "look" better to God, and we do not have to. We come to God clothed in the perfect righteousness of Christ. That is how we are acceptable to God. We sometimes feel so sinful. We may have just had a fight with our spouse, or gotten angry with one of our children, or done something that is, perhaps, far worse. We may feel terribly guilty, and certainly do not feel that we can come to God in prayer at that point. In addition, we may simply not feel like coming to God at all. Well, that may be exactly how we feel, but these are not good enough reasons, not to come to God in prayer.

You can come to God even if you do not want to come to God. Jesus knows how we truly feel, and what we truly are, and if these facts are not terribly commendable, isn't that why Jesus came? We come to God just as we are. That means when we feel good and when we feel sinful. The fact is, that even when we feel 'oh so spiritual', there is still much sin, and so many areas God still does not control. How we feel is not the criteria for coming to the Father in prayer. Our need and Jesus' righteousness however, are.

Nevertheless, we are not accepted by God, simply because we come "just as we are". We are accepted by God because we come trusting in his righteousness, and in that righteousness we can come just as we are. We can come to him because we are perfect in a righteousness that is not ours. Indeed, the guarantee of God's answer to our prayers is that we come, "in Jesus". Do you remember we died in him, and then rose in him? At no time are we not, "in him" Prayer in Jesus' name is not simply a ritual or magical phrase. To do anything in someone's name is to act as if that other person was present, as if you were the person you represent. When we come to God in Jesus' righteousness, we are coming in Jesus' name. This is because it is as if Jesus himself is also coming to God, (and he is) because we are in him and He in us. And in that name, the Father is sure to hear our prayer. Our position in Christ, and our perfection in him, is the guarantee of our acceptance, in every sense, by God. Coming to the Father, pleading the righteousness of his Son is praying in the name of Jesus. The only condition that can be applied to that blanket guarantee is that, as we come to know God more and more deeply, we become more sensitive to what we should be praying for, and what we should not. If we are not sure that something is the will of God, we may be completely correct and it may turn out that God does not grant us that request. However, when we come trusting Jesus' perfect righteousness, and acknowledging our sin, we are completely acceptable.

Jesus did not make God's standards any lower than they were in the Mosaic law. In fact, if anything, they became even more impossible. Prayer, in all its forms, and our approach to the Father based on the 'clothing' of Christ's righteousness, bring us to a place with God where we come to know him in his love, and power, and grace. And in this experience, brought about by spending time with God, that which was previously impossible, becomes possible.

CHAPTER 10
WHERE IS GOD IN A WORLD OF SUFFERING?

*The God who commands us to love,
even in the face of the failure of such love,
must also possess such a quality.*

This period in the history of humanity can be summed up, at least from one point of view, in the word 'uncertainty'. Philosophically and scientifically, we struggle to arrive at epistemologies that give us a sense that there are, indeed, things that can be known. In our day to day interactions this does not seem a very troubling matter, but in almost every area of academic study, the belief that there is a problem regarding the possibility of knowing something (anything) with any degree of certainty, has taken deep root. Not even science is immune from this questioning. For example, split photons that react similarly if one of the splits is acted upon in one way, and the far from new Heisenberg indeterminancy principle relating to the impossibility to predict the paths of sub-atomic particles, have taken us from the childlike confidence that we can possess a certainty about the world, and that knowledge is genuinely possible, to a world of doubt as to the possibility that we can have certainty about almost any of our understandings of the world around us . The power of these philosophical reasonings has naturally had an impact on the faith of many believers, and left Christian apologists in a weakened state. There are, however, reasons to believe, though they are not arrived at by some five and dime, ten minute reading of a book. Faith is arrived at, usually with at least as much suffering of mind and heart as Einstein experienced in generating his general and special theories of relativity.

The Problem of Evil: Can God be Trusted?

To ask where God is may seem a rather strange question as, for God to be omnipresent, that is present in all places, he must necessarily be everywhere. However, it is not in that sense that the question is asked. While the definition of omnipresence is correct, it is also true that God does not dwell in the heart of one who does not know him, who has never understood the salvific work of Christ and has accepted Jesus as her or his forgiveness and righteousness. God is also not present in the evil that people do to each other, or in the famines and earthquakes that kill thousands of men women and children. John 10:10 states, "the thief comes to steal, kill and destroy. I have come that people may have life, and may have it in all its fullness." God is not a thief, and though people in the past believed that both good and evil acts, particularly of nature, came from God, this statement by Jesus, along with others, proclaims that this is an erroneous perception. I do not know if God in (his) infinite wisdom ever instigates such events, though God has frequently used such things to get humanity's attention, but the overwhelming description of God's character portrayed in Jesus, argues against such an understanding.

Jesus himself, commenting on the collapse of a tower in Jerusalem that killed several people, denied that the event had any relationship to the level of sin in the people killed. The implication clearly was that the event was not caused by an act of God, arbitrarily meting out divine punishment. That natural events should not necessarily be seen as divinely caused is further reinforced by Jesus' reply to the disciples' question regarding the cause of the blindness in a man they encountered. Jesus stated that the blindness existed so that God's glory and power could be revealed (John 9:1-5). He was, in colloquial language saying, "no one sinned, but it does give me a chance to show you the love and power of God." I do not believe that Jesus intended us to understand that God went out of his way to make the man blind so that Jesus could perform a miracle, and so reveal God's power. Weren't there already enough blind people in Israel for Jesus to heal? Were the other blind people situated in other places in case Jesus missed this one? Not likely.

Also, such an interpretation implies that God did not particularly care about the suffering the man would experience as a result of his blindness, and that he was, more or less, a "lab rat", made to suffer to allow the miracle Jesus would later perform.

However, I realize that there are many who can find positive results from human suffering, and who argue that the man's suffering was beneficial to achieve his later (presumable) faith in the Messiah. That this may have been the result of Jesus' action does not necessarily imply that God caused it to bring about this end.

This need to explain suffering positively is understandable, but I would argue essentially inaccurate. Positive lessons can come from all human experience, including our many sins. This does not imply, however, that God causes suffering, or that we should sin in order to learn valuable lessons in right living. Such a view of God's love, or perhaps lack of it, is not consistent with the revelation of the loving character of God shown in Jesus Christ towards each suffering person. Indeed, even to say that suffering is one of the resultants of a withdrawal from the protection of the Kingdom of Heaven is not to say that God causes suffering, though there may be degrees of removal of the protection of God that cause varying levels of suffering.

Nor is this understanding consistent with the overwhelming love revealed in the very complete work of identification with a lost and suffering world on the Cross. Isaiah 53: 3,4 states, "He was a man of sorrows, familiar with suffering...He certainly has taken upon himself our suffering and carried our sorrows." It was not only the sins of the world that the Saviour bore in himself; it was also, and this is an amazing wonder in which his love is overwhelming, the total suffering that a world outside the protection of God has experienced and will ever experience. It is at the cross where the heart of God is clearly revealed. It is at the cross where the idea that God causes suffering is absolutely negated, and denied by God himself. Jesus, in bearing the suffering of the world, incontrovertibly proclaims his dissociation from human suffering as the cause of this suffering.

Further, as regards the presence of God in this world, does not Jesus' remark about the kingdom of God coming to a region suggest that it was not there prior to his coming? Once again, of course, God is omnipresent, but surely that is not the point. The kingdom of God is not simply a place. It is more importantly a state of being, where God and God's nature are expressed, and our sinful rebellion (all sin is an act against God) is at least admitted, along with some level of remorse. Whenever the Godhead (the triune God) enters any location, in the person of a believer, it can be said that the kingdom of God has come to that place, in the same way that an invading army enters a region that was previously "lacking" such an armed intrusion. In prayer we are powerfully bringing the kingdom of God to the world. Indeed, the possibilities of such a situation are only dependent on the faith, the spirituality of the believer, and the particular intention of God to act, at times independently of the believer, and despite his or her limitations. In the sense that the kingdom of God must be brought to this world (or was Jesus just playing with words here?) this is not God's world. Accordingly, what happens in this "Godless" world should not automatically be attributed to God, or to his intentions.

The coming of God to the world, or some part of it, is an intrusion into that world. It is air coming into that which is, in some sense, a vacuum; light breaking into night. The coming of God, in this world, is the coming of God into where God is not. If this is true then, in what sense is this world "my Father's world"? The hymn, despite its great beauty, has troubled me for a long time. If this is "my father's world" what does that say about God? What would the unbeliever, an individual suffering beyond the limits of endurance perhaps, conclude about such a God? The fact is that, in a very deep sense, this is not "my father's world". It is a world that is, not simply in terms of the sinful humans that populate it, but also in vast cosmic terms, a world of violence in nature, of death for all that lives, a universe in which there is the destruction of galaxies, and the very inevitable ultimate end of the universe in the distant future. I am certain that this is far from the "world" the Father has in mind.

The terrible horror of the dark side of existence simply can not be an expression of the nature of God. Is God to be blamed for famine, flood, disease, arbitrary accident, poverty, war, volcanic eruptions and earthquakes, the death of stars, and the destruction of galaxies as they collide with each other? As much as Christians would like to believe in the Garden of Eden narrative as the complete source of evil in the world, the fall of humanity does not adequately explain evil in the world and the metaphysical negativity that exists throughout the universe. If one accepts the angelic fall of Lucifer, the Fall occurred before the creation. After all, according to Genesis, Satan was already evil before Adam and Eve chose to sin.

The mystery to the existence of evil in the universe is not solved by a simple appeal to the fall of humanity. If it were, Paul would almost certainly not have written to the church calling it, "the mystery of iniquity". However, unless you want to imagine God as arbitrary, and perhaps schizophrenic, the destructive events that occur throughout creation cannot be attributed to the Trinity. The very arbitrariness of the events violently contradicts the love of God expressed in the Saviour. Of course, there are some "godly" people who seem to delight in the suffering of sinners, but God himself is not one of them.

God gets no satisfaction from our suffering. To refer once more to Isaiah, chapter 53:4,5 tells us,

> He certainly has taken upon himself our suffering
> And carried our sorrows
> But we thought that God had wounded him
> Beaten and punished him.
> [However] He was wounded for our rebellious acts
> He was crushed for our sins
> He was punished so that we could have peace
> And we received healing from his wounds.

That God is not the cause of suffering is seen from the fact that Jesus took into himself our suffering when on the Cross he took into himself all that was alien to God, and if suffering is alien to God, then (he) is not the cause of it. As mentioned before, does this mean that God never uses suffering to get our attention? On the contrary, it is all forms of separation from God that necessarily result in our suffering, and make us long for a different world. This is one of the points of the parable of the prodigal son. Just as the prodigal son realized he did not need to continue suffering in the far country when his father had all that was necessary and would provide it lovingly, when we suffer, we sometimes come to understand that we need to turn to God from our own sin and its consequences. Incidentally, if the father had been lacking in love, would it have ever occurred to the prodigal son to return to him? To use suffering is not identical to causing it.

Our state of being sinful in a lost world necessarily means that we will experience suffering. To be alienated from God implies the absence of those characteristics which are part of a state of being which is not alienated from God. That is, to be separated from God means that we will experience a loss of that form of perfect existence one would have if one were in a relationship of peace with God. According to the scriptures, the complete removal of suffering and sin from the created universe waits for the Second coming of Christ as Redeemer. For that reason, though the fact is patently obvious, even Christians suffer in this world. It should be remembered that Christ also suffered when he was living among us. That God did not obliterate evil in all its forms after the resurrection is perhaps a problem. The second coming can sound like an excuse for an incompletely successful job. One thing is certain. God does not make faith in him a simple affair.

The idea that God causes suffering comes, at least in part, from the belief that nothing can happen unless God allows it, and therefore God must be responsible for all that does happen, and this is indeed a very powerful argument. According to this line of reasoning, if something happens, it must be God's will. Is sin the will of God? Indeed, that God is not the cause of all that happens to us particularly, but not only, in the area of health is seen in the book of Job. Job, like many of us, believed that God was the cause of all that happened to him and he made a remarkable and praiseworthy confession of submission and faith in the face of the loss of everything he possessed including his health. "If we accept good from God, shall we not accept evil?" (Job 2:10) He was, nevertheless, incorrect in attributing his suffering to God, as chapters one and two of that book clearly show. If sickness is the will of God why did Jesus heal all who came to him, and even some who did not actively do so? This is simply a general statement of biblical truth. And why some people are not healed is an issue that can only be dealt with sympathetically. Perhaps it is true that we do not have enough faith. It is also true though that the people usually making such a condemnation can be accused of the same failing. Jesus never fell back on such an accusation towards a sick person when he "tried" to heal someone.

Jesus also knew that with every confession of faith there was a deep well of unbelief still remaining in the heart. Further, he did not condemn the man who said to him, "I believe, help me in my unbelief." Nor did Jesus refuse to heal the man's child when this confession was uttered. Why is it that we think sin can be forgiven so easily, that we have faith for that, but we have great difficulty believing that sickness can be healed? And why do we in this situation feel compelled to find reasons why either the sick are no longer healed today, or that there must be a reason why God wants a particular person to remain ill? Yet that is the way we are, and thank goodness God truly understands just how weak we really are, and acts in grace and love towards us.

Clearly, if we are willing to accept that these destructive things are not caused by God, then it is logical to assert that not all things are caused by God. If this is so, then we should not believe that whatever happens to us is the will of God, or that God is the cause of the evil that occurs in the world. What then, however, do we do with I Thessalonians 5:18, "In everything give thanks for this is the will of God in Christ Jesus", and Romans 8:28. "For we know that all things work together for good with those that love God"? What is Paul trying to say here? Either the evil that happens to us is caused by God or it is not caused by God. If it is caused by God, then if an individual sins against us, causing evil to happen to us, God causes that individual to sin.

Now, if the argument is made that the sinner is responsible for the sin done, and that God did not make the sinner do such a thing, and that the act was only an evidence of the sin already existing in the sinner's heart, and that God simply created an environment in which the individual was certain to sin, does that free God from responsibility for the sin? Matthew 18:6,7 states, "But if a man is a cause of stumbling to one of these little ones who have faith in me it would be better for him to have a millstone hung around his neck and be drowned in the depths of the sea." Luke 17:1 states, "Causes of stumbling are bound to arise but woe betide the man through whom they come." Surely what these verses teach is that those who cause one to sin are held responsible in some sense for the sin that another commits. It is, thus, a sin to cause another individual to sin. This being the case, it is impossible for God himself to be the cause of another's sin, by *any* means. If it is a sin to cause another to sin, then God does not cause any individual to sin. That is to say, God has no input in the sins that people commit towards other people, for to have such input would imply a violation based on the principle of causal responsibility.

That this is so means that whatever these two bible verses do mean, they do not mean that the things done against us are from God, and that, as such, we should give thanks for them. If we read earlier in chapter 8 of Romans we see Paul's litany of events that cannot separate us from God. Rather than thinking that events can overpower us, that negative events have a greater power in our lives than the power of God, Paul wants us to see that in any situation of sin, God is still Lord, and that ultimately, evil against the believer can not be victorious. It is this, I suggest, that we should be thankful for, the overall and ultimate victory of God in Jesus Christ over evil, and not for the evil that is being done to us.

Indeed, earlier in the chapter Paul speaks of the metaphysical impact of evil on the entire universe. He writes that even this all pervasive "mortality" of the universe, in which we also, despite being Christians, are in bondage, will be obliterated with the final "revelation of the children of God" (8: 19,20). He goes on to speak of the "hope," the confidence, of the Christian (v25) because of this final victory. Hope as mentioned in this verse is not solely the psychological attitude that enables one to press on. More truly, it is the factual basis of this confidence which is the ultimate victory of universal wholeness over universal chaos. Our hope then is the content of God's promise. It is thus, within a description of the pervasiveness of evil and its ultimate total defeat, that Paul makes the remark regarding "all things working together" It is, to reiterate, the ultimate victory of Christ over evil, and an expression of faith in the ultimate goodness of God that is the background for the remark, and not a statement that we can expect God to send evil to us and that it, nevertheless, will be for our good. God can use evil for our good, as we learn in the story of Joseph being sold into slavery in Egypt, but he does not send it.

Does this answer the problem of the existence of evil? Unfortunately it does not. If this issue is not a problem for you then my remarks will probably have little or no importance, but if the existence of evil is a cause of great consternation and distress, let me regrettably suggest that almost certainly, there is no philosophical or even theological answer that will be ultimately satisfying, and I doubt that we will ever discover one, on this level and in this form of cognition, this side of the grave. Furthermore, for those who see free will, whatever that is, as an answer to the problem of evil, free will also does not provide a satisfying answer. Psychology, our own experience, and the teachings of St. Paul all lead one to the conclusion that we may be guilty of falling short of the glory of God, but that it is also true that we are all decidedly not free to do otherwise. But even if free will were a reality, it would still not be adequate to explain the existence of evil and the theological problems this causes.

Given the dimension and complexity of the universe it seems clear that God is far above our level of intelligence. Yet, to believe that God is essentially good, that is in his essence, and can be trusted, there must somehow be an answer to this unbelievably troubling logical paradox of God's involvement in a flawed universe. I know that there are questions that have not been addressed here, and that they are deeply disturbing to some who are troubled by this problem. If I have not raised them it is only because of the destructive effect they may have on others who are not troubled by the implications of these questions. Whatever the questions, I suspect that there is part of an answer in Jesus' cry on the cross, "My God, my God, why have you forsaken me?" There is much in that cry that echoes the confusion of a silent God in a suffering world.

In all seriousness I suspect that we discover an answer by following one of two paths. The first is that we decide we cannot live with the tension we experience in believing that God himself may be evil, and choose to deny the logic of our doubts in a "leap of faith" that will no longer tolerate any thought that questions the goodness of God. In effect, we do not receive any answer to our questions. I do not believe that this maneuver actually frees our minds of its doubts, but we appear to be relieved of conscious and troubling questions. I also do not believe our faith in God is genuinely strengthened or increased by this move.

The second path we can follow is one that is more time consuming and requires more of us than most are willing to give. This path involves our seeking of God with our heart, waiting silently on him, or even crying out to him, and eventually discovering for ourselves, and in reality, the God of Abraham, Isaac and Jacob, the God of the prophets, and the Father of the Lord Jesus. On this path our doubts do not need to be repressed into our subconscious; our intellect is not dismissed and denied, and our religion is not turned into a shallow mental statement of religious beliefs that have no foundation in genuine experience. On this path we discover what God is, from coming to know him as a person, and consequently coming to trust him. If we follow this path we come to *know* that God is good, not because the bible tells us he is, but because that is how he has revealed himself to us. Following this path, our questions receive an answer that is interpersonal. A god who is like the God who is revealed to us could not be the kind of God that the logic of an ambiguous existence and the conclusions one can derive from this, would lead one to posit. That is to say, the revealed God, as unfathomably loving, rules out the possibility of an evil guilty God that our conclusions would lead us to fear.

That this individual discovery will also be what we find recorded in scripture, however, does not preclude the necessity that we must discover this for ourselves in a genuine relationship with God. For each of us, scripture must become real through a continually deepening relationship with a God who wishes to reveal himself to our hearts. And until the evangelical wing of the church comes to understand that the crucial truths of the scripture can only be held to be true, because they can be revealed and experienced in the life of each believer, and until believers realize that genuine faith in the scripture can only flow from a knowledge of the Godhead revealed to the heart and mind, the Christians who are part of this dynamic wing of the church, will be forced, by the teaching that faith in the scriptures must be total and unconditional, to pretend a belief that is based predominantly, and at least theoretically, only on teaching and tradition.

I am not suggesting that faith is not necessary in order to experience God. On the contrary, what is being said is that a false faith, one based on a condition prior to a certain level of experience, will NOT experience the power and revelation of God. As human beings, we have NO faith in God. We have no faith in him because we do not know him, and have no experience of him. We may confess to certain beliefs about God, but this is not the same as faith. It is only as we gradually, in an ever widening expansion into our hearts and minds, experience God, that we develop a genuine faith. This is a faith that is based on knowledge. However, it is not a knowledge generated by logic or tradition, but rather on the expanding understanding of the God- person we have begun to know, consistent with and based solidly on scripture. Indeed, the relationship between scripture and experience is one of interdependence. To assert the primacy of either over the other is to invite error and spiritual shallowness.

This is not, as some will assert, the deification of the ego over God, or even the instituting of experience as supreme over scripture. What it is, however, is the honest admission that the God of the scriptures is not the God of a book, but the God of the human heart and mind, and the God of true reality. To refuse to accept that the scriptures are proven in the experience of the believer is to seek an assurance that will forever be beyond our grasp, and is based only on mind games and intellectual denial.

We were not given scripture so that God could bypass individual revelation and direct experience. Rather, we have the scriptures in the same way that we have textbooks, for example, so that we do not have to go through the complicated process of the discovery of mathematics and engineering every time we want to build a bridge. The scriptures are, at least in part, the template that directs and instructs us. However, imagine an engineer studying bridge building and finally asserting he or she knew how to build a bridge, yet never once going out and actually building one. It is like possessing the text describing Einstein's discovery of relativity, and defending this with our lives, yet never attempting to put the theories into practice by employing their "truths". *The church should ideally be the living incarnation of the "word of God" continually presented to the world as the verification of scriptural revelation.*

The scriptures are a precise guide for us, but they are not a substitute for a personal experience of God that each of us must have in order to have faith in God. Moreover, this "personal experience of God" cannot be seen simply as the experience of the new birth, or identified with the time when this occurred. This experience is merely the first "baby" step on the path to knowing God. Indeed, one of the tragedies of North American Christianity is that one's "personal experience" with God has been limited to this one moment of rebirth, and there is frequently a dearth of solid teaching on the ongoing life of the believer as a continuing and expanding knowledge of God based on continued incursions of God into the life and consciousness of the believer.

In regard to the problem of evil, a true knowledge of God and his character, discovered in personal experience, gives us reason to have confidence in the goodness of God, despite the incredibly terrible moral and logical issues surrounding a universe where evil exists. All too often there are facile answers given to questions about the existence of evil by religious people who sincerely believe they are defending God and the truth. Unfortunately, some of these explanations are given by true Christians who do not understand that, for those who question the character of God because of the existence of evil, this is an issue that is not simply an intellectual puzzle, or evidence of a rampant ego. Indeed, if religious people see it as an issue at all, they often see it as merely an indication of spiritual weakness in the person asking the question, and, for example, quote Psalm 14, as if that is an answer. Nevertheless, spiritual weakness is not the cause of such a concern, or at least it does not necessarily imply such a failing. To one who is troubled by this question the issue is deeply disturbing, and can shake one's confidence in existence to the foundations. I suspect that even St. Paul felt the power of the problem.

C.S. Lewis, in his book "God in the Dock", writes, " The ancient man approached God...as the accused man approaches his judge. For the modern man the roles are reversed. He is the judge. God is in the dock."(p.100) For Lewis, this seems an unthinkable situation, and for some believers, such a position is inconceivable. Questioning God, however, is an experience that is not identical with each doubting individual. Malicious rebellion is not always in the heart of one who feels compelled to question God. To question that which is obvious, moreover, is equally unlikely. We question what we do not know and understand. Even those who seek to impute evil to God are doing so of a God who is presumably not the true and living God we claim to have faith in. In this sense they are not accusing God of anything, but rather are addressing these accusations to an "image" of a God who does not exist.

Indeed, frequently, the faults with which they accuse this "God" are based on failures by "God" to exemplify characteristics which believers hold inhere in the true God. As such they are not impugning God at all, but asserting by implication, the very characteristics we accuse the doubters of denying. We have learned, and not simply since the Renaissance, that powerful figures are not to be simplistically trusted. In a world of suffering and evil this distrust of the powerful extends to the God one does not know. And the truth is that most of us, including those vociferous defenders of divinity, do not know God. I believe that the passion to question God is more godly than the thoughtless acceptance of qualities of godhead professed by supposed believers. Passionless "faith" is much more dangerous than passionate doubt.

I also believe that God looks with understanding and love on one who struggles with the question. Yet, if one comes to the very brink of blaming God for the presence of evil, sees no reason why this terrible conclusion is not false, and yet refuses to make the final conclusion of making God ultimately responsible for evil, if only from an agnostic position, that is, because one simply does not have enough information, I believe one has shown great intellectual wisdom. In the face of a paradox of such existential enormity one should exhibit some intellectual humility. Such a position, i.e. deciding not to decide for lack of data, is not the same as agreeing to the unquestioning mind-frame.

Doubt does not occur in everyone's life. But for those who do journey along this path, it is not usually the result of a conscious choice, but rather an unavoidable inner debate that one would have preferred to forgo. Further, ironically, if one sees existence as a serious ethical problem, one may be less likely to rashly attribute to God causation and responsibility for the evil that occurs. This is so, simply because one is horrified by the extent of evil throughout and within the very nature of the universe, and not only in the individual or collective acts of sinful humans, and cannot bear to imagine God as being the source of such a state .

I believe there is an answer to the question at the beginning of this chapter, and part of that answer is that in a world of suffering, God can be found in the presence of Jesus, the suffering servant. In his love of the prostitute, in his compassion for the deformed and leprous, in his patience with the "little faith" of his disciples, in his understanding of Thomas' doubt, in his pain at the unhappiness caused by death, in his understanding of the slavery of sin, in his refusal to identify the Father with the collapse of a tower on a group of people, and in his control of the destructive forces of nature on the stormy lake...In all these, and in our own lives, and in our own times of pain, he is there as the revelation of God's mind, God's attitude to what Jesus was also confronted with. God was not only in Jesus reconciling the world unto himself. He was also in Jesus revealing himself to the world. In this world of suffering we find Jesus, a man of sorrows and acquainted with grief,... a man of sorrows and acquainted with grief.

We need to take Jesus' statement that he was the perfect revelation of God seriously. How did Jesus act? What does that say about the Father? Do we have a God like Jesus, and another God who acts contrary to this? Of course there are not two differing Gods, playing "good cop, bad cop". Moreover, Jesus is not the official property of the institutional church, an archaic and irrelevant idea that is found only in dusty books. He is, in reality, the presence of God with us in all that can, and does happen to us. What did Jesus mean when he said, "Look, I am with you always, even to the end of the age."? If we could only come to realize the implications of that remark, to the same degree that we believe the chair we go to sit on will not collapse under us, it is likely our entire lives would be changed, improved, made more dynamic, and our relationship with God would be unrecognizably transformed.

It is doubtless true that we may not be able to generate a philosophical answer that will meet the needs of the current atmosphere of doubt, though this would be a priceless intellectual contribution. On the other hand, the removal of intellectual props that can not stand the weight of examination does not have to imply the end of one's intellectual confidence. When an inadequate system is removed we are forced to a greater dependence on God to provide assurance that faith is not unreasonable. In this quest we do not have to make leaps of faith that attempt to ignore, or drown our intellectual confusion.

The biblical description of a relationship with God is one involving the existential revelation of God to the individual, such that doubt is removed and faith is generated. The faith God seeks may be tested, but it is a faith that is supposed to be based on a knowledge of the creator derived from experience, just as our knowledge of the world around us is based on such experience. Faith is not a belief in the unknown, but a sure knowledge of the usually unseen. Elijah may have doubted God's goodness but he was absolutely convinced of God's power and willingness to use that power, because he had discovered these facts from God himself. It is from within a relationship with God that we will discover an answer to the problem of evil. From within that relationship we will be able to trust. It is understandable that to some the solution offered here will be unacceptable. The problem is immense and answers are not easy to discover, and frequently miss the point. However, despite the horror of negativity in the universe, I believe God comes to us and asks us to discover what he is like. And in that discovery is the answer we cry out for and must have.

Lord...it is easier to call you this than Father, though that is what I have also been taught to call you. Sometimes I become aware of your love. I see it, and for a moment I believe you are one who loves me. But just as someone who falls in love, and is one moment filled with wonder that this love seems actually to be returned, only to be overcome by doubt and cast into despair the next, fearing that the thought can only be the product of one's imagination, so my experience of you is also sure, and the next in the depths of despair. My belief that you are a loving father is just as fragile. Take me, who will not be taken. Reveal yourself, so that I may know you, in the same way that I am known, so that I may truly love you.

Chapter 11
FORGIVENESS

Whenever we think of forgiveness, we think of anger, resentment, and perhaps the impossible demand Jesus made to forgive our brother seventy times seven. But mostly we think of anger. We are also aware of the phrase "Oh yes, I forgive you, but I will never forget", the person thus giving with one hand, while taking back what was given with the other. That kind of forgiveness is worth about as much as a counterfeit thousand dollar bill. When we think of forgiveness from God we also think of anger. We all know about the wrath of God. And yet what God is really like, despite this image, is not like this at all. God longs to forgive, to remove sin. He longs for a restoration of the sinner to himself, and the last thing God wants to do is punish someone.

If you think this is wrong, then ask yourself why Jesus came to live among us. That 'boringly' well known verse in John, "God so loved the world that he gave his only begotten Son that whoever believes on him shall not perish but have eternal life" tells us clearly why Jesus came to this earth. It also tells us what God's attitude to sin is. God wanted to get rid of sin so much that He came Himself, in the person of Jesus, solely in order to die and destroy sin by doing so. Recall also the parable of the ninety nine sheep that were safe, and the one sheep that was lost (Matt. 18: 12, Luke 15: 4). What was Jesus' comment on this? Doesn't Jesus say "I tell you there will be greater joy in heaven over one sinner who repents than over ninety nine righteous people who do not need to repent"? And what does the parable of the prodigal son show us? When the father knew his son had messed up his life terribly, he went out day after day, to see if the son was somewhere on the horizon on his way home. Was this so he could vent his anger on the reprobate son? We know this was not so. Luke chapter fifteen tells us that Jesus said:

> So he set out for his father's house. But while he was still a long way off (the father didn't even wait for him to get all the way to the house) his father saw him, and his heart went out to him. He ran to meet him, flung his arms around him, and kissed him. The son said, "Father I have sinned against God (and the son knew just how much that was true) and against you. I am no longer fit to be called your son." But the father said to his servants, "Quick, fetch a robe, my best one, and put it on him... (Luke 15: 11-24)

Perhaps we imagine that God is the kind of person who commands us to repent or suffer the consequences. But that is not the picture of God that Jesus presents us with in this parable. The Father, who is a God, waits. Day after day he waits, not impatiently but in love, for each of us to realize that the only place of security is with (him). God is not a resentful forgiver. He does not say "ok, but I won't forget what you did" For the prodigal's father it is as if the son had never left. All is forgotten in the joy that he had returned and was safe. That is the God we have to deal with. Jesus even takes the risk in this parable that we may think he is soft on morality. He makes absolutely certain that we understand the moral failure the prodigal has been (verses 13, 30). Yet there is no moral harshness in the father. That is found in the unforgiving other son. The father's behaviour is focused on the restoration of the lost son. The most dangerous thing about sin is deciding to live in it. In Joseph Conrad's "Heart of Darkness", one of the characters exclaims "The horror, the horror". But it is not just the horror of evil out in the world. The horror is the horror of sin that exists within the heart of the one reading this. Yet, even though our failures and sins are so hard to face sometimes, even though we may be overwhelmed by the horror of what we have done, God the Father waits for us to come to him so that he can cover our sin with his best robe, so he can fling his arms around us, and pour out his love on us. And his robe is the perfect robe of the righteousness of His own Son who died for each one of us, not despite our sin, but because of it.

We are sometimes far from convinced that even Jesus is totally trustworthy on the score of approachability as regards moral failure. We (Christians) often see Jesus, and definitely the God of the Old Testament, as morally outraged, and as a terrifying being who, rather than filled with love, is ready at an instant to send down punishment. We derive this sense from our reading of the scriptures. Let us admit this. And it is true that God is a holy being. It can also be concluded from the emphasis that is placed on holiness as an absolute state in the scriptures, that God does not understand or have a true sympathy for the actual experience of sin and failure, as opposed to the moral evaluation of that sin and failure. In fact, God, and even Jesus, can be seen at times to absolutely fail to understand the reality of the life we live on this earth as enmeshed in sin, our own and others. The story of the woman taken in the very act of adultery is crucial to a removal of this fear.

That the story is not found in all extant texts of John's gospel, or in the same location within the gospel, and is even found in some texts in Luke, does not imply that the narrative is not genuine, or that it is not authentic scripture. Its omission from some texts does not weaken its truth, and the ideas present in the story are in agreement with other gospel teachings of Jesus. The respective weights that Jesus placed on morality in relation to forgiveness and restoration are clearly seen in the piece. It is not simply that Jesus and the woman were opposed by religious groups focused on morality and family values. The scripture was obviously on their side. They had chapter and verse to back up their position on what should be done.

Jesus did not dispute that they had the bible on their side. He did not question their interpretation. We are not talking about a liberal preacher who is trying to minimize the bible. The person involved in this narrative is the Lord Jesus Christ. He does have some weight in this moral issue, does he not? Jesus did not reject the morality of those who wanted to stone, pillory, punish, discipline, reject, execute the woman. He simply made the strong and irrefutable claim that sinners do not have the right to execute judgement on another sinner. In fact, he went further. By implication, only he could stone her to death, as he was without sin. He is God. "Woman where are your accusers? Has no one condemned you? No one Lord. And Jesus said to her, neither do I condemn you. Go and sin no more."(John 8:10,11) There is deep understanding here. There is no callous indifference to human experience. There is no moral outrage. There is love, and there is forgiveness. Having the scripture on your side as defense for a position of punishment is conclusively shown here to be irrelevant to the behaviour Christians are expected to exhibit towards sinners. It does not matter how many verses can be marshaled against this position, and in defense of outrage.

God's forgiveness, and therefore by extension ours, and the soul's redemption trump a supposed moral response.

Nevertheless, if God is so willing to forgive our sins, why did Jesus say immediately following the "Lord's Prayer", "For if you forgive others the wrongs they have done you, your heavenly Father will also forgive you. But if you do not forgive others, then the wrongs you have done will not be forgiven by your Father." (Matt. 6: 9-15)? What does this say about God, and what does it say about us? Is God just as ready to be cruel as we are? Is this what it tells us?

Though there appear to be limits to the level of chaos and violence this world generally operates at, the world of humanity does not continue within the protection of an existence in which the nature of God is the dominant feature. In other words, God is essentially absent from the world in the way it 'works'. To be unforgiving to those who have wronged us, is to operate in the fashion of the world without God. It is to remove oneself from that rule of God, which is the rule of love. It is not that God does not want to forgive one's sins in this situation. Rather it is that we wish to remain in rebellion to God. God is unable at that point to forgive one.

There are those who find in Jesus' teaching on confronting the wrongdoer in Matthew 18:15-17 support for an aggressive response to other's wrongs. This advice should not, nevertheless be understood to be a blanket direction to confront all sinners with their sins. Such an understanding, in fact, violently contradicts the ministry of Christ. In any case such instructions are found only in Matthew 18, and in a shorter form in Luke 17. Firstly, the section does not advise us to go through this procedure with everyone. Verse 15 states the limiting conditions, "If your brother commits a sin against you". The sinner involved is specifically a brother or sister, and secondly the advice only involves the sinner and the person directly wronged. What is being discussed in the verses is predominantly the fracture in the relationship between these two, as we see in verse 15, "If he listens to you, you have gained your brother." In the narration in Luke we are told that if the offender repents we are to forgive (him).

Is the implication in Luke that if (he) does not repent we are not to forgive him, or that we are under no obligation to forgive him if he does not repent? What then are we supposed to make of Christ's warning that if we do not forgive, our heavenly Father will not forgive us? Indeed, both in Matthew and in Luke, this example is immediately followed by Christ's command to forgive the offending person 70 times 7. How then could it be acceptable to harbor unforgiveness in our hearts? 2 Corinthians 2:7, Ephesians 4:32, Colossians 3:13, Matthew 6:12-15, all command us to forgive those who wrong us. When Paul speaks of forgiveness in 2 Corinthians he is referring to a restoration of fellowship, as the context indicates, and as is the essence of forgiveness. Neither Ephesians 4:32 nor Colossians 3:13 alludes anywhere to repentance in anyone, but only urges us to forgive as Christ has forgiven us. Further, if there is any implication in the verses, it is that there should be forgiveness, independent of the wrongdoer's reaction to the wrong. While we are commanded in Luke to forgive the one who repents for the wrong done to us, it is not a logically necessary conclusion that we are justified in withholding that forgiveness, if there is no repentance.

Clearly, when we forgive an individual this does not mean that he or she has, as a consequence, found forgiveness with God for all his or her sins, and has peace with God. If an individual does not turn from their sins, and with faith in Christ becomes a child of God, that person remains under the burden of sin and continues to be alienated from God, despite our forgiveness. The reason why this is so is that the dominant New Testament understanding of forgiveness, as far as we humans are the "givers" of this, is that forgiveness is an attitude of love and the abandoning of all resentment towards another individual. It does not have to imply the annulment of the sinful act, though this seems to be also what occurs as we see in Jesus cry from the cross (Luke 23:34) and St Stephen's similar dying cry (Acts 7:60). Forgiveness, *as it is given by us,* is the attitude of love towards a sinner. It is not a "get out of hell" card. We are directed to forgive, whether the offending sinner regrets what has been done or not. To imagine that if the sinner does not repent we do not need to forgive is to distort the teaching of Christ beyond recognition.

Matthew 7:5,6 warns against attempting to correct another person's sin. It should be admitted, however, that simply because someone confronts another person with their sins does not mean that they are breaking Jesus' command. However, neither does it indicate that they are not breaking it. Given the human weakness to condemn, such an activity should not be naively accepted as innocent. Before we start pointing out other people's faults, we need to be deeply aware of the magnitude of our own sinfulness.

Further, it needs to be restated that Matthew 18, and Luke 17 are both concerned with healing an offence against a wronged individual, and that this sin has caused a break in the individuals' relationship. The passages are not advice to anyone who seems to think another person has sinned and needs correcting. We are not directed to continually bring other people's sins to their attention in this very mechanical and socially limited fashion. Further, scriptural practice by both Christ and the apostles supports this understanding.

It is true that unless one repents there can be no forgiveness. However, the supposed "gift" to the church of the powers of forgiveness does not add to this reality, but only reflects the condition that would have pertained, even if

Jesus had not said Matthew 18:18. If we do not pronounce that there is forgiveness for one who has not repented, this is simply describing the reality. And if we refuse to give forgiveness to one who has genuinely repented, this does not mean that the person is not forgiven. God cannot forgive one who has not repented. Matthew 18:18 is not the expression of the granting of extraordinary powers to the church. Moreover, our attitude to the sinner is not open to such possibility. Whether the one who wrongs us repents or not, our attitude to them can only be one of forgiveness.

The scripture does not allow us to harbor resentment in our hearts towards those who have wronged us. This is strikingly clear from the fact that we cannot ask God to forgive the wrongs we have done against him, while simultaneously refusing to forgive another human being their sins against us. Even with God, the forgiveness God offers is not a mathematical crossing off of our sins but the expression of the love God has for the sinner, restoring that sinner to a relationship of union with God. God's forgiveness, like ours if we act and live in love, has already been given, and God waits, as do we, for the sinner to seek the relationship that this love-forgiveness passionately desires. We need to ask ourselves what God's forgiveness actually means? Does it mean that God suddenly stops being angry? Is that what goes on?

That God's attitude is already one of forgiveness is seen in the incarnation, the coming of Christ into the world in human form, and in Christ's willing sacrifice of himself on the cross. In that he died for all, tells us that he has indeed forgiven all, even before the sinner repents. That the sinner does not experience this forgiveness is so only because he or she either does not know of the forgiveness, or chooses not to live in the kingdom of God's love.

In addition, we should not look at forgiveness as a kind of divine account book, and that God mathematically crosses out sins as they are confessed. If we think about how forgiveness works, isn't it essentially an attitude in which one does not withhold love from another human being? Forgiveness is an attitude as much as an act. That is why Jesus said in Matthew 18:25 that forgiveness had to be from the heart. Surely this is also God's attitude to our sins. How do we imagine the last judgement? How many sins does it take to separate one from the presence of God? When God forgives, do you think he goes through each sin and checks it before he forgives? Isaiah 43, verse 25 says, "I am he who wipes out your transgressions, and will remember your sins no more." He wipes them out, he doesn't do a bookkeeping of our wrongs. Isaiah 44:22 states, "I have blotted out your sins like a cloud." Psalm 103: 10-12 states, "He has not treated us as our sins deserve, or requited us for our misdeeds. For as the heaven is high above the earth, so is his love. As far as the east is from the west, so far has he removed our sins from us." God starts out with an attitude of forgiveness. That is God's permanent attitude to us. It is we who do not allow this attitude of "forgetfulness" to operate towards us. Not forgiving another person, apart from the logic of fairness, (God has forgiven all of our sins, therefore it is reasonable for us to forgive a few, in comparison.), is a placement of ourselves outside the nature of God's "kingdom". If we wish to live outside the quintessential characteristic of God (love), it is impossible for God to have a relationship with us, because we have not turned away from sin. We have chosen not to live according to this characteristic of love.

God waits for us to come to him. He waits for us to have had enough of sin so that we turn to God for a wholeness we have been missing. We do not need to listen to the voices of shame and rejection that, throughout our lives, we have learned to hear. All that needs to be heard is the words of an all embracing love, from the one who came to bring an understanding and gentle forgiveness.

> *Father forgive me for the sins that weigh so heavily upon me. I am so conscious of the degree to which I have failed you and others, particularly those I should have loved more truly, and I let down so many times. I am so aware of the way I have treated those I did not love as I ought to have, that I can not even face thinking about it. I hide from the memories inside me, and from anything and anyone who reminds me of how much I have failed. At times I am so horrified at what I have done that I cannot confess these things to you. And yet you are forgiving, and what I could not trust others to see about me, you already know, and want to forgive. I'd like to believe that, but it's really pretty hard. Forgive the sins I can face, but also the ones I cannot even mention. Help me to face what I have done in the knowledge that, despite the horror of these sins, you love me. Give me grace to know that you are the Prodigal's father, and that nothing I have ever done causes you to hate and reject me. Help me to understand that I do not need to fear you, that you love me.*

Chapter 12
THE POWER OF GOD

For most of the people in the world God is silent and does nothing. If it were somehow discovered that God did not exist, this information would not change their lives in the least. Why is it then that expressions of the power of God breaking into the ordinary powerlessness of human experience are seen as normal in the bible? How do Christians explain this apparent contradiction, both to themselves and to any of the rest of the world who happen to take the trouble to ask? In the scriptures, manifestations of the power of God accompany any one who has a close relationship with God. The miraculous, indeed, is a standard evidence of God's presence in a society, and within an individual who has a heart that is open to God. These ideas notwithstanding, it is beyond contestation to assert that, without such occurrences we would have absolutely no reason to believe that we are not alone in the universe, and that the divinity that is suggested by existence is not a schizophrenic being, unsure whether to build or destroy, whether to be just, or arbitrarily and mindlessly cruel.

The fact is that without the ongoing intrusion of God into the world, and not simply the "historical" intrusions of the past, there is little reason to continue to believe that these putatively historic events have any facticity, or for that matter, any life changing reality. If the scriptures are correct, the gamut of divine intrusions into our quiet existence, from the quiet and little known to the healing of the sick, and any other otherwise unbelievable event, should be seen as part of the normal religious life of the church. There is no biblical teaching to controvert this assertion. Religious life that exists only in occasional feelings and lofty thoughts is not the religion of the bible, and is even more definitely, not a religion that gives assurance that the teachings given us in the scriptures are of any significant worth.

Such a claim is not an assertion that God needs to be tested in the sense taught against in scripture. Rather, it is simply a description of the environment that the scriptures themselves describe as normal for those who have a relationship with God the Father through the Son and made real by the Holy Spirit. A sense of the reality of God is essential, even to the most basic experience of the new birth. It is the Holy Spirit who makes real the things of God, and it is the Holy Spirit who convinces the soul that Jesus Christ is the Lamb of God. A faith based on anything less than the revelation of the Spirit to the human soul that Jesus is indeed the Saviour, is one that will almost certainly not stand the test of time, and not result in any genuine growth, based as it is on a 'faith' that has virtually no substance. God's religion is one in which people worship him in spirit and in truth. How can anyone worship God in truth if they have no real reason to believe that God even exists, other than the memory that they were taught so by parents or society?

To worship God truly is to worship a God one truly believes exists. A second hand faith does not so truly believe, as the only reason such a proposition is assented to is that it has been taught to one. Such a faith is incapable of changing the individual, and it is certainly incapable of transforming the world. If the teachings of the bible are to become anything other than interesting and noble cultural artifacts, it is essential that God becomes genuinely real in our lives. And he is truly not that for most people. Without the reality of God breaking into the world we have no reason to believe that the biblical teachings are correct. And perhaps even more importantly, we have no ability to bring the life of God to a suffering and lost world.

Sections of the church find any discussion on miracles either past or present, disturbing. Personally, I find such reticence quite understandable. Apart from being troublesome, miracles are the kinds of events, like true love and world peace, that one longs for, while believing in one's heart they will never occur. They are avoided because they are so deeply desired. For those who believe that miraculous events no longer occur, one might ask where such a belief was derived. Miracles, like the continued experience of God communicating with his people, have no time limits, both according to the scriptures and in the experience of the church. That one can expect the miraculous to occur at this present stage in human history, is both tremendously liberating and terribly disturbing. Along with the wonder that such occurrences can be expected, can come feeling that one's spirituality is not up to the level where these events are likely to take place. Nevertheless, just as progress in science is often preceded by an awareness that a certain result is possible, while the theoretical basis of that result has not yet been derived, the awareness that the miraculous is possible, can be part of the heart's preparation for the experience of these intrusions by God.

Rather than being signs for an unsophisticated and primitive society, miracles are acts of divine love in situations beyond human help. A miraculous healing is not a paternalistic and condescending act of the divinity for the person healed. Money that miraculously arrives at the last moment of necessity is not an act of God for a primitive and uneducated culture, but the real meeting of a desperate human need. Miracles are events that God brings about because humanity is unable to achieve or possess all that life demands.

However, miracles also serve another purpose related to our ignorance of God. Following the healing of the cripple at the Beautiful Gate, Acts 3:10 tells us that the inhabitants of Jerusalem who recognized the healed man, " were filled with wonder and amazement at what had happened to him." Miracles fill people with wonder because such events are not expected to occur. They are not everyday occurrences, and they are not events that are believed possible. Miracles are happenings where the level of probability of their occurring is zero, or close to it.

Miracles also open people's hearts to the word of God. Acts 4:4 relates that after Peter preached, following the miracle, "many who had heard (Peter's) message became believers". A combination of godly living and manifestations of the power of God was enough to cause the early church's reputation to become widely known throughout Jerusalem and beyond. Acts 5:14-16 states,

> People in general spoke highly of them, and more than that, numbers of men and women were added to their ranks as believers in the Lord. In the end the sick were actually carried out into the streets and laid there on beds and stretchers...and the people from the towns around Jerusalem flocked in, bringing those who were ill or harassed by unclean spirits, and all of them were cured.

Miracles act as proofs of the veracity of the message preached. Humanity has been inundated by charlatans pretending to meet society's needs from the beginning of recorded time. As a race we are a skeptical lot, and with good reason. Why should people believe the good news of salvation, merely because we present it orally? However, skepticism is a log jam in the human psyche that the power of God can break through in a moment.

When Philip went to a city of Samaria and began preaching in the power of the Spirit, "the crowds, with one mind, listened eagerly to what Philip said when they heard him and saw the miracles that he performed. For in many cases of possession the unclean spirits came out with a loud cry, and many paralysed and crippled folk were cured, and there was great joy in the city." (Acts 8:4-8) We should remember that when Jesus had stopped at Jacob's well in Samaria, it was his miraculous knowledge of the woman that had opened her heart and led to the town's invitation to him to stay longer.

Later in Acts, after Peter called on the Lord Jesus to heal a paralysed man in the town of Lydda, verse 35 of chapter 9 tells us that "all who lived in Lydda and Sharon saw him (the healed man) and they turned to the Lord." When Paul and Barnabas, on their first missionary journey preached to the governor of Cyprus and were opposed by Elymas, a sorcerer, Paul made the sorcerer temporarily blind. Acts 13:12 relates, "When the governor saw what had happened he became a believer, deeply impressed by what he had learned about the Lord." It was the revelation of the power and reality of God that convinced the governor of the truth of the preached word. Finally, Luke, the presumed author of Acts, states, "Paul and Barnabas stayed on (in Iconium) and spoke boldly and openly in reliance on the Lord, and he confirmed the message of his grace by causing signs and miracles to be worked at their hands." (Acts 14: 3,4). Once more we see the combination of preaching being authenticated by the presence of miracles. It was not Paul and

Barnabas who confirmed this. The text states that God confirmed their words with these signs.

It is not we who seek the co-presence of miracles with the spoken word to confirm what we preach. This, rather obvious point, somehow needs to be made. God confirmed his word with his own power. It is not we, but God who seems to feel that miracles are necessary. Why then should we continue to act as if miracles are either unimportant, or at best aberrant activities for an immature faith? Indeed, such a statement may have some credibility if the ones making such a claim had a mature faith. Our problem, however, is that we have an excess of belief, and virtually no genuine faith. The book of Acts seems quite clear on this point. Miracles associated with the preaching of the Gospel convince people of the veracity of the words spoken. Surely we would do well to take this lesson seriously. We are quite aware of the difficulty of evangelism, not only in the mission field, but in our own "Christian" countries. Have we become so blind to the scriptures that we do not see that experiences of the power of God witnessed by ordinary people open their hearts to the Gospel? Are we really so intellectually and culturally sophisticated that miracles are unnecessary?

The Acts of the Apostles is not merely a brief history of the early church. More importantly, it is a blueprint of what the normal Christian church should be like, and how it should act. We have become so used to the non-miraculous in the life of the church, and this must now also include the Pentecostals, that this is what we take as normal. But it is not. It is the sub-normal, and it is a hindrance to the spread of the Gospel and the spiritual growth of the believer.

The Pentecostals can take but little comfort in the 'fact' that they already have such a position as part of their orthodoxy. However, dynamic movements of God have a history of entropy. Their spiritual power gradually decays. This can be seen with the Methodist movement begun with the amazing preaching and hymn writing of John and Charles Wesley. To some degree it is true of the Salvation Army created by William Booth, though perhaps because they are outside the "normal" church, the Salvation Army has retained a spiritual presence. This decay of spiritual power can even be witnessed in the Christian and Missionary Alliance church which was founded under the dynamic preaching and administration of A.B. Simpson, who had a deep belief in the power of God to heal and empower preaching. The founders of all these denominations possessed a spiritual power and anointing that must be admitted to be relatively absent in today's church.

For their part, the Pentecostal churches of today give the appearance of wanting the acceptance of the mainstream churches, not in itself a harmful thing, and at times express a diminished valuation of their Pentecostal doctrines, perhaps because these teachings are a source of difference and embarrassment, or because the experience of the spiritual gifts has ceased to be as normal an occurrence in the congregation as it once was. The reality is that, apart from some strange behaviour and teaching, that some claim to be Pentecostal, but which has little biblical support, the presence of miracles and evidence of the gifts of the Spirit in Pentecostal churches appear not to be as evident as even twenty years ago. The possibility that Pentecostal churches could cease to be Pentecostal at all is a distinct historical possibility. However, this section of the church at least still proclaims the value of miracles. The tragedy of the loss of this witness would be such that if charismatic support for miracles were to cease, it would be all the more difficult to garner support for the biblical teaching of the need to experience the power of God, except as this occurred in the interiority of an individual's soul and mind .

It is not only the New Testament that describes acts of God that are clearly not normal happenings. The Old

Testament is also full of such events. Samuel's call as a child, Elijah's many divine experiences, God's conversations with the Patriarchs, God's revelation of himself to Hagar in the desert, all reveal a God who can break into human life and communicate with normal, and sometimes not very spiritual people. The Psalms frequently refer to the power of God, but Psalm 146 particularly speaks of a very existentialist view of human life that includes the activities of God in the world. The author clearly has a deep sense of his or her own mortality, and the inability and unwillingness of human government to meet the needs of ordinary people. I quote it in full:

> O praise the Lord
> Praise the Lord, my soul
> As long as I live I will praise the Lord
> I will sing psalms to my God all my life long.
> Put no faith in princes
> In any man who has no power to save.
> He breathes his last breath
> He returns to the dust
> And in that hour all his thinking ends.
> Happy the man whose helper is the God of Jacob,
> Whose hopes are in the Lord his God,
> Maker of heaven and earth,
> The sea and all that is in them;
> Who serves wrongdoers as he has sworn
> And deals out justice to the oppressed.
> The Lord feeds the hungry
> And sets the prisoner free.
> The Lord restores sight to the blind
> And straightens backs which are bent;
> The Lord loves the righteous
> And watches over the stranger;
> The Lord gives heart to the orphan and widow

But turns the course of the wicked to their ruin.
The Lord shall reign forever,
Thy God, O Zion, for all generations.
O praise the Lord.

That this should not be understood merely in metaphoric terms is seen in the ministry of Jesus, where the hungry were fed, the demonically held prisoners were set free, the blind were given their sight and the woman's bent back was straightened. It is improbable that such images in this psalm could be generated only from the author's imagination and not from experience. They could, nevertheless, have been the poetic imagination of the writer. This must be admitted. The actions of the Saviour, however, belie the idea that God does not act in this very literal way to ameliorate human suffering. Although, even this could be literary embellishment, intended to convince the skeptical reader of the authenticity of the "story". However, such events have occurred throughout the last two millenia, and continue to occur in the present.

God, in a very real sense, must reveal himself this way because in our hearts we do not believe that God can do the "abnormal", or even that God is actually real, though the confession that God exists rolls off our tongues, as if it were the most obvious of realities. That such miraculous acts are not only acts of compassion but verifications is clear from Jesus own words: (John 4:48) "Will none of you believe without seeing signs and portents?" In addition, John 10:37 states, "If I am not acting as my Father would, do not believe me. But if I am, accept the evidence of my deeds..." Jesus clearly understood that his miracles were an evidence of the truth of his statements. As one translation puts it when Jesus delayed going to Lazarus when he was mortally ill, "Lazarus has died, but I am glad that I wasn't there so that you can grow in faith." (John 11:15) An arrogant demand to prove God to be true, that comes from a hard heart that has no gentleness or hunger for truth, is not the same as the need for proof for ideas and realities that are not part of normal human life.

However, God is perfectly able to use the miraculous, even with those whose hearts are hard and arrogant. God knows that we do not trust him. It would be a step forward if, despite all our protestations of faith, we could come to a similar realization. Then perhaps God could begin to plant genuine faith in our hearts. Unbelief lies just below the surface of our carefully worked out protestations of faith. It is not that we do not have any faith at all. Rather, our knowledge of God is so shallow that we do not really know the spiritual reality we call God sufficiently, to know with certitude that "all things are possible". In 2 Kings 6:16,17 Elisha's servant, in great fear at being in a city surrounded by an attacking army, cries out, "O, master which way are we to run? Elisha answered, 'Do not be afraid, for those who are on our side are more than those on theirs.' Then Elisha offered this prayer: 'O Lord, open his eyes and let him see. 'And the Lord opened the young man's eyes, and he saw the hills covered with horses and chariots of fire all around Elisha." This is the predicament in which most of us live. We do not see the armies of God. And our eyes need to be opened, just as the young man's eyes were, so many years ago.

One of the problems is that we are taught not to confess our lack of faith. We are encouraged to say words of faith, and not allow negativity, but the fact remains we do not have faith. The words we say may be the most powerful one could imagine. They may be the truest words we could say. But the truth is also that we do not believe them in the depths of our hearts. Jesus said in Matt. 17:19,20, and Luke 17:5,6, "If you have faith, even no bigger than a mustard seed you will say to this mountain, 'move from here to there' and it will move;

nothing will prove impossible for you." I think that what Jesus was saying here was that it is not really the size of your faith that makes things happen but the simple presence of genuine faith. Faith is a response to the experience of coming to see God. Elisha's servant had to see the power of the God he served, and we need to discover for ourselves the reality of the God we so shallowly believe in.

Saying words of faith again and again is no substitute for actually believing. We must draw near to God, and let him reveal himself to us, and then the words we say will have effect. 1 John 1:9 says "If we confess our sins he is faithful and just to forgive us our sins and cleanse us from all unrighteousness." If we admit to ourselves that our faith is small, and lacks constancy, and confess this to God, then God promises to remedy this lack. As long as we refuse to acknowledge our lack of faith, our experience with God, and of God in the world, will be equally lacking in reality. Jesus is not hindered by honesty. In Mark 9:24 Jesus asked the father if he believed. The father's answer is "Lord I believe, help my unbelief." Jesus did not walk away. This confession did not stop Jesus from healing the child. In the strange way of the human heart faith exists along with unbelief, and struggles with it. We Christians do have a certain level of faith. But it is also true that this faith is often extremely shallow, and we are stopped from both experiencing the power of God in our own lives, and demonstrating God's power to the world.

Nevertheless, an experience of the power of God in the life of the church and in the world is not simply to increase our faith. The power of God must be expressed in the world because without God's intervention, healing, inner freedom, and even the removal of evil opposition will not take place. This is a world essentially without God. If we were to imagine a world in which God was perfectly known and experienced, what kind of world would that be? Would it not be a world without the limitations of ignorance, sickness, fear, and in which we could successfully achieve redemptive and healing social objectives? It is for that reason that the power of God needs to be revealed.

John chapter nine is the story of the blind man sent by Jesus to the pool of Siloam, where he was healed. But it is even more so a story of contrasting religious attitudes, one that is solely based on inherited ideas, and one that is based on a present and experienced relationship with God. It was not that the Jewish hierarchy at that time had the wrong texts. It was that they had permanently ossified their relationship with God so that they were unable to see the working of God when it was presented to them, in this case, in the healing of the blind man. Their religion had no place, except in pure theory and as historical events, for the miraculous intervention of God in their world. The power of God was not a part of their presently lived experience. They believed in miracles, but only as they were related in the scriptures, not as events that were to be expected in their own time. We need to be very careful that we do not fall into this mistaken understanding ourselves, and as a result fail to see the kingdom of God when it is revealed in our own time.

The world desperately needs to see the power and love of God revealed. However, it seems equally true that the church, individual by individual also needs this revelation. If the believer's faith is so fragile, what must the faith of the unbeliever be like. It is reasonable and necessary to speak of the unbeliever's faith, because the truth is that while society has lost almost all "belief", and that which they do still possess is confused and full of doubts, there is still a degree of faith, or at least a hope that there is a reason to have faith. It is not sufficient for the church to have a solid evangelical faith. It is not even sufficient for the people who are evangelical. And it is definitely far from sufficient for the lost world outside the church who usually see no reason to believe what they are told by religious people. This problem has been exacerbated by the change in the demographics of the West, which is now becoming more and more racially and religiously pluralistic. This of course is a great opportunity for a spreading of the gospel. The mission field has come to us. However, with this has also come a wide range of religious variation which impacts on the consciousness of the nonbeliever. Christianity is now no longer the only religious choice that can be made, and it is no longer the religious system, and automatic home for even a Western unbeliever's religious understanding of the universe.

We religious people often take for granted the faith of other religious individuals. We also take our own faith for granted, as if it were rock solid and unassailable. This, however, is not the case. A faith that is not grounded in the strong reality of God and his power is a house built on sand. It is a faith waiting for either a disaster, or a growing intellectual doubt to sweep it away. How many thousand new believers, inadequately taught, and virtually left to their own devices, have drifted away from an active faith, and no longer regard themselves as Christians? We who continue in the church must take some responsibility for this loss. The loss is not simply one of numbers, but of individuals who no longer experience a perhaps previously warm relationship with God. With solid teaching and an experience of the presence of God's power, maybe many of these weak Christians would now be strong in the faith, would still be worshipping in the church and taking leadership roles in the life of the congregation they were once part of.

This kind of language is unfortunately not melodramatic. A faith that does not have a continually growing knowledge of God as a real, powerful and loving entity, is not likely to withstand any serious test. The problem of a dearth of the knowledge of God is particularly real in relation to the children of Christians. I have heard the children, of even exceptionally good Christians, express strong reservations as to the truth of biblical propositions that are essential to Christian growth. If these young people have such a weak hold on their faith, what about the children of unbelievers, who were not brought up in an environment of faith? Without manifestations of the power of God in the lives of believers and in the church, what reason do the children of believers, even children of the clergy, have to accept the faith? Without evidences of the power of God, the religious beliefs of parents are just "mom and dad's religious ideas", no more demanding of acceptance than their political ideas, and perhaps even less compelling. Faith is not transmitted genetically. It is taught, and shown, and revealed. And if there is no degree of reality to the ideas believed by Christian parents, these ideas will almost certainly not be carried on in the hearts and lives of their children.

Despite what religious people would like to believe, faith in God is not easily supported by either normal experience or reason. The character of God is not clear cut and obvious. The nature of the universe is not obviously good, and therefore indicative of a good God, and the biblical narrative about the origins of evil in the world is far from being rationally unproblematic. Of course, if one does not question, there is no problem. However, the moment one begins to question what one has been taught, one finds that the issues that previously seemed simple, are far more complicated. The complexity of this issue is sometimes seen, even for those who do not usually entertain doubts, when an event occurs, and one wonders if the event was caused by God or the Devil. The fact that such a causal confusion can occur surely reveals that the universe is anything but unambiguous.

What response does the church have to radical doubt? Do we simply blame the ones having these doubts for their lack of spirituality? What answer does the church have for individuals who cannot see past these questions? Do we ignore these people, and condemn them for having such a lack of faith, or is there something that can be said or done to remove such questioning? One danger is that if we really do have nothing to say to these people, the questions that they have raised with us may well find a home in our own hearts.

When the Sadducees questioned Jesus on the reality of the resurrection, the Lord provided not simply an answer to this theological question, but a paradigm for authentic spiritual life. Jesus said to them," You are mistaken, and surely this is the reason: you do not know either the scriptures or the power of God." (Mark 12: 24) What is being asserted here is that one may know the scriptures (as the Sadducees almost certainly did) but arrive at incorrect conclusions. It is further being asserted that without knowing the scriptures it is unlikely that one will arrive at correct theological beliefs. The other variable in this paradigm seems to be that correct conclusions can be derived if one has a relationship with the Godhead which reveals the character of God such that one becomes aware of and experiences the power of God. Rather than being open to pure intellectual unpacking, the scriptures are at times able to be understood only in the light of, and in the environment of a close relationship with the God and Father of the Lord Jesus Christ. Rather than being necessary only for a nascent church and an immature faith, Jesus proclaims that a true understanding of God is possible only with the combined experience of biblical reflection and deep spiritual knowledge of God.

Only a faith that is grounded on a real experience of God, and knows God's power, has an answer to the problems of doubt. If our faith is built only on an intellectual understanding of certain theological tenets, ultimately one can defend the truth only by asserting that the tenets are correct. On the other hand, an individual who truly knows

God and his power to intervene in this world, can speak with an authority that comes from genuine knowledge, and with the authority of the Holy Spirit. It is not that the one without such an experience does not possess the truth. Rather, the problem is that such a one finds it virtually impossible to defend his or her positions with any sense of certainty. To the degree that one has had an experience of God, even if that experience is very simple and initial, that person is not at risk from one who has had no experience of God. Most of us are more talk than walk. Our experience frequently lags behind our understanding, and yet, in our hearts we understand that the God we have but dimly begun to know is far bigger than the God we have only been taught about .

Even if we have had an experience with God, this newfound knowledge must be continually built on by study and further experience, for we are all, mostly a vast ungodly territory, over which God's rule does not hold sway. And this unconquered territory of the heart, despite out frequent religious protestations to the contrary, has no real faith, and does not believe that God has the power to do what, in our religious moments, we say he can and wants to do. The 'fifth column' of the believer's heart is really its ignorance, not about God but of God himself. We have little or no faith because we have little or no knowledge of God. We have no problem believing that our car will take us to a desired destination, but we have a mammoth problem believing that the God who causes the car to continue to exist, is able to do what is said about him.

When we speak of miracles we usually think of great expressions of the power of God. This, however, is not a very accurate understanding. A miracle is simply the coming of God through some kind of action, into a lost world. A miracle may not be seen by anyone, or may be recognized by only the individual to whom it was directed.

On the other hand it could be the stilling of the tempest on the Sea of Galilee, or the healing of the blind. What is important for us is that we come to understand in the depths of our being, that all these occurrences are possible.

For too long the church has been satisfied with defining unbelievers as sinners from whom one can not expect spiritual understanding. We have placed the blame for the evil that happens on the unsaved and been content that we have been describing them from a biblical standpoint. We have believed that we have been describing the world because we have employed scripture to define the world of these outsiders. Indeed we have focused so much on what we have understood as the spiritual dimension of life that we have not taken seriously the objective changes in the societal level of belief in spiritual realities, satisfying ourselves with moral critiques and a trite use of scripture. The fact is, however, that a societal belief in the spiritual dimension of reality is paper thin, and God is an irrelevance to the majority of people in the Western world. The world is not interpreted in terms of religious beliefs, Christian or otherwise. This is so, not because these unbelievers are determined to rebel against God, but rather because they see no evidence that God is relevant in their daily affairs. In such an environment, to assert that manifestations of the power of God are unnecessary, is surely to miss the severity of the epistemological crisis regarding a belief in God that the West finds itself in.

If we truly understand that God can move a mountain, such an event will occur if this is needed. The book of Acts teaches us that expressions of the power of God bring success to evangelism by generating faith in the observer. It also implies that the Christians, through whom this power was manifested, had genuine faith. Yet the truth remains that the shallow spiritual life of the church, both as this impacts on itself, and in relation to the world, shows just how little faith we truly have. We are no different to these early disciples. They did not start out with great faith. In fact, the gospels show how weak and vacillating their faith actually was. On the whole, the church today, however, simply does not expect to see the power of God revealed. It is not only the unbelieving world that needs to experience this power, it is even more so, the church, that claims to believe in such a God of power.

Chapter 13
MISSIONS AND THE MISSION FIELD

One of the most easily recognizable indicators of the church's health has been its passion to spread the gospel, (or its indifference towards this task). Periods of church expansion have frequently been followed by times of inactivity and introspection. This focus on the self has usually been followed by growing dissatisfaction, an increasing realization that there was a missing component to church life, and the sense that there was something selfish and unacceptable in such an individualistic gaze. Alterations in national or state political activity have not always coincided with a widespread church paradigm shift to the lost world, but this has sometimes been one of the motivators for an outward looking church vision. The 19th and 20th centuries, for example, centuries of rampant imperialism, saw a concerted missionary outreach around the globe. However, there is a growing feeling within the church today, I believe, that the task of missions to the 'non-Christian' world is almost complete, that most have been reached, and that the bible has now been translated, and is now in the hands most of the scattered tribes of the earth. If this is correct, though, why is it that the church, in most of the world, is statistically irrelevant?

After the missionary expansion of the early church there was a second missionary push with the Celtic evangelization of pagan Europe. This was followed by a hiatus in the level of outreach activity, including in the period of the Reformation, during which further significant missionary work did not take place. Missionary activity on a large scale began once more with European economic and national expansion and exploration, beginning in the fifteenth and sixteenth centuries. With a growing awareness of other lands and peoples, the church slowly began to see these new territories as areas of responsibility for the spread of the gospel. At times there were conflicts between the ambitions of the nation states, seeking to expand their global empires, and the church as it sought to protect the indigenous peoples from the predations of the state and its agencies. Not all bearers of the cross, as one should realistically expect, were exemplary in their presentation of the gospel. However, to varying degrees, the church attempted to teach the saving power of Christ to these recently 'discovered' nations of the globe.

The nineteenth and twentieth centuries were the greatest centuries of missionary activity, and the evangelization of distant peoples became a dominant part of virtually every church's agenda. With the growing awareness of the magnitude of a lost world, there was a proliferation of both church and non-denominational organizations devoted to this task, and thousands of Christians gave themselves, to often heroic work in all parts of the globe. Missionary activity was seen as a "going" to foreign countries, often within the sphere of the worker's own national empire. Many died in these foreign lands, some of simple old age, but others from exotic diseases, and still others killed by the indigenous people who saw the missionaries as invaders, threats and barbarians. With the dismantling of the European Imperial system, missionary work altered dramatically. Newly formed states were often not as willing to accept religiously oriented workers, evangelization was sometimes severely curtailed, and there was a move among native Christians in these newly created states to become independent of the foreign church's administration of the national church.

There was, however, another social change of immense global significance occurring concurrently with the diminution of these European empires. Citizens of these old imperial colonies began migrating in vast numbers to the European "mother" countries, and to the countries like Canada, the US, and Australia that had relatively recently been peopled by Europeans. From the church's perspective, at a time when missionary activity was being denigrated as virtually identical to European imperialism, and devalued in an ecclesiastical environment that saw no reason for missionary evangelization, the mission field was coming, in vast numbers, to the Western church in Europe, North America and Australia. Sometimes this was as a result of political turmoil, such as when thousands of Vietnamese refugees fled Vietnam to Western nations all over the world. At other times the move was simply the result of relaxed immigration policies and a governmental policy of family reunion. This movement of populations is probably the greatest migratory event since European migration to the less populated continents of the world following their discovery, and has impacted these "migrant" and imperial states in ways that may take decades to assimilate.

According to an internet demographics site, Migrant Information Source, in Canada during the period 1991-1996 there was a net increase of migrants, ignoring movement from the United States, of 571,485. That is to say, migration, in the period mentioned, from countries previously targeted for missionary work, including the newly opened areas of Eastern Europe, was more than half a million. The site did not have the numbers for 1996 to the present, but if the trend has continued, that would mean a mission field of more than one million people from around the world has entered Canada. The numbers for the US are even higher. Between 1995 and 2002, excluding migration from Canada, 7,850,000 people entered the US. For North America, excluding Mexico, this represented an increase of more than 8.5 million people. There was not one area of the world from which people did not come. And yet there is no concerted, and organized move to evangelize these people who previously lived in countries to which missionaries have traditionally been sent. In addition, the numbers are not completely up to date, and only begin at 1995 for the US, and 1991 for Canada. The real numbers, therefore, are much higher. There are thus, approximately ten million people in English and French speaking North America alone, from virtually every ethnic and linguistic background on the planet, to whom no large scale programs of evangelization are directed.

To the present, the church has not taken this global shift seriously, and has not instituted any significant programs of evangelization directed to this transported mission field. The early nineteenth century saw a delay in response by the church to the "expanded" world, and the twenty-first century is experiencing a similar delay to the recently "contracted" world. Migrant communities can be found in all major cities of North America, Europe, and even the previously "white" Australia. These communities function as islands of their native land, run schools, publish periodicals and papers in their own language and conduct religious services that follow the religious practices of the home country.

If I were not already a white, English speaking Christian, I would do the same. Seeking to replicate one's homeland is a natural reaction to migrating to a foreign country with a distinctly different form of culture. Christians must be extremely careful not to encourage reactions that reflect the sinful nature of impatience, intolerance and hate. For those who have never migrated to another land, the behaviour of these new immigrants must be difficult to understand, and perhaps at times even more difficult to accept. One may wonder why the migrants came, if they "so clearly" do not want to blend into the dominant culture. One may ask, for example, why these foreigners persist in speaking their strange languages when they are surrounded by English or French speakers. One may even feel that one is losing one's country to people who speak, act and look so different to the people one grew up with, and who one understands. One must also, however, continually remember that a sharing of the love of God is the only behaviour a Christian should engage in.

Despite one's fears regarding new migrants, history shows that after a period of time all migrant groups become assimilated into the culture of the land they move to. Older people may retain their language and customs relatively unchanged, but the children of migrants will, almost certainly, begin to speak the dominant language, adopt local customs, and gradually see themselves as belonging to the new nation rather than to the country of their parents and grandparents. Gradually, the elders find that their children cannot speak the older generation's language. Or they may understand it, but find it difficult or impossible to speak. Slowly the language of one's grandparents becomes a foreign tongue, as strange to the grandchildren of the migrants as it is to the children of the migrants of four, five or seven generations previous, and who now see themselves as "original" inhabitants, and not the descendants of the migrants that they really are. This is both sad and inevitable. It is sad because the generations feel themselves separated from each other, and because an understanding of another culture only enriches the possessor of these differing cultures. However, this leaving behind of the ancestor's culture is virtually inevitable, and even necessary to harmonious relations within the new nation's communities.

What is not at all inevitable is that any of these new migrants from previous missionary countries will ever become Christians. At a time when even overseas missionary activity is under fire, the church must refocus and redefine its missionary goals so that the unevangelized, non-Christian communities, among us, become the object of an organized, rational, widespread and understanding penetration by the Gospel. Historically, missionary work has been difficult and expensive, requiring the regular and sustained movement of finance and personnel around the globe. The regularity of this support can not always be depended on, missionary families need schools for their growing children, holidays after lengthy periods away from home, and occasionally rapid evacuation in times of war or local conflict. With the presence of large communities of migrants from countries to which missionaries were previously sent, these logistical difficulties no longer exist to anywhere near the same extent. Nevertheless, the call to young and old to go to the lost continues to exist; and the need to learn a foreign language and understand a foreign culture will frequently continue to exist. However, the huge logistical problems associated with missionary work in the past are no longer an issue for evangelization in one's own land.

These new migrants are too numerous for the small number of Christian churches pastored by people from the same foreign language groups. Experience has shown, in fact, that these foreign language churches (a) have so far been unable to make a significant impact on their own, despite much faithful efforts, and (b) that these churches undergo the same generational difficulties as the normal migrant population with both children and adults who are not fluent in the home language asking for services in the language of the dominant culture. This naturally makes the foreign language church less attractive to new migrants, and essentially integrates the church into the mainstream of the non-migrant world.

The outreach may not have the same heroic romance attached to it that it did in travelling to a distant country, though that soon wore off in the heat and dust of actually living in a foreign land. However, the same call of God to go, the same urgency to harvest the field that Jesus spoke of, and the same reason for such an exercise of love in leading the lost to their Saviour most certainly remain. These migrants from so many countries of the world are the same people to whom thousands of missionaries have been sent by so many missionary organizations and churches at such great cost in lives, careers, health and even money. Is it not reasonable to think that having become so much simpler with their coming to us, the church can initiate an effective and wide ranging missionary program to continue the work begun by generations of God's servants who worked and died in foreign lands all around the globe?

It is time for the traditional missionary societies to reorganize, in a way that, granted, may prove even more difficult than the task they already find challenging. Missionary activity does not have the urgent priority it had fifty or a hundred years ago. Many churches do not have a dynamic missionary society anymore, and the sense that there is a call to the lost in foreign fields is muted, even in those churches with a moderately active missionary orientation. Organizing, therefore, for both the foreign field and the home, will almost certainly prove challenging, to say the least. It may be that new organizations will have to be formed. But they will only be formed by people with a burning passion to reach out to the lost of this world. They will also, only be formed with a renewal of the practice of calling for workers, and not simply waiting for individuals to offer themselves for ministry. Further, they will only be formed when we as a church realize that these new migrants are not, and will never be, the "market" for new churches that are being built in our expanding suburbs for at least three generations.

The Call of God

Why should Christians go to the trouble of telling others about a different way of living? What right do we have to attempt to introduce those from other religions, or none, to see things the way we do? Quite frankly, isn't it a little insulting to tell another person that their religious system is inadequate? In a society where we are attempting to institute respect for all people and reduce ethnic and religious discrimination, isn't evangelism a return to intolerance and disharmony?

A response to these questions is found, in part, in outlining why we do not engage in evangelism. We do not attempt to tell others about Jesus Christ because we are better people, either morally, religiously, ethnically, or even spiritually, than they are. As odd as it may sound, we do not tell others about Jesus because our religious system is better than any other religious system. It is not a religious system that we seek to spread. Rather it is a relationship with God through Christ that is a gift of grace. Moreover, we do not seek to convert people, but rather we seek to introduce them to the Saviour who loves them, and wants to lead them to a life of peace and meaning, in Him. Rather than implicitly seeking to control other people's lives, we attempt to tell those we meet about the Saviour in order that they might discover a true and living freedom in Jesus. There are many reasons why we do not attempt to influence others towards faith in Christ, but the over-riding motivation for why we do is a love that seeks to share a relationship with a friend, that seeks, even passionately, to introduce them to the person who died for them.

We are all called to perform this evangelical role. The New Testament does not teach that it is the role of the clergy to spread the gospel. Indeed, biblically speaking there is no such thing as the division of the church into clergy and laity. St. Peter writes " Come, and let yourselves be built as living stones into a spiritual temple; become a holy priesthood to offer spiritual sacrifices acceptable to God through Jesus Christ…you are a chosen race, a royal priesthood." (1 Peter 2:5,9) According to these verses we are all priests in God's eyes. How one can accept this idea and then proceed to support a theology of a unique priesthood separate from the remainder of the church is difficult to understand. To do so involves an ignoring of the theology presented in the verse in Peter, and the construction of a contrary theology based upon particular interpretations of other passages, while suggesting an interpretation of the Petrine position not based upon its intrinsic semanticity. Yet this should not be the basis of division within the church. Rather, all of us, as Christians, can work together and respect the faith and spirituality, even of those who hold such views we find difficult to accept and understand, and who may passionately disagree with the logic of the above interpretation.

We are all called to serve God and represent him to the world. What does exist, however, is a variety of ministries that each in its different ways serves the body of Christ in order to make it strong, to edify it. It is true that we are all called to tell others about the saving grace of God in Christ, but some are called to specific full time "career" tasks within the church, and beyond it, in the spreading of the gospel. In New Testament times St. Paul was occasionally a tentmaker, but usually these days the clergy are supported by the local congregation or a specific organization, so that they can devote themselves completely to ministry. However, while one does not need a specific call to tell others about Jesus, one perhaps does need such a call to go to Brazil or some other far distant place, if only for one's own sense of certainty.

There are then, specific ministries to which God gives a special invitation. In 1 Samuel chapter three, God called Samuel while he was still quite young and acting as the servant of Eli the priest of God. Samuel was sleeping and hearing the voice of God, awoke and went to Eli, thinking he had called him. Eli told him that he had not. Samuel heard the voice once more, and Eli realized God was attempting to speak to Samuel and told Samuel what to say. Verse 10 relates, "The lord came and stood there and called, 'Samuel, Samuel' and Samuel answered, 'Speak, your servant hears you'", just as Eli had told him. From then on, as Samuel grew, the scriptures say none of his words were unfulfilled. Samuel didn't simply hear God's call. He placed himself at God's disposal.

This is not an age in which the church, to any significant degree, feels a strong sense of urgency about reaching the lost. At the services you attend make a note of the amount of time, and the frequency with which the services refer to reaching out to the lost. Does your congregation have a genuine and regular outreach service? What is most surprising is that this dearth of gospel preaching is clearly evident in churches that claim to be evangelical. If one listens to the service, one may be struck by how much time is spent in preaching about the spiritual life and problems of the believer, but how little time is devoted to either calls to the believer to serve in outreach ministry, or in specifically evangelistic sermons to the unconverted. In many churches, the Sunday night evangelistic service has been abandoned, and replaced by a youth service on Saturday night that, apart from catering only to one segment of the congregation, and only one section of the social demographic map generally, is frequently only a worship service under another name. Further, when it is evangelistic, the service is oriented almost solely to youth. Has the church simply given up on anyone above thirty?

Have the lost ceased being lost? Why have we decided that if the unconverted are not going to come to the Sunday night service on their own we will simply stop having the service? Or have we actually come to believe that the evangelistic service is so uninteresting, that people are not going to choose it over the Sunday night TV movies? It would seem more correct to believe, that if people are not coming to our services we should examine and confess our lack of spirituality to God, and admit that it is our failure to be Spirit filled that has caused this decline in attendance. If the book of Acts is to be believed, Spirit filled preaching is, if nothing else, not boring. Surely Acts is not suggesting that people became Christians because there was nothing better to accept?

When the Soviet Union collapsed it was not a state that was seen to have failed, but Communism itself. If evangelical churches continue in their decline, and fail to present the Gospel and the spiritual life in Christ effectively, to the extent that people no longer gravitate to these churches, then it will not simply be a church that is seen to have failed but, to a great degree, Christianity itself. As it is, the majority of the world does not take the historic churches seriously, and regards them as bastions of a past era, with certain aesthetic aspects that are worthy of praise, but having little or no spiritual consequence. This is not a criticism of the traditional denominations, for which I have a great affection and respect, but an appeal to evangelical churches to act and believe as genuine evangelicals, to go beyond the mere confession of evangelical orthodoxy to an experience of it. He that hath ears let him hear. Of course there are genuine Christians who long for, and genuinely do experience, the presence of God, but it is not to these faithful souls and congregations that this is addressed. Indeed, I would suggest, that if one's reaction to this paragraph is one of anger and frustration, this reaction in itself may be a proof that the comment on the general spirituality of the church is accurate.

Two closely related questions come to mind when thinking about the need to reach the lost, (a) what motivates one to go into all the world and preach the gospel, and (b) why should this have to be done? The first relates to the personality and character of the person going (or not going), and the second speaks about the nature of the people we have been told we should go to. Human beings, Christians included, are a self centred bunch. We are not motivated by the needs of others unless they are staring us in the face, in which case their need cannot be avoided, and it is true we generally attempt to respond to this need in compassionate ways. We appear to be locked in a "prison" of thought processes that simply do not see the needs of others. Our needs are real, and other people's problems are "words" that do not reach into our hearts. We see a homeless street person walk by, and are not particularly motivated to act in any fashion that would cause us to sacrifice, even our time.

However, to some degree, that experience is a key to why we fail to respond. The objective need of the person, whether it is psychological, economic or spiritual is simply not real to us. When preachers tell us the world is lost without Christ, we hear the words but they have no impact on our behaviour, no reality. Does it not seem reasonable to conclude that the spiritual lostness of the world has very little objectivity to us, partly because the spiritual dimension of the world has very little objectivity to us in the first place? And this is true even when we are religious or confess to be Christians. In such a case, how could the lostness of the sinner motivate any of us to action? Despite this, however, God can sometimes get to us in this regard, through the only area that we truly do regard as real: our own lives and our sense that we, for our own benefit need to be in a positive relationship with God.

This is a start, and God has always been kind towards us, and patient towards our spiritual limitations. As Christians we hear that we should be surrendered to him and discover that part of being surrendered is to obey the command to reach out to others with the gospel. We do not necessarily have any great love towards these others, but we see the need, if only as it relates to us in our need to be at peace with God. Please do not think this is a cynical attitude to the whole affair. Examine your own heart, and see to what degree this describes the thought processes you yourself undergo. The sinfulness of the human heart should not be a shock to a Christian. It is the realization of this sinfulness that leads us to faith in Christ. It is, on one level, simply a fact. The important point in all this is that unless lostness becomes "objective", or real to us , we are never going to be genuinely motivated to go out in to the world with the gospel.

It was suggested that God uses our self centredness to achieve his goal of reaching the lost. As we surrender our hearts to the Father we make steps to obey (him) by telling others about the saving work of Christ. This forces us into contact with people, the reality of whose lives we have no knowledge. These people, in sharing their stories of pain and failure, give dimension to the idea of lostness that begins to develop in our hearts and minds as a consequence of this contact. We find that we begin to feel pain at their suffering, and long for an answer to their need. Almost certainly, we begin to pray for them, for their salvation, and for the relief of their suffering. Thus, by essentially doing something for our own benefit, i.e. surrendering to God because we "should", we come to enter the lives of other people in a compassionate way that expands the boundaries of what we sense as real, and what we feel of others pain. There are several paths we must follow to be changed into the image of God, but I believe this is one of them.

If you will forgive a personal story, especially because my own life has more often than not failed to conform to the character of God, something interesting happened to me when I was in bible college. I was praying in my room one day, and asked God to give me love for other people. As soon as I had prayed this, a voice in my head, my consciousness, call it what you will, said to me "Go to the insane asylum." A few days before this, we students had been asked to volunteer to go to a mental institution the coming weekend. I had had no interest in such an activity, but didn't feel guilty about my lack of interest. I thought no more about the request until the "voice" spoke to me. Yes, I know, "Field of Dreams", "If you build it he will come." Anyway, I went, didn't really do much while I was there, and nothing happened. I have thought about this in the years since, and have come to believe that what God was trying to tell me, was that if you go to people, if you enter people's suffering, you will come to love them. It is as simple as that.

The second question asked was, "Why should we go out to preach the good news?" What is it about unbelievers that should make this a driving passion? Indeed, if it is not a passion, it is doubtful it will be engaged in with any seriousness or effectiveness. People can tell when you don't really care for them. Is that one of the reasons they have stopped coming to our churches?

Matthew 9:36-38 says," The sight of the people moved him (Jesus) to pity. They were like sheep without a shepherd, harassed and helpless; and he said to his disciples, 'the crop is heavy but the laborers are scarce; you must therefore beg the owner to send laborers to harvest his crop.'" The idea that the harvest is 'heavy' speaks of the vast mass of humanity, and that it is ready to be harvested. You do not send out the harvester to grain that is not ripe. According to Jesus, the world is ready, and even longing to be saved. This idea is repeated again in Luke 10:2, and again in John 4:35,36, which states, "Do you not say, "Four months more and then comes harvest"? But look, I tell you, look around on the fields; they are already white, ripe for harvest." The state of the harvest and the reaction this had on Jesus needs to be our attitude and our reaction as well. Why was Jesus moved to pity? Wasn't it the helplessness of the people? Do we see the people around us as helpless and without a shepherd? God forgive us for the hardness of our hearts.

The suffering of the lost was one of the great motivations of Jesus' behaviour. He went out to them, to where they were, spoke to them, expressed his love for them, and spoke the words of life to sinners. Luke 4:16-21 includes the words of Isaiah, spoken by Jesus in the synagogue, "The Spirit of the Lord is upon me because he has anointed me; he has sent me to announce the good news to the poor, to proclaim release for prisoners and recovery of sight for the blind, to let the broken victims go free, to proclaim the year of the Lord's favour....He began to speak, "Today, in your very hearing, this text has come true." There is nothing legalistic about this speech. There is no heaviness of an obligation one would rather not take up. There is a sense of what it means to be away from God and the suffering that this entails, and there is a heart full and overflowing with love for those who are in this state.

And who is in this state? Who are the ones to whom this longing to heal is directed? It is sinners; people who would cheat you if there was a chance; people who accumulate wealth for themselves and have no concern at all that in another part of town a family cannot find enough money to buy the food to eat for the next meal; it is the person who grasps at political power and walks over the lives and bodies of people to achieve this goal; it is the child who hates a parent, and for good reason, and the wife who hates the husband, also for good reason; it is the husband who causes all this hatred because of the suffering and hatred that also exist within his own heart. It is the person who knows there must be something better in life, and yet can never achieve it, and the one who longs for goodness, but knows also the bitterness of continual moral failure. It is you and I, who know that without forgiveness we would forever be unable to come into God's presence, as it was also the people who would later arrest Jesus, betray him, and nail him on a cross. In the divine words of Charles Wesley,

> And can it be that I should gain
> An interest in the Saviour's blood
> Died he for me who caused his pain
> For me who him to death pursued
> Amazing love, How can it be
> That thou my God shouldst die for me?

Jesus had a love for the lost that was so true and strong that he was willing to go to the cross and suffer death and the weight of humanity's sin and suffering, in order for this love to overcome evil, and redeem those he loved. Do we see the lost in anywhere near a similar way?

To go into God's harvest we need to see the harvest in the same state of need as Jesus did. How would we feel if we had a thousand dollars and knew that a certain stock was going to increase fifty or a hundred fold, and yet did nothing? (For the moment forget insider trading laws.) What a wasted opportunity that would be. The way Jesus sees the world is that it is like a field ready to be harvested, but with not enough workers to bring in the crop. Without these workers the risk is that this plentiful crop, or part of it will also be wasted. We are still confronted with Jesus words spoken to his disciples. There are still not enough workers to go out to reach the lost and suffering world. The world still cries out in need, and the desperate scarcity of workers still remains.

The truth is, you see, that unless a Christian breaks the silence, and tells the story of forgiveness to a lost and hurting world, it will never know that God has met their need in Jesus, and has provided, not just forgiveness, but also freedom from the power of sin. How clearly the necessity to go is expressed by St. Paul in Romans, chapter 10:

> For there is no difference between the Jew and the Greek:
> for the same Lord over all is rich unto all that call upon him.
> For whosoever shall call upon the name of the Lord shall be saved.
> How then shall they call on him in whom they have not believed?
> And how shall they believe in him of whom they have not heard?
> And how shall they hear without a preacher?
> And how shall they preach unless they are sent?
> As it is written, 'How beautiful are the feet of them that preach
> the gospel of peace, and bring glad tidings of good things. (vv 12-15)

We are all commissioned to take this gospel of peace to the people around us, to our neighbours, and to those in the cities down river, and across the prairies and mountains. We are commissioned to take the good news of reconciliation to lands and people far away, and who may speak another language to ours. And if they come from around the globe to our neighbourhood and land, we are commissioned to tell them this good news here as well. "How beautiful are the feet of them that preach the gospel of peace."

God is looking for people who love him, and desire with all their heart to serve him. It is usually to these people that God speaks, telling them what he wants them to do. One of the most powerful calls by God is found in Isaiah 6: 1-9. Isaiah sees a vision of the Lord and in great fear because of his sinfulness, thinks that he is about to be destroyed. "Woe is me! I am lost, for I am a man of unclean lips and I live among a people of unclean lips." An angel comes and touches his lips with a glowing coal saying, "See this has touched your lips; your iniquity is removed and your sin is wiped away." There is no one who is worthy to speak the things of God to other sinful people. We will never be good enough to take the holy things of God and present them to a lost world. If you imagine you are not good enough to be God's messenger, either in personal witnessing, or as a missionary, or in some clergy related role, you are completely correct. And you never will be worthy. But our God is a god of forgiveness. The Father has sent Jesus to make us what we could never be by our own efforts. Jesus gives us a worthiness, his own worthiness, so that we can stand before him in confidence, and so that we can speak of his holiness and love without fear.

The angel told Isaiah that his sins had been removed, and this is what has happened to us as believers in Christ. Then, having forgiven Isaiah God gave him a chance to offer himself in service. The Lord of Hosts (the way God is named in this chapter) did not say to Isaiah "Go for me!" Rather, in admittedly anthropomorphic language, we hear God thinking aloud. Verse eight says, "Then I heard the Lord saying, Whom shall I send? Who will go for me?" God gave Isaiah a choice. He did not try to force Isaiah. He does not try to force us. He asks, and waits for us to offer ourselves. We may have an experience similar to Isaiah's. Or we may hear or read this very piece of scripture, and feel that God is specifically speaking to us from this text that has been passed down through the millenia. It could even be that we want to serve God, and this text serves as a confirmation that our desire conforms to the will of God. Or we may experience a growing and uneventful conviction that we should offer ourselves to the church, and so be called in such a quiet way that is totally different from this dramatic story in Isaiah.

There are many reasons to hear and obey the call of God to tell others of his saving power. These are reasons of love and fellow feeling for the lost, just as one was once lost also, and is even now, conscious of how far from the character of God one is still. But there is one more reason that must be added to this. This last is given without comment. Indeed, no comment is needed.

> The Lord came to me: Man I have made you a watchman for the Israelites. You will take messages from me and carry my warnings to them. If you do not warn a person to give up his wicked ways , and so save his life, the guilt is his. Because of his wickedness he will die, but I will hold you answerable for his death.. (Ezekial 3:16-18)

God waits for us to respond to his call. Isaiah says, "And I answered; Here am I; send me. He said, Go and tell this people." (Isa. 6:9) God uses sinful people, people who are willing to follow him, to take his message to the world. As Paul tells us in 2 Corinthians 4:7, "we have this treasure in earthen vessels." We are the earthen vessels, and the treasure is the gospel. Despite our failings, despite our unworthiness, God will use us if we are willing to follow him. Indeed, the fact is that God cannot use those who rely on their own strength, who see no reason to feel unworthy. The disciples were anything but perfect beings. Nevertheless, God can take the weak things of this world to do glorious things for his kingdom. We do though, need to agree to his call

Who are the Lost?

The question remains, nevertheless, as to who the lost actually are. There is a quite strong social disinclination to condemn anyone, and an assertion that someone is lost seems to many with these feelings, just such an accusation. The answer to the question, though, is quite inclusive. If I am going to describe one individual as lost, then I am forced to describe myself in just such terms as well. The answer is actually that we are all lost. The world is really divided into two groups, both of whom share many behavioural characteristics.

These two groups are the "it is so" group, and the "were it not so" group. The "were it not so" group has a relationship with God based solely on a gift of righteousness (goodness) made possible by the death and suffering of Christ who took the sins of the world into himself on the cross. Were it not for this sheer gift of God we would be eternally alienated from God because of our sinful natures and the plethora of our sins. This gift, and the new birth that occurs when we are reconciled with God, are the sole reason we can claim to have a relationship of peace with God. The "it is so" group are lost, unfortunately in a much more critical sense, because they have as yet not realized the need and wonder of the gift of God in Christ. They are 'so' because they are indeed alienated from the source of goodness, both as a perfect gift, and in the transformative possibility that the indwelling Spirit of Jesus permits.

I can hear many saying, "Oh yes, but.." and I both understand and agree. Yet there is truth in this simple identification of all humanity in an ascription of lostness. Despite the fact that through faith in the saving work of Christ we are born again into the family of God as daughters and sons, ... the covering of righteousness that has been given us, and that allows us to come into God's presence with confidence, as it were, "as Jesus", does just that. It covers. So much of our mind, our behaviour, the way we feel, our reactions to other people, the deep hurts we carry around inside us, so much of us is really unholy ground. We know God to a truly shallow degree, we have an absolutely tiny faith, and our ignorance of how God actually wants us to live in this world is humblingly huge. To that degree, and in that sense, we Christians are also lost.

And yet, it is also true, in the way that a person rescued from a burning building is now safe from a terrible death, that Christians are in this sense, no longer lost. And it is also true that in this sense, those who have not yet put their trust in Jesus are still in that burning building. They are still lost.

Some people feel that if Christ has died and solved the problem of sin, then all are already saved as a result of this salvific work. There are then no genuinely lost people, but only those who have not realized or discovered their true spiritual state. If this is true, though, why do the Gospels and the Epistles repeatedly speak of acts of faith that lead to forgiveness and salvation? Indeed, if salvation is already everyone's, simply by what Christ did, why did the apostles go to so much trouble, even to the point of martydom, in a spreading of the good news? (Acts 8: 1-17; 1 Cor. 9: 1-27, et al.) Further, why was the baptism in the Holy Spirit seen as evidence that the people who experienced this must have experienced the new birth (Acts 10:44-48), the implication being that not everyone had experienced the new birth? John 1:10-13 states that people became children of God as a result of seeing Jesus as the Messiah (see verses 10,11, and 12). This is not described as an intellectual understanding but rather as a new and spiritual birth.

Moreover, that there remained the necessity for a turning in faith, even after the crucifixion and resurrection, is seen in Peter's sermon on the day of Pentecost. Peter, in response to the crowd's asking what they could do to avoid displeasing God, says to them, "Repent and be baptized every one of you in the name of Jesus the Messiah for the forgiveness of your sins." (Acts 2; 37,38) Clearly the forgiveness was dependent on their repentance and faith in Jesus (after all they were to be baptized in his name). If salvation is the blanket gift of God to the world, in the sense of a standing before God, irrespective of what the individual thinks of Jesus, then repentance and faith are not necessary.

This does not, however, seem to be the case. The early chapters of the book of Romans, and particularly chapter ten, teach that reconciliation with God follows an act of faith, and that this faith has a definite conceptual content that needs to be accepted, in order for this new status to be achieved. Verses 13 and 14 state, "For whoever shall call upon the name of the Lord shall be saved. How then shall they call on him in whom they have not believed? And how shall they believe in him of whom they have not heard?" It is completely true that the experience of reconciliation is universally available, but for that reconciliation to become personal, one is required to accept this offer in an expression of faith. However, though this is a condition on which all else is dependent, a requirement without which no relationship with God is possible, it has nothing to do with the number of people who will experience this.

If, in that case, the experience of repentance and faith is necessary in order to be reconciled with God (and whatever other results there are as part and parcel of this experience) then without this spiritual 'change' one can quite accurately be described as being 'lost'. Of course this term is metaphorical, and there are other words that could be used to describe the state of being separated from God (another metaphor). Nevertheless, "lost" is an exceedingly good description, and one that fits, not just those who have never experienced the new birth, but also us who, in much of our, at times very confused lives, have only begun to know the God who cared enough for the lost to die for them.

Chapter 14
FAITH

For a Christian, one of the most important concepts in the New Testament is faith. Indeed, one New Testament verse bluntly states, "without faith it is impossible to please Him (God)" (Hebrews 11:6). If faith is so important, what is it, and why are we continually confessing that our faith is so small? We are taught to pray in faith "for he who doubts must not expect the Lord to give him anything" (James 1:6,7). When the sick are prayed for, but do not recover, there is a desperate searching of the heart to see if there was sufficient faith, or whether doubt had remained secretly hiding in the recesses of the mind while faith statements were repeatedly expressed. Moreover, the possession or lack of possession of faith is taught to be crucial to the healthy spiritual life of the believer. Apart from congregational preachers, church teachers ranging from St. Thomas Aquinas, to Blaise Pascal and Søren Kierkegaard have attempted to define or explain its operation in the life of the Christian for centuries.

Surrounded as we are in North America, Europe and other traditionally Christian countries by centuries of

Christian tradition, we in the church usually take for granted a belief in shared doctrines, without questioning why these doctrines are so readily believed. The people of the Mediterranean in St Paul's day would not have been so quick to make this judgement. Their cultural and religious beliefs were not like ours, and St Paul's message would have struck very few cultural chords they could have identified with. Yet the church was founded in this alien environment, and grew to dominate its religious landscape. Why did people come to believe the gospel at the beginning of the Christian era? Why, in fact, do we? Dangerous as it may be to suggest such a thing, it seems reasonable to believe that the faith of most people is paper thin, and continues only because no serious threat to this belief has occurred in most people's lives.

If one reads 1 Corinthians 2:3-5, Paul believed that the converts to 'his' gospel believed because the Holy Spirit had made the truth of the ridiculously sounding words he spoke, real. According to Paul, the faith of these early Christians was based on the revelation of the Spirit to their hearts and minds. Why do we believe the Christian teachings? What life changing reasons do we have for our faith?

A discussion of faith is a discussion of the hidden trails of the human heart. It has been categorized both as different from knowledge, and not an emotion. That, it seems, does not leave faith much room in which to maneuver. Its presence in the heart can be evidenced in the achieving of the goal asked for from God. On the other hand, one may possess faith without receiving what was asked for. In addition, one person cannot evaluate the degree of faith existing in another individual, and at times even the person who possesses faith may be unsure if she or he actually has faith. With such vagueness and lack of certainty, while being held in such high existential importance by the church, it is no wonder we are so troubled as to the amount of faith we possess.

If faith is defined as something one believes, though there is no evidence for such a belief, then faith is definitely not knowledge. However, if knowledge is the deeply held psychological sense of the trueness of an idea, with that idea based primarily on sense data and rational thinking that is theoretically verifiable or reproducible, such as in mathematics and physics, then if nothing else, both faith and knowledge exist as psychological states. Moreover, if faith is *not* a belief in something for which there is *no* evidence, then faith and knowledge may come even closer together as states of mind based upon human experience. I will ignore the difficulties of epistemology (the ideas relating to how we come to know) because it is questionable that there is any philosophical consensus as to whether knowledge is possible at all. Ignoring the issue does not imply a scorning of the philosophical dilemma, but rather is a movement to an appeal to the common sense that, despite the real problems associated with "knowing", there *are* things that can be known.

Were this not correct, at least to some degree, we would not be able to function. We would not be able to get into our cars with any sense of confidence that the seat would actually support us, that the engine would turn over, once again, and that there would actually be the location we predict will be there when we drive over the roads we believe are the paths to this location, and that the complexity of social relationships we believe we have, actually exist. And behaviours and attitudes at this level of knowledge would have to include those acted upon by philosophers who somehow get to class rooms at universities to teach, despite any theoretical hesitations they may possess. Epistemological doubt is not a joke, but one must continue to live, and we do this based upon a vast array of simple and complex interdependent beliefs about the nature of the world, that we call knowledge.

The definition of a belief derived from this position, therefore, is that a belief which qualifies as knowledge is something that is held to be true based upon repeated experience. For the purposes of the definition, it is irrelevant as to the number of people holding a set of beliefs as to its truth or falsity. That a million people believe my car exists does not make the car either real or not real, any more than that a million people at one time believed the world was flat. From this definition it also follows that what we currently hold to be knowledge (in contradistinction to belief, as commonly understood) is also, in fact, a set of beliefs. That something is said to be an object of knowledge, is thus a matter of belief, and though there still remain certain ideas that can be understood as beliefs in the traditional sense of an idea for which no evidence is proposed, that which presently passes for knowledge does not necessarily exist on a significantly firmer, or different foundation than what may be termed religious beliefs. Devising a method for testing the veracity of a belief, beyond the definition given above, is not within the purview of this section, or the skill of the writer. Rather, that caveat notwithstanding, a simple point is asserted: that though there are claims to knowledge that are unjustified, as based, for instance, merely on opinion or tradition, there are some things about which one can say one has knowledge.

Knowledge is inextricably connected to the ideas of time and predictability. We may know that the sun came up yesterday, but to predict that the sun will come up tomorrow cannot be an object of knowledge but of expectation and probability. I may know a person's character, but I would be predicting a certain reaction to state what that person's reaction to an event will be in the future. Can expectations based on past events and past analysis be classified as knowledge? It is certainly true that a statement about the character of God based on no experience of such a characteristic is only the expression of belief. However, if one has a deep, ongoing experience of God that has led to insights into the nature of God, does that allow one to express statements as to the character of God as knowledge?

Perhaps, at least part of the answer to these questions can be found in the experience of the continuance of existence that we possess. The fact that a person can read these lines implies that life, for that person, has continued. The world also has continued for ages (let that statement be enough to signify great length of time), and as long as other humans continue with us we can expect that what they are will continue in roughly predictable ways also, along with the earth. The point is that, though it may be a rough thesis, the continuance of existence justifies the making of predictions about possible future events and situations based upon past experience and reflection on this experience. What I know about my friend will, in all likelihood, remain true for the foreseeable future. In this fashion we can possess knowledge from the past that allows us to make statements regarding the future. That these predictions and characterizations can not strictly be called knowledge, based as they are on tenuous ground to start with, perhaps is not important. They are as near to knowledge as humans can aspire, and given those limitations, there is no reason not to call them knowledge.

While it is true that knowledge of all kinds is epistemologically problematic, we continue to hold to a vast array of perceptions of the universe with a deep certainty, and appear to function successfully as we employ these beliefs. This situation being the case, it should not be unduly problematic to assert spiritual facts with as much certainty, given conditions of experience that are similar to the ways we come to knowledge in other areas. If it is granted, for example, that I can know that the structure I sit on, all things being equal, possesses physical characteristics which will support my body, then surely it is also possible that I can know spiritual things with an equal degree of certainty, also because of a variety of kinds of experience.

All knowledge is mediated through the mind, and is derived from a variety of human experiences. However, not all knowledge is reproducible and verifiable, independently of the human mind. Love is not verifiable externally, nor is fear. Biological signs may suggest such states but they do not, so far, positively indicate them. Nevertheless, if one were to limit knowledge only to those events that can be reproduced in laboratory conditions, this would reduce the practical and existential experience of knowing unrealistically. On the other hand, though it is admitted that knowledge is mediated mentally, the objects of our knowledge are derived in a variety of ways, some from "purely" mental activities, and others from incursions external to the mind, such as falling down a set of stairs. Nevertheless, it is not simply the degree of certainty that is important in affirming that one has knowledge. Indeed, certainty can be the product of a delusional mind. If experience is derived, however, from a multiplicity of sources, and in a variety of ways, only some of which are mental, it would seem reasonable to assert that one may well be justified in asserting that one has knowledge, and surely this could include a knowledge of God.

If the only evidences for the supernatural, for the existence of God, were derived from our mental activities we would probably have cause to be concerned. If the concepts we hold to be true exist only, and receive verification only from our own, or other's mental processes, what reason have we, not to question those religious concepts, or not to wonder if they are not the product of our own highly complex rational processes? In addition, that certain religious experiences are similar in different religions may not imply that there is a spiritual reality which is behind and shared by all these religions, but rather that the human mind is capable of producing similar experiences when put into similar psycho-physical situations. The complexity of an experience that appears to be religious does not guarantee that the source of that experience is God. One has only to remember the complexity of one's dreams to realize the creative potential of the human mind.

However, does this mean that all mentally based experiences lack genuine spiritual content? Surely such a conclusion would be as unreasonable as suggesting that rational and scientific errors imply that solid scientific knowledge is also impossible. The possibility of error does not logically lead one necessarily to the impossibility of true conclusions. In support of this line of thought, the fact remains that the revelation of God to the world has always been on a multi-dimensional level, and never solely via the mind. Indeed, a Christianity that limits itself to the mental aspects of the faith does so at its peril. From faith and epistemological positions, a Christianity that ignores or excludes the intrusion of God into the world, particularly into the contemporaneous, both misses the verificational benefits of this "intrusion", and also limits the experience of real faith in the believer to a minimal and potentially dangerous level. The faith of a "Christian" whose only reason for belief is tradition, or a solely mentally mediated experience, in an environment of stress, persecution, or separation from similar believers, eventually finds it difficult or impossible to maintain such a faith, unsustained, as it is, by any believable verification from God.

The revelation of God, by God, to the believer, whereby the believer comes to know the person of God, with as much certainty as we know and hold the reality of the world around us, places in the believer a knowledge of God that is the certain foundation for New Testament behaviour, on both the individual and social levels. If one knows God, this will change the way one acts in the world.

What then is faith? Is it not the cognitive response to data, from God, that gives one an understanding and knowledge of the being behind the word "God"? Is it not a confidence in the creator that (he) will do what he says he will do, and that he will answer prayer in ways similar to those described in both the Old and New Testaments? Faith is the psychological response we have to God, based on the knowledge we have of the creator as a person who can be trusted, and who has both absolute power and unending love (for what other kind of personality would justify such trust?). If one does not know God, how can one even pretend to have faith in him? We need to become correctly scriptural here. Knowing God does not simply mean having taken Jesus as one's Saviour. Knowing God means knowing God, just as you know the friend you can trust, just as you know your car will(or will not) take you where you want to go. Knowledge of God may be begun by a scriptural statement, but it is derived from ongoing experiences of God that potentially involve the whole range of living.

Knowing God should have as much certainty to it as knowing that snow is cold, and that the government will tax you each year. And surely it should be, and at best, can be as equally taken for granted, and not continually exist as a matter of question. Faith should be as solid a part of our intellectual and emotional understanding of reality as any other part of our thinking. Why do we imagine that knowing God should be something one is not sure of? Why should faith be seen as a perpetual struggle? Is this how Jesus operated with God? Does the scripture teach us that God does not want to be known? If, as St John states, "perfect love casts out all fear", how would such love be possible if there was not a very clear understanding and knowledge of God's love that went far, far beyond a mere conceptual possession of that fact. Indeed, if one does not possess such an existential knowledge of God, how can one, with certainty, call religious beliefs, facts at all?

The sad truth is that we have such weak faith because we have such a weak knowledge of God. If one knew that God was incredibly powerful, would one doubt that power? If one knew that God was perfect love, would one doubt that love? Acts of faith in God are simply the exercise, the operation of a knowledge of God. It seems that the question of whether we have faith or not, in the present stage of our lives where we really do not know God at the level of knowledge, is determined by the balance between any faith that we do possess, and the massive unbelief which exists inside us in regards to God, in that pagan part of our personalities that has not been transformed by the Spirit of God. When Peter walked on the water he certainly was exercising faith, but the unbelief that also existed in him won out over his faith, and Jesus had to rescue him. Because we have such a shallow knowledge of God, what we experience as normal, is similar to what Peter experienced on the lake when he started to sink. Though it is doubtful we could have mustered even as much faith as Peter did.

Jesus' description of the disciples, "O ye of little faith", is not intended to be the normal Christian experience. Don't you agree? It is not doubts that make our prayers ineffective. Rather, it is that the doubts overwhelm our faith and swamp it. The man needing Jesus' healing for his child admitted he had doubt as well as faith, but Jesus did not say to him, "O well, sorry, I can't do anything for you." Nor did Jesus let Peter sink into the lake when his doubts overcame him.

Finally, the words of Jesus on the cross must be taken into consideration. At his time of absolute suffering, Jesus cried out " My God, my God, why have you forsaken me?" We cannot know what Jesus was thinking, but clearly the enormity of the experience had shattered Jesus' confidence in the rightness of what was going on. At that moment, Jesus did not see the universe as "unfolding as it should".

The cry is an expression of doubt so huge, so tidal wavingly huge, he had lost control of the compass that had guided his entire life up to that point. If Jesus could experience doubt, then it is not so horrendous that we have our own supply of them, and not sinful that our mind cannot see the hand of God in what is happening in our lives. If the Son of God can wonder where and why God had disappeared, then we should not be condemned, nor condemn ourselves, for having doubts regarding the things of God, either theoretically or in the happenings of our lives.

God is not unaware that we do not trust him. And do we really believe that God wants to make life difficult, and is unwilling to reveal himself to us so that we know that he is what the scriptures say he is? In most of the world, including our particular part of it, God is almost absolutely absent and unheard. You may have been taught that God and his character are obvious to the sincere heart and mind, but if this were so the character of God would not be a contentious point, even among Christians. The existence of the world suggests a God, but it does not prove it. The beauty of the world is balanced by the destructiveness of the universe. To attempt to see the character of God from the creation one is forced, either to ignore the negative and destructive aspects of creation, or to provide a theological explanation of evil that an unbeliever could not be expected to hold as self evident.

This lack of evidence results in an almost complete absence of a knowledge of God, and makes faith virtually impossible. If it is true that without faith it is impossible to please him (God), it is also equally true that without a lived knowledge of God it is impossible to have faith. The unhappy truth is that we do not have faith in God, because we do not know God. Each of us must discover that God is a good and gracious God for ourselves. An intellectual "knowledge" of God's goodness is as motivating as knowing that the earth is round. Indeed, I would suggest that most of what we call knowledge of God is not knowledge at all.

If we truly did know the love of God we would not act as if the world were a dismal place in which to exist. If we truly did know that God loves us, our fears would dissipate like the fog with the coming of the sun. If we had a genuine faith in God that came from knowledge of him, we could well say to "this mountain ..Be moved, and it would be so" You cannot increase that which does not exist.

We are usually taught to deny our doubts, to act in faith, and regard our lack of certainty as unimportant. The scriptures do not necessarily teach such a mindless acceptance. Few would doubt that Elijah is one of the great spiritual giants in the Old Testament. With Moses he appeared to Jesus on the Mount of Transfiguration. The bible says that rather than dying he was taken directly to heaven on a chariot of fire. Beginning 1 Kings chapter 17 the bible relates how Elijah, acting alone as the representative of God, assembled the prophets of Baal, and that fire came down from heaven and burnt up Elijah's sacrifice. Moreover, after he had predicted that there would be no rain until he (Elijah) said there would be, he prayed for rain, and God sent rain to the dry land of Israel. At the time of the drought, Elijah was told by God to journey to the seacoast, to Sidon, where he stayed with a widow and her son. In the course of time, the son grew ill and died. This is what the scripture says with certain emphases added,

> Then she said to Elijah, 'What made you interfere, you man of God? You came here to bring my sins to light and kill my son!' 'Give me your son' he said. He took the boy from her arms and carried him up to the roof chamber, where his lodging was, and laid him on his own bed. Then he called out to the Lord, O LORD MY GOD, IS THIS THY CARE FOR THE WIDOW

WITH WHOM I LODGE, THAT THOU HAST BEEN SO CRUEL TO HER SON?' Then he breathed deeply upon the child three times and called on the Lord. O Lord my God, let the breath of life, I pray, return to the body of this child. The Lord LISTENED to Elijah's cry, and the breath of life returned to the child's body.

"O Lord is this thy care that thou hast been so cruel?" Now this does not seem like the words of a spiritual giant. He questions God, definitely a no no in today's "faith-filled" church. Whatever you do, you can not question God. Isn't this what we are repeatedly taught? But this is exactly what Elijah, the man of God, does. Indeed, he not only questions God's freedom to act but also God's loving character, "O Lord, is this thy care?". He also imputes cruelty to God.

We could simply say that Elijah was wrong to impugn God in this way. His theology was in error, and we know better. I'm sorry to say this, but I don't think we do know better. Our knowledge of God is mostly in our heads, and as far as Elijah is concerned, I think it is safe to say he knew God better than most of us do. But that is not the important point. What is interesting is the attitude of God to Elijah's doubts. God did not attack him for believing incorrectly, or even for imputing some degree of evil to the Godhead. Elijah functioned, within his relationship with God, doubts and probably anger, and all. His doubts did not stop his interaction with God, and God did not refuse to answer Elijah's prayer.

We do not need to deny our doubts. God is not horrified by them. In fact he knows we have them even if we are not willing to admit them. Despite what we have been taught about not questioning the character of God, scripture here indicates that God is quite capable of accepting that doubt is part of the ongoing spiritual walk, and that we are not struck down for having such thoughts. One last thing that we can learn from this passage is that doubt should not stop us seeking God and interacting with (him). One can over-evaluate, or perhaps it should be said, misinterpret the verse that says, "without faith it is impossible to please him." Elijah integrated his doubts into his relationship with God, and did not allow radical questions as to the character of God to stop this relationship, and neither did they stop God.

Indeed, it was not Elijah's confidence in the power of God that was at stake, but rather his confidence in the very character of God. This seems a much worse area to have doubts about than those regarding God's power. Though, it is doubtful we would even reach to that level of faith. Perhaps this is not how it really happened, but Elijah seems to have decided to present God with any doubts which generated conclusions that came to him, so that God would have a chance to answer them. Perhaps that is why he had so much faith. He did not deny his doubts and repress them, but rather brought them right out into the open before God, for God to deal with. And God seems to have done just that. It also must be remembered, however, that he took his relationship with God absolutely seriously, and was committed to his obligation of faithfulness to the covenant.

Elijah's confidence in God had a level of certainty that allowed him to act heroically. It is highly unlikely that Elijah made the altar, sacrificed the bull, poured huge amounts of water on and around the altar, and gathered the 450 priests of Baal, and then said to himself " I wonder if God will really do what I have in mind? I wonder if God really is as powerful as this plan requires?" Do we think his confidence in God mysteriously existed with no prior cause? If Elijah had not known God, prior to this event, to the same degree of certainty that he knew that pouring water on what was supposed to burn was a bad idea, he would never have confronted the prophets of Baal, by himself to prove whose God had power.

Elijah does not seem to have been a naturally brave person. Perhaps God had not told him what would happen after he had dealt with the prophets of Baal. He courageously confronts and then annihilates the Baal leadership, but when the queen threatens him he immediately runs off to escape her. If he had not been sure of God, it is highly unlikely he would have summoned Israel at all. Elijah's relationship with God gave him the faith to act in the heroic way he did. Without a knowledge of God the believer will not have faith. He or she will want to have faith, because this is what has been taught, but it will not be there. When Jesus said "if you have faith as a grain of mustard seed you will say…and it will be done", I do not think he was referring to the size of that faith, but merely to its reality.

As far as humans are concerned, the problem is not the amount of our faith, but the probability that it will not actually exist. To have faith means you trust God. To trust God you have to know God. To know God, God has to reveal (him)self to you. If God reveals himself to you, then to the degree, and in those areas that God has revealed himself, you will have faith. If one knows God, this knowledge is as impossible to deny as it would be to deny the existence of any object around you that you can see and feel. Just as the scripture says we love him because he first loved us, so we trust him because he first reveals himself to us as one who can be trusted.

We then act on that knowledge in the situations of life where God's presence and power are necessary. Faith is not believing something for which there is little or no evidence. I know my chair will support me, and believing this I sit on it. I have seen other people sit on it (the importance of the church in the faith life of the individual). I have sat on it myself, repeatedly, and it has supported me. It is something that by repeated experience I have come to have an unquestioned reliance on. One sits because one believes. Faith is simply the religious term for knowing what God is like, and acting on that knowledge.

What is truly amazing is that following a revelation of God, the result of which may be a previously unknown sense of faith in God, this new confidence may be quickly followed by an equally deep doubt as to the reliability of the God one was trusting, perhaps only moments earlier. To understand this flow back and forth between faith and doubt, it may be useful to recall the experience of falling in love. Each expression of love by the one loved brings an increasing sense of confidence in the lover that this love is returned. However, our confidence is fragile, and successive expressions of love that open one up further to the loved one, are usually accompanied by fear and a decided lack of assurance that the loved one will continue to respond in the positive fashion that has been experienced up to that point, in the face of these further expressions and self revelations. There is, in addition, a simultaneous fear that the love desired and previously expressed by the one loved may not be genuine, and that one has misunderstood the "attentions" of the loved one. Thus both faith and terrifying doubt coexist in the lover. This seems illogical, but it is a fairly accurate description of falling in love, nevertheless.

For those cynics of this wonderful and life affirming experience, all this will seem trivial. Yet, it explains the experience of coming to trust God fairly well. We do not begin with faith in God, and each revelation of God surprises us with its authenticity. With each discovery of the character of God our confidence in the dependability of the Godhead is strengthened. However, we have lived our lives not particularly aware of the active presence of God, just as we have lived our lives experiencing the lack of love in that sea of others in which we swim, so that it is a lack of love in others that we have "confidence" in, and a lack of the relevance of God that we have trust in. Indeed, it is this lack of love that makes it so difficult for us to believe in the continuity and depth of love that another seems to be giving to us. With other humans we fear to share both our love, and the truths about who we really are. We believe that this wonderful love is being given, and at the same time, are terrified that it is not.

When one comes to understand this, perhaps seemingly contradictory process, one should not be surprised to discover that the struggle to trust does not go unchallenged, either by the forces of darkness, or our own divided heart. Trusting another person, including God, is the result of coming to know that other person. If we do not know the other person well we will continue to question that trust. Faith in God, and in other people, is a matter of degrees of probability as to the dependability of that other person. This may not sound very spiritual, but in the experiencing of trust in another person, that is what it is. One may, in fact, be deluged with reasons to doubt. These "reasons" usually exist in the realm of possibility, and they can eat away at our trust in the other person. It is at this point that a decision to base one's confidence on the character of the person that has been revealed to us by them must be made. God understands our fears and lack of full knowledge and can strengthen us in these times of, what may well be an experience of incredible stress in relation to this trust. If we are able, we can commit our lives and situations to God so that he controls these, and then wait patiently for him to work. God does not despise an honesty before him that even includes doubts as to our having any real faith in him. Once again, God knows what is actually in our hearts.

It is this same dynamic that we experience when we begin to know God. It is this simultaneous experience of faith in God based on the revelation of himself to us, and an accompanying unbelief in God that has been our entire understanding of reality up to that point. The growth in true faith is no different from the growth in our confidence in the love of the one we love. In both our love for another person, and our discovery of God, surely only another kind of relationship of love, our trust and confidence progresses and deepens as hoped for expressions from the desired other are confirmed in word and action, our faith and confidence increasing as our fear and doubt grow less and less believable.

The experience of faith in God and the doubt that accompanies this is, it seems, qualitatively no different from virtually all our relationships with other human beings. Faith, expressed as either trust or unbelief, is the basis of all human relationships. Our confidence in others is dependent on the degree to which we know that their character is dependable or not. We have no real faith/confidence in those we do not know. We have partial confidence in those we have some reason to trust. And there is a third category made up of those, for one reason or another, we want to trust, and in which we suffer from a conflict between faith and doubt because we desire strongly to have our confidence confirmed in some kind of behaviour. It is love, or a similarly strong desire, which often "creates" the situation that reveals the conflict between faith and doubt to us and in us. However, all our dealings with people reveal a faith that is based on some level of knowledge of, or rational faith in the other person. Nevertheless, the struggle for faith, the struggle to believe the other, is made additionally more difficult by the terrible openendedness of life and language to misunderstanding.

Undesirable though it may appear to some, one of the foundations that human society is based on is a radical belief in the lack of love towards others that exists in all other human beings. It is this negative (not in the sense of not existing) faith that troubles all attempts to love. It is this negative faith that causes us to see undesirable intention in innocent behaviour. It is this negative faith which discovers lack of love, though no such lack exists, in words and actions, and even silence, in the one whose love is sought. Faith then, as the basis of all human interaction (even without misunderstandings) lives in a struggle between confidence in what has been revealed of a person (including God) and the unbelief and doubt that also exist because of previous experience and an incomplete knowing of the other person.

In this sense then, faith in God is not essentially different to the faith we employ towards the people we interact with each day. Just as our faith in our friend is dependent on a deepening knowledge of our friend's heart, so our faith in God depends on an ever deepening discovery of the heart of God. Thus, our faith in God will at times coexist with the doubt that comes from an imperfect knowledge of God, and will coexist with that well of unbelief in us as a result of the irrelevance of God in our lives up to the time he first found us. Over the centuries, faith has become a debated theological term, with the result that it has lost its simple and interpersonal meaning. Perceived in predominantly theoretical ways, an understanding of faith as a response to the revealing of one person to another, has virtually ceased to be considered.

The entertainer, Jewell has a beautiful line in one of her songs that says, "Have a little faith in me". We imagine we understand the line because we recognize each of the words as containing a certain meaning. Why, however, should this imagined other person have faith in her? Without reason there is no justification for making such an appeal, and no reason for having such a faith. If, nevertheless, (Jewell) has revealed herself to be someone who can be trusted (this does not need to be perfect trust, or a complete revelation of the self) then this faith she asks for is based on a knowledge of (her) that can overcome the calls of doubt and unbelief as to her dependability. We may then understand faith in God in a similar fashion.

One penultimate point, however, still needs to be made. It is in times of crisis, times of stress and need that we discover our need for God. In these times, in our time of need (unless, of course, one continues to attempt to convince oneself that one has a faith one may not, in fact, possess) that we unwillingly find ourselves given the possibility of actually experiencing God. In such times we may become unpleasantly aware of the depth of our unbelief and doubt, even a radical doubt that most of us have a passion to deny to ourselves. In these times, specifically in these times, we can and should be honest with God. We can share the depth of this doubt we are experiencing with the lover of our soul, and ask God, probably desperately, that we need his guidance, intervention and grace if we are to survive. Existing at times in a struggle with doubt and unbelief, we turn our mind and heart's attention to what we know of God from the revelation we have of him to our hearts by the Holy Spirit. Faith is not a cold theological term but a warm, living, psychologically active experience. We have faith in what we know to be true, not in what we are simply told is true.

This dynamic psychological experience may, however, in some experiences be almost terrifying. In Genesis, beginning with chapter 12, we discover Abraham's journey of faith. In chapter 15 God promises Abraham a child who would be his heir. Sarai, Abraham's wife, was infertile. The problem was not an unimportant one for the two of them. Culture, the inheritance of Abraham's wealth, and even shame at not being able to produce children obviously caused them great suffering. The matter was so important that Sarai offered Abraham her slave girl as a concubine so that a child born to the girl could be thought of as Sarai's. This hunger for a child was not a superficial wish. Social respect, the continuation of one's name and family line, and even the human hunger for parenthood ate away at their hearts unsatisfied. And then God came to Abraham and said, "Your heir shall be a child of your own body." God took Abram (Abraham's original name) outside and said, "Look up into the sky, and count the stars if you can. So many shall your descendants be." (Gen. 15: 4,5)

Fantastic! Abraham has a promise from God. No worries. The next verse, however, tells us "Abram put his faith in the Lord, and God counted that faith to him as righteousness." (v 6) Why, "however"? Abraham and his wife are elderly. She is past the child bearing age. This is the one thing they passionately want. What if it does not happen? After God "goes away" Abraham is left with the reality of the world around him. What he can see is what the world has always been without the intervention of God. What does he know that could possibly give him a reason to believe such a promise? If he chooses to believe God, he does so with all the futile reality of how the world actually works swirling around inside his head. Abraham wasn't the infallible bible character of perfect faith and no inner turmoil. When he went to new locations he would get his wife to say she was his sister so he would not be killed by covetous foreigners. Do we imagine God accounted Abraham's faith as righteousness because this faith was just so easy for Abraham he couldn't have done anything else but believe God? The whole world of impossibility roared around in Abraham's heart, every day telling him of the stupidity of such a faith, telling him that he was deluding himself, and that nothing would come of his trust. God attributed Abraham's faith as righteousness because it existed, and continued to exist in the flames of doubt and terror at the stupidity of such a faith. Each day Abraham had to seek strength from God, and remind himself that God had actually spoken to him. Each silent day that seemed to prove that his faith was pointless, Abraham had to focus on the revelation and not the apparent reality of life, a reality that included his still infertile wife.

How else can we understand the next statement Abraham utters, "O Lord God, how can I be sure that I shall occupy it (the land)?" (v 9) Do we imagine that Abraham had no doubts? Abraham then makes a sacrifice and waits. All day he waits and nothing happens. Birds of prey (symbolic of doubts and fears, if nothing else) swoop down on the sacrifice to eat it. And he drives them away. He does this all day and still nothing happens. The sun begins to go down and Abraham falls into a deep sleep or trance, "and behold horror and great darkness fell upon him", as the NKJ puts it. Why might this have happened? Could it have been that the struggle to continue trusting had exhausted him, and his fears had overwhelmed him so that he could not stand? It was not necessarily that he gave in to them, but that they were simply more than he could cope with without the help of God. It was at this point, when he could endure no more, that God spoke to him.

You are free to interpret this as horror at the news that his descendants would be slaves, if you wish, but this does not say anything about the darkness, or even take seriously the situation Abraham had been in for hours, and that must have been exhausting, if only from a physical point of view. I think Kierkegaard got it right when he described Abraham's experience as "fear and trembling". The passionless, almost entirely intellectual relationship we have with God, in which we never find ourselves at the end of our intellectual, physical and spiritual resources does not describe a biblical experience of coming to know God. I think, also, that at such times, and in specific situations, we cannot endure, and we will not continue to have faith, unless God comes to us, as the sun goes down, and as we are overcome by a reality that does not include God. And each of us must find this

God who comes to us in our darkness, in our time of despair, and strengthens us.

This outline is the general principle dealing with both what faith is, and how it is achieved. If it were easy to achieve this degree of insight there would, in all likelihood, be no problem either with regard to the nature of faith or its outworking. The key to the developing of faith is, on the surface, really quite simple. A deepening relationship with God, which really means coming to know God, results from time spent before God in prayer, and in waiting silently in his presence. It is this that is the problem for most of us. We do not spend time with God, and the time we do spend is brief. We come to God in the way we come to McDonalds or KFC, to the drive thru window. We don't want to spend time in prayer, and we want immediate answers from the short time we do spend.

God forgive us for the ignorance and short-sightedness of our hearts. This short-sightedness, of course, is one more evidence that we really do not see God as honestly and truly relevant to our lives. Moreover, it shows that we really have an incredibly small perception of God. In fact, it comes very close to revealing a level of thinking that does not genuinely believe in the existence of God at all. Our behaviour honestly reveals what we truly believe, and our lack of prayer reveals that a sense of the reality of God is not one of the pieces of information that is involved in most of our decision making. Despite our protestations to the contrary, we Christians are, in the main, atheists in our hearts.

Claiming that Christians are atheists may appear odd and a little ridiculous. However, this is not an assertion that there is no genuine faith at all in the hearts of Christians, but rather, that in most of our beings, we are, in reality, atheists with no faith. If the faith to be saved were evidence that one had perfect faith there would be no discussion on the topic. There would be a spiritual level in the church that would be glorious, and God would be freely manifested to all around us. A New Testament description of the church would be the description of the church in our day.

One should imagine the human heart as territory that begins to be transformed (conquered) with the new birth, but which is clearly enemy territory in the main. Those parts of us that have been transformed by the grace of God view reality through the eyes of God. However, those vast parts that are not, view existence through the eyes of the unbeliever. It is not words alone, but words and actions that prove we have faith. This is not an argument asserting that salvation is by both faith and good works. Indeed, the epistle of James describes the situation quite well. If we say we have faith but we have no actions that support this claim, it is doubtful we have genuine faith. As James notes, when the people he gave as examples really believed, this faith was followed by an action that verified (not added to) this faith.

All that is being claimed here is that what we claim is faith, given a lack of results, does not appear to be genuine. This is not a mild claim. Our actions, or more correctly, lack of actions, prove we have very little faith. Describe this situation any way you will, but it must be described accurately, or we will, almost certainly, never get beyond our weakness. And it is decidedly possible to do just that.

It *is* definitely possible to discover the power and reality of God. St Paul in 1 Corinthians chapter 2 states, "The word I spoke, the gospel I proclaimed, did not sway you with subtle arguments; it carried conviction by spiritual power so that your faith might be built upon the power of God." According to this passage it is the revelation of the things of God by the Spirit of God that generates faith. As Paul goes on to state, "God has revealed (these things) to us through the Spirit." (v 10) and, "Only the Spirit of God knows what God is. This is the Spirit we have received from God, so that we may know all that God of his own grace has given us." (v 12).

What God wants to reveal is not only interpretations of the scripture, but even more so, Himself. If we are to have a workable faith it must be based on a knowledge of the God of the scriptures, not the scriptures. We do not have a relationship to a book but to a person. And the Spirit desires that we know that person intimately. As verse 11 tells us, "Among people, who knows what a person really is, but the person's own spirit. In the same way, only the Spirit of God (an identification of the Spirit with God) knows what God is." Not only do we, without qualification, need to know God in order to have the kind of faith that is grounded on knowledge, the Holy Spirit, who dwells in the heart of the Christian, wants us to have this kind of knowledge, so that we *do* have such a faith.

Before we conclude this look at faith, however, there is one kind of exception that must be considered. In 1 Corinthians 12, Paul lists the Gifts of the Holy Spirit. Among those gifts is "the gift of faith". In the same way that the other gifts should not be thought of as simply talents different individuals possess, and indeed are possessed by non-Christians as well, so the gift of faith is not simply an almost accidental quality someone possesses. Rather, these gifts are specific abilities that the individual does not naturally have but are given to the person for the building up of the church. These gifts should not be confused with natural talents, which are the result of a combination of genetics and the social environment one has experienced. Non-Christians possess certain of these qualities, but the bible speaks of the gifts in 1 Corinthians 12 as gifts of the Holy Spirit. And as exclusive as this unfortunately sounds, only Christians have the Spirit dwelling in them.

In addition, the gift of faith should not be equated with the faith that all Christians possess to one degree or another, and which grows as one draws closer to God. The gift of faith is a faith implanted in a particular believer (as

Paul explains, not everyone has this gift, just as he states that the other "gifts of the Spirit" are not possessed by everyone), yet all Christians clearly possess some degree of faith. The gift of faith exists virtually independently of the level of the relationship that person has with God, and is given, as are the other gifts, for particular times and specific needs. This explanation, vis a vis one's relationship with God, is not, of course, completely correct. One must have some level of relationship with the Father. The gift of faith is like a quantum leap of faith from the personal faith one possesses, to a powerful confidence in God that God has intentionally, and in grace, planted in the particular believer who is given this, perhaps uniquely New Testament experience.

Apart from the gift of faith, however, as we begin to grow in our faith I believe we experience a continual flow between faith and unbelief. With the chair, for example, the first time one sat on it there may have been a lack of assurance that the structure would actually support our weight. Then, as one repeated the experience over time, that initial hesitation faded and disappeared. Likewise in the area of faith. *If God truly has revealed himself to us,* based on this revelation, though with a hefty amount of unbelief still existing, one attempts to act, and is surprised to discover that God has come through. As with the chair, repeated acts of discovery reinforce the belief that the God who reveals can be depended on, until, as the relationship with God deepens, there is no doubt remaining. The dynamics of this description are not fixed. The revelation of God to an individual may indeed be so overwhelming that there is no transitional series of steps to perfect faith. Each person will experience God in his or her own way. But the overriding principle is correct. We have faith as God reveals himself, and this faith is reinforced as we continually discover the reliability of the Revealer.

We do not usually need to create crisis situations to get God's attention. Moreover, there have been enough public tests of faith that have brought shame on the Kingdom of God by being either self instigated or completely beyond the spiritual depth of the person placing both him/herself and others in untenable positions that did not reveal the power and love of God.

Certainly it is true that for most of us our faith is very small. However, if we realize this, if we accept that this is where we truly are at this moment, and understand that the solution to our problem is a continually deepening relationship with God, then we have a chance to increase this faith. If we can develop a relationship with the Triune God, we can go beyond the depressing, maybe-maybe not kind of faith we presently have, to one, unbelievable as it sounds, like Elijah's. We can then have a faith that knows.

Chapter 15
SOCIETY AND THE CHURCH

There is considerable talk today about the decay of morality in society and its impact on the behaviour of individuals as they interact within this society. St Paul also saw morality, not simply as an individual affair, but as that which had both individual and interpersonal implications. There was not always, nevertheless, an interpersonal dimension to Pauline morality. He also understood that parts of one's morality might be made up of individually held beliefs, not necessarily shared by all others, and whose only 'other' connection was to the Godhead, as all morality ultimately is. In this situation one could act without disturbing one's conscience, despite the fact that other believers would regard the behaviour as absolutely unacceptable (see 1 Corinthians, Chapter 8). On the whole, however, there is a shared system of values within the church, and to some degree within society, by which one's life can, in terms of those values, be evaluated.

Along with this dialogue on the topic of social morality, there is some discussion on the biblical topic of covenants, as binding relationships among and between individuals and society and God. However, biblically speaking, there are essentially only two wide-ranging covenants the bible proclaims. One is the Mosaic covenant with the nation of Israel and God, and the other is the New Covenant between God and humanity mediated through the salvific work of Christ. These are the only covenants the bible teaches in relation to specific societies. God's covenant with Abraham was limited to the giving of land and Abraham's descendants; God's promise to Noah was limited to a promise not to flood the world, and the promise to David was restricted to conditions for the continuance of his kingly line. To speak loosely of societal covenants, and societal-divine covenants, that have no foundation in scripture, as if to claim the existence of conscious and historical relationships of alliance and obligation between individuals or groups, and societies and God, is surely misleading and certainly erroneous.

Indeed, it is erroneous, I would say, to regard the situation in which we as individuals in society live, as having anything to do with any form of social agreement. We are born into a society, or we place ourselves in one for economic advantage or survival. We are, in reality, not offered the choice of rejecting (or accepting) the social and political structures of the society we find ourselves in. And at the risk of sounding ridiculous, we are not offered the choice of submitting to these arrangements, except as they are forced on us in citizenship rites, over which we have no free control, and so are essentially coercive. We may live in a de facto relationship of interdependence with the society and government in which we dwell, but this does not constitute a social contract between the citizen and the rest of society. Indeed, until the government and the populace perceive each as possessing genuinely equal power, any relationship between the two is one based on coercion and the threat of violence.

Nor does society have basic tasks that it must or should conduct towards its members, as if these responsibilities were given to it in some kind of divine or secular moment of employment. Society acts in its own interest, and it is only at times that these interests coincide with goodness and decency. A societal task is not a metaphysical reality inherent in the gathering of individuals in groups. Any task society takes upon itself is either surrendered to an administrative unit within society or appropriated by force from the individuals who make up society by a group within it. Neither is it the task of society to deal with evil. Evil is a theological term and implies a relationship to a divine being. Society is not the representative of any such divine being.

Moreover, from a biblical perspective, God does not have a covenant(s) with general nation states (other than perhaps with Israel) or even communities. God does not, for example, have a covenantal relationship with the United States, anymore than one existed with the Soviet Union. The difference between the New Testament understanding of sin and that in the Old, is that the New Testament does not teach that nations sin against God, but rather that individuals do. Nations are not homogeneous aggregations of individuals such that to be in a formal relationship with one individual is theoretically to be in some kind of covenantal relationship with all. Neither can moral guilt or virtue be imputed to the entire nation. If fifty-one percent of the population is sinful this does not make the nation sinful. And in addition, the New Covenant, the only biblical New Testament covenant, is not directed to societies and states at all, but rather to individuals who then constitute a totally new body, the church, which is unrelated to the society in which the individual is simultaneously and accidentally a member.

Society is not the church under another name. Furthermore, the church's mission is not to prop up society as it sinks into immorality, but rather to spread the Gospel, and in doing so, transform hearts and lives, so that personal and public behaviours become more and more conformed to the nature of God. This is not to assert that individual behaviour does not have a societal impact, but rather that the battle to reinforce societal morality is the wrong battle for the church to be engaged in. This claim does not imply that the church should not engage in public opposition to certain specific moral injustices such as racism, child labor, or unlivably low wages. What is opposed in the church's contemporary battle against immorality is the widespread nature of this religious opposition. It is the virtually universal range of this opposition to societal decay that is rejected. Not because there is no immorality to decry, but because the goal of this opposition is merely a moral society. And this is believed to be distinctly possible, despite the two thousand year history of the church, even when the church, both Protestant and Catholic, possessed political power, and was clearly incapable of such a victory. The fact remains that a battle with societal immorality suggests and may well indicate an understanding of human nature that is not biblical. It further implies a redemptive and sanctificational possibility in society that the New Testament claims does not exist.

What is particularly troubling about today's church in this regard is its passionate emphasis on morality, particularly social morality, and its almost equal non-emphasis on a biblically based spirituality as an expression of the resurrection life and character of Christ as derived completely by an act of grace brought about by the life of the Spirit, and not by the strength of human commitment. Further, there is frequently a dangerous identification of the church with the state accompanied by an understanding that the state not only can or should be, but actually is under the special umbrella of God's blessing.

One wonders, given the long history of sinful, completely pragmatic social and foreign policy behaviour by a whole array of state agencies, why God should be viewing our particular state with such a benign eye. Coupled with this identification, or at least friendly association of the church with the state is an apparent inability or refusal to admit and condemn the wrongs and sins of the state, as opposed to the individuals making up the state, in any meaningful fashion, and a perception that to attempt such a stance is unpatriotic, and possibly even sinful. That the church should be preeminently loyal to the truth, and at times even take a prophetic position in regards to all governmental action is ignored in the rush to approve the spiritual credentials of one's nation and its leaders. The church thus engages in wide-ranging condemnation of individual morality, while completely ignoring the morality of governmental behaviour, an area which we Christians, because of the nature of Christianity, have historically been weak on.

Moreover, if there is indeed a proclamation of sin by the church, the intent of this proclamation should be to awaken a consciousness of the individual's alienation from God, and the need for reconciliation. The proclamation of sin is not a proclamation of morality. Biblical moral behaviour relates to God and salvation. The church does not have two tasks: one to evangelize, and the other to preach a moral behaviour that is amenable to public reformation, independent of the sanctifying work of the indwelling Spirit of God. Rather, the biblical position is that completely acceptable behaviour will always be beyond human ability. Attempting to improve societal behaviour is like putting one's finger in the proverbial hole in the dike. If the water stops at one place, it will start leaking out somewhere else. At the risk of sounding too old fashioned for words, what society needs is not reformation but regeneration. Religious discussion of public (im)morality fails to be Christian if it is conducted outside a discussion of the salvific work of Christ. And if the work of Christ can be understood to have impacts on societal morality, what does it mean for the church to discuss public morality outside of this paradigm? As strange as it may sound, the vocabulary of ethics is not necessarily the vocabulary of biblical and New Testament morality.

Further, human social interaction is so thoroughly penetrated with non-godly behaviours, that to attempt to correct one layer of non-Christian action, while not resolving the interconnecting web of other non-Christian behaviours, would result in overall failure. To succeed, indeed, would necessitate a virtually simultaneous social transformation of reactions to human failure that would imply either a negation of the need for the Cross, or be equivalent to the work of the Cross in the human heart on the social scale. Demanding morality of the individual, while not demanding a reciprocal morality of love in the society against which the individual has sinned, appears neither fair nor efficient. Moreover, the church's quest for a moral society seems to ignore both the depth of sin that fills the human heart, and the necessity of the cross as God's transformative answer to this sinfulness. To reiterate, it is the wrong battle on the wrong battlefield, the theological implications of which, from a Christian-New Testament perspective, are enormous.

CHAPTER 16
COMPARING OURSELVES TO OTHER CHRISTIANS

Comparing oneself to others may be a characteristic we share with every other human on the planet. We compare looks, our cars, our bank balances, our houses, even at times our relative worth as producers of children. We also do this in relation to our spirituality. This may not be entirely spiritual, but it is very natural. John tells us towards the end of the scene where Jesus appeared to the disciples at the Sea of Galilee after the resurrection, that Peter looked around and saw the disciple whom Jesus loved following. When he caught sight of him, Peter asked, "Lord what will happen to him?" Jesus said, "if it should be my will that he wait until I come, what is that to you? Follow me" (John 21: 21,22).

The spiritual danger in comparing oneself with another is remarked on in Galatians 6: 3,4 where Paul warns, " Each person should examine his own conduct for himself. Then he can measure the achievement by comparing himself with himself." Our level of success is not measured by a comparison to another person's spiritual level. If the water level in a lake rises six inches (about fifteen centimetres) when the original level was fifteen feet (five metres), the increase in depth is large or small relative only to that particular lake, and not to any other lake. Our spiritual improvement can not be measured by comparison to another Christian's spiritual level. No matter what the level of another's spirituality is, no matter what that other Christian brother or sister is doing "for the Lord", their particular path has no essential relation to you, or God's expectations for you. Nor should another's spirituality necessarily be a cause of either pride or shame. God's only wish for each Christian is that they follow him.

What this means in regard to making personal comparisons, is that each person stands individually and solitarily before God. Is there another sense, in which we are all the body of Christ and united in God's family? Of course, this is true. However, we also have a solitary relationship with the triune God. As Paul states in Romans chapter 14: "Why do you pass judgement on your brother? And you, why do you hold your brother in contempt? We shall all stand before God's tribunal...So you see, each of us will have to answer for himself." In Christ, not only should we not compare ourselves to other Christians, at times it is dangerous to our spiritual walk to think in these terms. We need neither to think ourselves more spiritual than a fellow believer nor be depressed because we see ourselves as less spiritual.

Other Christians can be role models, encouragements to faith, and even those to whom we go to confess sin and seek prayer. However, our spiritual state and its evaluation have nothing to do with these other Christians. We stand before God perfect in Christ, and as long as our hearts are surrendered to Him, and we desire to conform our lives to him, we are in perfect conformity to His will for our lives. This does not suggest that we are perfect. It further does not imply that we should not be saddened by our lack of spirituality, and the great distance we see we must go, even to arrive at the level of spirituality we believe to be perfection (though only a vision of God would approximate this true perfection). As John tells us in the gospel passage above, what Jesus wants us to do is follow him, and not concern ourselves with what God is doing, or has done, in the lives of other followers. If we follow Jesus we will be pleasing to God. That surely is enough.

CHAPTER 17
MY CLEAR CONSCIENCE, AND YOUR REFUSAL TO AGREE THAT I SHOULD HAVE IT

Even if St Paul had not written 1 Corinthians chapter 8 on food consecrated to heathen gods, we probably would have discovered that some Christians do things that we think are absolutely sinful, while they claim to have a clear conscience. Of course the 'we' in that sentence might, on occasion, be the 'some' of the rest of the sentence. St Paul in this chapter is not really discussing the issue of how this can occur. Rather he is particularly concerned with what the Christian with the clear conscience does in relation to the other Christian who does not feel so free.

The question seems clear and easy to St Paul. If a person would be influenced to sin as a result of doing what I do not think is a sin, I should not engage in this in the presence of this other Christian. We have a responsibility to other Christians to act in such a way that they are not led to do that which they believe is sinful, even if we do not share their understanding of the action as a sin. We do not have the right to claim intolerantly that the other believer should not limit our personal freedom. We may, nevertheless, have the right to attempt to show the other believer the error of his/her thinking. However, we run the risk in doing this of coming to understand that it is we who have been in the wrong.

It is probably inevitable that other Christians would hold beliefs about daily behaviour that differ from our own. People, even Christians, frequently see issues from different perspectives. Paul, in Romans 14 speaks of one who is "weak in the faith", and as a result holds beliefs that differ from those of a more mature Christian. In an interesting reference to vegetarianism, he asserts that it is the weaker person who does not eat meat. Personally, I think he was wrong here, and it is the reverse, though I confess I eat meat myself. However, his lesson is based on love, and the realization that we stand, individually before God, and that not all moral decisions are universally obvious. He tells us in verse three, "The man who eats must not hold in contempt the man who does not, and he who does not eat must not pass judgement on the one who does; for God has accepted him. Who are you to pass judgement on someone else's servant?" Paul was not so much interested in these differences of opinion, and how such differences were possible, but rather in how and what these two groups thought about each other as a result of the differences.

Is it that there is no absolute truth to which we can appeal? Such a conclusion does not follow from the

Pauline remark. However, we all use our minds to arrive at that which we believe is true, and Paul is very clearly telling us that different people arrive at different conclusions to the same issue. Further, we have no right to assume that our conclusion is necessarily God's. He does teach, however, that having arrived at a conclusion, we are obligated to act, in our own lives, as if this were the truth of God. Verse 14 states "if a man considers a particular thing impure, then to him it is impure." Verse 23 provides the result of such a conclusion, though expressed in a failure to follow one's thinking. "But a man who has doubts is guilty if he eats because his action does not arise from his conviction, and anything that does not arise from conviction is sin." Not only is it how we think of something that makes the action right or wrong for us, it is how we act in relation to this conclusion. No wonder St. Paul said, "Happy is the one who does not condemn himself in the thing that he allows."(Romans 14:22)

We may be convinced beyond the shadow of a doubt that we are correct in an evaluation. This does not mean that the person who does not share this conclusion is sinning. Nor does it imply that they are wrong. God knows the truth, and it is before this God we all stand, as individuals. It is God's prerogative to teach a truth, and correct error, and the clear lesson in this passage is that we do not have the right to hold in contempt, or judge, a brother or sister who, with an apparently clear conscience, acts in a way we believe, nevertheless, to be wrong, and even sinful. We are all at different stages in the Christian walk, and we need to humbly acknowledge that it may well be ourselves who are in the wrong. Different beliefs that do not relate to the essential core of the gospel should not preclude our fellowship with "differing" Christians.

Does this truth leave us with no assurance that what we believe is correct? Surely this does not follow. What is being presented here is not that we should view our beliefs as merely tentative, but rather that while believing certain ideas for reasons we hold to be valid, we also must acknowledge that other people may hold contrary beliefs for other reasons that are convincing to them. Not every theological belief is a tenet of essential teaching. Whether I drink alcohol or not is not central to the doctrine of salvation, nor is it clearly stated that I should or should not drink. Drunkenness is taught against, and with good reason. However, simple drinking is not taught against in scripture, though one may abstain, for perhaps equally good reasons. The fact is, however, that this idea of Christians having contrary beliefs on certain issues is clearly stated in scripture by St. Paul. If the above interpretation of Paul is incorrect, what then did he have in mind?

The Christian's attitude to other believers with differing opinions should not only include a non-judgmental spirit. We also need to be concerned that we do not knowingly cause a weaker brother or sister to sin. Perhaps it is impossible to achieve this goal perfectly. The media is part of virtually every aspect of contemporary societal thinking, and has critically reduced privacy and the private life of anyone who becomes an object of media attention. St Paul's teaching was intended for a society in which one had the freedom to act, unless one was aware of an individual who would be tempted to sin as a result of that act, without such media attention. Society was not so exposed to the intense public scrutiny of the "famous" as it is at present. On the other hand, most of us do not endure such attention and when we are not under intense public examination there is an almost complete sense of anonymity. How can we know when an individual Christian who would be offended is present? The church in Paul's time was small, and most Christians probably knew most other Christians in their region, at the time he was writing.

We, however, live in a mass culture, in which most of the time we have no idea whether the people we meet are Christians or not. Further, there is a wide range of what is acceptable Christian behaviour throughout the church, and it is relatively easy to offend someone in another group, simply by doing what is acceptable in our group. Some Christians think it is acceptable to drink alcohol, while others see this as deeply sinful. Certain Christians believe movies are worldly and sinful, and others have no problem seeing a film, and even being involved in the movie industry. How is it possible to know with certainty that we are not causing another Christian to sin, simply by doing that which we believe is acceptable to God? The scripture plainly teaches us that we should be slow to judge a fellow believer's actions.

Whether we are correct or not in our understanding, the one attitude that is indisputably required of a Christian is that of love. Christianity is not expressed in the formulation of criteria whereby we evaluate each other's behaviour. Rather it is seen in the development of love. This is not the abandonment of righteousness but its establishment, as we see in Galatians 5:14, "For the whole law can be summed up in a single commandment, 'Love your neighbour as yourself.'" It may well be that you have a clear conscience about something that I regard as sinful. But I need to be quite careful that my response to you, while not ignoring what I see as truth, expresses this love.

There is, perhaps, no easy answer to this dilemma. It is clear that if we are aware that what we freely do is causing another Christian to sin we have a responsibility, based on love, to refrain from continuing in that action as long as the other Christian can be so influenced. As far as the 'grey' areas of the issue are concerned, however, if we are surrendered to God, that is to say, if we desire the will of God to be done in all our actions, and understand that as Christians we stand in the perfect righteousness of Christ, acceptable to God, then in that state, and in that surrender to God, we should live in the world untroubled in conscience, and open to whatever the Holy Spirit attempts to teach us in regards to behavioural change. God does not expect us to live neurotic lives. If our hearts seek the Father's will, and acknowledge our known sin to God, we can live at peace, and with an untroubled conscience as we interact with others in the world, at least until God tells us otherwise.

There exists, nevertheless, one more aspect to this troubling situation. There is the need to love and withhold judgment, and there must be a sensitivity not to cause others to sin, if that is at all possible. There must also, however, be a realization that others, perhaps society as a whole, can impose a heavy condemnation on one for acting on beliefs contrary to these others' beliefs. For one's own protection there are times when, despite one's clear conscience it is unwise, perhaps in the extreme, to act on one's beliefs. Both for Pauline and purely practical reasons, one's intellectual freedom with regard to an issue may not be sufficient to allow one the exercise of that freedom. Apart from the need to think of one's impact on others, one should carefully consider the possibility of others' "impact" on oneself.

CHAPTER 18
GUILT AND SHAME

It is doubtful that there is a single human on the planet who does not have the feeling, deep in (his) heart, that no matter what (she) does, it is not enough. That if others could look into the deepest recesses of one's being to see the moral failure, and selfishness, he/she would be cruelly rejected. The feeling of guilt is an experience, almost certainly shared by every human being who has walked this planet. Guilt can be the legal evaluation of a court, an objective state of having broken a legal or moral code, or the diffuse and pervasive feeling, that lives in one's heart as a result of one's moral self evaluation. This feeling, that we may unwillingly carry with us until our death, can indeed, be grounded in fact. There is, perhaps, an almost innumerable list of wrongs we have actually committed, apart from those done of which we are unaware. However, let me suggest that most of what we experience as guilt is, in reality, shame in the face of a society that has the terrible potential to reject us. The guilt that is frequently expressed by people found out in some, perhaps nefarious act, has more to do with social rejection than the perception and the need to admit that one has done wrong.

Society is not a harmless, or even usually positive entity within which the individual can safely reside. Rather, it is the accumulation of all that is good and evil, kind and violent in people, potentially arrayed against the individual who strays from society's narrow confines. Society is not essentially an organization for the protection and building up of the people who make it up, though that is frequently the claim made for its existence. It is not constituted to act compassionately to those who fail, and given that those who act compassionately are outnumbered by those who do not, society does not usually act for the betterment of the individual, nor should societal opprobrium be understood as equivalent, or even similar to God's attitude and reaction. This dark and gloomy understanding of society is perhaps balanced to some degree, nonetheless, by the values of forgiveness and compassion that are part of Christian teaching, and similar teachings that are held to be crucial to other religions, and that are controlling values for individuals within these religions or philosophical schools, in society.

One of the most destructive aspects of society is the violence with which it evaluates and rejects those who break, or attempt to break, its "laws". We see this, for example, in the comedy that makes fun of famous people's failings, and brings humiliation on them and their families. Such "fun" is overwhelming in its self righteousness, but even more so in its insensitive brutality. The message in the supposed humor is that the comedian, and the audience laughing at the failed person, are beyond such sin, and that the person's actions, if they are in fact a sin, are things that deserve to be laughed at. The act of failing appears to be something that others can derive pleasure from, partly perhaps because these 'amused' people's failings have not been so publicly revealed. What is being implied, even more significantly, the lesson that this teaches us all, is that if one fails, if one commits an infraction of a societal value, the person who fails will be humiliated by the very society in which he or she has taken, and must daily take refuge. The power of society's opprobrium towards an individual is such because both society's values, and the fear of social rejection, simultaneously exist, cancer like, in each person's heart and mind, throughout a person's life.

To claim that we all daily take refuge in society is not to state that we live in fear, and regard ourselves as protected by the society in which we dwell. Though even that understanding is not completely incorrect. The simple test, as to the degree to which we take refuge in society is the level of dependence we have on others for our daily lives. There is a psychological sense in which this is also correct. Despite our best intentions and desires to be unaffected by the thoughts and reactions of others to our behaviour, we are radically affected by other people's responses to us. Depending on the level of our self confidence, this negative threat is limited. Apart from self confidence, and the walls we build to insulate ourselves from the others in society, perhaps through wealth or a place of "recreation" in the wilderness, it is indeed others who supply our need for friendship and communication, and it is others who, through the expression of their gifts meet the mental and spiritual needs of the human heart. It is not biblical to state that we need no others, and the image of the body of Christ is the support for such a position. How else then can it be stated than that we daily take refuge in society?

Society has power over the individual because we, as individuals, need society in order to survive as human beings. It is others who meet most of our needs. It is frequently others who inform us of our value and the sense of who we are, and it is others who provide the emotional sustenance human beings seem to need in order to function. The fear of being alone is enormous, as we discover in

"Robinson Crusoe" and in films like "Castaway", and societal rejection results in an absolute realization of one's aloneness, while one is forced to continue to live among those one needs. The fear of social rejection is not based only on a particular idea or ideas that we are taught, but rather on our experience of living with others, and discovering their reactions to others', and our own failure to meet their expectations. This reality has nothing to do with the expectation that we should be pleasing to God. It is not only God who has standards which the individual must satisfy.

We learn this initially from our parents, who express anger at behaviour that frequently does not have any relation to an external body of moral laws, but instead is simply contrary to their personal whim. We learn this as students from teachers who express dissatisfaction in a variety of ways, not excluding sarcasm and physical violence, and even in the simple fact of not performing perfectly in examinations, and from fellow students whose rejection one may fear even more than one does the displeasure of one's parents. We learn this also in our interactions with strangers who feel safe to abuse us, and in the abusive reactions of people, directed to those who break laws and contravene societal values.

Shame is not, as much as it is believed otherwise, the perception of guilt in an individual, but the sheer terror that one has become exposed to societal repulsion. Shame is not an expression of regret at a wrong done, but a reaction to being seen to have failed in society's eyes. It is also not repentance, because repentance implies an attitude to the wrongness of an act, in itself. Rather, shame is a reaction to society.

Some societies, such as Japanese society, are held to be shame driven. The West is troubled by this, because it perceives such an attitude as a failure to see actions in objective moral terms. What the West fails to recognize, is that it is similarly, if not just as shame driven as Japanese society, but that because of its Judeo-Christian heritage, the West couches its understanding of social failings in strictly moral terms. The Japanese are not ignorant of values that exist independently of the societal reaction to them, and the best of society in Japan seek to conform their lives to these values, just as the 'best' of society in the West do. What we in the West have tended not to see, is that the fear of social rejection (shame), is just as powerful in our culture, as it is in any society that overtly emphasizes shame.

The destructive power of shame even has impacts on the safety and stability of our democracy. It is the motivating force that generates repeated lies in bureaucrats, the military, and politicians when actions, both private and official, that have turned out badly, run the risk of becoming known and repudiated. Shame and public humiliation are some of the weapons used by individual and official government blackmailers who seek to control, and at times subvert the right course of justice and legislation. It is shame that is actively sought when political parties seek dirt, real and fabricated, on opposition candidates. If we were, on the other hand, a society that understood its own deep and individually ineradicable sinfulness, and lived the life of love, there would be no room for such deceit. There would be no room for blackmail. There would be no room for the political manipulation of powerful officials through the fear of disclosure. If we did not reject others for their failures, it is just possible that we could live in a truly safe and viable democracy.

Now, I am fully aware that there are some reading these lines who completely believe that those who fail should be made known, and should bear the humiliation for their sins. There are some who believe that those who fail deserve such humiliation, and that God approves of this attitude. I also understand that for these people nothing short of a miracle would ever change their minds on this score. Not only is this true. It is also true that those who derive gain from either the control of information that could cause shame, or who could financially benefit from such disclosures, would see no positive result from such threats in an environment of love. Such an environment would remove the power of their information. If one were confronted regarding failure in an attitude of love, where would the need for denial and deceit be? If a government official believed that those who pointed out his or her failings did so in an accepting attitude of love, what would the chances be that they would frantically seek to deny their mistakes, or put the blame for such failure on someone else?

However, these are only pragmatic reasons for operating in love. The question about God's attitude to this point remains. Personally, I believe that God is more interested in bringing about repentance than in causing shame, and further, that the social rejection that is the power of shame is least likely to achieve this goal. Shame forces the individual into a corner where denial is seen as the only escape. Examine the Gospel stories of the tax collector, and the woman taken in adultery. Was shame Jesus' method for bringing about their salvation? What does the scripture mean when it states that "there is more rejoicing in heaven over the one sinner who repents than over the ninety nine who do not need to repent"? Is this the attitude of a God who desires the humiliation of the sinner? What kind of society does God wish to establish, right now, on the earth? Is it one of love and forgiveness, or one of anger and humiliation?

An accusation that one is trying to make another individual feel guilty is usually a confusion regarding genuine guilt and social rejection. The fact remains that before God we are all guilty. We have all fallen short of God's moral character (Romans 3:23). So what we have is two "voices", each accusing us of wrongdoing. One is the voice of God, and the other is the voice of society. Because we are used to societal rejection, we almost invariably interpret God's evaluation of our acts in the violent terms of societal rejection. We are almost certainly viewing God in terms of society. Nevertheless, the societal perception of a sinner is not necessarily God's perception. Can you imagine a society in which moral failure was received in an attitude of love, where love was the prism through which all human acts were filtered? You see, love does not reject.

We, as human beings, want God to be angry, because we ourselves are angry. It suits us very well that God be incensed by the failures of others, because we are so incensed. We do not want, on the other hand, God to be angry with us. Towards us, we desperately want (him) to be kind and forgiving. The wrath of God is perfect when it is directed towards our enemies. But is that how God really is? Fortunately, the answer to that can be found in the life of Jesus. However, that begs one more question. Was the life of Jesus a full revelation of God, or only his nice, friendly side? Based upon your answer to that last question you will perceive the character of God. If you conclude that Jesus' life represented only one side of the character of God, then I suspect you will never feel really confident about the God you worship. You will never be really certain that you are dealing with a loving being, and will always be wondering when you will inadvertently trigger his anger.

If, on the other hand, you decide that Jesus is the perfect revelation of God, you will have a basis for an understanding of God that includes an inability to arbitrarily and violently reject. Our sin does not disappear in this understanding. We still fall short of God's standards, and without the forgiveness and cleansing won on the cross we would forever be alienated from God. Our problem on earth is just this, that we are alienated from God. This is the cause of the human dilemma. There are other ways this dilemma can be described, but the essential characteristic is that we are separated from the life of God. The other, undeniably important aspects are evidences of this.

There is, thus, an objective sense (as far as one accepts that there is an abstract body of values that are independent of subjective human formulation) in which the fact is that we are guilty of having broken God's law. In a truer sense it is more correct to understand that we have acted contrary to God's character, that our behaviour is not in conformity to God's behaviour. Our natures are not his nature. It is not simply that we have broken a set of laws, but rather that our lives testify that we are not like God. We can live these ungodly lives, but we can not live them with God. We can also not live them with any sense of joy, unselfish happiness, love and fearlessness. If God were like us, he would not care that we are in this state of ruin. He would not care at all, and would abandon us to our suffering.

When we attempt to make others see that their lives do not conform to the character of God, we are genuinely attempting to show them that they are objectively guilty. What we are not attempting to do is make them feel ashamed, particularly before us. Nor is this all that we are attempting to make them see. We are also attempting to allow them to understand that there is a better life, and that repentance, the turning away from sin, is really a turning to the life of God, that sin is not only wrong, it is also destructive. It would be nice to think that all who repent do so because they come to understand the terrible ungodliness of evil, because they see the holiness of God, and feel sorrow for their terrible shortcomings, that they regret what they have done. The truth is usually, however, that we see the destructive effects of remaining in sin, and turn away from it to avoid this destruction. Isaiah saw the holiness of God and confessed his sin, but his reaction to the holiness of God was really based on his fear that 'he was undone', that his sin would result in his destruction. It is, however, enough, as a beginning, to turn from sin because one sees the result of not repenting.

As Christians we should both not make people feel guilty, and at the same time seek to make them feel a terrible guilt. When one pulls a person from a burning building one does not deny that the building they were in was actually on fire. We have all been trapped in the burning building, and we have no right to act towards another unfortunate sinner, as if we are or were not sinners ourselves. What a shame it is, and indeed it is a great shame, that the society of saved sinners is probably the worst place to find oneself a revealed sinner, especially if one is a believer.

Society should be a place in which the weak, the failure, and the sinful are wrapped in a blanket of love, in an environment where all are conscious of their sin, the sin that nailed Jesus to the cross, and recognize other sinners as like them, and as worthy recipients of the same love that God has displayed towards them. However, this is frequently far from the case. The church, particularly the evangelical wing, to which I admit a membership, is apparently obsessed with morality and virtuous behaviour, to the extent that many within the church cannot view the real sins of others, particularly in the faceless public domain, with any other attitude than that of anger and moral outrage. Far from the love that Jesus displayed towards sinners, we as the church want these human failures to be punished to the full extent of the law, and the full extent of the societal power to exclude and reject, and delight when this occurs. As a church we are so focused on proper morality, that we are unable to see other sinners as like us, and as objects of divine love. If Jesus were to return to earth, the Pharisees he would encounter would be the Evangelicals, and the Sadducees would be the liberal wing of the church, and if this understanding is correct, both groups would attempt to crucify him, the liberals for attempting to suggest that the power of God should be experienced, and the evangelicals for suggesting that their minutely worked out teachings on spirituality were not exactly God's attitude to the subject.

Indeed, this focus on morality, in its broadest meaning, as this is directed to society generally, and our passionate rejection of failure in this realm, is not only a failure to love, it is even more importantly, if that is possible, a theological symptom of a serious misunderstanding of soteriology, the teaching on salvation. To focus on societal and individual morality is to (a) miss the point of the kenosis, the Messianic emptying of the use of godhead, (b) negate the doctrine of human weakness to achieve the law as taught in the Pauline epistles, and (c) fail to recognize one's own sin as deep and pervasive in the heart. Finally, such an attitude is a strategic failure to see that rejection of the sinner is an almost certain way to cause the sinner, and a sizable section of society as well, to reject both the church and Jesus himself as places of sanctuary and as the source of redemption.

That the church has an equal obligation to teach ethical positions to those who are within the church is equally correct. This is so because within the church such teaching is part of the teaching of salvation. However, were the church to proclaim ethical standards without an accompanying teaching on the work of the Cross and the function of the Law, it would not be functioning as a New Testament body. Indeed, it would not be functioning as the Church, for it is not the mission of the church to preach the Law but to present the Gospel. And while part of that presentation is the preaching of the universality of sin, if that alone is the message, especially as this regards society, no "good news" will be understood to be part of this message.

Rather than as a place of sanctuary, the sinner most frequently experiences the church as a place of extreme personal rejection. Rather than being known as a place of love, the church is known in society as the place of the most stringent social rejection of ethical failure, or at best, only as the moral barometer of society. In the name of a supposed righteousness, the church has lost sight of one of the primary reasons for its existence in the world, and that is not to teach morality but to lead other sinners to a relationship of love and forgiveness with a holy God, who is more interested in reconciliation than rejection and moral indignation. We are so concerned with social morality, that when failure presents itself, as for example President Clinton's failures and sins, we miss the redemptive possibility that this offered the church in terms of a public confession of the church's position on sin, forgiveness, (not only or necessarily President Clinton's) and salvation.

Instead, we circle the academic wagons to put out interpretations on just how evil the moral failure was in terms of its social impact and as a societal expression. We express doubts about the sincerity of the President's 'confession', and are concerned that it was public. We cannot look into the heart of an individual, but perhaps his confession would have had a better chance of sincerity if his sin had not been so published abroad and his humiliation viewed around the world under the glare of public awareness and societal rejection. As it is, he was forced, I believe, to make a 'public' confession, because the investigation had been such a public expression of the colosseum mentality. It would take a saint, as the Catholics understand the term, which Clinton definitely is not, to be unaffected by the humiliation of such public disclosures. Society got a message from the church, but it was not that we particularly care for the sinner. Perhaps responsibility for the "low" level of public morality can actually be laid at the doors of our churches. If society does not see the impact that sin has on further societal behaviour, perhaps it is our, the church's fault. Perhaps we need to evaluate the content of our preaching, and examine the level of our own spirituality as this impacts on society.

It is, and was, love that sent the second person of the trinity to earth to die for the sins of the world, and reveal what God was really like. It was love that made God inject himself into our suffering, and provide an escape. If our theological positions generate a hatred, a despising, or a devaluing of any other human being, then there is an extremely high probability that our theological positions are absolutely unscriptural. One scriptural interpretation cannot violate another scriptural interpretation that is of primary or greater importance, or contradict the very nature of the Godhead. Any anthropological interpretation, that is an interpretation of humans, supposedly based on scripture, cannot violate the New Testament revelation of Jesus Christ, or the teachings on holiness and love (two sides of one coin) as expressed by St Paul in Romans and Corinthians, if nowhere else.

An understanding of humanity, or any sub part of humanity, which contradicts the nature of Jesus, so expressed in his earthly life, and which does not conform to I Corinthians chapter 13, is an unscriptural interpretation, no matter how logically structured, no matter how many verses are appealed to in its defense, and no matter how long the particular interpretation may have been in currency. A theological position that finds its expression in rejection, hatred, repulsion, and a devaluation of another human being is a demonic interpretation. Though a Christian who is living a blatantly ungodly life should not be permitted to participate in the operation and ministry of the church, it must also be remembered that one of the accusations against Jesus was that he socialized with sinners (Luke 5). If we are to seek the lost we will have to spend time with them. Of course this does not mean that we put ourselves into situations where we will almost certainly fall into sin. What is at stake here is the psychological rejection of another human being because of their sin. The practical wisdom of protecting oneself and one's loved ones is another issue entirely.

Before concluding this little discussion one last question needs to be asked. Both now and in the future kingdom of God, where we shall all hopefully end up, how shall the bitterness of shameful discovery be overcome? If we who have scorned and humiliated the one who has failed are not changed in our attitudes and responses to this failed person, how shall that individual ever be able to raise his or her head to look his accusers in the eye? What could alter the equation of shame that we have caused to be generated by our humiliation of this other individual, we profess to call our brother or sister? We live our religious lives protected by the belief that others do not know our secret sinful life. We acknowledge that we are sinners, but we have little or no genuine sense that others truly believe that we are so, or even that we ourselves truly believe it. Our sins are not published, and we rest in the confidence that others see us (as we, in the depths of our hearts, see ourselves) as decent human beings, despite the rather odd religious belief we say we hold that we are in fact so sinful that it took the death of the second person of the trinity to exculpate us from the great weight of these our sins. But there is a minority for whom a public revelation of their inner being has already taken place, to one degree or another. For these people the sense of sin and failure is palpable. Both now, and in any future world, until each one of us discovers how truly sinful we decent Christians are, other people are not safe from our lovelessness, and neither are we safe from the condemnation and shaming of others.

It must be, and can only be, in love that we correctly represent this loving God to those who are still in sin. Seeking to incur shame, and the rejection of a person for ethical and religious failure are not behaviours that are taught in the New Testament, and are not reflective of the ministry of Jesus. The pursuit of shame does not advance the kingdom of God, nor does it promote repentance. The humble heart of the one who has seen into his or her own heart and discovered a heart of darkness, finds in this discovery that only compassion is a fitting response to another's failings.

Chapter 19
WORLDLINESS AND THE BELIEVER

For many people in the Western world, to be 'worldly' means to be experienced in the ways of the world, and to be sophisticated, perhaps a little "too" sophisticated. For many Christians, especially evangelicals, worldliness is a sign of spiritual weakness and sin. To be worldly is to be involved in activities that though not mentioned in the bible as sins, are activities that non-Christians engage in, but which one drops when one becomes a believer. Indeed, worldliness is evidenced by participation in particular activities that many church leaders have stated are unchristian, for example dancing, going to movies, wearing make-up, and listening to rock and roll. To avoid an activity that is not specifically understood as evidencing sinfulness, however, on the basis that it has been defined as worldly, appears to involve one in a rather circular form of argument. We do not do the act, and regard the act as sinful because it is worldly…and we decide it is worldly (sinful) because it is not spiritual. Thus, it is sinful, not because it is sinful but because it is not spiritual.

That we engage in numerous other activities which are not spiritual, but which we regard as necessary for *our* existence, is never questioned. We then look for any destructive effects of participating in such activities, and assert that if any of these results are ever evident, the act in itself must be destructive and sinful. That these results do not always follow from such activities is rarely examined. The power of the assertion rests in the frequency of its assertion. The term, nevertheless, is a term that we have taken from the bible, though perhaps with inadequate reflection.

The bible does indeed refer to the 'world'. In Matthew 13:22, Mark 4:19, Romans 12:2, Galatians 1:4 and 2 Timothy 4:10 the word used is *aion,* to refer to the age, the dispensation, the period we live in. John 1:10, 3:16, 15:19,17:15, Acts 17:24, 1 Corinthians 5:10, and 7:31-33, Galatians 6:14, Ephesians 2:2, Colossians 2:8, 20, James 1:27 and 4:4, 2 Peter 1:4 and 2:20, and 1 John 2:15-17 employ the word, *kosmos*, which refers to an arrangement, beauty, or the cosmos, the world. Titus 2:12, and Hebrews 9:1 use the adjective *kosmikos,* meaning worldly.

As a reading of the texts will indicate, where the Greek word *kosmos,* or its variants is used, this refers to the physical world or the world of humanity, human activities and interests that are simply not spiritual but not necessarily sinful (John 3:16, Acts 17:24, and 1 Corinthians 7:33). It is also employed to describe reasoning that is not Christ based (Colossians 2: 8,20), or as the source or location of sinful behaviour (James 1:27), and the living of an unholy life and under the control of sin (James 4:4, 2 Peter 1:4, and 2:20).

The First epistle of John presents one with a text that appears to support the idea of particular acts that should be avoided. Indeed, verses fifteen and sixteen seem to suggest that one's entire life in the world is one that should be of no interest to the wholly committed believer. John states, "Love not the world neither the things that are in the world.

If any one loves the world the love of the Father is not in him. For all that is in the world, the lust of the flesh, the lust of the eyes, and the pride of life is not of the Father, but is of the world."

An incorrect interpretation of these verses is not simply disconcerting, it is positively dangerous. John 3: 16 tells us that God loved the world. Genesis tells us that God looked at what he had created and saw that it was good. Further, we are commanded to love all people who inhabit this planet, and are informed in the Sermon on the Mount that God is concerned that natural life be provided with daily food. We are also told in the Gospels that God, as our Father, will provide us with the things we need in this worldly life we live so that we can be fed, clothed and sheltered. Moreover, there are countless Christians who have sought the guidance of God for direction in what they should do in their lives and who have been guided to distinctly non-spiritual vocations in which they have not only attempted to serve God but have diligently labored in this world's economic activities to pay mortgages, buy clothing for their families, and even purchase cars so they can get to work, go shopping, and occasionally go on holidays. Not to love the world does not mean to completely devalue the activities that are involved in daily living. Nor does it mean that one should not enjoy living in this world.

What John was attempting to teach was the use of the "world" as indicating the world of sin, not the world as the location of human activity that was not sinful. In addition, "For all that is in the world...is not of the Father" surely includes all those Christians who claim a relationship with the Father. All means all. Therefore if we are not to love anything that is in the world we must also, logically, not love the Christians who are clearly in the world. It is not valid to assert that this is not what is being claimed. The verses do not say that some things (which the church can feel free to delineate) in the world are not of the Father. Further, if we are claiming that these verses are teaching that all (the whole set) of life in this world is to be rejected, we must also assert that these Christians, including the individual making this universal claim, are not "of the Father".

For these reasons, verse sixteen, which repeats the "all that is in the world" theme, must only be referring to those aspects of human life that are expressions of direct and observable sin as described throughout the scriptures, and not to activities that are simply expressions of human life and creativity that are not overtly, or even at all spiritual. There is probably not one human activity that is not susceptible to sin. Susceptibility to sin does not make that activity sinful. And the church needs to be extremely careful not to create a false spirituality that is based on incorrect interpretations of biblical terminology.

A spiritual set of regulations that appear to have only the most tenuous connection to biblical teaching, and which are based on an individual's particular perception of behaviour that is not mentioned in scripture should not be unreflectively accepted. The teaching of the Pharisees appeared logical and based on biblical "positions", yet Jesus denounced it as invalid reasoning. As Matthew 15: 9 tells us "They teach as doctrines the commandments of men." This possibility to arrive at incorrect but seemingly true conclusions in relation to godly behaviour is also mentioned in John 5: 10-18 with the healing of the man at the pool at Bethesda. The Pharisees had concluded that carrying anything (in this case the man's bed) on the Sabbath was work, and therefore a controvention of the Law of Moses. This is not a ridiculous conclusion, but clearly it was incorrect. Neither was it not a sin simply because Jesus had told the man to do so. The work Jesus claimed to be doing was not the "work" the man was doing. The Pharisees were simply incorrect in seeing this activity as work. It is extremely easy to arrive at a body of spiritual behaviours, or activities that should not be engaged in, that appear to be correct implications of scripture, but which are not. This mistake is often made in relation to deciding that an activity is "worldly".

It is one's sinfulness that has been crucified, not human activity in the multiplicity of its expression. Indeed, if such a universal rejection were intended, as Jesus implied in his prayer in the Garden of Gethsemane, we would have to be taken out of the world. John 17: 15 states, "I do not pray that you should take them out of the world but that you should keep them from the evil (of the world)" . Clearly, such a move was not Jesus' intention. Worldliness is not the participation in activities that are non-spiritual. Rather, worldliness, as described in all the above verses, is the participation in sin, and in a life of sin that is clearly portrayed and rejected throughout scripture.

There is yet one more reason why our understanding of worldliness is flawed. All human sin is committed in this world. Further, a sin is, by definition, a negation of the behaviour that should have been undergone. The implication in this is that theoretically a positive sinless world is "contained" in the existence of the sinful world, a perfect world in which sin is not the norm, for the negative implies the positive, just as the positive implies the negative. That sin exists in the world asserts then that the world has a positive value, and that in a sinless world, this world is perfectly acceptable in all the multifarious forms of human interaction conceivable. This position is strongly supported by God's words at the beginning of Genesis in 1:4, and repeated in 1:10, 18, 21 and 25, "and God saw that it was good."

That God saw the created universe as good, that the domain of human interaction was deemed good, puts paid, once and for all, to the idea, powerful though it is in

Western, and even Eastern thinking, that this world is of little or no value, and that activities in it have no intrinsic moral or metaphysical worth if not directly associated with religious/spiritual matters. This imprimatur of acceptability was given, based solely upon the simple fact of existing and experiencing life. In fact, sin and creation both direct the mind to the worth of ordinary human life lived from within an environment of love, and even, ironically, from an environment of sin.

The existence of sin does not necessitate therefore a rejection of the world, but rather, in sin's removal, an acceptance of it as the place of divine and human enjoyment, for to live in perfect love is to live in perpetual enjoyment, without limit and without exception. It is not justified then to devalue the world and the activities humans engage in, simply because they do not appear to be specifically spiritual. For in the *random and ordinary* activities of being human are found the acts, and opportunities for acts, which, either sinful or holy, define the individual who performs these acts and gives positive or negative value to the acts themselves. Consequently, in all such worldly acts is the potential for the revelation of the kingdom of God, or of unrighteousness.

Part of the confusion, and the unhappiness that often results from this confusion, comes from an inappropriate categorization of particular activities or other realities. We imagine, for example, that if playing football cannot be immediately seen as a spiritual event, then it must be an event of no spiritual worth. Indeed, we go further and decide that such "non-spiritual" events, because they are not spiritual are therefore unspiritual, and should be shunned if one is to be truly committed to God, and in a search for holiness. It is as if we are saying that if apples cannot be oranges, they are unworthy to be eaten. But that an earthly act is not an overtly spiritual one does not necessarily imply that the earthly act is of no value. To denigrate such an act in this way would be to attempt to force one kind of reality onto a definition of the category of another kind of reality. And in terms of a denigration of "worldly" activity it is to miss the intention of the creation as a domain of the kingdom of God.

Now apart from the potential for true spirituality, which is love, that exists in virtually every moment of being human, there are overtly spiritual events. Praying, reading the bible, telling someone about the forgiveness of Jesus, are all decidedly spiritual events. But it is not logical, or even good biblical exegesis, to go from that to the conclusion that because being part of the athletic team at school, for instance, does not appear to be spiritual, it must therefore be worldly, and therefore sinful. There is much in human life that is not overtly spiritual, but we must not make the mistake of confusing non spiritual with sinful, which is at the heart of the error in deciding some acts worldly. Human friendship, a love of a beautiful beach that we have frequented, even the enjoyment of a relaxing cup of coffee may not be deep moments of spirituality, but this does not mean that they are without value, or that the happiness they bring should be felt to be evidence of our low spirituality, or even that, because in death they shall be lost, the happiness we feel for them is empty and wasted.

And yet, while all this is true, it is also correct that there are only twenty-four hours in every day, and life, despite the feeling of immortality we have when we are young, is actually quite short and swiftly passes. There are finite limits on what we can do as human beings, and we are forced by the limitations of being human to treat the time we do have as a valuable resource which should not be wasted. If one were to spend all one's time in activities related only to this world, how would one discover the reality, power and love of God? If we spend no time in God's presence, how will we ever become transformed into his likeness and be freed of the sin and pain that exist in all of our hearts? Thus, while a rejection of the world and a categorizing of certain acts as unacceptable to Christians, though they are clearly not sins, is unbiblical and unreasonable, one must also not fill one's life with activities which allow no time for a deep and satisfying knowledge of God, such that we have, in effect, no real relationship with the Lord.

Chapter 20
HAVE YOU EVER BEEN TOLD JUST HOW BAD YOU REALLY ARE?

In asking this question I am not asking if you have been presented with biblical verses that show you your sin. Rather, I am thinking of something that hits home a little harder: being told just what you are by friends and relatives. The bible verses seem more theoretical and dispassionate than the comments of our friends, and we are more able to integrate them into our thinking about ourselves without the pain that a friend or relative causes when the same thing is said. The differing levels of perceived reality usually stem from the fact that society has an extremely visceral impact on us, and additionally, we don't really have a particularly strong perception of the reality of the world of the spirit. This does not, of course, make the bitter comments of our friends and family any less hurtful.

Now it is true that these people may well be wrong in their evaluation of our being. It could be that they are interpreting our behaviour and motivations incorrectly. It could also be true that the remarks are not being made from an attitude of love. They may also not be at all aware of our communications with God where we confess our sins and where we are heartily regretful of the low spiritual level of our daily lives and sanctity. The error of their ways really has no connection to the correctness of how we should respond to them.

Our response to these accusations by others is usually one of hurt and anger, and we want to strike back and show them just how mistaken they are. Unfortunately this is not always possible for any number of reasons, one of these being that they may be close family members and the cost of completely alienating ourselves from our family is far too high.

The power of these attacks, apart from the overwhelming power of society to reject, rests in our very understandable need to be liked and valued. In addition, human cruelty to other humans, especially those "close", is often deeply painful, and so any advice must be given with this in mind. There are two approaches that can help lessen the pain of these attacks. The first is found in an old hymn. One of the verses says:

> Do thy friends despise forsake thee?
> Take it to the lord in prayer.
> In his arms he'll take and shield thee.
> Thou wilt find a solace there.

God can remove the pain of human cruelty, and in bringing our anger and hurt to the Lord we give God a chance to reveal his love to us, and thus deepen our relationship with him.

The second path we can take is to acknowledge the truth of the accusation. The fact is that we really *are* deeply sinful beings. Nevertheless, unless we have just recently been converted from a life of crime, the chances are also that deep in our hearts we actually believe that we are really quite decent people. It is this belief that is being attacked when we are hurt by the criticism of our friends and family. Isn't it the case, however, that when we consider the life of holiness and love that God expects from us we are dismal failures? Doesn't the fact that we are hurt by these accusations show that in our hearts we are evaluating the level of our goodness by comparing ourselves to other people, and not according to God's standard? Do we love others as we love ourselves? Do we love God and have a deep faith in his power and character? The secret we keep carefully hidden (often even from ourselves) is that we have a depth of sin that every other person we know is totally unaware of. It may help to realize that this depth of sinfulness exists in them also.

Admitting our sinfulness is a confession of the truth. Confession is also not what most people expect when they accuse another of some kind of personal failure. Actually, when people are accused of some wrong this is usually done in anger, and a response of any kind is not the intent of the remark. Nevertheless, what is most surprising, and may actually soften the other person's anger, is an admission of the correctness of the accusation. We are so guilty of spiritual failure that it does not really matter if the specific accusation is actually correct. If they are wrong about the specific charge, does this make us sinless? It might be useful, and would certainly be truthful to say, "Oh, if you only knew the half!" "You are right. The only confidence I have is God's forgiveness in Christ. If I have wronged you, I am sorry. Please forgive me."

On the other hand we are under no obligation to confess to acts of which we are not guilty. The people who accuse us may do so out of a malevolence that does not need encouragement. Jesus did not admit to the failures he was accused of by the crowds. In fact Jesus was often accused of failing one or another of society's expectations, for example, taking meals with socially unacceptable people by those who did not believe he should, and eating with sinners. Whatever level of frustration Jesus may have felt at these claims, his responses to them clearly pointed out the hypocrisy and error of the claim.

We should not, nevertheless, be surprised when people find fault with us. If they are wrong some of the time, they will be correct at other times. View yourself firmly from God's perspective. We all have so little to recommend ourselves to God. Understand that we all have a depth of sinfulness that is momentous. Yet, our value is not altered by false accusations. The sin of others does not increase our sin, no matter how vituperatively we are accused of wrong. If we are falsely accused, it is their relationship with God that is at stake, not ours. Our real and truest (and not merely the only) goodness is that perfection with which God views us in Christ. Expect other people to find wrong in you. It is in the nature of those who do not experience love to attack others around them. View those who attack you as those who are weak. It may be that your strength is a threat to them in their ambition to control the behaviours of those around them. Do not be shocked when they fail in their Christian obligation, and even protestations, to love you. In these painful situations we must draw close to God. Only God will not disappoint. Only in him is our heart truly safe. And only in him, the perfect one, are we accepted as perfectly lovable.

Chapter 21
WHAT GIVES A PERSON VALUE?

As Christians, and simply as members of society who share a collection of similar values, we generally accept the idea that pride is not a commendable trait. With Jane Austin we disdain Darcy's proposal to Elizabeth, recognizing in it the ugliness of his pride. However, we are frequently far less self critical when it comes to the attitudes we possess towards our own particular talents, abilities, and assets, and are often unwilling to see the pride we nurture about these, and how they let us feel superior to others who are less endowed. In this we fail ourselves, others, who consequently are not the objects of our love, and God. And yet, if we cannot be justly proud of our abilities and accomplishments, where can we discover a reason to think of ourselves as valuable?

The scriptures inform us that we all have gifts. Indeed, God appears to be so concerned about our sense of self worth and the human need to be valuable that he has given each of us some particular and necessary 'gift'. Ephesians 4:7,8 tell us,

"But each of us has been given his gift (*karis*), his due portion of Christ's bounty. Therefore scripture says: He ascended into the heights, leading captivity captive, and gave gifts (*domata*) to humanity." Moreover, it is the "job" of the church, one's family and one's friends to recognize and encourage these qualities. Talents almost always have a social dimension. We have them so that we can be of benefit to others, and so that we can realize that we are valuable in the lives of these others.

However, while there is no reason, I suggest, for not taking pleasure in the positive and good things we bring to the world, there is still no justification for a sense of pride that focuses on these gifts as reasons for feelings of superiority. Human behaviour, whether one is a Christian or not, is ultimately paradoxical. While we are beings with the ability to act, yet we are constrained, even enslaved, either by sinful nature or by the limited data with which our brains must make decisions. One is reminded of the Holy Sonnets of John Donne, in which he describes our enslavement to the enemy of our souls and the need for Christ's conquest of our hearts, if we are ever to be free.

Our knowledge is limited, yet it is the only source of information that we have to make the ofttimes faulty decisions we must arrive at, each day of our lives. If we are not given further, adequate information, we are forced to continue to arrive at erroneous conclusions, and live out possibly destructive behaviours. The gospel is the most radical infusion of new information that an individual can be given. For with this new 'good news' a person can realize God's escape plan from death and futility, and begin a new relationship with the creator that carries with it the life of the risen Lord. The Gospel is that set of new data which breaks into the closed set of our limited thinking, and sets us free from thinking processes that are radically flawed and inadequate. The new information is not enough, in itself, to achieve this, but it shows us how to enter into a relationship of peace with God and experience the new birth through the Holy Spirit, so that we do achieve this freedom. To reiterate, before being given the information on the new birth we are enslaved, not only by a nature that will result in qualitatively inevitable behaviours, but also by life threateningly limited thinking. These radical limitations should cause us to hesitate when we are pleasantly tempted to consider our knowledge and skills above those of more ordinary people.

Why then, if we are so frequently tempted by feelings of superiority, do so many of us simultaneously believe ourselves to be useless, stupid, and valueless?

Sadly, we live in a destructive world in which one's personal worth is so frequently attacked and devalued that the danger when we think about our abilities is not a temptation to pride, but the feeling that we are quite worthless, both to our families and to the society around us. Many teenagers and young adults grow up with little sense of their worth, either as a result of verbal ridicule, or an unintentional lack of adequate praise by significant adults who may not realize the damage they have been causing, and who indeed would be horrified to discover the lack of self confidence they were generating by their failure to praise.

I do not believe that either spirituality or humility is attained by personally abusing another individual so that they believe they lack any worthwhile abilities. Despite the fact that God may be the ultimate source of the talents we possess, and that we have no right to be proud, I also believe that God takes pleasure in the building up of one's self confidence as one comes to realize that one actually does possess talents and abilities that are useful and necessary to the group in which one lives.

I do not understand this apparent contradiction, but I strongly believe it to be true. While we derive our strength from God, there is also the paradoxical sense in which we are all different, valuable, and if given the chance, beautiful beings. We are not God's robots, nor does he wish to make us such. We are all different in certain ways, and though we are highly determined by genetics, our culture and our social environment, there is still the sense that we are the agents and origins of our actions, and can take pleasure in the abilities and talents we bring to the world.

Not only are we devalued as children, young people and as adults, and as a result come to see ourselves as of little importance, it is also true that in the developed world as a whole, there seems to be little room for a widespread expression of individual gifts. The level of education and the standard of living that seems to parallel this development, have created a society where, though creativity flourishes abundantly, and even extravagantly, this creativity can find only a partial success among the people to whom it could be offered. How many Shakespeares have there been, whose genius will never be known, whose works lie locked forever in unopened drawers? How many Byrons, and Shelleys, how many Donnes and Austins, and Hardys will we never read and know? Moreover, how many within the church have gifts, both natural and spiritual, that go unknown and unexploited because of the lack of desire by the church leadership to discover and utilize these gifts, perhaps as a result of the structure of church "governance" at the congregational worship level, or from the almost innocent ignorance of the clergy of the need to foster such talents, and so strengthen the church.

The creativity of the human heart is rich and plentiful. Yet it appears impossible for us all to be aware of the gifts so many possess, that could enrich our lives, and minds, and hearts. This is, to a large degree so, simply because of the vast numbers who live on this planet with us, and who all seek to be heard amid the din of the earth's billions. It seems that while we have so much of what we do not need, we waste the treasures of the heart, mind and spirit we do.

In Grey's "Elegy in a Country Churchyard" there is a line, "some Cromwell guiltless of his country's blood", speaking of some unknown man buried there, who simply because of the obscurity of his existence, had not been tempted by power to acts of violence. We live in a world of chance, of inefficiencies, where what could be is often not what is. It is not only human brains that are inefficiently used. In the small populations of the past there existed the possibility that creativity and information could be shared and known by virtually all within that community, and that which was superior could be filtered through to become a cultural heritage. In a mass population such as ours, this is neither possible nor likely. Could it be, that in a world obsessed by globalization, we need to return to the smaller model of the village, or the town?

It may be that we need to see our place in society, in relation to our gifts as predominantly oriented to our moderately small corner of the world. This clashes with the television mentality of an interconnected global "community". Yet perhaps efficiencies of "gifting" are to be found in a turning away from the paradoxical limitations of such 'enlarged' thinking. We live in communities. Perhaps it is in and to these communities that we need to refocus our attention, and redirect our gifts. Perhaps by looking around us, to those who are our neighbours, we can regain the sense of value that an over-populated world seems to deny.

The Basis for Individual Value

One of the valuable lessons one learns when one travels is that there are whole societies around the world that view the world in different ways to the way we have been brought up to understand it. We also discover that many of these cultures have different views on what makes a human being successful. However, whatever the dominant value in a culture is, this will be the way in which an individual is judged, as to the level of their success in life. In a predominantly religious culture, a deeply religious person will be held in high regard, whereas in an economically based culture such as we have in the West, particularly in North America, one who is successful in business, or has succeeded in accumulating wealth, will be viewed highly. It should also be noted though, that the opposite side of the coin will also hold, such that those who do not achieve their society's goals will be held to be failures.

There are three major variables that work together to cause a person to achieve their culture's particular goal for the individuals in a society: (a) the objective environment that an individual encounters, (b) the level of effort that an individual puts into the achieving of this goal, and (c) the particular personality that an individual brings to this process. The objective conditions a person encounters include the family and class one is born into, one's geographical location vis a vis the rest of the world, and the macro economic condition that prevails at the moment of one's existence. All these essentially uncontrollable variables work together to assist or make difficult the quest to succeed in one's culture. For various reasons some people exert more effort in their attempts to succeed in their particular culture than others appear willing to. With all the other individuals in a society similarly competing for the culturally determined 'objects' of success, it usually requires a deep commitment to 'win'. The last variable, one's personality, is even more open to variation, and to a great extent completely beyond the individual's power to control.

Perhaps we should consider the words of that great pessimist of the Old Testament, the writer of the book of Ecclesiastes, when he wrote, "One thing more I have observed here under the sun: speed does not win the race, nor strength the battle. Bread does not belong to the wise, nor wealth to the intelligent, nor success to the skilful. Time and chance govern all." (Eccl. 9: 11) Moreover, given the fact that various societies hold different forms of achievement to be the criteria for social approval, and that each individual in these respective societies has almost certainly accepted his or her society's perception of success, and given that the vast majority of any given society does not achieve their society's level of understood success, in what way and on what basis can a person understand him/herself as worthy of self respect, independently of this set of criteria?

We are certainly the products of a combination of genetics and the environment, and the positive and negative implications of the kind of personalities that result from this existential and random development will make it either likely or unlikely that we will succeed in the cultural quest to succeed, or even that we will have the desire to do so. The multiplicity of these variables in this cultural competition, and the extent to which one is incapable of genuine input, surely lead one to question the value and validity of the results.

It is not simply that one must struggle to overcome obstacles (the endeavour we frequently focus on to justify our belief in the objective's worth). The truth is that we come to this struggle with qualities that make its success either likely or unlikely, regardless of the effort. Indeed the reality is that the cultural objective, that provides with its attainment social respect, is both geared for certain social classes and personality types only, and is essentially created by that group. The problem exists for the rest of the population in that, while they are incapable or unlikely to achieve these goals, they are socialized to accept them as the criteria for a personal sense of worth. The knightly values of the Middle Ages were of little worth to the peasants, but it is unlikely that, to the degree that the peasants were aware of them, they were not affected by them. When the church was the dominant force in Europe, the clergy and those in the religious orders were the successful and admired individuals. Cultural ideas of personal success are inextricably connected to societal power, and not necessarily to intrinsic values.

It should also be noted that a goal that can be easily attained is not likely to be seen as an expression of personal success. That this is so can only mean that most persons in a society will fail to achieve their culture's perception of success, or will evaluate their performance, only according to the degree that they have attained this form of success. To put the first sentence in other words, this will necessarily be so, in that a goal that most can achieve will be viewed as one not worthy of high social valuation. Society will, thus, be inevitably divided in a continuum, in which one is placed, or places oneself, according to one's (perception of) achievement. Society, by instituting the particular image of success it possesses, builds into society, for all practical purposes, an alienating principle that puts each member of society in competition with all other members of society. This is not an evaluation of this process as essentially destructive, but is simply an objective description of the process. The criteria that could be used to evaluate such a process could be evidence that such a process is or is not beneficial to society, and that the majority of its members are either helped or hurt by such a value process.

However, I would assert as an axiom, that it is essential that all members of a society value themselves positively, and that if a success model makes it impossible for all members to thus value themselves, this model is either flawed and requires modifying, or is intrinsically destructive and needs to be rejected. The rejection option should not be the choice one immediately decides on. Society must have a certain level of efficiency and production in order to achieve its goals, among which are the protection and provision of the individuals in the society. The abandonment of a model that provides these necessities, at least to some degree, may result in an even greater reduction in the provision of such needs. On the other hand, models of success that inevitably alienate members of society from each other, make widespread societal success objectively unlikely, or make a universal positive evaluation of an individual similarly unlikely or impossible, cannot be seen as viable models of human and spiritual worth.

It is also axiomatic that a society which does not perfectly express the values and characteristics of the kingdom of God in the hearts and lives of the populace is inherently incapable, because of this lack, to universally encourage and provide value to all individuals in that society. That is to say, that while it may be possible to give positive value to a segment or segments of society in a secular society, this will never be the experience of the entire society. As long as the dominant values of a population make it unlikely for all members of society to achieve the objective(s) the society deems to be the criteria for success, those values will similarly ensure that this society is incapable of bestowing positive value on all of its members.

Other value(s) therefore must be determined where there exists no necessity for competition. Such a set of values does not preclude the continuance of previously held values, though these values would be held to be of lower importance. Whether, at that point they would maintain the motivational power they had previously held is, perhaps doubtful. Further, a society which is not motivated by competition for scarce resources, which could include power and prestige, in addition to wealth, appears, under certain conditions to run the risk of collapse. Nevertheless, among those who had integrated this new set of values, previously held objectives could then be relegated to a secondary or lower position, such that, at least on the surface, there could be a continuance of normal societal behaviour. Early Franciscanism, where work was seen as an act of love in the provision of goods and services for one's community, could be an example of this, as could a wholly owned company whose primary objectives, for example, were not self aggrandizement but the well being of the employees and the genuine benefit of the consumers.

For Christians, if for no one else, the question that could be asked is, "what are God's criteria for determining success in this world, and do these relate to one's sense of personal value?" However, based on the understanding that God sent Jesus into the world to die for each of us, while we were still sinners, the question of value and success can apparently only be considered two entirely separate issues. One may not be successful from God's point of view, while simultaneously being of inestimable worth. The degree to which we are individually valued, that is the degree to which each one of us, at this point in time, possesses value, is seen in the depth and height of the sacrifice made by the Lamb of God to redeem each one of us. No CEO could acquire the value that such a sacrifice implies. No one could accumulate wealth and social prestige that would be equivalent to the value possessed at this moment by the poorest, most insignificant person, because of the love that God has for that insignificant individual.

Indeed, we can measure the value that each of us possesses by the suffering and humiliation that Jesus endured in order to redeem us from our lost estate. The incarnation is the divine assertion that nothing this world proclaims as signifying personal worth can approach the value that God places on each and every human being in every corner of the planet. The command to love others is merely God's attempt to 'get' his people to express that same love which God has for his creation. In human society, value is ascribed to those who have achieved societal goals. However, from God's perspective, value does not result from success at all, but from simply existing. It would be impossible for God not to love his creation, and the dimensions of this love are seen in the extent to which God went to impart healing and peace. For our part, the love we share with others, irrespective of what they do, helps them understand the importance they have, without any regard to any criteria for success the particular society may have attempted to inculcate in them. Just as salvation does not depend on our efforts to achieve it, so likewise, one's positive value does not depend on our personal achievements. The truth is that when we give value to those we love, we are simply giving them that which they have always, unknowingly possessed.

Yet we cannot leave this section on personal value without looking at the experience many have of viewing life as a wasted activity, in which nothing of any true worth was ever achieved. Though it is true that human value is derived from the spiritual value which God ascribes to each human being, might it not also be true that if we do not achieve anything of spiritual worth, our lives have been terribly wasted? In fact, as we have seen, to fail to achieve whatever set of values we set as of primary importance will inevitably result in a sense of personal failure. This must also include that set of expectations (not necessarily and only destructive) inculcated in us as children by our parents, and that we have miserably failed to live up to, but which we struggle to fulfil throughout our lives, frequently without success.

How many of us look back on lives devoid of a sense of achievement. We may have brought up children, attempting to avoid the mistakes of our parents, and seen them go off to college or get jobs and start families of their own. We may even have achieved some degree of economic success, or become educated, even highly educated while at the same time feeling in the depths of our hearts that we have achieved nothing. That none of these achievements merit satisfaction and a sense of accomplishment. On the other hand, worse still, we may have lived lives of almost total failure, in which there are not even these paltry evidences of success. We see the end of our lives, and not distantly, while we have nothing that can be remotely described as a justification for having lived, nothing that, in our hearts, we can feel any sense of pride in having attained or even attempted.

What, indeed, is the justification for having lived? Or is it that there is absolutely no need for such a justification? Certainly, by glorifying personal success we are only expressing the level of existence that we value positively. Nor does the standard of perfection God demands appear to make this problem any easier. Yet, paradoxically, the answer to our terrible feeling of failure is found in this very God who does demand this perfection. There is very little that is more devastating than an infestation of locusts. Virtually all plant life is eaten. And this image is used in scripture to describe a life from which all joy and satisfaction have been lost. In such a life there is little or nothing that can be regarded as worthwhile. Perhaps this also describes the feelings of one who, looking back on life, sees nothing of worth. Perhaps, not necessarily, but perhaps this negative view is entirely justified. Yet there is hope. Joel 2: 25,26 states, "I will restore to you the years that the locust has eaten. You shall eat in plenty and be satisfied." The Father of a lost humanity does wish to make the remaining years of a wasted life filled with the satisfaction that all the previous emptiness has been unable to give.

I believe that many, many people live with a sense of wasted life. It is not always as terrible as may have been described above, but it is similarly unhappy. So what does God expect of us? What does the complete picture of salvation tell us about God's attitude to success? Turning from the struggle to be good, to the gift of perfect goodness Jesus offers, shows us that God is pleased with us, as we are, in Christ. We do not need to improve on the goodness of Christ that covers us. As we live our lives, day by day surrendered to Him, seeking through the Spirit of Jesus to be transformed into his likeness, being transformed into the likeness of Jesus, we can rest, completely content that we are pleasing to the Father of all life. We do not have to be famous. We do not need to have built a dam across a raging torrent to bring hydroelectricity to a city of millions. We do not even need to have directed and acted in an epic film that is loved by millions. We simply need to live before God, and be allowing him to change us day by day, into his image. All other achievements may be wonderful, and even pleasing to God, but one's life has had value and been worthwhile if we have only turned in faith to Jesus, and given the rest of our lives to be molded into his image. Then the years that the locust has taken can be restored. Then we can have joy in a life completely ordinary. As Isaiah tells us, "They that wait upon the Lord shall renew their strength. They shall mount up on wings like eagles. They shall run and not be weary. They shall walk and not grow faint." (Isaiah 40: 31)

CHAPTER 22
INTELLIGENCE AND TALENTS

A long with wealth and a high paying prestigious job, intelligence is one of the most valued possessions human beings take pride in. The realization that one is more intelligent than one's colleagues and friends can give one a deep sense of satisfaction. Believing that one is more intelligent than most other people is similar to the feeling one has in seeing that the car one drives is classier than the car one is being passed by. Intelligence is a characteristic that society holds in high esteem, and therefore one that can be thought of as indicating one's superiority over others, even those one loves. Superiority over others is one of humanity's highest goals. It is, of course, important to have a sense of value, particularly in relation to a society that is ruthless in its rejection of failure. And that which gives us a sense of worth is not, perhaps, without some merit.

However, the rather humbling reality is that the products of our intelligence, and our intelligence itself, are not the results of a conscious decision we have undertaken, but rather, more in the line of an unasked for gift. We are not intelligent because we chose to be so, or as a result of diligent effort on our part. Rather we find ourselves intelligent, to one degree or another, as a result of what may be termed chance, or if you wish divine intention. Intelligence is delightfully foisted on us in the random manner that beauty has or has not been our lucky lot in life. One can blame it on the genetic shuffling of the deck. We really did nothing to achieve the intelligence that we possess.

If one reflects on the smart ideas that have popped up in our heads or on the screen or paper on which we write, we will invariably fail to discover any intention to be intelligent. Our mental hardware, working with the data that was before it, came up with the creative leap that resulted in the perhaps brilliant concept that we produced. Did we produce this beautiful string of ideas? Yes, the truth is we did. However, the piece of brilliance was not the result of a decisional process, but rather was the end of the efficient interpreting of data that our brain is capable of, to the degree that it is an efficient data processing unit. Can we say to ourselves, "Wow, that is really quite smart"? Yes, we can. Whatever it means to be human has the ability to evaluate the creativity of an idea, just as we are able to evaluate the visual data that we receive and say that something is beautiful.

Often the development of an incipient idea results in conclusions that one did not expect or imagine. What was the seed of an idea may produce content that is as surprising to the writer as it is to the hoped for reader. Pride, in the traditional understanding of the term, is the feeling of superiority over others, as a consequence of the possession of an object or quality that the rest of society does not possess to an equal degree. In this sense, pride is not the simple feeling of pleasure and satisfaction experienced when a task is done well, but is rather a self reflection of superiority over others. If one performs a task well, it is illogical to imagine that there will be no pleasure in the successful operation and completion of that task. Nor is it wrong to evaluate the task positively.

One may also be well aware that something one has done will have a powerful effect on the society in which one acts. St Francis was almost certainly conscious that his behaviour was both good and remarkably different to that of those around him. Few would claim to have discovered an unacceptable pride in Francis as a result of this realization, and Francis would have had to be extremely unintelligent not to have realized his impact on the society of his time. To realize one's difference, and even one's intellectual superiority to others is not an evidence of pride.

Nevertheless, one's intelligence should not be the cause of sinful superiority for two reasons: (1) such a sense reveals a lack of divine love for one's sisters and brothers, and (2) the intelligence that one possesses, reflecting, as it does the degree of efficiency of our brains, is not something that we have, in any fashion caused to exist as a result of any thought, desire, or behaviour on our part. Indeed, such mental behaviours themselves depend on the efficiency of the brains we already possess, prior to any ambitions for intelligence one could imagine. If we are as smart as we imagine we are, we can view the results of this intelligence with pleasure, but we can take no pride in it, as if we independently brought into being the intelligence that gave us such creativity. And in this realization there is comfort for those who see themselves as less intelligent. The unintelligent are not inferior for possessing less efficient brains. It is not that one should be humble because this is a demanded moral characteristic. Humility is not a false move, or an expression of a false modesty to hide, what is otherwise a justifiable source of pride. There are reasons, in fact, for why humility is asked of one.

If we cannot choose the brains we possess, we likewise cannot view the products of these data processing organs as reasons for either pride or inferiority. Moreover, given the multifaceted sources of human limitation that accompany this gift, not to mention the scriptural call to humility, we really have little reason to see our talent as a justification for superiority. While we may have been very diligent in the development of our intelligence, there is also the strange sense in which we have been developing a quality that we actually had no hand in acquiring.

Chapter 23
PEOPLE ON THE STREET

One of the most interesting experiences for someone curious about how people regard others in society is travelling on a city bus or train. Most of the people one observes seem intent in creating the illusion that there are no other people around them, despite the fact that the bus or train might actually be full of other passengers. What one observes appears to be fear, suspicion, mistrust, and a careful avoidance of direct contact with all other people who press against them. In our society the stranger is not immediately viewed as harmless and seeking our good, but rather, at best, as careless of our wellbeing. People are afraid to be singled out in a crowd, and seek the direct opposite of what close contact with another human being seems to call for. Rather than human communication, most people in the company of strangers implicitly communicate the desire for a social isolation that living in a city would seemingly make impossible.

If my reactions and feelings are any indication of what most other people experience as well, we humans view virtually everyone we do not know as threats to our possessions, our sense of safety, and even our lives. Indeed, most of us seem to live in a continual state of fear, or at least suspicion of others. On the social level we appear to live at "Defcon 5", continually vigilant when we leave the comparative safety of our houses lest others seek to do us harm. This psychological vigilance is so perpetual and common that most of the time we are not even aware of its existence.

This attitude to others is exceedingly peculiar because most of us live in cities surrounded by hundreds of thousands of people, and would be utterly lost if we were suddenly to find ourselves alone. Moreover, if we live in rural areas we go out of our way to make ourselves known to our neighbours. The usually solitary nature of rural life seems to cause us to create an extended self made up of the community of similarly isolated people around us, and this group becomes the "trusted self" that the solitary individual sees him or herself as in the city. The stranger or the newcomer is still viewed, however, as suspect, and socially excluded from the sense of oneness that rural communities feel for those who live in them.

We avoid the eyes of the person walking towards us, while carefully checking to evaluate their potential for danger, act as if the person does not exist, and usually do not acknowledge the person's presence, even with a simple greeting. We probably, quite rightly, assume that this other person does not care about us. The level of fear involved in this ignoring of the stranger, the human in front of us, or sitting across from us on the train or bus, must surely be exhausting. It is the rare person indeed who will engage a stranger in conversation, and consequently, in fact, risk being thought strange and slightly "potty", as the English would put it. In fact, the person engaged by this human rarity will frequently feel uneasy and embarrassed by being the beneficiary of such "friendship", be uncomfortably conscious of the people around them listening to the unusual conversation, and thank his or her lucky stars when the offending "friendly" conversationalist finally has to get off at the next stop.

Why is it that Christians are not known for being different in this regard? Why is it that we are not known as the people who can be trusted, as the people who are friendly as they walk down the street? Why is it that people do not stop us as we are walking and ask us why we are so friendly and happy? Why is it that we are not different to the "pagans"? Was Jesus afraid of the people around him; the people he met? What is it in our hearts and lives that allows this fear to dominate our relationships with the stranger across the aisle? If perfect love casts out all fear, as St. John tells us, then we are apparently not living in this state of perfect love. The world will not change as a result of our experiencing this love, but perhaps the absence of fear in our hearts will be perceived by some of the people we meet, and will help these equally fearful others to become a little more trusting, at least of us. I believe that the love Jesus felt for others was frequently evident to those around him, and attracted usually fearful people, like the woman with the issue of blood, and despised lepers, to him as one who could be trusted. While we can't be friendly with everyone we meet doesn't it seem that our reticence towards strangers is not a particularly Christian reaction?

Chapter 24
THE SOCIAL GOSPEL

I first thought of including Isaiah 58 without comment, a ticking nuclear device that was so powerful such remarks would be unnecessary. Here, however, is the chapter:

> Shout aloud without restraint
> Lift up your voice like a trumpet.
> Call my people to account for their transgression
> And the house of Jacob for their sins,
> Although they ask counsel of me day by day
> And say they delight in knowing my ways,
> Although like nations which have acted rightly
> And not forsaken the just laws of their gods,
> They ask me for righteous laws
> And they say they delight in approaching God.
> Why do we fast, if thou dost not see it?
> Why mortify ourselves, if thou payest no heed?
> Because you serve your own interests only on your
>   fast day
> And make all your men work the harder

Since your fasting leads only to wrangling and strife
And dealing vicious blows with the fist
On such a day you are keeping no fast
That will carry your cry to heaven.
Is it a fast like this that I require,
A day of mortification such as this,
That a man should bow his head like a bulrush
And make his bed on sackcloth and ashes?
Is this what you call a fast,
A day acceptable to the Lord?
Is not this what I require of you as a fast:
To loose the fetters of injustice
To untie the knots of the yoke
To snap every yoke
And set free those who have been crushed?
Is it not sharing your food with the hungry,
Taking the homeless poor into your house,
Clothing the naked when you meet them
And never evading a duty to your relations?
Then shall your light break forth like the dawn
And soon you will grow healthy like a wound newly
    healed;
Your own righteousness shall be your protection as
    you advance
And the glory of the Lord your rearguard.
Then, if you call, the Lord will answer.
If you cry to him, he will say, "Here I am."
If you cease to pervert justice,
To point the accusing finger and lay false charges,
If you feed the hungry from your own plenty
And satisfy the needs of the wretched
Then your light will rise like dawn out of darkness
And your dusk be like noonday.
The Lord will be your guide continually
And will satisfy your needs in the shimmering heat.

He will give you strength of limb;
You will be like a well watered garden,
Like a spring whose waters never fail.
The ancient ruins will be restored by your relatives
And you will build once more on ancestral foundations.
You will be called the Rebuilder of broken walls
The Restorer of houses in ruins....
The Lord himself has spoken it

What this section of scripture certainly is not, is a political address. Isaiah is not attempting to straddle a fence and ensure that no one is offended. The chapter begins "shout aloud...lift up your voice...call my people to account". We in North America are very often exposed, I think, to two types of preaching: one that is so balanced and bland that sleep is the preferred refuge of the soul who is under its sway, and the other is the dramatic shouter, walking up and down, raising and lowering his speech, seemingly for theatrical effect, and virtually irrespective of the topic being presented. This second type of preacher raises his voice habitually, and appears not to have any other method of presentation. However, whatever the form employed, the relationship between the method of presentation and the spiritual content of the sermon is frequently either tenuous or non-existent.

While it is true that many pastors genuinely seek to teach their flock the way of God, it remains the case that, overall a cool detachment seems to be the general criteria for acceptable church leadership. Perhaps in the same manner that the British are caricatured as, " No emotion please, we're English", the clergy frequently come across as guarded, and not given to a deep emotional attachment to the ideas and beliefs they hold, apparently fearing to be viewed as immature and unsophisticated. And yet, given passages such as the above, and the very gospel itself as the only escape from a world of sin, such detachment can only be seen as entirely inappropriate.

Nevertheless, not all passion is a genuine expression of a love for God or a high regard for the truths being presented. Passion in preaching can come from an erroneous sense of one's importance and position. It can arise from a general anger at humanity in general, in the guise of putting people straight. It may even be a sign of psychological imbalance. It could also simply express one's love of the theatrical. The passion that God seeks for the healing of the soul, which the world needs, is one which consumes the heart in a love that springs from a close and genuine relationship with God. A passion for God may not even reveal itself in a raised voice or a restless gaze. It is doubtful that Jesus was ever confused with John the Baptist. Such a passion does not see ministry as a job in which one negotiates one's salary and refuses to take a pulpit if certain economic requirements are not met. Rather, a passion for God and humanity makes one a shepherd who is willing to lay down his or her life for the flock.

Genuine passion (and not simply shouting) is a rarity in churches and among the clergy in most parts of the historic Christian world. Indeed, on the whole, it is not wanted. And yet the prophet here, not only cries out "shout aloud" once, but repeats this in various forms, three times. Our passionless preaching must surely indicate a general level of satisfaction with the world. Either this is the reason for such a state, or it is that we actually do not believe that what we are preaching is radically important. Indeed, what can it indicate other than that despite the content of some of our religious statements, we are not particularly troubled by the general condition of the world, and just a little tinkering, pretty much at our own level of interest, is sufficient to make things go as they should?

Surely, if we genuinely believed that the world was suffused with deep suffering, fear, and spiritually lost, and that we Christians were not much better, our attitude to life would be somewhat more intense. If we had loved our "lovers" as passionlessly as we regard the spiritual state of the world, and indeed our own souls, we would never have been able to convince our spouses that we were truly serious about them. It is, though, completely understandable that such a vision, and the presence of such a person in whom God is genuinely, sanely, and completely central should deeply disturb us. Unfortunately, it remains true that as long as the church exists in a low state, and as long as there are few in the clergy who are genuinely filled with this kind of passion, we will not be troubled by God's vision. Nevertheless, as uncomfortable as such a vision and passion make us feel, this is exactly what we need.

The next little section, verses 2 and 3 is directed to the nation of Israel, but we, the church, can see ourselves in these verses as well. "They ask counsel of me day by day, and say they delight in knowing my ways…and say they delight in approaching God". Doesn't this sound very much like us? Don't we go to church, listen to the word of God and pray, while the true level of our seeking of God is far below, even that which we dimly understand to be necessary? The problem that Isaiah saw was that the people of his day related to God, mainly for the benefit it would have in their own lives (verse 4). Chapter 58 is a terrifying critique of the selfish heart. If you don't want to see the inseparable connection God makes between spirituality and unselfishness/good works this is the chapter to avoid.

Verse six states, "Is not this what I require of you as a fast: to loose the fetters of injustice, to untie the knots of the yoke, to snap every yoke, and set those free who have been crushed". Snapping yokes, setting people free? This is not how we Christians have been taught to identify spirituality. In fact, we have been taught that these verses, and others like them, are meant to be understood as the freeing of the soul from spiritual bondage. And they can indeed be understood in this fashion. However the context of the rest of the chapter strongly indicates, not merely a spiritual release, but a release from real economic and social bondage, from real suffering and stress, a release brought about by the people of God, whom God expects to work to remove these yokes.

In order to make this biblical language somewhat more meaningful, perhaps we should imagine the legal system that we have, and those parts of it that remove the right to withhold labor from certain workers, or that limit the minimum wage to amounts that barely allow one to stay alive, while making it virtually impossible to escape from this insecurity and shame. Or perhaps, as it is in Canada, the situation Christians should be struggling to alter is the forced deduction of relatively large amounts of the worker's pay, along with the employer's income, into an insurance fund against unemployment, which the government regards as general revenue, and indeed has long been evaluated as over-funded, while the government, at the same time, makes it extremely difficult for the average worker to get any benefit from these pay deductions except in extremely limited circumstances. Almost certainly there are other, perhaps even more important injustices we should be seeking to remove.

It is not simply injustice in general that is mentioned in this chapter of Isaiah. The following phrase in this verse states, "to untie the knots of the yoke'. As part of the yoke that puts the poor in bondage there are discrete systemic realities that need to be addressed. What keeps the poor at the low level that they are? Let it be clearly stated here. Nowhere in the bible does scripture blame the poor for being in the state they are. Nowhere are they accused of laziness or stupidity.. On the other side of this coin, scripture, here and in other sections of the bible we so love to assert is divinely inspired, commands us to support the poor, remove that which keeps them in such a state, and encourages us to divest ourselves of our wealth in this very task.

Before unions and enlightened legislation forced businesses to share their profits more equitably with their employees, many of the present middle class were in just this state of penury. This sharing of the vast wealth of the western developed nations has accomplished much in the amelioration of societal suffering. But there is still much that needs to be done, and the same cry that higher wages will put businesses out of operation is heard every time increased minimum wages are discussed, one move that would at least improve the situation of the working poor. Indeed fair wages have never resulted in economic collapse, and the only event, to memory, which has come close to this has been the sudden rapacious increase in the cost of petroleum which dislocated, and continues to send ripples through the developed world, and which has resulted in the virtual destruction of many viable social programs for the poor and weak in society, radical price increases which were instituted, not by workers but by companies and various states.

We are told to "untie the knots of the yoke". What are the knots? What needs to be done for this to occur? What systemic structures need to be examined and refashioned? What kind of education do we need to acquire in order to deal with this issue? Should we organize to achieve this goal? What actually needs to be done, of a concrete nature, to address this command? And it appears that God cannot rest until all yokes are removed. The last small section of this verse tells us, "To snap every yoke". Partial success is unacceptable. As long as one individual is still held in socio-economic bondage, not free to enjoy life to the same extent as others do, God expects us to work for this person's release. This is not left wing, Marxist, or socialist clap-trap. This is simply a partial exegesis of these verses in Isaiah, a book we Christians love for its Christological and soteriological content. If evangelical Christians want to be biblically loyal, they must be biblical, even when this contradicts their political and social theories.

And just in case we are tempted to spiritualize this, the next verses tell us exactly what God has in mind in these previous verses. "Is it not sharing your food with the hungry, taking the homeless poor into your house, clothing the naked poor when you meet them, and never evading a duty to your relatives." If you do not think these verses are terrifying in their implications, you must be at the level of Catholic sainthood. These verses cut to the very heart of our self centredness and self love. The words of the Gospel immediately come to mind. "And he went away sorrowful, for he was very rich" Luke 18:23.

God is not simply supplying us with specific things we should mechanically do, and be doing. That is the mistake we often make with scripture. We confuse examples as rituals we should follow word for word. Yet despite this, we are given specific things here that we should be doing. Things that we find almost, if not totally impossible to do. Things we are downright unwilling to do. Even the preachers of the social gospel would balk at this level of love for others. And on the other hand, those who pooh pooh the social gospel must find these verses extremely difficult to spiritualize away. However, this is the kind of people God expects us to be.

Why is it, do you think, that the scripture says in Luke 1:53 "the hungry he has satisfied with good things but the rich he has sent empty away"? If one is tempted to interpret "the hungry he has satisfied with good things" as the hungry are those who long for God, and the good things are spiritual blessings, why then does the next verse say "the rich he has sent empty away"? If the hungry is meant spiritually, doesn't that surely mean that the rich must also be interpreted spiritually as well? And if that is so, why did God send them away empty? Indeed, that is the question that must be asked, "why did God send them away"? Simply because they were rich? And rich in what sense? Almost certainly not. As Isaiah 58 indicates, and Jesus' words to the rich young man suggest, the problem with having possessions is not so much that one has them, but that one regards the possessions more highly than one does one's brother and sister who are in need. Indeed, it gets worse. In scripture, one's brother and sisters are not necessarily one's family, or even one's fellow believers. The scriptures see one's family as the entire human race, every one we meet, without exception.

When St. Francis was alive, if a person had no belt and he did, he would give away his. And one needs to know that what St Francis possessed was usually only the clothing on his body. I do not believe that God wants us to be so impoverished. It is not easy to know, however, how much of what we possess (mountains compared to St Francis' possessions) we should give to those who have so little. If there is an area in which one is alone before God, and in which another person has no right to condemn, this is probably it. St Francis saw impoverishment as the removal of a vast impediment to a real identification with Christ in his poverty, and as a doorway to a true love of the Saviour. The truth remains, you see, that while our brothers and sisters suffer in poverty and psychological bondage, we do not have the right to be wealthy, in comparison to them.

How we Christians have been ignorant of God's attitude on this for so long is remarkable. It is not as if the scriptures are not clear. St Paul, in 2 Corinthians 8, verses 12-15 writes,

> God accepts what a person has, he does not ask for what he has not. There is no question of relieving others at the cost of hardship to yourselves. It is a question of equality. At the moment your surplus

meets their need, but one day your need may be met by their surplus. The aim is equality.

Do you find these verses as terrifying as I do? What are they saying? Well first, that God does not want us to become impoverished by our giving. God wants a removal of suffering. He is not seeking an equal sharing of it. Second, the standard of living that one enjoys should be the standard of living that all enjoy. Paul mentions equality twice. Can you think of another interpretation of the verses? If this is not a radical critique of our capitalist thinking I don't know what is. Yet, while it is not a rejection of the capitalist system per se, it is, nevertheless, a rejection of the elitist and self obsessed aspects of the system.

We should raise the poor closer to our level by a diminishing of our wealth. This does not imply that all should be raised to the highest level. Nor does it imply that we should be lowered to the lowest level. Rather, it demands that we give our surpluses to the poor so that their suffering is reduced, and further, that systemic structures which make it difficult for the poor to escape their poverty are removed so that they themselves have the opportunity to access the means of improving their lot in life. I feel though, that I have been too kind to us. The major idea contained in these verses is, and unchangeably remains, that we give to the poor so that their suffering is reduced and so that they achieve some level of equality with us. Don't let us deceive ourselves by focusing on the systemic changes that need to be made so that the poor can help themselves. These changes are needed. However, Paul is writing here about giving other people our surpluses. The question then for us is: "What surplus do we have?".

Verses ten and eleven of this chapter in Isaiah say, "If you feed the hungry from your own plenty, and satisfy the needs of the wretched, then your light will rise like dawn out of darkness, the Lord will be your guide continually, and he will satisfy your needs in the heat of the day". At the very best, the possession of wealth is viewed in scripture with an extreme ambivalence. More often, it is seen as a source of great temptation. In 1 Timothy 6:5-10 Paul very bluntly states,

> People who have lost their grip on the truth...They think religion should yield dividends, and of course religion does yield high dividends, but only to the one whose resources are within him. We brought nothing into the world; for that matter we cannot take anything with us when we leave, but if we have food and covering let us be content. Those who want to be rich fall into temptations...The love of money is the root of all evil things.

Rather than encouraging the belief that a spiritual Christian will be blessed with material wealth, this section of the New Testament teaches us that we should be content with that level of possession that provides us with economic security. This is the teaching of the Lord Jesus Christ on poverty and wealth, not the one promising a Cadillac in every driveway of the faithfully giving believer.

Indeed, if this is the correct understanding of these verses, we should be a little hesitant to proclaim that God has made us wealthy. God allows a great many things to occur, and in regards to our respective wealths, in the light of the verses above, there is no indication that God has the slightest interest in making the members of the body of Christ wealthy. If it is a matter of relative hermeneutical "weight", ethical and spiritual positions given us in scripture far outweigh any interpretational implications we feel are inherent in statements in scripture indicating that God has made a particular individual wealthy. If we are to pick verses that assist us in spiritual development, those that suggest the crucifixion of the self in a life of selfless love seem more appropriate than searching for a justification for our desire for personal aggrandizement.

Moreover, the materialistic motivation of charitable behaviour is totally antithetical to the teaching of giving that is presented here. It is, in fact, an absolute denial of this teaching. The reason the rich are sent away is that they do not love their neighbour as they love themselves. They do not do to others as they would have others do to them. Their lives are, despite any religious covering that may be attempted, self centred. They do not have love for others, and therefore, inevitably, they do not love God. And that is why this chapter is so terrifying. That describes my heart at this moment, and it probably describes yours as well.

CHAPTER 25
THE RICH AND THE POOR

Personally, I do not believe God wants anyone to be poor. Despite the ascetic mentality that the church has generally accepted since the Eremitic fathers walked away from civilization and into the desert in an attempt to free themselves from the corruption of society, an overwhelming body of scripture indicates that God expects those with economic security to reduce the suffering of the poor, not necessarily by becoming similarly poor. There is another aspect of poverty, however, which has nothing to do with such obligations. God is also concerned with the attitude of the poor towards the rich.

Psalm 73 is the therapeutic confession of one of God's people who felt envy at the lifestyle of the rich and famous, and discovered that this attitude separated him (or her) from peace with God. With omissions, the psalm reads:

My feet had almost slipped
When I saw how they prosper
No pain, no suffering is theirs
They are sleek and sound in limb
They are not plunged in trouble as other men are.
So it was all in vain that I kept my heart pure
And washed my hands in innocence.
I set myself to think this out
But I found it too hard for me
Until I went into God's sacred courts.
When my heart was embittered
I felt the pangs of envy
Yet I am always with Thee
Thou holdest my right hand.
Whom have I in heaven but thee?
And having thee, I desire nothing else on earth.
I have chosen thee, Lord God, to be my refuge.

It is not easy to suffer the worries that swirl around one's life when one is poor. It is not easy to be driving down the street in a wreck of a car and be surrounded by Mercedes, BMWs, and other beautiful new cars. If one is single, there are enough economic demands to concern one. However, if one has a family and children, these concerns are multiplied, and finding enough money to pay all the bills that accumulate every month can be an endless struggle which gradually destroys any hope that there is a way out of the dark pit one is in. There is a vast array of goods and services that must be paid: rent, food, medical bills, utilities, school supplies and clothing, gas, and car insurance so that one can get to one's employment, if one does have a job. Poverty is not a vacation from responsibility, but the experience of struggling to meet needs that fortunately, three quarters of the society we may be part of, do not have to seriously worry about. Is it wrong to spend millions of dollars on a house while millions of people are dying of starvation, aids, and live in grinding poverty? Certainly it is. And this is not altered by one's personal philanthropy. It is natural that in such a situation, one might feel envy, and even anger towards those who do not have such seemingly endless pressures.

Nevertheless, bitterness and envy at those who have more than enough are as equally unacceptable as the misuse of wealth. They are not emotions or attitudes that promote peace with God. Although the wealthy have a God directed responsibility to support the suffering in society, there is no guarantee that they will accept this opportunity to express love in this way. Fortunately, God has promised to supply our needs, and we need to take these needs to our heavenly Father/Mother in prayer. The faithfulness of God to meet the needs of his children, however, does not negate the scriptural expectation that those with "plenty" have, as a general and continual practice.

Nevertheless, to conclude that one's devotion to God has been a waste of time because it has not removed one's poverty, while being understandable, is a sad mistake. There are lessons found in the psalm, however, that we can take from this misunderstanding, whether we are poor or not. First, from this erroneous understanding we discover that it is a mistake to assume that God promises wealth to those who follow him. Second, faith in God, and devotion to him, as seen in godly behaviour, have no necessary connection to one's economic position, nor does this reflect one's spiritual state before God. We follow God because a relationship with the Father has a positive value, unconnected to any earthly reward. Third, an attitude of resentment and envy causes the cessation of one's untroubled peace with God. Fourth, the poor need to be encouraged by their having chosen God to be their refuge (v 28). As verse 27 so lovingly states, "God is (their) possession".

Whether, one way or another, one ultimately is provided with those things one needs as a human being, God does not forget the tears of the poor and their suffering. Luke 1:53 states, "the hungry he has satisfied with good things, but the rich he has sent empty away." I have no idea how this redistribution gets worked out in the land where there are no more tears, but God will certainly find a way to heal the pain that unfairness, and our unfaithfulness to the cries of our brothers and sisters, have caused. And further, I will not take refuge in an unfeeling middle class interpretation of these verses as "spiritual satisfaction for the spiritually hungry" (though this also is a valid interpretation).

The rich are not without problems, though they are not at the survival level of the poor. Yet it is impossible to find inner peace, or peace with God if one's heart is consumed by bitterness and envy. The poor and the wealthy together do not have the right before God to judge each other. This right to judge is God's alone, and he will act with mercy and truth. 'You alone are my possession', the poor can cry out to God, and the great Shepherd of the sheep, he who had only one garment as his possession at the end of his life at the Cross, will lovingly, and truly understand.

Chapter 26
CHRISTIANS AND THEIR FAMILIES

Industrialization, and the consequent increase in the migration of populations to the cities, essentially destroyed the extended family. Traditional families were trans-generational institutions in which not only three or more generations of relatives lived together, but where siblings often shared the same large household. Industrialization reduced the family to the nuclear form we are familiar with, and gradually destroyed ties of closeness and obligation that had been the mainstay of the traditional form, and which had generated support and security for each member of the family. There were often benefits to this fragmentation of the family in increased household harmony and a greater sense of privacy, but the sense of security and belonging was, in the main, lost. The biblical model of the community of God is based on the model of the family, and indeed, on a horizontal view of this structure. The terms of relationship within the family of God are brotherly and sisterly. The hierarchical nature of the extended family is not strongly alluded to in this model, and relationships are those of love between essential equals.

Strangely, though the model of the people of God is the family, the family itself, as a model of a greater unit, is infrequently referred to in Christian, or even Old Testament teaching. And yet, though this may be so, it is inconceivable that the affectional and obligational aspects of family life that have become the model for the household of God, should not reflect back on the source of this model. Indeed, if one has obligations of love to those to whom one does not naturally have close ties, should it be unexpected that there are also such expectations towards one's natural family members?

Although it is possible to cut oneself off from most other human beings, it is quite difficult to do this with one's own family members. Even if one does separate oneself from a brother or sister, or even one's parents, they remain in one's memory, and the sense of failure evident in this lack of family harmony continues to prick one's conscience. Family members, as has been pointed out by many, make one aware of one's sinfulness more acutely than almost every other person we have contact with. Family hurts can be the deepest, and memories of insensitivity, selfishness and cruelty can last for a lifetime, and be the cause of family tensions in almost every family, not excluding Christian families. Families are like the Mosaic Law. They make us bitterly aware of our sinfulness, and our shortcomings before God.

If, however, one is a Christian, broken family relationships should never be taken for granted or allowed to continue in an attitude of resentment. If healing cannot be easily achieved, then God must be sought so that one's deeply hurt heart can be healed, and love can flow between separated family members. At times only the Holy Spirit can bring this about. If one is enjoined to seek a renewal of relationship between one's fellow believer and oneself, would it be right to imagine that one's relationship with a family member were less important?

Life is a struggle, and achieving security in the world is a long process. The nuclear family certainly has its share of economic pressures. However, if one member has attained some degree of stability and economic prosperity, while another family member suffers, does it seem reasonable that the more secure member has no obligations of blood and compassion to assist the poorer family member financially, or in other ways possible? The reader can make up his or her own mind, but it seems decidedly, unchristian to treat brothers and sisters, and definitely parents, in the same economic fashion as one treats one's clients and other strangers, that is to say, impersonally.

Nor is this so, solely on the basis of simple logic. St Paul clearly indicates responsibility to one's family members in 1 Timothy 5: 8 where he states, "If anyone does not make provision for his relations, and especially for members of his own household, he has denied the faith and is worse than an unbeliever." This verse seems tailor made for our particular time. There is a specificity to the verse that is compelling, and from which there appears no escape. The family is not simply one's nuclear family, or even the family that resides within one's walls. According to this verse, one's family is one's entire relations. And towards these relations there are obligations of support. In passing, the only way one who fails to meet these obligations could be "worse than an unbeliever", would be that the unbelievers, on the whole, were fulfilling these familial obligations. Paul was essentially suggesting that if even the unbelievers acted in this fashion, would it not be shameful, and a stark evidence of a lack of Christian love, to ignore such obligations? If the unbelievers act properly out of a sense of social obligation, should not the Christians, even more so, act similarly from a sense of love?

Verse 16 of the same chapter states, " If a Christian man or woman has widows in the family, he must support them himself." Paul was writing in a period when there was no social "safety net". However, the existence of this support system does not abrogate one from the responsibilities Paul was teaching. The safety net of Paul's time was the church, and church funds were not to be used to meet the needs of the church members who had family who could look after these needy. The scripture is teaching, therefore, that the existence of an economic safety net does not necessarily remove one from an obligation to look after one's relations.

This is not, however, an inflexible law. That one does not have the economic resources to meet even one's own needs, surely suggests that one is not expected, to any significant degree, to supply the needs of extended family members in need. And yet one must sincerely search one's heart if one is tempted to apply such a proviso to justify not supporting one's family. Indeed, if one would sacrifice to assist one's daughter or son, such a sacrifice may be demanded in relation to other family members. As in virtually all other human behaviours, the presence or absence of love is the litmus test by which we evaluate our actions and decisions.

In fact, to treat one's brothers and sisters in Christ in the fashion one would a business client needs serious reflection. Indeed, the biblical ascription of pseudo-familial relationship titles to non-family members makes the economic relationship one has with both clients and fellow believers one that demands a biblical reexamination. The scriptures do not differentiate between the obligations one has to one's fellow human beings, one's fellow believers, or even one's family. Behaviour to one is described as identical to the behaviour of love that is demanded to the other. Indeed social distinctions become lost in a biblical description of how one relates to all others. Psychologically, culturally, and scripturally there exists an inescapable obligation to support one's family members when they are in need. However, most of the bible, if not Jesus in his summary of the Law in the Golden Rule of "do unto others as you would have them do to you", sees no social distinctions as motivating any special kind of compassionate action, either to the Family of God or to one's particular family. Rather, those obligations of love and support, traditionally understood to be part of family membership, are expanded to the entire human race, without differentiation.

The question then seems not simply, "what are my obligations to my extended family?" but more troublingly, "in what way do the scriptures impact on how I interact, on many levels, with society at large?" Moreover, in what fashion is a Christian business person, member of the military, policeman/woman, factory worker, salesperson different to one who is not a believer? What scriptural principles, other than honesty, should be included in how a Christian does "business"? Surely it is simply not enough that one is a Christian, that she or he is successful, or even that the individual believer contributes to religious and philanthropic causes. As with every other area in which the Christian must discover the Christian path in the world, "In what way is a Christian different from other people?" Are there distinguishing characteristics to Christian economic and social activity, or are we all simply capitalists, who just happen to be religious?

As Christians, it is difficult enough to satisfy the scriptures in relation to our family members. This alone is an area that needs substantial rethinking in the age of the isolated nuclear family. There are, in addition, the implications of our Christian faith in regards to the rest of society, and how we interact economically and behaviourally to it. The problem, it seems, is not the clarity or ambiguity of the scriptures themselves. Rather, it is that we Christians frequently compartmentalize life into at least two sections: our faith, and the rest of our lives in the world. We live in these two domains, and seem not to realize the implications that flow from certain aspects of our faith, to the way we react to the world and its people. And with this division, our economic obligations to the suffering, for example, have been understood in extremely limited terms.

This is actually quite understandable, because the implications of the scriptural teaching are a radical critique of the self love that is the true motivation of most of our lives. When Jesus asked the rich young man to give away his wealth he was not asking for his money. He was asking for his heart. And that is something that most of us have not, in truth, given to Jesus. On the other hand, it should not be understood that Jesus did not really care what the rich young man did with his abandoned money, as if appeals by God to assist the poor to live humanely are not the true intent of the Godhead, but only tests of our self love. Such an interpretation would come exceedingly close to an understanding of God as essentially dishonest and manipulative, or to an accusation that God's love towards the poor was not completely genuine.

That we cannot but fail the Law does not mean that the Law is not an accurate description of the mind and character of God. It remains the case, however, that God seeks our hearts, the control centre of our natures. And in this area it remains true that without the sanctifying work of the Holy Spirit, through which we are given new hearts, we cannot achieve, even this one thing. The ethical demands made by St Paul are no different from the demands of the Law or the positions taught by Jesus, for example, in the Sermon on the Mount. Behavioural demands are no more achievable, simply because they are found in the epistles and not Leviticus and Deuteronomy. All are, in their entirety, impossible to fulfil without a transformation of our hearts. Family obligations, both in relation to our relationships and our resources, remain ours to obey, and as with other divine behavioural expectations, the need for God's grace is both our desparate need and the divine promise.

Chapter 27
THE CHURCH TODAY

Music: How Should We Sing?

One of the most important creations of the human race has been the expression of the heart in music. In ways, very similar, and parallel to those of poetry, music has expressed human longing, love, oppression, fear and worship for thousands of years. Indeed, there is probably no human thought or feeling that has not found an outlet in this artistic form. Music varies from culture to culture, and what is believed to be valuable in one culture, is often unappreciated in another. Even within one culture there are musical forms that are not understood and not valued by one or another group within that culture. Probably the more complex a culture is, the more varieties of musical form there are within this culture. The church is essentially no different, and within the church there is a variety of avenues whereby God is worshipped. There are also, as we would expect to see in a situation of diverse musical expression, groups in the church that do not appreciate and value varieties of worship music that are loved by other sections within the church. Unfortunately, this very democratic and acceptable plethora of avenues of expression, does not describe the musicological environment in which many sections of the evangelical church now find themselves. Rather, what often exists is an environment in which one particular form is forced on the entire congregation, and the hymnody of, at least the last three to five hundred years, is essentially abandoned in a move, it is claimed by those who support this imposition, to adapt the church to contemporary musical styles.

The church is a social environment in which open conflict is not valued, and in which, in the name of peace, a consensus is sometimes arrived at that does not necessarily reflect the sincere thoughts and opinions of the individuals allowing such an apparent consensus. This is especially true when the minister or pastor is strongly in support of a particular change. Of course, willingness to support ministerial innovations does not automatically occur. However, when theologically based changes are contemplated, such as a radical change in worship styles in the name of contemporary acceptability, the likelihood that such a change will be agreed to by the church board is relatively high. Appeals to the relevancy of the church in today's society, and the need to attract outsiders, are difficult appeals to gainsay.

Musicologically, the situation many congregations find themselves in today is one in which a 'rock' based musical style dominates the worship life of the church, and other, "traditional" musical forms are virtually non-existent. In terms of the congregation, this results in the silencing of voices in opposition, who fear that they are in the minority and must be unacceptably "old-fashioned". However, it also results in at least two other consequences that are even less desirable. A percentage of the congregation that can not accept this form as the only way worship will be conducted gives up, and slowly stops coming to church. The other result is that members leave the congregation, to which they may have belonged for a considerable length of time, and try to find a new home congregation where, what is now called "traditional" worship is conducted, and the church's hymnody is not limited to songs composed, only in the last fifteen or twenty years.

Personally, I do not find anything wrong with rock based music. I grew up with rock n roll, and though some Christians have rejected this form as evil, I do not find its rhythms any more disturbing than any other form of music that causes happiness and expresses human feelings. Specific songs may be unacceptable, but the form itself is not, at least from my perspective. However, I would find it rather odd to attempt to express the gentleness of love, for example, by using the melodic forms employed by Steppenwolf, or some other hard rock band. For myself, I still think that love should be expressed in soft and gentle music, at least to some degree, and I believe that society, which we say we are attempting to attract, finds a deep and lasting attachment to certain love songs like Unchained Melody, or Brian Adams' love songs. This surely reinforces the idea that love is best expressed in softness and slowness, rather than loudness and rapid tempo. If I am happy and want to express myself enthusiastically, Bachmann Turner Overdrive, or some other fast and noisy rock band of your choice is, on the other hand, perfect.

Surely that is the point. By imposing a rock model on all musical expression in the church we are simply ignoring the psychological realities of the totality of the human experience. Once, in bible college, I was raked over the coals for singing a hymn to a faster beat. There does not seem anything wrong with music that is fast, produced by a multiplicity of musical instruments that include guitars and drums, and is even loud. But there is surely something terribly wrong with a worship service where all music includes this instrumental variety, and all is sung in an "upbeat" fast manner (the politically brilliant term used to describe this kind of service, other forms, by implication, being depressing and downbeat) that absolutely precludes any ability to gently worship and express a tender love for the God to whom we are presumably expressing love.

I have spent most of my adult life listening to contemporary music, and what happened following the initial explosion of rock n roll onto the world was that there was felt a need to re-introduce love songs that were not enfolded in the frenetic melodies of simple rock. The result was a transformation of the traditional love song, but with connections to its historic roots, and an enriching of rock to include a variety of rock forms and improved instrumentation that had more musical sophistication than simple rock n roll. We as a church need to understand that (a) psychologically, slow and gentle is necessary at certain times in the human experience, and (b) that there needs to be a variety of musical forms beyond the supposed "upbeat" that dominates churches where "contemporary" music is employed. We need to be a little more sophisticated ourselves.

This enforcement of one form is not only musically and psychologically mistaken, it is an act of violence on a section of the congregation that can not, and will not worship in this fashion. The demographics of a congregation will certainly show an age breakdown that includes old people, people in their fifties to seventies, more middle aged people, young people who are either married or single, youth, and children. It is almost certainly erroneous to assume that all youth, children and young adults will always choose a rock model for their religious expression. It is definitely incorrect to assume that middle and older generations will always choose such a musical form, and it is totally incorrect to assume that the post-youth generational levels do not care that the music which they have grown up with, and which they have employed to worship God, is never allowed. The use of an occasional hymn from the traditional collection, frequently sung too fast to have any sense of adoration, often with verses left out, and usually accompanied in the rock mode, does not meet the needs of those who would like to worship, sometimes at least, with a little less noise, less haste and the feeling that they and their desires were not being patronised by such an inclusion.

What should also not be forgotten, is the accompanying fact that in contemporary services, young and old are usually kept standing for extended periods of time, as if this makes the worship more authentic. Despite the occasional encouragement to feel free to sit, there is no real choice as to standing or not. Frequently, the overhead can not be seen if one sits down, and it is feared that the removal of oneself from the communal act of standing and singing, will be understood as a tacit rejection of the majority attitude, or worse, as an expression of a spiritual inadequacy. Indeed, the upset to the individual and on the service that can accompany the imposition and use of the contemporary form of worship is almost unbelievable in the multiplicity of the aspects that it negatively impacts.

Not only is such a uni-form service, in effect an act of violence, it is also an abandonment of hundreds of years of the church's musical confession. That not all historic hymns are really worth singing is well known. This fact is registered in that they are so infrequently sung. However, there exists such a rich treasury of hymns that express the inner experience of the believer, the need of the church to engage in particular ministries, and that form the basis of a genuine worship of God in (his) three persons, that it is truly irresponsible to ignore the church's historic hymnody. Contemporary hymns, more usually they are simply choruses, often lack theological depth, are at times indulgent, and sometimes could have been generated by any religious group, and not necessarily the Christian church. This is so far from being simply a matter of a difference of taste, that it is a tragedy. The loss of a hymnody that has strengthened the church for varying lengths of time extending into the Middle Ages is similar, in this particular area of faith, to the loss of civilization as a result of the barbarian invasions of the Roman Empire. As a church we could very rapidly become (and I believe already are becoming) almost totally ignorant of any of the biblically based, beautiful, and soul stirring hymns of the church, prior to this movement to the supposed contemporary.

The virtually total abandonment of traditional i.e. not fast paced, rock based recent hymns, in the name of an adaptation to contemporary musical forms is, ironically, a major error in the evaluation of contemporary music. Contemporary church music does not, in fact, reflect the real diversity of the contemporary music scene. Contemporary music is composed of everything from pop country, traditional country, to hip hop, classic rock, and an almost endless number of genre variations in between. For all these musical variations there is an audience that loves this particular kind of music. Contemporary music is no more the monolithic model that "contemporary" churches present than the traditional musical presentations of the church were unidimensional, before this hymnodic coup/revolution. Pentecostal and other dynamic black and evangelical churches have long had a variety of musical instruments employed at various parts in their services. The only difference between then and now is that, previously there was always a variation in the kind of music that was sung in these churches. There was a variety of traditional music, country, and even fast paced and 'loud' music. It is amazing that this abandonment has been so widespread. It is an extreme, and social extremes, by their very nature, do not express the broad demographic spectrum of interests and needs.

Throughout the centuries there has been a sifting of the hymns the church has produced to a relatively small number that express the deepest thoughts and feelings of believers. The beauty of hymns is that they say, often in music that seems perfectly fitted to the sentiments, ideas that we as individuals are too limited to express. Bach's Jesu Joy of Man's Desiring, the wonderful hymns of the Wesleys and early Methodism, the outpourings of the nineteenth century religious awakenings, and many more from around the world, have all contributed to the spiritual life and service of the church. It is a contribution that must not be thoughtlessly left behind. This flight from a deeply biblically based hymnody that is the heritage of the church is of such great importance that it is time for mainstream members of churches to pray for, demand and work towards a restoration of a more balanced worship model. No one is asking for old fashioned organs, and no contemporary hymns or instruments. Such a demand would be as ridiculous as the demand that the service be completely contemporary. There should not be a radical dichotomy between contemporary and traditional congregational worship models. Both have a place, both are important, and both reflect the life, the ongoing life of today's church.

Technology, Christian Teaching and Programs in the Contemporary Church's Life

Technology

One of the things that mark the 20th and 21st centuries is an apparent obsession with technology. Information technology is changing so rapidly that, in addition to being almost impossible to keep up with, we derive a sense of pride and shallow superiority in being part of the cutting edge revolution. The changes are confusing, and sometimes terrifying, but in many ways these new tools are wonderfully useful. The church has been part of this revolution, at least in terms of attempting to adapt to it, and information storage, formatting, and presentation has made aspects of the life of the church easier and more efficient. On the other hand, one wonders what the advantages are of a computer driven over head projection system that costs more than $20,000, to provide the words of hymns, over a hymn book. Coupled with an unbalanced use of contemporary music in worship, in many churches there is a rush to have the latest information delivery system, with little more apparent reason than that the church down the block has just such a system. After the investment in such a complex and potentially useful system it frequently ends up being used, in the main, simply as a non-paper hymn book, that, during the long periods of standing to sing, if one sits down, one can no longer access, because the people who continue to stand in front of one, block the screen.

Please do not accuse me of being a Luddite. Every tool that can be used in the advance of the gospel, and to improve church life should, if possible, be so used. This does not mean, however, that an inadequately thought through investment of church funds that involves modern technology should be undertaken. Technology will not, in itself, raise the spiritual level of the church, and indeed, may be a hindrance to this. An excessive focus on a tool, as a means to achieve a spiritual goal is surely to miss the whole nature of the spiritual world. It is not that these advances should not be used, any more than the use of paper to make bibles is sinful. Paper, after all, is also a product of technology. What is disturbing about the church's employment of modern information technology is its almost faddish nature. It is there to be had, and so it must be purchased and installed. Other churches are using it, so it must have an intrinsic and necessary value.

Surely the value of a technology is not in its potential applicability, but in its actual usefulness in a specific context. New technologies have such value, in that the existing technologies in these contexts are clearly seen to be markedly less efficient. But is this always true? In many churches the employment of expensive computer driven information delivery systems not only does not increase efficiencies, but actually reduces the level of information delivery to the congregation. Indeed, at times its use within the local church is unnecessary, and it is as if having bought the equipment, we now must find uses for it, if only to justify its cost. Moreover, especially just prior to the beginning of services, the ongoing 'news items' distract and discourage a preparation for worship that is difficult enough to create, as it is. We have bought the toy, but we are just not quite sure how it should be utilized.

Theoretically, this in itself, is not a problem. It usually takes time for any new technology to become successfully integrated by a society. Where we, as churches, do have a problem is that we have not allowed for the time to discover the weaknesses of the potential tool. Rather, we have rushed pell mell to implement it. We have focused almost solely on what it can do, without seriously questioning whether it is *actually* needed, or what the deleterious effects might be. Indeed, we appear to have such faith in our new technological wonder that we have failed to consider the negative impacts it may, and indeed does have. We take time before we buy a car. We take even more time to purchase a house, or before we invest in particular investment funds. How then should we explain our rush to implement a technology that can so radically impact the place where we worship?

The Commercialization of Christian Teaching

There is yet another area in which, not technology but another adopted secular "philosophy", related and dependent on technology, has impacted the church to its detriment. The church has always engaged in programs of spiritual education. On a congregational level, this has been focused on either the Sunday services and midweek bible studies, or on a larger scale, at retreats where many gathered to hear the word of God, often in relation to a particular area of the Christian life. Keswick conventions, for example, frequently combined a hunger for a deeper life with God and the call of missions. The people who came to these classes in spirituality etc. approached the services with hearts open to the Holy Spirit, who was held to be the real teacher. At times they would write notes and research the scriptures, but all of this was done on an ad hoc basis, for the meetings to which they had come were not held to be predominantly informational, but rather a time of meeting with God. This is not the model of church teaching that is carried on in many of today's churches.

The model of today's church teaching is the business model. People no longer simply come to the church to hear special teaching sessions. First they must register, and fill out applications that demand that they do not make tape recordings of the meetings. These tapes, they are told, can be bought following the meetings. They then pay a certain amount of money for the lessons they will hear and participate in. If one is poor and cannot afford this, the applicant can identify him or herself as poor and ask for a financial subsidy. The humiliation that this may entail is not considered in the commitment to the business that teaching the scriptures has become, and those who run the program feel confident in the feeling that they have been generous to those less wealthy. The money that one pays is said to cover expenses, and of course, as in all conferences one leaves with a handbook, along with space for notes that deal with the speakers and the topics they will cover, often complete with graphs, flow charts and an array of taxonomic diagrams to explain the points of the discussion.

I am tempted to cry "shame", but I doubt this would prove very effective in halting the sale of spiritual truths. Jesus may well have said "freely have you received, freely give" but this does not enter into the calculation. The fact that Jesus drove the money changers from the Temple is ignored as irrelevant to the need to generate income from prepared and organized teaching packets that cost those who prepared this material, both time and money. The commercialization of Biblical teaching is justified under the banner of "the laborer is worthy of his hire". This sale of spiritual truths is not new. Even as St. Paul was travelling around the Eastern Mediterranean preaching the gospel, there were those apparently following his route teaching the word of God for money. The KJV translates the word used in 2 Corinthians 2: 17, *kapeleuontes* as 'corrupt'. However, this is perhaps not entirely the best translation. The word actually means "hawking", which in the Oxford dictionary means "to carry about for sale". I do not think St Paul misunderstood the situation, or that he was not correct in rejecting the idea that these people had a biblical right to commercialize the word of God. I further doubt that the reader thinks Paul was wrong either. There is a line between the laborer being worthy of his hire, and what is increasingly the commercial fashion in biblical teaching "seminars" today. They are not the same. This sale of spiritual truths is shameful.

Nevertheless, simply put, biblical truths are not for sale. If one believes that the scriptures were inspired for the education, correction and the building up of the saints from this body of teaching, then any spiritual insight that one has gained along the way should be freely available to any member of the congregation in its total teaching outreach. Biblical truths are not the property of an individual, and spiritual insight is equally a gift both to the person with the experience, and to the greater church beyond. The congregation should be able to freely access any teaching program put on by the church, particularly without the humiliation for asking for monetary assistance. The enforced sale of tapes and program material makes the teaching, in effect, merely an avenue for the generation of money, and this process is only minimally less shameful than the economic aggrandizement of some television evangelists who become enormously wealthy on the backs of the poor and ordinary people who send in their $5 contributions believing it goes towards genuine spiritual outreach.

Not only do the materials so prepared for these "spiritual conferences" become proportionally less expensive in relation to increased sales. The real truth is that they are not necessary. That last, apparently excessive claim is based upon three simple truths: (a) the essence of genuine spiritual teaching is found in the teaching of the Holy Spirit to the individual hearing the lesson, (b) if information is desired by an individual he or she can easily write down the aspects that genuinely interest them as they listen to the preaching/teaching, (c) for two millenia biblical teaching has gone on without this enforced purchase and minute organization, and has been effective to the degree that the Holy Spirit has been listened to. Compulsorally bought material does not make the teaching more effective, and even the individual with a high level of memory retention will forget the majority of what has been heard, and almost inevitably, soon leave the material untouched in a bookcase for years.

No one is asserting that the material should not be sold. What, however, is being argued is that the compulsory nature of this purchase changes the nature of the experience from being one of spiritual development to that of a commercial arrangement that brings shame on the church in the eyes of a world at large that looks to the church for a more unselfish model of behaviour. There is no problem in offering the material, and even tapes for sale after or during the conference. There is also no problem in asking for an offering towards the ministry of those presenting the teaching. But what is most certainly true is that spiritual truths should not be for sale, such that if one does not have either the money or the humility (or the willingness) to pay for these truths, they are denied the possibility of hearing them. Registration for conferences does not achieve anything that a simple list of those intending to come could not achieve. In fact, registration is actually, merely the psychological ploy that justifies the attitude of commercialization to the conference. We are registered so that others, not registered, will not be permitted entrance.

The difference between buying a book in a bookstore, or at a table following a meeting, and being forced to register and pay for material at a church sponsored series of meetings, is neither subtle nor insignificant. The combination of church sponsorship and enforced registration stamps the teaching, that supposedly is the primary objective, as radically exclusive. Only those who are willing to pay have the right to hear the truth. All others, and especially the poor, are excluded because they cannot afford to hear the truths that one is told in the pre-meeting advertising, are crucial to successful Christian living. Biblical exposition then, becomes a commodity that is shared, only with those willing and able to buy it. Biblical truths, the gifts of God to a lost world, are taken out of the hands of the believer and put into the power (and pockets) of those who share it out, in as many divisible parts as possible, at monetary levels related to supply and demand. To drive present day money changers from the Temple Jesus would have to make a thousand whips, and spend years going to thousands of churches, and one wonders, even then, if they would actually get the point.

And yet the kinds of operations that I have been describing, existing as they usually do around the local church, are almost insignificant, compared to the economic fleecing of the church that certain televangelists engage in. Surely we must understand the enormous potential for accumulating vast amounts of money that television creates, and that among any population there will be unscrupulous and intelligent individuals who are totally willing to seem to provide us with what we appear to need, and who have studied our beliefs and preaching styles so that they may come across as absolutely genuine. Under the guise of spiritual ministry, these people amass huge fortunes that, in the US, are beyond the reach of the IRS, and are apparently tax free. So convinced are we that these people's hearts are pure, that we hang on their words, accepting them as the revelation of God, while they increase their personal wealth, sometimes to the extent of a hundred million annually. The bible does not allow the accumulation of wealth, untrammelled by social obligations . Indeed, the scriptures give clear responsibilities to those who have such wealth, as to its use as a means to ameliorate the suffering of the poor. While there are those in the world who suffer from the lack of this world's necessities, no one, *especially in the ministry*, has the right to be personally wealthy.

That this particular section of the clergy has exploited the church's largesse to become enormously wealthy is shameful, and a reason for society to lose faith in the church, as indeed, it does. What does Zechariah 11:16 mean if not that there are those who heartlessly feed off the wealth of the people of God deceitfully? What does Matthew 7: 21-23 mean, except that there are those who falsely represent the Lord? What does Mark 12: 38-40 mean, if not that there are religious leaders who deceitfully take the assets of the church for their own personal aggrandizement, while hiding behind the most holiest of spiritual sentiments. Why do we then so willingly trust the sincerity of all who appear before us on television and in vast evangelistic gatherings, when the Saviour himself has warned us to beware of such people?

That this economic exploitation of the church is conducted by those who pretend to exercise the power of God is overwhelming, resulting as it does in society's rejection of the church, and its loss of belief in the possibility of genuine expressions of the power of God. It is in just such conditions that "the love of many does wax cold." If we but doggedly sought the truth regarding these individuals, instead of credulously believing their every claim to *Divine* spiritual power, perhaps we would begin to see these spiritual hucksters for the deceivers they really are. We long for genuine spiritual revelation and power so desperately (as indeed, we should) that we willingly cling to almost anyone who claims to possess these qualities, while they see the church and its teachings merely as a vast source of great wealth, and apparently gullible enough to believe them.

There is a significant difference between viewing the teachings of the word of God as a source of revenue and working in the ministry and expecting to be supported by the church or the congregation to which one is attached. Matthew 10 presents both these models. With regard to the use of the power of God to bring healing and liberation, Jesus states, "You received without cost; give without charge." (verse 8) The Gospel and the power of God that accompanies its presentation are not items that can be exploited to make money, nor should such activity be undergone at a price. Later, in verse ten, Jesus says "the worker is worthy of his food." The people of God do have an obligation to support the ministry God has provided, and the clergy can expect the church to attempt to meet their needs. Ministry, however, as Jesus presents it here, is not a business where spiritual truths and power are the source of profit or given in exchange for money or goods. Indeed, from these verses we are led to understand that the spiritual assets we handle are not ours to sell. Spiritual ministry is not a business.

Church Programs

What is probably the most disturbing aspect of contemporary church life is the rather large disjunct between its confession of biblical orthodoxy and its usual behaviour. We all fail to live up to the standards that God has shown us, and we are all in need of (His) grace and forgiveness. The church's failure does not exist, however, in its inability to live up to its ideals. Rather, the failure of the church is even more harmful and exists in the church's inability to see that what it professes, and how it operates, are inherently contradictory. The church, and particularly the evangelical wing of the church, confesses a faith in the scriptures and the complete dependence of the individual on the grace of God for salvation and sanctification. Then, week after week, in congregations across the continent, sermons are preached extolling the virtue of commitment as the path to a holy life. As if St Paul, for example, was not committed before he was confronted by Jesus on the road to Damascus. Salvation by grace, and not works, is certainly proclaimed, but then that having been accomplished, a vast raft of sermons that are marked by a total absence of biblical emphasis on the Holy Spirit to live an acceptable Christian life, a dearth of preaching on the work of the cross in sanctification, and a deathly silence on the radical inability of the human heart to achieve a truly godly behaviour, is preached, that lead the new believer back to a dependence on anything but the salvific accomplishments of the Cross.

The church's abandonment of solid biblically based teaching on this central issue of the New Testament is not the church's only point of confusion. According to the scriptures, coupled with the message of the Cross, there also exists the need for a total dependence on the Holy Spirit to achieve spiritual results. The preaching of the cross, and all other expressions of the church in its witness, are of no effect if the Holy Spirit does not also confirm the word. The Holy Spirit is the one who causes new life in the heart of a believer. And it is, furthermore, the Holy Spirit who deepens this spiritual life and creates in a congregation (body of believers who are filled with spiritual power, and are seen by the community in which they dwell) the ability to live lives motivated by love.

If, on the other hand, one listens to "church talk", one is very quickly struck by its overwhelming focus on the implementation of successful church programs, and not by a dependence on the Holy Spirit. Indeed, successful programs might well be the staple of pastoral-congregational discussion in this period of the church's history. Programs on how a mega- church is built, and the nature of church programming to meet the needs of the generational divisions within the church, for example, are the major thrusts of the church's self-reflection. Conferences are held to discuss the latest book on the local congregation's vision. Then the congregation is given multi-layered questionnaires necessary to discover where the church is as a congregation, and where it would like to be.

It may, of course, be claimed that though there is much discussion on programs, there is still faith in the work of the Holy Spirit. And this argument would be convincing if the programs discussion was at least equalled by discussion and solid teaching on the place of the Spirit in the life of the church. But this is not the case. Program discussion is accompanied by a faith that an implementation of certain programs will result in increased attendance, more relevance, and other goals that, at best have only a tenuous relationship to the criteria for a Spirit filled church. A simple statistical examination of the amount of time spent on the discussion of programs indicates where the real point of interest and faith lies. And it is not, unfortunately, located in a confidence in God.

This, perhaps unconscious lack of a genuine spiritual focus is a symptom that requires careful examination. What does it mean in regards to the true level of spirituality that the church pastoral leadership has ceased to focus on the spiritual dimension as the source of its congregational success? And if, in fact, the goal of a large church is attained, what might the result of this be on the spirituality of the pastoral leadership? Indeed, the complexity and variety of church programs conducted by a congregation can become of such importance that church reputations are based on the size of one's congregation, and not on the spiritual level of one's preaching and the evidence of the working of the Holy Spirit in the life of the congregation.

In such situations, pastors cease being simply preachers, and are transformed into ecclesial CEOs, administering multi-million dollar budgets, overseeing large staffs and numbers of assistant pastors, and basking in the adulation of an admiring membership, amazed at the size and power of the church that they have had the good fortune to join. The temptations in this are huge, and not a few genuinely excellent pastors have run tragically aground in such situations.

At the same time, and even in churches that are not burdened by the temptations of size, there is an ever decreasing amount of time spent on the Holy Spirit, the call to missions, and the sanctified life (except where sanctified equals the "moral" life). Moreover, historic conference centres, which in the past preached the inner life of Christ, encouraged the individual's love for the Saviour, and had a global impact by being the cause of numbers of missionaries being sent to the field, have either closed, or have slowly and inexorably been transformed into church social meeting places, which now and then discuss religious themes. At times, the contemporary church's method of outreach appears to be to hide the gospel, as much as possible, within a seemingly non-religious package, in an attempt to seduce outsiders into the church by appearing not to be particularly religious. A successful church is identified as a large church, and programs that develop these kinds of churches are studied for whatever may benefit the small local congregation which sees itself as a failure in the quest for "mega" status. A sense that we, as a church, need to seek the presence of God in our services, is only given lip service, or not mentioned at all. A dependence on *God* to achieve *God's goals*, and not simply our own, is not genuinely considered, as long as we see ourselves as reaching, or attempting to reach, what *we* conceive are God's goals.

That these two objectives might not be identical is not seriously taken into consideration. The seeking of a true spiritual life of devotion, a love for the Saviour, and a hunger for a transformation into God's likeness are markedly absent from most congregation's Sunday services. Morality, by itself and not as part of the message of the Cross, successful interpersonal relationships and a good dose of humour are, however, staple sermon material. We close our Sunday evening services because no one is interested in coming, and reschedule our Saturday nights as a youth oriented service in an attempt to stop, at least that generation's abandoning of the church. Rather than depending on the Holy Spirit to generate spiritual life, we put our faith in carefully crafted programs that are claimed to have been proven to result in larger and happier churches. We will blame almost anything, except our own lack of spirituality, to explain the decay of the church, and its increasing irrelevance in today's society. In addition, the church's leaders frequently blame the congregation for its lack of support for the clergy, and for the people's depressing tendency to go to other churches in an often desperate search for a congregation where there is some semblance of spiritual life.

However, what is, perhaps, the most truly depressing fact about our inability to seek and trust God to build the Body of Christ is that the part of the church which, surprisingly, is most guilty of this, is the evangelical denominations which most ardently professes an allegiance to such principles, and pride themselves on their biblical loyalty. The historic churches may fail to express a consistent and truly Reformational theology, but they are at least consistent in operating on the theological assumptions that they do profess. Moreover, within these traditional churches, both Reformational and Catholic, are cells of individuals who seek, within the limits of their understanding, as we all do, to know God and serve him faithfully.

It is not that the church has no need of programs, or that programs are intrinsically antithetical to God's work or presence. St. Paul had a program of going to the synagogue first when he arrived at a city on his missionary journeys. The church in Jerusalem had a program for supplying the material needs of the believers. Fortunately, most sermons are not spontaneous utterances. Preparation is a necessary activity for most events that the church participates in. This does not, in itself, imply that the Spirit is absent from these exercises. In addition, there is not a missionary organization on the planet that could continue if it did not have a regular process for decision making.

Particular programs may be "unscriptural" but programs, in themselves, are not necessarily spiritually unacceptable. We need, nevertheless, a rebalancing of program with genuine faith in the work of the Holy Spirit, a reemphasizing of scriptural truths, and a confidence that true spirituality carries with it a power that attracts and transforms lives. Rather than placing our faith in carefully analyzed church models, we need to return to the rather old fashioned idea of the Spirit filled life. Both scripture and church history suggest that a congregation led by and filled with the Spirit of God is dynamic and attractive. What more do we wish to aspire to? And are not these the realities that we are actually seeking in our misled quest for effective programming?

Certain truths remain. A Spirit filled church will be successful. A Spirit filled church with a complexity of church programming will also be successful. Such a church with such a program complexity, however, runs an incredibly high risk of slowly turning its focus from the Spirit filled dimension, to the running of the nuts and bolts of its programming. There is a historic tendency for spiritual movements to decline, and this is increased if there is a complexity of programming to mask the signs of spiritual decay. An emphasis on programming demands great amounts of time and money that, given human nature, almost inevitably result in a diminishing emphasis on solid biblical teaching. Three things are of absolute necessity in a church: (a) solid biblical/theological teaching, (b) regular bible studies, and (c) a strong prayer life, and an emphasis on such prayer. If these are maintained they will result in a deepening of the spiritual life of the congregation, and the anointing of God on all outreach activities. It is not a well programmed, but a Spirit filled church which is successful.

Preaching: What Can be Said?

There is a lot of talk today about moving away from preaching, and that this form of spiritual communication is relatively ineffective. It is said that the example of a life of love, or a variant description of this, is what is needed, that preaching is essentially an antiquated rhetorical method that has outlasted its day, and that people simply do not want to be preached to anymore. The problem with such an understanding is that it is a mixture of truth and serious error.

Preaching has always been an inefficient method of communication. It has, in fact, been an ecclesiatical failure from the beginning of the church. However, this is so, only if there is no spiritual experience backing up the preaching, and secondly if there is no anointing of the Holy Spirit empowering the sermon. One could preach on a tree stump, or from the pulpit of Westminster Cathedral, and if the power of God is present, the preaching will be equally effective, and the people will be deeply engaged in what is being said. Why, one may ask, do people go in the thousands to hear Billy Graham, if preaching is a useless method of evangelism and teaching? I doubt that anyone could be more traditional in their presentation of the word of God. It is true that words are not enough. Nevertheless, lives without words are equally ineffective. The gospel, indeed all biblical teaching, has conceptual content, and this content needs to be expressed. No matter to what degree of love one lives one's life before the world, one will eventually be forced to use words to tell people about Christ.

On the other hand, there are serious faults in much of what goes for preaching in many of our churches. The danger in this contemporary move away from preaching, however, is that what replaces an organized sermon is often equally vacuous and superficial, or even more so, and the church is not adequately presented with solid biblical teaching. There are many ways to conduct a service, and we need most of them, formal and informal. What we do not need is vacuous and shallow preaching. The answer to the church's sleep inducing sermons is not to stop preaching. Rather it is to return to a place with God where there is power in what is said, and what is said is taught to the preacher, at least in part, by the Holy Spirit.

I believe it is impossible to be boring if one knows God. As a church we are in grave danger of casting aside both the good with the useless in our attempt to be successful in communicating with the world. We have been deceived into thinking that methodological innovation will solve the problems of empty churches, lack of community interest in the church, and congregational boredom. Our error in this is that we focus on process, and not on the God of the Acts of the Apostles.

It has been said by some (actually leaders in the Pentecostal movement) that "Old methods have stopped working". And while this does reveal a correct understanding that the church truly has a problem, and that there needs to be some kind of "correction", the remark seems to indicate that the speaker sees no immediate solution to this problem, and that the New Testament solution, if one accepts that the New Testament does provide solutions to church dilemmas, is not understood to be the answer. We need to conduct a rigorous evaluation of the content of our preaching. Is our preaching Christ centred? Do we teach a biblical understanding of behavioural transformation (holiness/sanctification)? How often and how consistently do we teach the necessity of prayer? To what degree do we teach a total dependence on the Holy Spirit for the success of our ministry and our preaching? Just how biblically centred is our preaching? Do we use the biblical text of our sermons as merely the jumping of point of a talk that has no significant connection to the text as its central core? And finally, to what degree must this communication failure be laid at our feet as a result of the low spiritual level of our lives?

Indeed, what old methods are we talking about? Are God's "old methods" unsuccessful? If we are saying the old methods are not working, are we not saying that God's methods are not working? You see there are two areas of "methodology": ours and God's. So which one is not working? And if we say that…"No, it is not that God is failing", then what failure are we worried about? If God's methods are being successful then we have no problems. We are being successful.

There does not seem a way around this issue. We have problems because we have, unintentionally for sure, abandoned the ways of God and attempted to achieve spiritual goals using methods that, while continuing to be presented in a religious vocabulary, have excluded the very spiritual presence (God) that would ensure the achievement of these objectives.

The problem with our preaching is that it is too frequently not truly biblical in both its content and in its emphases, and that it is not preached in the power of the Holy Spirit. Preaching should not be seen as an opportunity for the preacher to act before the congregation, get laughs, or tell personal anecdotes that reflect well on the preacher's qualities or spirituality. Preaching is a communication between the congregation and the pastor. However, it is preeminently an exercise in edification. If spiritual truths are presented in such a way that the people are not presented with a felt challenge, they will all too often let the words wash over them leaving no permanent residue of changed attitudes or behaviours. It is not enough simply to preach an adequate exegesis of the text (though in some cases that would be a significant improvement). Nor should we be holding conferences in an attempt to discover new and effective methodologies. What we should be doing is getting on our knees and seeking God, so that God can effectively communicate through us to a spiritually hungry, often seriously confused and even intellectually unsatisfied humanity.

We are really like the people of Judah in the time just before Josiah (2 Kings 22,23). When they finally read the Book of the Law that had been discovered in the Temple during renovations, they were amazed at how far from its teachings their religious life actually was. They thought they were doing the right things. The problem was that what they thought was covenantal practice, actually wasn't. We could learn something from them.

A Pastoral Job Description

From the beginning of the church there have been criteria that had to be met by anyone desiring to be a leader in the church. The Acts of the Apostles and the Pauline epistles are relatively explicit, regarding qualities necessary for pastoral ministry. Coupled with this criteria, and inextricably connected to it, has been the job description for church leadership itself. In today's church the criteria required for a pastoral position are also extremely varied, and implied in such criteria is the role that a church sees the pastor or priest fulfilling. The problem with today's criteria is that it is frequently neither overly spiritual nor particularly biblical.

Spirituality, as a "job requisite" for this ministry, is either virtually ignored in such a search, or regarded as lower on a list of priorities than other, usually human relations and organizational skills that a church seeks in a candidate. One's theological positions may or may not be regarded as important at all in this evaluation. Being Spirit filled, a requisite for distributing food in the early church, is virtually unthought of, and the prospective minister must often be prepared to initiate or continue programs for church growth that are the result of attendance at conferences on this question. Frequently the pastor is seen as a member of a church management team, and the process of hiring a minister is often not significantly different to that conducted for any business managerial position, including the negotiation of acceptable salary and benefits packages.

Indeed, the hiring procedures reflect this methodology, at least to some degree, because of the business and professional backgrounds of the people who are usually chosen for church board positions, and to gain advantage of these particular backgrounds. Church board meetings are, on the whole, not discussions of spiritual issues, but rather of financial and administrative problems which form the core of the day to day business of the modern church. I would assert, though I do so sadly, and with the hope that somehow I am mistaken, that we have no genuine interest in God's criteria for pastoral and other church ministry , and that we have adopted, to varying degrees, a model of church leadership that is virtually identical to leadership in any secular and multifaceted business organization. The congregation leaves the selection of the minister to the committee, and its input is minimal. In such a situation the voting by the membership of the church on a candidate, who has already been, to all intents, chosen by the selection committee, is almost always a farce, and no more than the rubber stamping of the candidate selected by the leadership.

If the New and Old Testaments teach us anything in this regard, it is surely that it is the heart, and the call, and the divinely described role that we should take as our starting point in selecting a minister. If we assert that the bible is divinely inspired, should we not take its direction a little more seriously? In Zechariah 11: 15,16, the prophet states, "I am about to install a shepherd in the land who will neither miss any that are lost, nor search for those that have gone astray, nor heal the injured, nor nurse the sickly, but will eat the flesh of the fat beasts, and throw away their broken bones." If we remove the negatives from this section we discover the job description for pastoring that God desires.

A godly pastor misses those who have become lost; he or she searches for them if they seem to have abandoned the congregation. He/she heals the injured soul, and patiently and lovingly nurses back to health those who have fallen or are broken by life. The godly pastor is not satisfied that his/her congregation is reasonably filled each week that the church programs are generally ticking along fairly well, and that the pay cheque is deposited in his account regularly. The godly pastor does not administer a congregation. He/she seeks out those who are not experiencing the healing of God. This is his/her passion. If there are ninety-nine "sheep" who regularly attend prayer meetings and Sunday services, he/she will not rest until the one who has perhaps stopped being a faithful attender, is restored to fellowship.

The godly shepherd knows that, almost certainly, behind the smiling faces of many of his/her parishioners is a well of suffering, confusion, and ignorance, and that the job of the pastor is to reach out into that pain and bring God's healing. This is the job description of pastors, from God's point of view, and it is these qualities that should be preeminently sought in the search for a pastor. Such a person may make mistakes on the organizational level. However, in terms of the spiritual progress of the church, and the imprint of love that they will leave in the hearts and minds of the people they come in contact with, it is these ministers of grace who will ultimately be accounted as successful.

Chapter 28
PRAISING GOD: WHAT'S THE POINT?

The dictionary defines the word "praise" as to "express approbation or admiration of, and to commend, or glorify." We are told, in fact we are frequently told, that we should praise the Lord. Why would God ever want us to praise him? Is God unsure of himself? Does God like to be told he is wonderful, like an immature child? Is God so proud of himself that he wants us to tell him how wonderful he is? Do any of these questions sound reasonable? Then why does God want us to praise him?

Despite what we have been taught, i.e. that God wants us to praise him, throughout the scriptures praise is almost totally a human reaction to what God has done, or an expression of wonder at the discovery of what God is. It is a reaction of wonder and of love. Many of us have been in services where we are told to praise the Lord because God "inhabits the praises of his people". We therefore say words of praise because we think that, if we do this, God will reveal himself in some way to the congregation, or that there will be an expression of the power of God, or even, simply, that this is the right thing to do. Do we honestly think that God can be flattered, or that he cannot tell if the praise is genuine or not? Do we think that mere words with no sincerity satisfy God? If we are not already motivated to praise God, if praise is not already in our hearts, do we genuinely believe that mere words that lexically mean praise will be pleasing to God?

God does not need us to praise him so that he can know what he is like. God is not an oriental (or other) monarch who must be flattered, so that we can get what we want from him. Do we imagine that God's attitude is that we must praise him, or we will be punished? Or that praise is one of the duties of the follower of God? Do we honestly imagine that all God wants us to do in heaven is praise Him? God creates a universe of incredible complexity, but that heaven is only an eternity of adulation to the divinity?

Jesus told the Samaritan woman, "The time approaches, indeed it is already here, when those who are real worshippers will worship the Father in spirit and in truth. Such are the worshippers whom the Father wants." (John 4: 23). God is not impressed with words that masquerade as praise. Actually, what the lack of sincerity in this reveals is an absence of a genuine love for God. If one does not really love God, then words of praise directed towards God are either only attempts to manipulate God, or are cultural expressions of a historic religious heritage. As expressions of one's culture they may be almost innocent, in that nothing religious is truly intended. They may even reveal an openness to God. The other reason for praising God does not bear close scrutiny.

God is possibly infinitely above us. Were we to know even a fraction of what God actually is, we would be overwhelmed. That, at least seems to be the universal reaction to visions of God. Yet this is also the God who emptied himself of such powers and became a weak human being so that we could understand his heart. God does want people to worship him, though the word worship may be an inadequate human attempt to describe deep expressions of love for God. Is it not the ultimate paradox that the Almighty came to earth as a servant? Is such a God likely to prefer the role of Almighty potentate when he is finally surrounded by those who love him?

When we are in love, do we not enjoy, almost more than anything else that could be said, hearing the one we love say that they love us? Is this too human an example to use to describe the Divine lover? John says that God loved the world so much that he sent his only Son. Is it not reasonable to believe that the return of that love, from one who was previously God's enemy, gives God pleasure?

The almighty God, before whom we exist, only because he wishes the universe to continue to exist, is not diminished when he reaches down to our puny attempts at gratitude and love. If it is true that God inhabits the praises of his people, it is true because *his people* are those who love him, and that such praise is but the sincere expression of that love. I doubt God derives much pleasure from his people who are praising him, only because they have been told to do so, or because they want something.

Chapter 29
FEMINISM: A DISCUSSION ON VOCABULARY AND REALITY

Feminism has been one of the most influential movements of the last hundred years, and yet on the surface, at least, it has had almost no impact on the evangelical wing of the church, and to the degree that it has, it has been denigrated, and unbelievably misrepresented, or consciously left unexamined. Feminism is actually a multifaceted critique of civilization, and not simply Western civilization, regarding the devaluation of half of humanity. That it has not had a deep impact on this section of the church is not overwhelmingly startling, as it has not been markedly victorious, even in secular society. Feminism is not about women taking power away from men, though with some feminists this may well be the objective. Rather, feminism is about the devaluation of women in a society in which the only humans with power have been men.

In addition, there is not "one" feminism but rather many, in which there are moderates and extremists, as in virtually all social movements. What concerns me most about the church's reaction to the feminist movement is its patronizing indifference to the concerns that feminists raise, and its seeming delight in acting as if the individuals presenting such concerns are intellectually or spiritually inferior, and there is no validity at all to their claims.

The difference between a man and a woman is determined by the simple and single presence or absence of one chromosome at the time of conception. What could have been Sarah turns out to be Sam. Now, I admit, this is somewhat flippant. However, if we want to strenuously argue that there are definite differences between the sexes, we need to remember this chromosomal fact before we get too excited. I will not attempt to argue for the feminists. I would not know which group I should defend. Further, I will not argue, either for or against any traditionally understood Pauline teachings on the subject. In terms of church harmony, this would simply be too controversial and divisive.

What is extremely important, however, is the attitude to the issue that we present, and the degree of love and respect for at least fifty percent of our congregations that we show. It is neither holy nor biblical to act as if there is nothing of value to feminist issues, particularly Christian feminist stances, that do not violate a biblical position on men and women. And this is true even if vast numbers of Christian women do not presently see the issue as important.

There are several points that should be considered: (1) In any marriage it is only a male lacking in wisdom who seeks to dominate his wife. Whatever the Pauline interpretation on family roles actually is, a dynamic sharing of ideas between husband and wife is not precluded by such an interpretation. That a man should listen to a woman, and that this does not contravene God's thinking is seen from both David's dealings with Nabal's wife, and Abraham's obedience to Sarah, his wife, in regard to Hagar, Abraham's concubine, (the very first human who is recorded in scriptures as experiencing a theophany, and to whom God appeared twice). That God does put women in ministry positions where their words are to be taken seriously, and even obeyed is clearly seen in Judges 4:4-24. The scripture here states, "At that time Deborah, wife of Lappidoth, a prophetess, was judge in Israel. It was her custom to sit beneath the palm tree of Deborah between Ramah and Bethel, in the hill country of Ephraim and the Israelites went up to her for justice." (Judges 4:4,5) This section does not say the Israelite women went up to her for justice. It says the Israelites went up to her for justice. These biblical passages show that it is not unscriptural to do what a woman suggests, or even directs, and that women can have leadership positions within the people of God. (2) From the picture we get in Genesis three, Adam does not present a spectacularly strong picture of "manhood". Rather than woman being the weaker, this chapter shows the man to be the weaker of the two. Surely, in the only sense that is observable, women are weaker merely in physical strength. If women are supposed to be subject to men because they are the "weaker" sex, scriptural narratives involving women, such as this chapter in Judges, do not present them in this fashion. (3) In the history of missions, the overall majority of missionaries were female, often single women who went out, did courageously, often became heroes of the faith, and preached the Gospel to all who would listen. Unless one is willing to deny that God called these women to preach the Gospel, it seems clear that whatever St Paul did have in mind in Ephesians, God does want some women to preach. One cannot send a woman, convinced of the calling of God, to the mission field with the church's blessings, and then deny at home an equally qualified woman the right to "speak in the church".

Finally, it is surely about time we became a little more sensitive to the language we use in church as it relates to gender. Initially, God should not be understood as male. The bible says, "At the resurrection men and women do not marry. They are like the angels in heaven." (Matt. 22:30) Gender is entirely of this earth. Its function is to procreate the species, as it is with virtually all the biological forms of life present. Further, Paul, states in Galatians 3:28 that, "There is neither Jew nor Greek, there is neither bound nor free, there is neither male nor female, for you are all one in Christ Jesus." Clearly on earth these categories do exist. However, in the new creation, in the new person in Christ, gender, among other divisive categories, ceases to exist. Why then do we so vociferously believe that God is a male? This is as illogical as the perhaps only half jest that used to be made in the British Empire that, "God is English".

Gender is not a heavenly characteristic, and we fail to understand both God and the limitation of language if we assert that God is male/ he, or any other gender based item of vocabulary. That the vocabulary of the original texts which refer to God employs male nouns and pronouns has nothing to do with the "gender" of God. If gender does not exist in heaven then the use of male gender terms is only an accommodation to human linguistic limitations. How indeed would one imagine a male God? In fact, even if we were to assert, on a strictly literal basis, that "man" was made in the image of God, and that woman came from within "man", then we can only believe that God participates in both male and female characteristics, and is thus clearly not "male" as we understand the term. Unfortunately English does not have a gender neutral pronoun. That is, we do not have a pronoun that does not indicate gender. Until we somehow generate one, we will have trouble describing God and (his) actions, as I just did.

On the other hand, God is also not female, and it is equally wrong to speak of God as "she". Sadly, there will be those who read this and think angrily, " Great! The whole thing is a stupid idea anyway!" I say "sadly" because to have such a reaction is not to express any admirable level of holiness. Rather, it is an expression of a lack of love. If one has love for one's brothers and sisters one will be sensitive to the effect that one's words, in this case gender based vocabulary, have on them.

The bible frequently uses the term "man" to speak of humanity, and in the New Testament the term "brethren" to speak of the people of God in Christ. This is culturally understandable. However, it has never meant only men or only brothers, and there is no reason we have to continue to employ these gender based terms when we live in a society which is becoming ever more aware of the non-inclusive nature of the terminology. Our stubbornness only unnecessarily alienates those we say we are attempting to reach. We have no reason to pride ourselves on our refusal to be sensitive to the feelings of half the population of the world, let alone our congregations. And if a male reading this thinks this is all rather too much, imagine that the roles were reversed, and instead of saying he, himself, brethren, and whatever other male terms there are, the bible and our hymnbooks used she, herself, Mother (for God), and the sisterhood. That last word in itself is an example of the unequal nature of our language. We don't have a "comfortable" female equivalent for "brethren". I doubt very much that we men would feel completely happy about such a vocabulary reversal. And yet we are perfectly willing to make women endure the male forms of such an inaccuracy, as if their thoughts and feelings on the matter were of no importance. Further, that some of our wives, sisters and female friends in the church find no problem in the continuance of male vocabulary is not a biblically grounded justification for its continuance.

For some, this attempt to change the way we speak will seem either pointless or disturbing. I understand both reactions. But for those who seek to conform their thoughts, actions and feelings to the one who became a selfless servant, so as to lovingly reach all, there will be an understanding that love and sensitivity are more important than tradition, and that this has nothing to do with a traditional Pauline understanding of the Christian family. The section of the church to which this is predominantly addressed has appeared, on the whole, to believe that there is no problem here that needs attention. However, such a lack of concern reveals an incorrect understanding of scripture, society, and the feelings of many, many women, but perhaps even more importantly, such an insensitivity ignores the obligations of godly love.

Chapter 30
THE DISCIPLINE OF CHILDREN: PHYSICAL PUNISHMENT

There are those who believe that a child crying in pain after being disciplined is a sign that their disciplining is effective. The question that should be asked, however, is, "How do they know that what is really occurring is not extreme psychological damage, the inculcation of the idea that the solution to social problems is found in violence, and the forming of a deep resentment at the painful physicality of the process which will ultimately result in a streak of cruelty that, because of the other religious training that the child will receive, will be repressed and denied, but which will nevertheless find occasion to break out, perhaps later towards the child's own children?" Physical punishment is not the only method to develop "good" children. There are traditional cultures around the world where physical punishment is never employed, and where the child, nonetheless, grows up to be obedient, respectful and loyal to the family. Whether one punishes one's child physically is very much a function of the cultural or social group in which one grows up.

Indeed, there are only two places in the bible where one appears to be directed to physically punish one's child: Proverbs 13:24, and Proverbs 23:13,14. And on this limited foundation, virtually an entire philosophy of child rearing has been built up. That this may be, in fact, only a cultural belief, like Old Testament polygamy, never seems questioned. In the bible the rod is a symbol of one's position in society, a weapon of defense, and a means of punishment. The word "rod" was used in Proverbs because that was the means of inflicting punishment at the time. We see this in many other sections where the rod is referred to. The term had a metaphorical, as well as literal meaning, simply implying punishment. It does not necessarily mean that a rod is especially and eternally the best and, indeed, God's method of discipline.

People in the Old Testament were also instructed to stone various sinners to death. Do the people who advocate physical punishment also wish to adopt this method of punishment? If one is going to take one passage as literal and absolutely essential to the diminishing of evil in a person's nature, what reason could there be for not following other equally physical forms of behaviour control? And if one is unwilling to stone another to death, though that also is commanded, why is the advice to physically punish a child of such power that it must be carefully observed and defended, virtually as a human right? Are there no other methods of behaviour control that are available that could be used instead of inflicting physical pain on one who may not even be aware of the reason for the punishment?

In addition, even if one is commanded to administer this form of punishment, when does one know that enough pain has been caused? Does the child have to exhibit some degree of repentance? What if they do not? Does one then continue to inflict the rod until they, until they what? Black out? Begin bleeding? What is the correct extent of this physical punishment? Frankly, the degree of punishment seems to depend on the person doing the punishing. Does that sound like the wisdom of God? The age of the person being punished also seems to depend on who is doing the punishing. I have seen children of two or three being hit with a belt and grow up to be extremely nice people, except that they appear to enjoy hurting other people and animals.

The fierceness with which people cling to this belief does not seem connected to either reason or experience. Surely we have learnt that a child in a violent environment grows up to be psychologically disturbed. The arbitrariness of physical punishment is no less dangerous than the unpredictability and violence of growing up with an alcoholic parent. Both lead to insecurity, fear, and at times a repetition of the environment that the adult grew up in.

Some may respond that they would never, and have never hit a child as severely as I have appeared to describe. That may be true, and it is also true that not all parents who discipline their children physically are cruel. That does not remove the problem. The open-endedness of the two quotations in Proverbs gives no adequate direction as to the application of the advice. Indeed, it appears to be completely arbitrary. If, however, we interpret these verses, not as prescriptions for violence but as directions to lead, guide, at times control and limit, and act in love toward one's children, then the verses become wise directions for parents.

Children need limits, or they may believe there are no reasons to control their emotions and desires. Children need to know that a behaviour has offended and upset a parent, and even that there will be a consequence to that behaviour. Children need to know that the parent's attitudes and responses to an infraction will be predictable and fair. But more than discipline, more than limitations, children need to know that they are loved by their parents with a passion that is lasting, and that even when they do fail, as fail they will, that the parent clearly and openly loves the child, and will continue to love the child. If the Prodigal son had not grown up in an environment of love it is unlikely he would have risked coming back, and the father's actions, when he did return, suggest just such an environment.

Extreme forms of discipline, even if physical punishment is an option, should not be the method of first choice. Children can be reasoned with, and there is nothing particularly spiritual or biblical about the attitude that a child's will must be crushed. Crushing someone's spirit does not lead to the new birth. Neither can I find this idea expressed in scripture. Nor does it develop characteristics equal to those produced by the new birth. Were one to discipline a child to one's heart's content the child would still become a sinner in need of divine forgiveness. Discipline, at best has significantly limited positive results. Patience in the face of impatience and rebellion need to be willingly employed before extreme measures are taken. Children need time to grow, and it is usually by making mistakes that they grow. Why then, especially given the absolute rejection of violence as a response to evil, throughout the New Testament, is physical violence to a child seen as perfectly acceptable for a Christian family?

CHAPTER 31

HERMENEUTICAL PRINCIPLES: UNDERSTANDING THE SAYINGS OF JESUS

It does not take one long to discover, when one begins to read the Gospels, that Jesus made some incredible statements which seem impossible to follow. It should be remembered, however, that Jesus lived in the Middle East, in a culture that we unwisely assume to be similar to our own, and in a time now almost two thousand years distant. Cultural and literary usages were certainly different to our own, and he almost certainly expected his hearers to recognize and understand most of the literary devices he employed. Nevertheless, despite whatever was mutually understood by Jesus and his hearers, the Saviour still couched his teaching, at times, in ways that were intended to shock and provoke people. John 6 where Jesus speaks of eating his flesh and drinking his blood is only one example.

In that example John obviously felt the need to include Jesus' explanation of the immediately horrifying instruction that we should become cannibals. Clearly, Jesus wanted to startle his audience into a reflection on what he had told them. Clearly, it is physically impossible for humanity to eat the flesh of a physically finite human body. This paradox is especially significant if, as Jesus said, this eating is necessary in order to "live for ever" (verse 51). I am aware that we have had more than a millenium of theological debate regarding this passage in relation to the Eucharist, but I will not enter into it. We do not really know when the explanation was given, because if it was in the synagogue where Jesus made these remarks, the explanation sounds as if Jesus suddenly realized he had said too much, and needed to backtrack. For myself, I do not believe Jesus would make such a mistake, and the remark is similar in its "shock appeal" to other "unbelievable" comments that Jesus made. I suspect the interpretation was given later to his disciples, and John included it in this location to prevent future incorrect interpretations being made. However, Jesus intended the remark to be shocking, and on the face of it, it most definitely is.

Not all of the Lord's unacceptable remarks are so fortunately explained for us. Matthew 5: 29,30 are well known verses which exist in the consciousness of many Christians as verses on which one does not dwell. Jesus states, "If your right eye is your undoing, tear it out and fling it away. It is better for you to lose one part of your body than for the whole of it to be thrown into hell. And if your right hand is your undoing, cut it off and fling it away; it is better for you to lose one part of your body than for the whole of it to go to hell." Did Jesus actually expect people to disfigure their bodies in this fashion? Did he regard this as a satisfactory method of sanctification? Did he believe that a person with no eyesight was thereby free of unlawful sexual desires?

Did he believe that the amputation of successive body parts freed one from sin? Did he envisage the church as one populated by mutilated believers?

Given that what Jesus was warning against was the loss of one's soul in hell (incidentally, an appeal to self interest) his remarkable words in these verses can be seen as a statement of ultimate significance. Indeed, this can be taken as a principle by which this and similar statements can be understood. From this perspective, Jesus is not suggesting, or even worse commanding, that we mutilate our bodies. Rather he is teaching that there is nothing more important than the health of one's soul. Nothing is more important than one's salvation. Jesus is saying, "If you regard the loss of a body part as so horrifyingly unthinkable, how then could you not regard the loss of your eternal soul as infinitely more horrifying?" In this case an extreme and virtually impossible action is used as an indicator, a "flashing light", that it is a rhetorical/literary device pointing to the greater significance of a second more significant action, along the lines of "If x were done this would be better than y".

For Jesus, allegiance to the Father was of absolute importance. Jesus was, in fact, in much of his teaching, conducting an "educational" exercise in relative values and was acting within an environment, in some ways quite similar to our own. His society was almost completely predicated on a religious and spiritual understanding of life. Ironically, this made it extremely difficult for Jesus. His audience was inured to the idea that they were religious people and children of Abraham. This is to say they believed they had the answers to life's theological questions, and that they were God's people. One of Jesus' approaches to this problem was to shock them into a reexamination of their, essentially unspiritual thinking. They were spiritually self-satisfied, and Jesus had to speak a new spiritual language in order to get them to see the truth, both about God, and about their assumed relationship to him (see John 9:40,41).

We, also, seem to be satisfied with our spiritual position. We, also, believe we see moderately well. Most of us do not experience any deep sense of sin and separation from God. Moreover, so much of this world, our values, and the perceptions we have of ourselves, are frequently the values of an existence that simply does not include God, in either its thinking or its daily experience. We often, in fact, have a set of assumptions about our knowledge of and relationship with God, which may not be accurate at all, and by which we govern our behaviour. We Christians ignore, to our peril, the possibility that we possess this worldly set of values and attitudes, and that these attitudes and beliefs are just as ossified and difficult for God to deal with, as those that Jesus had to shatter in order for his words to have any impact.

One other verse that troubles us with its apparent insensitivity is Matthew 8: 22. In this verse, Jesus tells a potential follower to, "Follow me and leave the dead to bury their dead." This is one more example of Jesus employing a rhetorical device to indicate the level of significance. Jesus was not suggesting in this verse in Matthew that he had no sympathy for the loss of a loved one's life. What else can be seen in the raising of Lazarus, (John 11), and in the shortest verse in scripture, "Jesus wept" (John 11: 35)?

Jesus was clearly not teaching that we should be indifferent to the loss of loved ones. He was not! Rather, Matthew 8 was teaching that if one was called by God to some activity, this was more important than any other claim that could be made on one, and that, for this individual, following Him was of more importance than any other demand, even that of familial obligations. Jesus made use of one of the most highly emotive human events, both then and now, to shock people into an understanding of the divinely higher importance of obedience to the heavenly Father. Consequently, as the verse utilizes a rhetorical teaching device, it is invalid to interpret the verse in any surface, literal sense. Yet, it is not simply that the above is the proper understanding of the verse. Jesus was employing a linguistic device to make a point. If we understand the Messianic methodology of relative significance, this and other troubling sections in the Gospels will both make sense and remove the usual perception they present, either that Jesus was irrational, or that he was heartless.

The principle of ultimate significance, for want of a better term, is seen also in Matthew 12:46-50, where Jesus is told, in the middle of speaking to the people, that his mother and brothers have come and want to speak to him. On the face of it what Jesus says is a callous thing to say to one's mother and family members. One must ask, however, if there is any evidence that Jesus did not love his mother. At the cross, in the midst of experiencing the pain of crucifixion, Jesus tells John that Mary is now his mother, and that he must look after her (John 19: 26,27). For Jesus to say in these verses in Matthew that the disciples were his true family is to state a position of relative significance. It is not to assert that the secondary relationship has no significance. What Jesus was teaching here is that spiritual relationships carry obligations, existing as they do in a submission to God, that must transcend human relationships. In strategic terms this point was essential. Jesus was preaching and his family came and interrupted, saying they wanted to talk to him. It was necessary for them that they understood the degree of significance his work had.

Indeed, Jesus' words may have hurt. But it was something his family needed to hear, and the text suggests that, up to that point, they did not appreciate this significance. By stating that the followers of God were his mothers and sisters and brothers, Jesus was not stating that one could deny one's relationships and obligations to one's earthly family if they were not followers of God. Moreover, Jesus was not setting up an either/or situation. He was not saying that if a disciple was his mother, Mary was not his mother. Along with presenting a paradigm of the church as one of closeness and obligation, similar to that of the family and thus extending the love within the family to all who are the children of God, Jesus was teaching that the obligations he owed his disciples took precedence over those he owed to his earthly family. The words Jesus used here are shocking, and clearly Jesus understood them to be so, but they must be understood as a rhetorical device to force reflection, and produce understanding, not as a thoughtless and hurtful remark. I cannot doubt that Mary was deeply assured of Jesus' love for her.

The intention to startle and provoke reflection is seen once more in Jesus' remark of Matthew 10: 34, where he states, "You must not think that I have come to bring peace to the earth. I have not come to bring peace, but a sword." Given that the angels on the day of Jesus' birth proclaimed "Peace on earth, and goodwill", and that Jesus came to bring us peace with God, this verse in Matthew should not be taken in any literal fashion. What Jesus is saying is that discipleship will result in conflict, and even a passionate hatred of the follower of Jesus. Jesus employed the term "sword" as a metaphor for conflict and violence. He was further indicating that there would be a cost in following Him, and that any authentic presentation of Jesus would force a decision on those that heard which would generate violent rejection of his followers. As a result of the statement of cost, even his followers would be forced to evaluate their decision to be his disciples. A rhetorically representational understanding of the saying, thus, is necessary, as clearly, the earlier Sermon on the Mount is not a call to violent expansion, but, indeed, a call for a rejection of such means.

Perhaps one of the most disturbing sections in the Gospels is found in Matthew 19: 16-22, essentially identically in Mark 10: 17-22, and Luke 12:33,34. The rich young man asks what he must do to gain eternal life. Jesus eventually tells him, "sell your possessions and give to the poor, and then you will have riches in heaven, and come follow me." The young man was very wealthy and left Jesus with a "heavy heart". We are usually less honest than the rich young man. We Christians tend to practice a kind of cognitive dissonance, in which we read the verses, sense a demand that is overwhelmingly terrifying, and simply push the apparent obligation from our consciousness. We classify the verses as, a "difficult passage", and regard this as an adequate level of response. In actual terms we make the same decision the rich young man made, without the virtue of his heavy heart.

Did Jesus literally want the man to sell his possessions? I do not think there is any doubt that this is the correct understanding. Could the same demand be made of us? If our usual response to these verses is any indication of our hearts, it most certainly could. Are these verses, despite this "literality" however, an example of Jesus' disturbing teaching devices which were intended to force reflection, and reveal the heart's inner sinfulness? In other words, are these words of Jesus to the rich man an unconditional command to all his followers to sell their possessions, or are they a diagnostic device to reveal the selfishness of his and our hearts, and indicate what we do have as the true focus of our love? Luke 12: 34 adds the words, "For where your treasure is, there will your heart be also." It seems, given the verse in Luke, that the verses are primarily aimed at a revelation of the heart, and by implication, a statement on what the driving force of the heart should be. Further, that such a "radically other directed" heart is the requirement of the follower of Jesus also implies that such is the heart of the Saviour. God has such a heart.

Jesus was certainly not interested in allocating how much we could keep, and how much we should give away to the poor. This misses the point. And in this sense it is wrong to take Jesus' words literally. Yet, paradoxically, Jesus did mean the young man to literally sell his possessions. However, I do not believe that God wants his followers to be poor. This contradicts a vast scriptural body of teaching that commands us to supply the needs of the poor. In addition, given that one's clothing can be classified as possessions, do we honestly imagine God wants us to go around naked in minus 40 degree weather? And were we to give our clothing to the poor, would that not immediately require of them that they also give these possessions to some other poor person, in an irrational game of endless dispossession? The illogic of this forces us to reject such an understanding. Jesus always aimed at the heart. The teaching in Matthew 19, and other places, on selling one's possessions has the intent of showing us where our hearts really are. A heart controlled by the love of God will generate behaviour that has its own characteristics.

Nevertheless, this diagnostic intention does nothing like let us off the hook. In relation to possessions, most of us fail the test of a "correct heart" If we take solace in the understanding that Jesus was not actually instituting universal poverty, we only reveal the shallowness of our own spirituality, and that we are content in our selfishness. These verses are not a delightful section that we can exegete with pleasure and leave with the happiness that we have understood one more difficult passage. Jesus' remarks to the rich man are a terrifying indictment of the sinfulness of our hearts. There is no escape. One cannot spiritualize a refusal to sell one's possessions. And that is how the majority of us respond to these verses. There can be no final sigh of relief that he was talking to someone else, and that we are ok. It is about time we also found ourselves with a heavy heart.

We do Jesus hermeneutical injustice if we are willing to understand many of his remarks only in literal terms. Indeed, in John 16: 25 Jesus tells us, what was almost certainly obvious to his disciples, for they were continually asking him to explain his sayings. He says, "Till now I have been using figures of speech. A time is coming when I shall no longer use figures but tell you of the Father in plain words." To reiterate, Jesus apparently believed that the only way to break out of the dead religious language of his day, and get people to think of spiritual truths in living ways, was to speak in new and dramatic images that did not result in the hearer believing they had understood while, in truth, no genuine reflection had gone on. This is an idea that in this two thousandth year of our Lord, we could think about as well. There are life and death truths behind Jesus' unbelievably shocking remarks. We need thus, to think in literary terms, and not be misled in our interpretations of these, admittedly difficult Gospel passages that in their literality are unlivable.

CHAPTER 32
MARRIAGE AND LOVE

Of those complex things that exist in the world of human relationships, surely marriage is one of the most difficult to truly understand. We come to a marriage carrying with us all the wonderful talents and qualities we possess, and all the hurt and confusion we have picked up along the way. Frankly, it is a wonder any marriage stays together, given this terrible hurt and the self centredness that characterizes the unsanctified and unhealed human heart.

When Jesus spoke about marriage in Matthew 19 we usually focus on his remarks on divorce. However, when we do this we miss the point he was attempting to get across. Jesus, in verse eight says, "Moses, because of the hardness of your hearts, allowed you to put away your wives, but from the beginning it was not so." The beginning is referring to a state without sin. This is not some cold, abstract moral environment. The "ideal" Jesus points to is a situation where the human heart is characterized by love. With sin, human relationships became fouled by a lostness that cannot help but hurt those enmeshed in it. Jesus was not teaching that an acceptable marriage was one in which two unhappy individuals stayed together because the bible demanded that they not divorce. Jesus taught that in the beginning, a situation existed that would have viewed divorce as the most ridiculous suggestion imaginable. In the beginning, there was love.

In addition, as a result of sin, human beings began to view marriage, not as a state of love between individuals, but as the transference of property. Woman were used to cement relationships between families and groups, and as the biological requirement for the perpetuation of the male line. Men also did not usually possess the right to choose whom they would marry. Marriage was seen as one of the prerogatives of the male head of the family. It was not for the satisfaction and happiness of the partners, but for the advancement of the family. But human beings are not pawns in an economic or political game of chess, even at the micro level of social life. In the beginning it was not so.

Men and women have been made to love each other. The bible does not teach celibacy. On the other hand, from Jesus' perspective, marriage is more than just sex. And yet, is God not the creator? Is the whole confusing mess we call human physical relationships something apart from the creator? Men and women have been made so that they are attracted to each other on a multiplicity of levels. What is the purpose of beauty? Is it perhaps only love that allows one to "lose one's breath" at the sight of the person one loves? Indeed, there is an almost infinite variation in what one person sees as beauty, and what another is in awe of. Moreover, it is almost certainly not only that which is immediately seen which draws one person to another. What is the beauty that a good looking person sees in an ordinary, and at times ugly person? It can only be the inexplicable beauty of the person of this "other", recognized on these many levels, that causes this love to be experienced.

Love, as the basis for marriage, has been ridiculed, rejected and viewed cynically by vast numbers of people throughout history. And yet I believe that it is the gift of God, the possibility of great joy and mutual support, and one of the most enduring suggestions of what normal human relations should be from God's standpoint. It is not that love is a human dead end. It is not that love is the expression of any negative quality one would like to insert. Rather, it is that our sinfulness, selfishness, and personal hurt derail love, betray it, and in the end destroy it. In the beginning it was not so.

When Jesus presented ideals, as he did throughout his earthly ministry, he was not implying, with that, that we could all fulfill these ideals. Indeed, as St Paul teaches us, it is only in the heart of one who has turned in faith to Jesus the Redeemer and Sanctifier that holiness is genuinely possible. The continuation of love in marriage is difficult for most, and impossible for many. This must sadly be admitted. And the following is not a facile response to this tragedy. But God can replace hurt. He can remove resentment. Jesus can reimplant love in a loveless heart, as it was in the beginning.

Chapter 33
FRIENDSHIP

In all likelihood, everyone reading this has a cared for other we call "our friend". The paradox of friendship is that we are deeply unsure if friends are the most common social "entity" we interact with, or that they are as rare as a happily married couple. We can differentiate between a friend and an acquaintance linguistically, but we are far from certain as to whether the people we refer to as our friends are actually only acquaintances. One of our deepest beliefs about our fellow humans is that they do not truly care about us, and can be depended on only to disappoint us at our most vulnerable moments. We fear to reveal ourselves to others because we have discovered, in the course of our lives, that other people are not interested in those terrifying or even beautiful aspects of our lives we would love to share with even one person. We fill our potentially solitary times with others who, when we are absent rarely think of us, so that the emptiness and loneliness of our lives can be quieted by the chatter we substitute for conversation, and the laughter we accept in place of love.

One of the greatest difficulties we encounter with those who we hope could, in fact, grow into true friends is the cancerous fear, based upon our previous experience of others, that this "friendly" other could not possibly be genuine in their expressions of what can only be described as incipient love. I further believe, in addition to this fear of disappointment and rejection, that Satan takes delight in reminding us of the general lovelessness of the human race, sows seeds of doubt in our consciousness, and seeks to convince us of the impossibility that this other "friendly" person could truly and deeply care for us. Either from a diabolical hatred, or because of the terrible insecurity that we feel in ourselves and coexists with a hunger for true companionship, possibilities for misunderstanding are focused on as indications that the other has lost interest or, indeed, never possessed any real interest.

Whatever the source of our insecurity, (one doesn't have to find a demonic cause in every human trouble) one needs to seriously doubt one's doubts as to the friendship of one who has given every indication of genuine affection for one. Moreover, as with faith in God, and the love one feels developing for another person, friendship grows in an environment of almost simultaneous confidence and fear and doubt. Yet, if we are to experience the joys of love and friendship, we must be willing to open ourselves to the very possibility we most fear: rejection. We do this, quite simply, by revealing an affection for the other person that may, in its initial stages, be relatively low key. If we experience a reciprocation of this affection we need to trust the person and the genuineness of the response, and continue our expressions of affection.

Different people will respond with differing levels of affection. Fear rules the hearts of most people, and each person has a different level of ability to express friendship. Perhaps because we have been rejected and disappointed so often, many of us develop strategies of self defense to deal with our perceived (and actual) lack of companionship. Many behaviours, antisocial or not, are the human response to fear and loneliness. These behaviours are expressed in the creation of substitutes for the love the person does not experience, and are psychological defenses the self feels it needs in order to live in a world in which the individual believes more and more deeply, that love cannot be expected. If, however, genuine love or even true friendship can miraculously break into the heart and life of a personally isolated individual, these strategies of self defense can break down in a realization that they are no longer needed, and openness to the sunshine of returned affection can take their place.

For many of us the struggle may not appear so extreme. We all, however, need to understand that friendships do not appear full formed, and that those we care for almost certainly carry about the same fears we do, and require similar efforts of self revelation. We need to realize that just as we search for expressions of affection from those we care for and love, so these others long for just these expressions from us, and wait, at times in fear and hope, for indications of affection from us, mirror images of our own longings and doubts.

Except from Jesus, the truly passionate and gentle lover of our soul, we can not ever be certain that our love will be returned, and that the friendship we seek will flourish. I know you do not need to be told that at times we will be disappointed. However, if we continue to take the risk to be open and express affection, there will be those we encounter in life who do love us as we love them and who, as time goes on, will grow into those companions of the heart we need and watch for in this dangerous and lonely world, just as the colonists in an earlier time searched the horizon in longing for a friendly sail.

Chapter 34
MISUNDERSTANDING

I suspect that absolute clarity of communication is as rare in this world as true love. I do not say this because I am an essentially pessimistic individual. Rather, if this is correct, it is so because initially, language, the medium we predominantly employ to communicate, is so open to multiple interpretation, and secondly, because we, the recipients of the communications, must understand these direct and indirect messages, not only with the limited data we possess, but also from within a personal paradigm that includes all the hurts and fears that we have accumulated throughout our lives, and which cloud and often mislead us as to what we are actually hearing and reading. Given the nature of language and the human heart, misunderstanding is virtually inevitable. And if this is the case, should we not hesitate a little before we jump to a negative and potentially destructive interpretation? And yet this is exactly what we so frequently do.

The combination of the potential for ambiguity in language, and a hurt human heart not only affects our relationships with others, but also, and perhaps surprisingly, our relationship with God. We are used to misunderstanding other people, but the idea of misunderstanding a communication from God may somehow seem unlikely. Yet, why should we think such a thing? Assuming that we are perfectly clear in our intentions in communicating with others, and it is the "other" who misunderstands us, is it not possible that God's "perfectly clear" communication may be misunderstood by us? God speaks in many different fashions: to our hearts, through the scriptures, through other people, and even directly. We, however, are quite capable of jumping to (incorrect) conclusions, and even what may appear obvious, may not, in fact, be so. The scripture, particularly in the Old Testament, contains many incidents where the "man of God" essentially says to God, "Have I got this right? Did you really say what I think you said?" What else are Gideon's prayers and Moses' conversation with God at the burning bush? Not only can we misunderstand the words God may say to us, we can also misunderstand God's intention and attitude to us because of the fears and hurt that exist within us. If we expect people to be angry when they correct us, we are very likely to see this characteristic in God when he points out our failings.

What is odd about human interaction is that, while knowing that we are frequently misunderstood in our attempts at communication, we deeply believe that our own understanding of another's communication is perfect. We are quite willing to engage in conflict, argue bitterly, blame and vehemently accuse, give ourselves over to unhappy thoughts, and generally assume the worst regarding the communications we receive, as if misunderstanding another's communication is something that happens only to others. Indeed, misunderstanding is so universal that rather than assuming we have correctly understood, we should habitually take the position that we may well have gotten our interpretation totally wrong.

Does it not seem logical that, in the light of this, we should make genuine efforts at discovering someone else's true intention before we either act on our understanding, or come out with all guns blazing and destroy what little relationship we may have with another equally frail and fearful individual? It may satisfy the anger we sometimes surround ourselves with to simply accept our first interpretation of another's "message", but if this anger is actually unjustified, are we not wasting an opportunity for friendship and mutual caring? We carry around within us a distrust of others that often precludes the possibility of satisfying relationships, and on occasion destroys the relationships we do possess. Perhaps we should write on our desks, the walls of our houses, and even more so, our own hearts, the words, "I may have misunderstood what this person is trying to say."

Chapter 35
BIBLE COLLEGE

When I was eighteen I went to bible college. The college was in Australia, on the banks of the Brisbane River at the bottom of a little valley that ran down to the river. A few years after I graduated and migrated to Canada I learnt that there had been a major flood and the college had been almost washed away. The college board decided that wisdom did not lie in rebuilding, to wait for another flood, and moved the school about a thousand kilometres south to Katoomba, a town in the Blue Mountains, just west of Sydney, and where my father, uncle and grandparents are buried. Australia does not have many earthquakes and I guess they felt that at least up in the mountains they were safe from floods. Since graduating I have collected several degrees, one in theology, but bible college was perhaps the most important and life changing time in my entire life.

The college was laid out in a series of three buildings parallel to each other. The men's dormitories were on one side. The women's were on the other side, and running down the middle were the kitchen, the dining hall, and administration offices to keep apart these two factions, at constant risk of coming into contact if not separated. Each day before classes, either a student or a visiting preacher would lead a chapel service. It was a time of challenge, teaching, and worship, and we all took our responsibilities in this very seriously. There was some good preaching, and it wasn't always the men who were outstanding.

The students were not all wonderful people, but most were trying to find God's direction for their lives, and live as holily as they could. People became depressed at various times, for example because they felt they were not living up to God's standards, or maybe because they did not have enough money to meet their needs. Some fell in love and even got married. Some fell in love with people it would have been better they had not. When I was in first year I met a third year student who told me he waited on God every morning at about five. The way he told his story made me want to pray the way he did. He told me that the year before, the college had been taught about waiting on God by a visiting bible college teacher named Beutler from the United States. I told him I would like to do it too, so he said he would wake me up the next morning. He did, and I went straight back to sleep. When I saw him that day he angrily told me that if I was not going to get up, he was not going to waste his time waking me. I had never before been spoken to like that, at least not by a Christian. The next morning I got up.

There was a prayer room below the women's dormitory where the college met for prayer each Monday of every week. We would all pray for the length of time that was usually spent for classes before morning break. It was a time of seeking God, prayer for the college and for individual students, and for times of praise. I learnt that there were people who could pray the most beautiful and sincere prayers, and that I was not one of them. Anyway, each morning my third year friend and I went down in the dark to the prayer room and went to our separate places in the room. Waiting on God is not praying in the normal sense. It is not giving God a list of things we earnestly need or want. Rather, it is being silent before God, emptying our minds of conscious thought, as far as that is possible, imagining that we are in the presence of God. It is letting God have a chance to speak to us, and change us.

Each day at five in the morning I would go to this place and seek to be quiet before God. At times my mind wandered, and I thought about things going on in my life. At other times I lay my head on the bench I was kneeling before and found myself falling asleep. This routine went on for some time, at least six weeks or maybe longer. I can't remember. Some time in the period of seeking God I asked the third year student when God was going to do something. I felt desperate, even though I honestly think I slept more than I prayed. It was soon after this that my life began to change. The deep hatred I had felt for my father all my teen (and predominantly Christian) life suddenly disappeared. Many times I had prayed about this. I knew the verses in John's epistle about hating another person, and how sinful this was, but I had never been able to stop hating him. Then it was gone. I discovered I had more love for other people, and was patient with them. I began to understand the grace of God. He had blessed me with a changed heart, and I had done nothing to deserve this.

Most of the time when I should have been silently waiting upon him I was thinking or sleeping. The word grace had a new meaning. I felt the power of God in my ministry in chapel, and others commented on it. Along with the miracles I have either seen or heard of, from sources beyond suspicion, this time when God's presence and transforming power were real, are the only things that have allowed me to keep my faith in, not only the goodness of

God, but even his reality. Were it not that I have experienced God myself, I am almost certain I would not be a Christian today.

The bible college I attended accepted people from many walks of life and from every level of education. What was important to the college was not the individual's academic skills, but his or her devotion to God, and the student's belief that God had called them to that particular college. We had English classes to help students improve their written and spoken language, but mainly we had lessons in the bible, theology and pastoral care. It wasn't a perfect curriculum, but it emphasized a knowledge of God and surrender to his will. Some who had probably never finished high school became successful pastors of churches. Some became missionaries, and others graduated and went back to normal life, working and being members of local churches. I don't think God does something and then decides he has made a mistake, and changes his mind. There is no doubt in my mind that God called most of these people to that college, and that he wanted many of them to enter the full time ministry.

There has been a tendency over the last twenty or thirty years to raise the educational level for entrance into various professions and career choices. At times this has been rational and correlated with the increasingly complex nature of the occupation. At other times it has seemingly been done to conform to a perceived social trend, and has had little or nothing to do with the job requirements or skills needed for a position. I cannot believe other than that this tendency, where it does not relate to necessary skills, will and does have a deleterious impact on the actual efficiency of a society to supply services to a community. At times the addition of skills, knowledge, extraneous experience, and other requisites, rather than increasing the success which an occupation seeks to achieve, in fact results in the exclusion of people who possess other admirable skills and talents that have been ignored in the move to require arbitrarily imposed qualifications.

Teaching, for which an M.Ed. is now almost a requirement, though it does not guarantee any better teaching at all, is only one of these occupations. There are areas where higher degrees do not guarantee greater efficiency of performance, and may, in fact, result in a reduction of such efficiencies, where the qualities genuinely necessary for success, reside outside the purview of the academic domain, or are only tangentially related to it. Viewed objectively, higher academic requirements for entrance into the pastoral ministry are an illustration of the social tendency to unnecessarily add to those requirements that are clearly sufficient to achieve an effective ministry.

Seminary and university degrees are definitely good for some people. However, when we as a church raise the academic standard so that uneducated brothers and sisters cannot enter our institutions, we have taken the wrong path. Seeking accreditation from secular bodies is a temptation that results in the controlling of the course offering, and almost inevitably excludes some programs that are, and have been recognized to be essential to the complete preparation of the full time minister. University education should most definitely be undergone by some individuals, and it is both good and necessary for the complete ability of the body of Christ to function in its mission to the world. However, if degrees are what we aim at as an institution, if accreditation is what we seek above traditional programming, we have been tragically misled by the enemy of our souls.

The bible college that ended in the mountains, eventually went down to the plains below and became a degree granting institution that I know would never allow most of the people who went to bible college with me, to attend. I know the topographical allusions in my story may have some wondering if I am not waxing metaphorical, and that the story of the college is not true. However, every word is historical and can be verified.

This kind of institution is elitist. It closes bible college preparation off from the "under-educated", and it places an overemphasis on academic learning, frequently at the expense of spirituality. I know that the apostles were not educated men, and I know that the whole church, and not just its educated elite, can provide members of the clergy. It is not university education that makes the best clergy. It is spirituality and a dependence on the wisdom and power of God. As I have stated, some people really should go to university, but not everyone. We must pull back from this lemming like rush to degree granting status. There must be opportunities for those who would never be admitted to university to get training for the ministry. It is not enough to say that there are bible colleges where this is still possible, if the rush to accreditation is making it more and more difficult to find such colleges.

Bible colleges were founded to meet the needs of the church and the mission field when it was felt that traditional seminaries were inadequate in this regard. This situation has not essentially altered, and the assumption among evangelical churches that they would never fall into this position with regard to their tertiary level institutions, is unfounded. To some degree they are already in that position. In focusing on tertiary qualifications, the evangelical church has, in effect, turned away a vast portion of its congregations as potential students from its newly constituted degree granting institutions. There are some who will and can raise the level of their education to meet this new situation, but others will never do so. And they will not because they will become discouraged, or because they are simply not academically oriented.

If a denomination has a seminary, this is not a particular problem, and indeed may be necessary to the full teaching and ministry needs of the church. However, when virtually every bible college is trying to raise its standards to allow it to grant degrees, this is a major crisis in the church. I think that as Christians and as churches, we need to sit for a moment, and ask ourselves why we exist, and what part the Holy Spirit has in the ministry. We need to ask ourselves if we have not gone a little over board in our rush to higher education. If having no university education is a strategic mistake, having an overemphasis on such education is an even greater one. Let us return to a balance, and allow *all* who feel the call of God, to minister in his church.

Chapter 36
IN PRAISE OF NATURALNESS: SOME CONCLUDING REMARKS

Sadly, though I have attempted to show that a Christian can have a deep, honest, satisfying and life transforming relationship with God, it must also be clear (if I am correct) that the church (and we as members in it) is far from the place it should be. Rather than attired as a beautiful bride, as I suspect it imagines itself to be, the church is poor and in rags. We profess a relationship with God that is almost universally not borne out by our behaviour, our thinking, and especially our lack of joyful love. We follow too closely the advice and teachings of spiritual leaders who are either simply wrong, or who in the words of Shakespeare, "Show me the steep and thorny way to heaven, whiles, like a puff and reckless libertine, himself the primrose path of dalliance treads," and who while professing to be spiritual leaders use their "leadership", apparently as the path to huge investment portfolios, often gained from the sacrificial gifts of far from affluent believers.

The Successful Christian in a Failing World

As Christians, and even as citizens, we need to rediscover the power and necessity of individually seeking the truth, and critically evaluating what we are told. It is as individuals that we discover God, and though the church and its pastoral leadership are extremely important, this solitary state is the teaching of the bible, in both the New and Old Testaments. We have become like children, dependent on others for all our spiritual direction, while never going back to either God or the scriptures in any serious fashion for verification of this teaching. We generate virtually no ideas, biblical or other, from our own thinking or prayerful reflection and we repeatedly express views, as if we have genuinely thought them through, that are merely the regurgitation of those we have taken from our "spiritual" guides.

When I was sixteen or seventeen, I remember one Sunday morning on the lawn of our church saying to my very Christian friend, "If you were really spiritual you wouldn't look at her." Over the years I have come to believe I was wrong in saying that. How do I know what he was thinking? Further, what could be more natural than looking at someone or something that is beautiful? Would I ever have said that if he had been looking at the ocean? Truth is important. In fact, it is crucial. On the whole the church's thinking is in an ossified state, just as was the thinking of the people in the time of Jesus. We frequently do not recognize and accept truth if it is not couched in familiar terminology. Moreover, rather than examining the discrete aspects of situations that we take for granted we truly understand, we thought-less-ly place a biblical interpretation on the situation which, in point of fact, we have not adequately thought through. Indeed, our conversation and responses to others is so cliché based that we often fail to listen to the heart of the (person) confronting us, just as long as correct doctrine is "confessed".

The truth of the moment we are experiencing; the truth of what people say and do, and the reality of a situation (despite our thoughts on what we think it should be and, at times, what we may have been taught) are of prime importance. We simply must not force a theoretical model of what we think reality is on a situation without patient reflection on the reality confronting us. We must not interpret a situation without looking at the objective variables that really do make up that situation. We should always be open to the possibility that how we have habitually understood something, may not actually be how something really is.

Also, I believe that ideally there is a naturalness to God's spirituality. It is not brittle and defensive. It is not derived from the generation of countless rules and interpretations of how we should live, but from the revelation of God to our hearts and the transformation of these hearts into God's image. Constructing a great body of "spiritual" understandings of what is acceptable and what is not has the appearance of promoting spirituality, but it does not necessarily achieve this. Rather it tends to operate as a body of laws, in the same fashion as the Mosaic law. Rather than freeing us, they enslave us. What was meant to help, in actuality deeply hinders. Indeed, as we attempt to follow these spiritual laws we are generally attempting to produce a spirituality that is not the creation of the Holy Spirit but the product of our human resolve. And because this "spirituality" is our own, it is often fragile, unnatural, Pharasaic, and unattractive, both to ourselves and to others. We can, in fact, become actually neurotic in the production of these things we can and cannot do, all of which may seem to us to be logical and biblically consistent. They may indeed be logical; the biblically consistent part is another matter.

There are good reasons why Hebrew society and Jesus himself summed up the law in the two great commandments to love God with all one's heart and one's neighbour as oneself (Mark 12:28-34). For example, if you experience these two commandments you could never be accused of worldliness, even if you were to play football every night of the week.

Love of God and love of one's neighbour is the fulfillment of the law. For what purpose then would one need a plethora of supposedly spiritual do's and don'ts for the successful spiritual life? We need to be suspicious of "spiritual" rules that do not have a specific and solid foundation in scripture, and also, it would seem, of the people who generate them.

There is a very human inclination to look for specific recommendations that will tell one what to do in every situation one finds oneself in. The scriptures however almost always deal in general principles, and do not provide guidance for the specific details of one's life. For example, the scriptures do not give us instruction on whether we should buy one house over another, or even whether we should buy a house at all. Moreover, much of life is not open to a simple reduction to a biblical teaching or to a particular group of verses from scripture. We are clearly told how we should act, but not what the details of those actions should be. Nor does the bible teach that we should seek bible verses for every step we contemplate. On the other hand, we may well be directed by certain bible verses. We could also, as well, be directed by the words in an ad on a bus that rushes by. It is guidance that is promised, not the specific method that may be used to provide this guidance.

There is a tendency in the church, when we seek to follow scripture, to expect biblical direction for every decision. However, spiritual life cannot be lived under an umbrella of biblical verses for every possible situation. And New Testament holiness is not found in the formulation of interpretations of "spirituality" for every occasion. This is not how Jesus lived his life, and it should not be understood as the way we are intended to live. What this, ultimately mistaken understanding results in is a set of 'spiritual laws' that can be followed, but which do not reflect the super-naturalness of life in the Spirit. Though I am supposed to loosen the knots that bind the poor, the way God may want me to do this may not be the way you are supposed to, or even the way I think I am supposed to. We must be led by the Spirit as to how to act, and as we are transformed into His image, our "new hearts", under the guidance of the Spirit, will lead us to certain specific actions. The Christian walk with God is not a mechanical fulfilling of obligations we must bend our backs to. When our self is deposed as the core of our actions, our hearts, now motivated by love for others, to the same degree that we love ourselves, will naturally act in certain ways.

Christian spirituality is not the enforced obedience to a set of Christian laws. Rather it is the inner transformation of the heart which then naturally acts in the ways of God. We do not have to neurotically develop sets of behavioural codes to be spiritual. If we see ourselves "in Christ", are surrendered to God, do not seek to hide from our sin, and seek God in prayer, we can live entirely normal lives that are not psychologically exhausting, either to us or to the people around us. The New Testament walk with God is a walk in the Spirit. It is not the generation of a set of (evangelically accepted spiritual) laws that someone asserts are required for true spirituality. If one genuinely loves God, one will be truly spiritual. God definitely wants us to be spiritual, but he does not want us to attempt to become spiritual by seeking, in our own strength, to conform our lives to a set of biblical principles, accurate though they may be. The function of every single ethical and behavioural direction, either in this book or in the scripture itself, is only as a guide, a "highway sign" directing us ahead. Though it appears to imply a divine directive to immediately comply, this is not its purpose. Biblical spirituality, the *performance* of these directives, is the product of the resurrection life of Christ being "downloaded" into the human heart by the indwelling Spirit of Jesus. Indeed, when we attempt to employ our considerable human strength to achieve spirituality we are abandoning the Gospel. We do not have to try to be spiritual.

Printed in the United States
91388LV00004B/25-33/A

9 781597 816212